Sir Ernest Lemon

E.J.H. Lemon (date unknown).
National Portrait Gallery

Sir Ernest Lemon

*The production engineer
who modernised the LMS railway
and equipped the RAF for war*

A Biography by
Terry Jenkins

RAILWAY & CANAL HISTORICAL SOCIETY

First published 2011
by the Railway & Canal Historical Society

www.rchs.org.uk

The Railway & Canal Historical Society was founded in 1954 and incorporated in 1967.
It is a company (No.922300) limited by guarantee and registered in England as a charity (No.256047)
Registered office: 3 West Court, West Street, Oxford OX2 0NP

ISBN 978 0 901461 58 2

Designed and typeset by
Malcolm Preskett
Printed and bound in the UK by the MPG Books Group,
Bodmin and King's Lynn

Contents

Introduction

IN the summer of 1938, the Government of the United Kingdom finally reacted to charges of incompetence in the management of the re-armament programme for the RAF. Expansion had been approved and set in motion in 1935, but the programme had been dogged by controversy, monetary restrictions and delays. Revised targets and expenditure had been set in the intervening years, but the aggressive behaviour of Germany suddenly lent an even greater urgency to the situation.

Production of the much-vaunted new generation of fighter aircraft had stagnated and was months behind schedule. No Spitfires had been built and only a handful of Hurricanes. The defence of this country still rested largely on obsolete aircraft. To solve the problem, the Government appointed Mr E.J.H. Lemon to be Director-General of Production. Lemon was seconded to the Air Ministry by the London, Midland & Scottish Railway, and charged with the task of completing the programme by the scheduled date of March 1940.

Ernest John Hutchings Lemon was the son of a labourer in an obscure Dorset village who had risen to become Vice-President (Operating & Commercial) of the LMS Railway by November 1931. Throughout the 1920s and 1930s he revolutionised the way the railway worked, seeking to eliminate old and inefficient practices.

It was a time when the railways suffered great financial difficulties in the face of a nationwide economic slump and growing competition from other forms of transport. To combat this, Lemon introduced the principles of *Scientific Management*, a business philosophy first developed in the USA, to all phases of railway working and management. He was one of the first proponents in this country of the principles, and championed them throughout his long career. Indeed he was described, during his lifetime, as the father of *Scientific Management* in the UK.

Lemon applied the same techniques to the RAF rearmament programme and, as a result of his reforms, the targets were achieved ahead of schedule. When this country had to face the full might of German air attacks in the summer of 1940, the RAF was ready. The Battle of Britain was a close-fought affair, but the RAF did have sufficient aircraft – just!

With his work at the Air Ministry completed, Lemon returned to the LMS and his contribution to the war effort is now largely overlooked. The story of the Battle of Britain, the planes that defended this country, the pilots who flew them and the officers who commanded the strategy, has been told in innumerable books. What is not so well-known is the story of how these aircraft were produced in the quantities required – and the dynamism and urgency brought to the project by one man. Lemon's work at the Air Ministry, for which he was knighted, was of over-riding national importance. His contribution can be summed up in a tribute paid to him at the time of his knighthood in 1941. T.S. Chegwidden [later Sir Thomas], an official at the Ministry of Labour, wrote: 'As you know, I have always taken the view that what you did was nothing less than to save this old country from being overwhelmed. Some day the true story will be told, stripped of all the petty jealousies and intrigues, and then it will be realised how one man brought order into chaos and produced airplanes where before there was only air – and most of it hot!'

This is the story of Lemon's life, written with the full co-operation and encouragement of his grand-daughters, and with exclusive access to his private papers. The latter challenge many long-held beliefs and shed new light on the management of the LMS during this period.

The story has never been told in full before.

Terry Jenkins
January 2011

Acknowledgments

Every effort has been made to gain authority to print the pictures and photographs in this book.

My thanks are due to the following for permission to reproduce items in their collections:

Railway Gazette International; The National Archives, Kew; Highland Railway Society (Howard Geddes); Mitchell Library, Glasgow; Derby Railway Engineering Society; Chartered Institute of Logistics & Transport; Hertfordshire Archives & Local Studies; National Portrait Gallery; The British Library; Hurst, Peirce + Malcolm Ltd.; Patent Office; Derby Silk Mill Museum; Birmingham Central Library; Solo Syndication (*Evening Standard*); London Transport Museum; Bourne Hall Museum, Epsom; *Flight International*

Thanks are also due to Nelson Twells and Brian Radford for the use of photographs from their personal collections; Peter Tatlow, who drew the author's attention to Lemon's 'Jones Goods' article, and David Ahn for the picture of Bulls Green Cottage, Arkesden.

All official LMS photographs are reproduced by permission of B.R. (Residuary) Ltd.

Permission has been sought from Churchill College, Cambridge and Flightglobal to reproduce items in their collections.

ONE

Birth, origins and early life

THE *Railway Gazette* of 19 February 1943 carried an article about Sir Ernest Lemon on his retirement from the LMS Railway. This stated that 'he was born in Dorset, in 1884, of Cornish extraction'. After his death, his colleague Sir Harold Hartley also referred to his 'Cornish origins' in an appreciation published in *The Times* on 3 January 1955; and it is known that, in adult life, Lemon employed a genealogist specifically to try and establish his Cornish roots.

No connection whatsoever with Cornwall can be found in the Lemon family tree. His birth certificate shows that he was born in Okeford Fitzpaine, Dorset, on the 10 December 1884, the son of Edward and Martha Mary Lemon. Of course, it is much easier to trace genealogical records nowadays – a luxury that was not available to Lemon himself – and it is an easy matter to show that his family came from a long line of antecedents who had lived in the same small area of Dorset since at least the restoration of the Monarchy in 1660. This area, in which the name 'Lemon' can be commonly found, was centred on Stalbridge, about five miles east of Sherborne. Lemon's grandfather was christened there on 17 April 1808, and named Thomas, after his father. The young Thomas took up the trade of a shoemaker and, at some time, moved a few miles south-east to Okeford Fitzpaine where he married Elizabeth Pethen on 21 September 1834. She was the daughter of the village shoemaker, and it may well be that Thomas served an apprenticeship with his future father-in-law. Thomas and Elizabeth had six children who survived infancy, the youngest of whom was christened Edward on 11 December 1849. In July 1873, at the age of 23, Edward Lemon married Martha Mary Rose at Okeford Fitzpaine parish church – and it is the couple's sixth child, Ernest John Hutchings Lemon, who is the subject of this biography.

The censuses[1] give various occupations for Lemon's father, Edward: in 1881 he was a domestic gardener, and in 1891 an agricultural labourer. In the 1871 and 1901 censuses he was listed as a mason, but it is unlikely that he was ever a skilled craftsman, but merely a labourer, which was the occupation given on his death certificate. Life would have been hard for Edward and his wife. There were a total of eight children in the family, all crammed into a small cottage and, in order to supplement their meagre income; Edward's wife, Martha, took in washing from people in the village.

Everything which can be discovered about Lemon's ancestry in genealogical records points to the fact that he was the son of a labourer in a sleepy Dorset village. One wonders, therefore, why he claimed to have Cornish ancestry? He must have firmly believed it to be true, as his friends and colleagues can only have got the information from him personally. It is true that the name 'Lemon' is also found in Cornwall, but that is hardly a justification, and so one looks for other possible reasons. When Lemon married in 1912, his father's name and occupation were not entered on the marriage certificate, and the relevant boxes had a line firmly drawn through them. Although he had left his humble origins behind him, he could not have forgotten he came

Okeford Fitzpaine, Lemon's birthplace.
Keith Harcourt

from Okeford Fitzpaine. Nor could he have forgotten his father's name. So why the omission? If he was ashamed to declare that his father had only been a labourer, then 'Edward Lemon, deceased', would have sufficed. It may be that, for some reason, he already doubted his parentage and origins. Another curiosity is the choice of Lemon's third Christian name 'Hutchings'. It is not a name associated with either his father or mother's family. It is however a local surname, and one can only assume that it had some relevance at the time.

Nonetheless, it is quite clear where the six year-old Ernest was for the 1891 census. He is listed, with his parents and six of his brothers and sisters, at Upper Street, Okeford Fitzpaine. Apart from the one year-old Alice, the children were all attending the village school. The education they received would have been very basic. Such schools simply concentrated on the three 'Rs'; reading, writing and arithmetic together with religious education. Any other subjects depended on the skills of the teacher, though needlework for the girls was common. Unfortunately, the school records were all destroyed in a fire in 1940. Amongst those trying to put out the fire out was Lemon's youngest brother Albert, and Albert's son Fred told the author that he clearly remembered that all that was left of the school were the four walls.

There is therefore no way of knowing whether the young Ernest was an exemplary student or not! But there was certainly something about him that brought him to the attention of the local Rector and his family. We know, from Lemon's own account, that he sang in the church choir as a boy. However, the Okeford Fitzpaine web-site describes Lemon as a 'back-door boy' at the Rectory – a curious phrase – which, if we take it at face value, presumably simply indicates he had ready access to the Rector, albeit not by the front door! Fred Lemon notes that the house in which the family lived at the time had a back gate that opened into the Rectory garden, so access was indeed easy. The young Lemon probably ran errands for the Rector, and generally made himself useful. However, John H. Phillips, Rector of Okeford Fitzpaine, *was* a Cornishman by birth, and one cannot help but wonder if this is anything more than a mere coincidence?

Phillips had four children, amongst whom was Helena Agnes born in 1867. In a small village, she would certainly have known the youngster, but it is impossible now to establish how much direct contact she would have had with him. As the Rector's daughter, she may have been a teacher at the church's Sunday School, or possibly even a teacher at the village school itself. A few days after Christmas 1898, Helena was married, by her father in the parish church, to Malcolm Laurie. He was a Scotsman, the son of a distinguished academic in Edinburgh, and had held the post of Professor of Biology at St Mungo's Medical College in Glasgow since 1894. After the marriage, Laurie resumed his work in Scotland and the couple set up home in Kirkintilloch, Dunbartonshire. What is surprising is that they took the 14 year-old Ernest with them – subsequently arranging for him to take up an engineering apprenticeship in Glasgow. If their sole motives were to arrange an apprenticeship for the boy, then one would have expected them to find somewhere closer to home, where Lemon could have kept in easy touch with his family. Instead, they took him several hundred miles away to Scotland. This must have been quite a daunting experience for the young boy. Was there a reason for this? The couple obviously decided to take an especial interest in him, and there is no way now to determine their motives. When Lemon later applied for membership of the Institution of Mechanical Engineers, he gave his education as 'Okeford village school, and then privately with Professor Malcolm Laurie'. It could just have been that the couple wanted to give a gifted village lad the best possible start in life, away from the narrow-minded influence of parents and family. Nevertheless, one is tempted to ask whether there were any other personal reasons. The Lauries remained close friends of his for the rest of their lives, as will become apparent in the course of this narrative.

In the 1901 census, we therefore find Lemon, the young apprentice, boarding at 155 Renfrew Road, Govan. The enumerator actually recorded his name as *Reginald* Lemon – Reginald also being the name of the previous entry, another apprentice who was boarding at the same address.

This is an unlikely coincidence and, as all the other details fit the young Ernest Lemon, we can be certain that this was indeed him!

Change of shift at Hyde Park locomotive works c.1900. Mitchell Library, Glasgow

Apprenticeship

IT MUST have been some time early in 1899, at the traditional age of 14, that Lemon actually started his apprenticeship at the Hyde Park locomotive works of Neilson, Reid and Company in Glasgow. In 1903, the company amalgamated with Sharp Stewart of the adjoining Atlas Works in Springburn, and Dübs & Co. of Polmadie to the south of Glasgow, to form the North British Locomotive Company. The amalgamation meant that the Company became the largest locomotive producer in Europe. Production was not confined to the home market, and the Company built locomotives for railways throughout the world. Estimates from authoritative sources such as the North British Locomotive Society and others vary, but in their heyday the combined works could produce some 600 to 800 locomotives per year. According to the North British Locomotive Society, the company, at its height, employed some 8,000 people and its workshops occupied some 60 acres of land. Whatever the

Lauries' motives were in taking Lemon to Glasgow, this was an excellent place to nurture the talents of a young engineer, and he gained a wide experience in one of the busiest locomotive shops in the world during his apprenticeship.

While he was away in Scotland, his mother died, at the early age of 49, in 1903. It is not known whether Lemon was able to attend the funeral in Okeford. He completed his apprenticeship in 1905, and in his hand-written application for membership of the Institution of Mechanical Engineers in 1929 notes that he served his time 'in the following departments: Template, Pattern, Foundry, Finishing, Boiler Mounting, Turning, Smithing and Erecting Shops'. The form also details the fact that during this period, apart from continuing to study privately with Malcolm Laurie, he took 'Evening Classes at the Royal Technical College, Glasgow'. The document still exists in the Institution's Archives in London, and is the only first-hand source of information for his education and early career.

Inverness roundhouse was approached through an ornate triumphal arch containing a 45,000 gallon water tank. The turntable was a solid platform of the maximum size that space would allow, and was the only way in and out of the shed which had 31 radiating roads. Not only was the turntable in constant operation day and night, it must have been a continual worry to Lemon that it would jam and interrupt traffic flow. In 1914 it was replaced by a more typical turntable with exposed well. This photograph must have been taken before 1908 – the year that Lemon left the Highland Railway – as that was the year that No.62 (a 4-4-0 of the Duke Class) was scrapped. Highland Railway Society Hunter Collection (F. Moore)

With his apprenticeship complete, Lemon left Glasgow for Edinburgh, where he was employed by Messrs Brown Brothers, Hydraulic and Mechanical Engineers, of Rosebank Ironworks, Edinburgh. He worked in the Drawing Office, which gave him further valuable experience, as he had not been employed in such a department during his apprenticeship. It must be during this period, 1905–7, that he also attended a Diploma Day Course at Heriot-Watt College, possibly on a day release basis. Professor Malcolm Laurie's brother, Arthur Pillans Laurie, was Principal of the College and also became a

lifelong friend, as is shown by one extant letter from 1938 in Lemon's personal papers.

Two years later, in 1907, he joined the Highland Railway, and served as the Running Shed Superintendent at Inverness. Nothing further is known about this part of his life, although one source says that he often reminisced about his time in Inverness later in life. None of these anecdotes have survived or been passed down through the family. Lemon did, however, refer to this period in a paper[2] he wrote many years later following the preservation of the original 4-6-0 'Jones Goods' engine of the Highland Railway at St Rollox works in Glasgow. This locomotive was built in 1894, and was the first of a class of sixteen such goods engines designed by David Jones. It was taken out of service in 1934, but in 1936 six others of the same type were still in use. The paper was entitled: *Pioneer Work in Locomotive Standardisation*, and the thrust of Lemon's argument was that Jones was fifty years ahead of his time, and that with this design of locomotive he achieved a degree of standardisation and simplicity which had rarely, if ever, been surpassed either before or after. He wrote: 'I may be forgiven an intense personal interest in this subject because it was with engines of this class at Inverness that I gained much of my early Running Shed experience'. He continued:

On the Highland Railway, which comprised a lengthy and straggling system operated

under conditions of severe physical difficulty with the minimum number of engines (and much necessary double-heading at that), Jones's system of standardisation and interchangeable parts enabled engines to have defective parts replaced with the minimum delay, so that they were out of service for the shortest possible period. I may add that if engine failures developed in the height of the summer rush, the most ingenious, and often desperate expedients were resorted to in order to get them running again, and the craftsmanship both at Lochgorm Shops and at the Running Sheds – all hand-done – was of an exceptional standard.

Thirty or so years later, Lemon could still remember the size and position of every nut and bolt, and the paper describes in the greatest detail the operations involved in stripping down the engine for maintenance or repairs. He may not have fully realised it at the time but the practicality of Jones' design was an important influence – leading to his later ardent espousal of the principles of standardisation. He was still promoting these principles with undiminished fervour in his 1949 'Standardisation' report for the Government.

Lemon did not remain long with the Highland Railway however and, in May 1908, joined the firm of railway wagon builders and factors, Hurst Nelson & Co., in Motherwell. A few months later, in September 1908, he was able to make the journey down from Scotland to be a witness at the

Highland Railway No.112 on the turntable at Inverness roundhouse about 1900, looking immaculate in Peter Drummond's smart fully-lined livery. David Jones' highly successful Big Goods were the first locomotives with the 4-6-0 wheel arrangement in the British Isles, and the most powerful engines in the country at the time. They worked the heavy goods trains over the summits between Perth and Inverness even into the 1930s. No.112 was an Inverness engine and would have been under Lemon's care. It was built in October 1894 and survived until February 1940. Highland Railway Society Collection (K. Leech)

marriage of his sister Florence to Edwin Love at Burghfield, in Berkshire. Edwin Love, according to Fred Lemon, worked for the biscuit manufacturers, Huntley & Palmer in Reading, and had lost a finger in an industrial accident. It was a family joke to treat their biscuits with caution!

It is not known whether Lemon was similarly able to travel back to Okeford for the funeral of his father, Edward, who died on 26 April 1909 in a bizarre accident. His father's death certificate gives the cause of death as 'shock following injuries accidentally caused by falling from a timber carriage and being crushed by the wheels thereof passing over him'. The Inquest into this tragedy was reported in a local paper, *The Three*

Shires Advertiser, on 1 May. At the time, Edward Lemon was employed as a labourer by a local builder, Edward Rawles, and was returning to Okeford from the neighbouring village of Turnworth with a heavy load of timber. It was the third such journey he had made that day, and each journey involved climbing up and down the steep hill out of Okeford. For some reason, on this descent, the horse shied and started to gallop down the hill. The braking system failed and Lemon fell from the cart, which ran over him. He died from multiple fractures and shock. As the Coroner remarked in his summing-up: 'Lemon had done what most people would have done after having walked up the hill three times: he got up to ride, which was a very unwise thing to do'. Edward was 59 years old, and had not made a Will, and so Albert James, Lemon's younger brother who was still in Okeford, administered his father's estate.

Lemon stayed with Hurst Nelson until July 1911. Many years later his son Richard wrote a short note, which still exists amongst the papers inherited by his granddaughter Christine, about his next career move. It reads: 'Hurst Nelson & Co. were substantial builders and operators of private-owners' wagons (mainly for the carriage of coal). There were always arguments . . . between the wagon owners and railway companies over which party should bear the cost of damage to privately-owned wagons (e.g. caused by derailments, rough shunts etc.) while they were working on railway company tracks. Family lore has it that Father, when working for Hurst Nelson, was particularly good at getting the Midland Railway to accept responsibility for the cost of repairs to Hurst Nelson wagons. So the MR decided he would be better on their side, and offered him a job.' An article in the *London Evening Standard*, following Lemon's secondment to the Air Ministry in 1938, corroborates the story.[3] This states – and the source of this information must have been Lemon himself – that it was his duty at Hurst Nelson to prosecute claims against the railway companies for damaged wagons. Mr Bain, then the Midland Railway superintendent at Derby, found his company were being forced to pay out a great deal of money through Lemon's activities. He

advised the Midland Railway to take the young man on to their own staff. The advice was taken and so it was that, in 1911, Lemon started his long association with the Midland, and then the LMS Railways.

Only the bare bones of Lemon's life thus far can therefore be established. However, at some stage in his education and training, he was stimulated to develop his natural enquiring nature, leading to his constant questioning of every technique and practice that later came under his wide purview. His friend and colleague Frank A. Pope wrote in his obituary in *The Times*: 'His general approach to a phase of the work that might involve an expenditure of millions of pounds a year, was to get every detail set down in black and white, and then to examine the results with 'Why?' constantly on his lips. He accepted nothing on face value, and he was not a comfortable person to be with at any time. But he got results.'[4]

Nothing remains to tell us of Lemon's private or social life at this time except one letter, written to congratulate him on his knighthood in 1941. The writer reminds him that they had known each other in Scotland in their youth, and after congratulating him on his honour, concludes: 'What amazing times we live in! So unlike the peaceful days of Darvel [near Kilmarnock] and Machrie Bay [Isle of Arran]'.[5] Perhaps they holidayed there together – who can tell?

NB – It is worth noting, in conclusion, that this genealogical information corrects oral sources in Okeford Fitzpaine that describe Lemon's father, Edward, as the local carpenter, wheelwright, and undertaker. This error has been repeated in the village history printed in the Church leaflet and on the Okeford Fitzpaine web-site. Edward was a labourer: it was his youngest son, Albert James Lemon who was the village carpenter etc. Albert remained in the village all his life (the only member of the family so to do) and died in 1955. As this is now over 50 years ago, it shows how memories can easily become confused and distorted.

TWO

The Midland Railway and LMS, 1911–1929

O N 1 August 1911, Lemon joined the Midland Railway as Chief Wagon Inspector,[6] and found himself based at Chesterfield in Derbyshire. Just over a year later, on 15 October 1912, he married Amy Clayton at Chesterfield Parish Church. He was 27 and she was 25 – a daughter of Thomas and Catherine Clayton of Harewood Grange, Holymoorside, just outside Chesterfield. The wedding was a quiet affair, overshadowed by the death of Amy's father earlier in the year at the age of 89. Thomas Clayton had been a farmer, born and bred in the area, and Catherine was his second wife. She was 35 years younger than her husband, born in Ireland, and she bore him five children of whom Amy was the fourth: two older sisters and a brother (who inherited the farm) and a younger sister, Margaret.

The local newspaper[7] reported that the couple were well-known and highly respected in the area. They would appear to have met through their mutual sporting interests – family tradition has it that they met at Chesterfield Tennis Club, but it is also known that both were members of the Chesterfield Golf Club. Malcolm Laurie acted as Lemon's best man and, after the reception, the couple left for a honeymoon in Ireland. They returned to live at 3 Poplar Avenue, Chesterfield – a 'back' development of eight detached bungalows, leading off Chatsworth Road on the west side of the town. It was here that their first son, Richard Michael Laurie Lemon, was born on 19 September 1915.

No documentation or record of Lemon's work as Chief Wagon Inspector has been found in railway archives, but his work presumably meant that he spent considerable time away from

Lemon as a young man.
This photograph was still being used for publicity purposes in 1930, but must have been taken many years earlier.
Derby Railway Engineering Club

Chesterfield, travelling throughout the Midland Railway network. He must also have been a frequent visitor to the workshops in Derby where wagons were constructed and repaired; and, in January 1917, he was appointed Works Manager in the Carriage & Wagon Department there. He succeeded Robert 'Bob' Whyte Reid who, at the same time, was promoted to C&W Superintendent for the whole Midland Railway. Lemon and family left Chesterfield and moved to

247 Osmaston Road, Derby – overlooking the Midland Railway Works. The promotion and move was accompanied by a rise in salary from £260 to £350 per year. This was rapidly followed in January 1918 by an increase to £400, and in June 1919 to £700 per year. The salary increases continued, and in August 1919 the figure was raised to £985 and on 1 Dec 1921 to £1,200 – a five-fold increase within 5 years!

In June 1918, Lemon received an OBE for his work as Carriage & Wagon Works Manager.[8] Awards of one sort or another were being handed out at this time by the Government with what now seems profligate liberality. Lemon's award was listed on page 6,705 of a supplement to the *London Gazette*! It is curious that so many awards were made at this time, as it was not as though the war was even going well: in March 1918, the Germans had launched a major offensive, and by June 1918 the Allies had lost all the ground they had gained since 1915. This hardly seems an appropriate moment to have been handing out awards! The Allied line, however, had not broken, and was now being reinforced by American troops which soon swung the conflict back in the Allies' favour. Lemon had only been Works Manager at Derby for 18 months when he received his award, and it looks suspiciously like a recognition of the work of the Department as a whole since 1914, rather than a purely personal one. As part of the war effort, the Carriage & Wagon Works had built Hospital Trains, and one such train, No. 52 for the American Expeditionary Force, was completed at the end of 1917. A full description of this train was given in the *Railway Gazette*: it was made up of 16 coaches whose length totalled 913 feet.[9] Nine of these coaches were fitted out as wards, each with 36 beds, with a further coach for infectious diseases. Of the remaining six coaches, one was a pharmacy, two were kitchens, two were for nursing personnel and one carried stores. The weight of the train was compounded by 2,385 gallons of water carried in the roof (apart from drinking water), polished mahogany fittings and lead floors in some compartments. One wonders how many of the Midland Railway's small engines were needed to haul this behemoth out of Derby works!

Family group, Chesterfield c.1916. Son Richard on Lemon's shoulders as Amy looks on. Family

Peace returned to Europe at the end of 1918, and society had to face the fact that much had changed. Over two and a quarter million Britons had been killed or injured in the war, to which can be added the unexpected deaths of so many more people in the influenza epidemic of 1919. The social and economic costs of these two events, so close together, were high; and many pre-war industrial practices were unsustainable and under question. The railways had been controlled nationally, and successfully, during the conflict, and this lent force to a notion amongst public and politicians alike that, whilst not quite endorsing nationalisation at this stage, certainly would not allow the railways to revert to the *status quo* that had existed before the war. The eventual result was the Railways Act of 1921, which grouped the companies into four major undertakings from 1 January 1923. The London Midland and Scottish Railway (LMS), thus formed, was the largest of the groups. Indeed on the day of its inception the LMS was the largest joint stock corporation in the world, as the company proudly proclaimed. However, the benefits that were supposed to follow were not immediately realised, and the birth of the LMS was later described as 'one of the most disastrous corporate events of the twentieth century. In retrospect it was absurd to attempt to merge the LNWR and the Midland Railway'.[10] This radical statement is questionable, but it is certain the merger had consequences which many staff in the new organisation, steeped in the traditions of their old companies, found difficult to accept. Even the President, Sir Josiah Stamp*, committed as he was to the LMS, later voiced his doubts publicly about the reasoning behind amalgamation. In 1928, he was still striving 'to realise some of the economies of amalgamation in an earnest endeavour to justify some of the glibly given and blithely estimated promises of politicians'.[11] As will become apparent, each of the participating companies was too large and proud of their achievements to submit willingly to the ethos of another, and the difficulty of overcoming this internecine strife was a concern to the management as late as 1938 when the School of Transport was opened.

The Midland Railway had however, prior to 'grouping', already implemented some radical innovations at its Carriage and Wagon Works in Derby. They were inspired by the visit of Reid and J.E. Anderson, Deputy Chief Mechanical Engineer, to the USA and Canada in 1919. The pair went with the express purpose of obtaining as much information as possible on American practice in the construction and repair of locomotive, passenger and goods stock,[12] and travelled widely, going as far west and south as St Louis and Memphis. They were surprised to discover that the supply of skilled labour in the United States was extremely small and generally confined to tool, die and pattern making – i.e. the ingredients for labour-saving appliances and machinery. The majority of the work force,

Sir Josiah (later Lord) Stamp, Chairman and President of the LMS. *Railway Gazette*

they discovered, were unskilled newly-arrived immigrants. For this reason, American factories relied heavily on machinery to do what, in the UK, was still considered skilled work. They visited the Ford car works, which was producing 3,300 cars a week, and described at considerable length, in their Report, how an assembly line worked. These days, everyone is familiar with the concept, and there is no need to elaborate further. But these methods were new, and a comprehensive description was needed for the Midland directors. Reid and Anderson did qualify their enthusiasm, noting that the 'work is, of course, extremely monotonous if continued for any length of time, and it is very doubtful whether British workmen would stand such monotonous conditions, under such high pressure, which this imported labour does in the Ford Factory'.

In the USA, not only was the motor industry using unskilled labour for what, in this country, was still considered skilled work, but similar arrangements were found in most of the big railway-car building plants. Lewis Ord, in his book *Secrets of Industry*, claimed that mass-

---

* Sir Josiah Stamp became Baron Stamp of Shortlands in 1938. For convenience, he is referred to as 'Stamp' throughout this book.

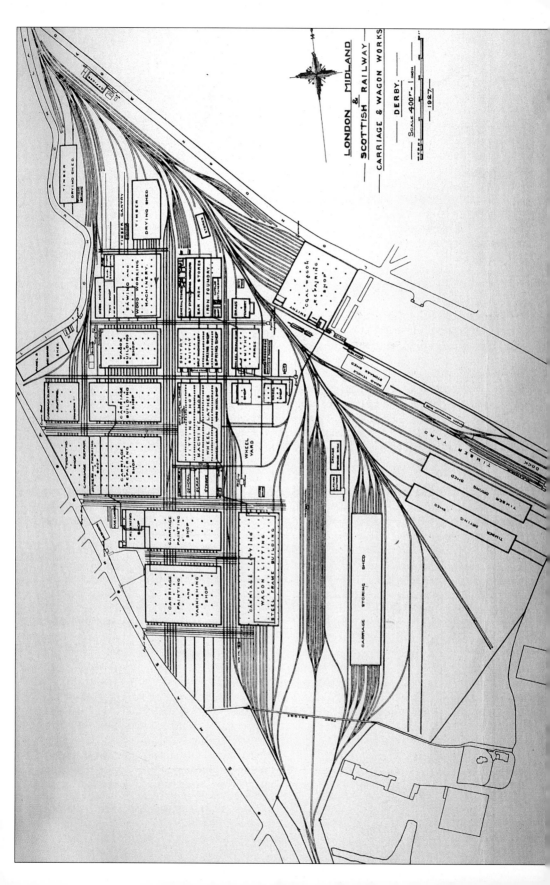

LONDON MIDLAND
&
SCOTTISH RAILWAY

CARRIAGE & WAGON WORKS

DERBY.

Scale 400ft = 1 inch

1927

production and assembly line techniques had actually been pioneered by constructors of rolling-stock for the American railroads in the 1890s.[13] When the trans-continental routes were opened at the end of the 19th century, there was an urgent need for large numbers of extra freight cars, which needed to be built rapidly, often seasonally for particular traffic, by unskilled labour. Ord maintains that it was only later that Henry Ford copied and developed the ideas for the construction of motor cars.

The use of labour-saving devices and machinery also gave the Americans an added advantage, as their factories were more adaptable. Not only were they able to increase their work force rapidly by employing and training any available unskilled labour, but they could turn readily from one design to another. Reid and Anderson saw large quantities of locomotives and wagons being built for Europe, although the specifications were quite different from American types. In this context they particularly noted the absence of blacksmiths in the railway shops, and that all forgings were produced by machine using unskilled labour.

The factories, as a rule, were much larger than in this country, and Reid described his overall impression of these factories thus:

The shops are lofty, well lighted by electric light. and are warmed in winter and cooled in summer by means of air delivered through overhead ducts with branches; air being passed over a nest of steam pipes or through ice boxes as required.

In all modern works there are large cloak rooms provided for the workmen, each man having a separate steel locker in which he can leave his street clothes and change into his working ones: there are also provided plenty of wash basins, also shower baths, hot and cold, and I noticed many of the men making use of these facilities. It is usual, too, to find

Plan of Derby C&W Works, showing the route taken by guests during the Institute of Transport's 1932 Buxton Conference.
Chartered Institute of Logistics & Transport

a large canteen and lunch rooms run on a co-operative basis in the works, and frequently there are booths in the shops where men may purchase tobacco, pea-nuts, gum, and sweets, during working hours; in many of the shops, with the exception of wood-working shops, the men were observed to be smoking at work.

The equipment of a shop for the economical production of steel freight and passenger cars naturally differs considerably from the present day equipment of British railway shops for building of wood vehicles, such as we have at Derby, but I was interested to learn that the men who were previously engaged in the building of wood cars readily adapted to the construction of steel vehicles.

There was much to learn – not only on the technical side, but also from the amenities and conditions of work given to the workers! Reid made several recommendations to the Board of the Midland Railway as a result of this visit. First he considered the problem of fire-proofing timber, and reported that American practice was 'dead against it' [sic]. He recommended, therefore, that if it be decided that carriages should be made as fire-proof as possible, it would be better to adopt either an all-steel coach, or one of steel and wood composite construction. This was preferable to the current practice of trying to fire-proof soft woods adequately. He considered it would be impossible to build steel cars on the same lines as American ones because of their great weight, and the limits placed on Midland locomotives. Nevertheless, he thought it would be feasible to build something of similar design. The cost and weight of such a vehicle would be prohibitive if the present side-door construction were maintained, and he therefore strongly advocated the adoption of vestibule-type cars with end doors for any steel passenger stock. In this way, not only would fire-proofing be radically improved, but coaches would be significantly safer than the present wooden vehicles which disintegrated into matchwood in a collision.

He also returned with other suggestions for improvements. American railroads had developed a far more widespread use of box cars (rigid wagons with a roof and closing doors) and containers (which could be packed by the sender and simply shipped on a flat wagon) – reducing the practice of covering open wagons with tarpaulins. Reid recommended that the Midland Railway should build a greater number of covered wagons which, he claimed, would reduce the damage to goods in transit. He also thought the idea of using pressed (i.e. corrugated) steel ends for these wagons, in order to give more strength, was worth a trial. He also hoped to obtain permission to purchase some modern bolt-making machinery: the Derby works used a quarter of a million bolts per month, and he had seen machinery in the USA that could produce them at the rate of 40 per minute. The wood-working machinery that the Americans used was also far in advance of anything that the Midland Railway possessed.

However, by far the most important recommendation, as far as this book is concerned, were the changes he intended to bring about in workshop practice, and he concluded: 'In so far as workshop practice is concerned, I am putting into operation some of the principles which I observed to be particularly successful in America, namely, the rearrangement of plant to give a continuous flow of work from one machine to another in one direction until the different operations are completed. My previous opinion is also strengthened that it is desirable at an early date to replace a considerable amount of our old machinery by modern equipment'.

When he made these recommendations, Reid was certainly not aware that he might be importing the germ of a whole new management philosophy. The suggestions and recommendations that he made were practical and eminently sensible. It was obviously highly inefficient for a railway the size of the Midland to continue to use traditional bespoke methods in their workshops. These new ideas were a logical progression – and, like many ideas that were considered revolutionary, seem to be perfectly obvious when viewed from a distance of years. However, this new approach to industrial efficiency had already been fused into a concept which Americans called 'Scientific Management'.[14] The basic principles had been developed by Frederick Taylor and Henry Gantt from the

experience of managing two American steel works at Midvale and Bethlehem, and it was Taylor's seminal book, published in 1911, *The Principles of Scientific Management* which formalised their ideas and presented them to the world. Taylor's four guiding principles have undergone considerable interpretation, as their original language was complex, but the following is a fair summary:

1. Replace rule-of-thumb work practices with methods based on a scientific study of the tasks.

2. Scientifically select, train, and develop each employee rather than passively leaving them to learn the job themselves.

3. Management must co-operate with each worker to give exact instructions in the performance of their individual tasks and supervise them whilst they are carried out.

4. Divide work nearly equally between managers and workers, so that the managers apply scientific management principles to planning the work and the workers actually perform the tasks.

In Britain this new approach was often simply called 'Rationalisation', though the complete philosophy was much larger than this title might suggest. The principles were gradually gaining acceptance in this country – undoubtedly hastened by the War. It is a sad fact that the necessities of war often prove to be the spur for new technological developments and inventions.

In order for Reid to carry out these reforms, he would, of course, need the help and co-operation of his Works Manager at Derby: Ernest Lemon. The concepts that were involved must have struck an immediate chord with Lemon, and he became an enthusiastic proponent of this way of thinking for the rest of his career. The principles of Scientific Management, or Rationalisation, were the unifying thread to all of Lemon's subsequent reforms, whether in production or management.

The first manifestations can therefore be found in the changes made by Reid and Lemon to the Carriage and Wagon Department throughout

1917–29. Standardisation of tasks, training, working to the clock and the participation of management were all present in the reorganisation of the shops. One of the basic fundamentals, which Lemon reiterated time and time again in later life, was that work should come to the man and not the reverse. Stocks of materials therefore appeared at each work station on the production line only as they were about to be used – a process known today as 'Just in Time'. The application of this new approach yielded an economy of effort for the worker, and a saving in time and costs for the employer. It also ousted the craft practices that had existed, and been jealously guarded, before. The Midland Railway were thus amongst the first to use these techniques in the UK and, as such, may be thought to be true industrial innovators. The use of the production line in railway manufacturing plants had been born and, by 1922, the hand-built methods of construction that prevailed pre-war had, despite the critics, given way to mechanised ones.

Lemon later explained how he and Reid

Carriages under construction at Derby c.1921 with a stack of pre-cut components ready to hand. J.B. Radford Collection

started their reforms in the Carriage & Wagon workshops. They went to visit woodworking companies who produced high quality goods such as 'furniture, pianos and gramophones, with a view to gleaning any methods of production which could be applied economically to the construction of the body or wooden structure of carriages'.[15] Lemon recounts the opposition that the proposals met: 'we were told that the methods adopted for the mass production of gramophone cabinets could not be applied to railway rolling stock, and we had also to oppose a great many objections based on the fear that owing to the timber shrinking and swelling it would be impossible to assemble the parts without hand fitting, and that we should not be able to carry through the scheme successfully'. In the old traditional method, tenons were always cut oversize to ensure that they would, whatever the movement in the wood, be adequate to fit the

**Wagon production at Derby c.1936
showing assembly of the underframe.**
J.B. Radford Collection

mortise hole. This necessitated a great deal of skilled hand-fitting during construction, and meant that, once shaped, the piece of wood had but one place where it could be used. The methods were labour intensive, craft based and uneconomic, as well as space absorbing.

Engineering magazine in 1923 carried two articles describing the new methods at Derby entitled 'Modern Methods in Railway Carriage Building' and 'Mass Production of Railway Wagons' which included photographs of the workshops, and a detailed set of drawings of the wagon-building production line that was set in place.[16] From these it can be seen that the wagons were assembled in a sequence of ten operations. The works were equipped with compressed-air powered screwdrivers and nut-drivers, rather than the hand tools which were still in use elsewhere, even in the early 1920s. All of the components were ready to the hand of the workers, having been transported to their appropriate bins and stacks, by slides, conveyors or in the case of small items, such as screws etc., in containers on small electrically-driven trucks. The construction of the underframe, which was built upside-down, occupied the first three distinct operations. The frame moved from one operation to the next along roller runways. Hoists then inverted it and placed it on the waiting wheels, which carried the completed chassis through the remaining operations. By the use of these new methods, a new wagon left the assembly line every 30 minutes of the working day; and the time taken to build a carriage was reduced from six weeks to six days.

However, these reforms were not instituted arbitrarily and without advice from the craftsmen who built the carriages, as the following anecdote relates: 'There is a story about Lemon that he called a conference of his foremen in the carriage shops and asked them which part of a body would be most difficult to produce in mass. He was told that it would be the tumble-home* bottom of a door. Very well, he said; a start would be made with the doors, and they could go on from there'.[17]

* The expression 'tumble-home' refers to the curved shape of the doors when viewed in profile.

Price Abell Medal presented to Lemon by the Derby Society of Engineers, 1922.
Family

Not only were the methods of production reformed, but Reid and Lemon also became exceedingly interested in the standardisation of components. Their aim was to have a standard set of parts from which a wagon or carriage could be built. Although the new woodworking machines were extremely efficient, cutting parts to an accuracy of four-thousandths of an inch, they needed careful setting-up for each part they were required to produce. Current designs called for a large number of individual parts, all of different dimensions, and the constant changing of settings to produce short runs of parts was therefore uneconomic. Subtle changes were made to the designs, particularly to the necessarily more complex carriage parts, in order to standardise them for mass production. It was discovered, for example, that the components of a sliding compartment door could also be adapted to form the whole of the corridor partition. Just this one example meant that huge runs of standard components could be undertaken, thus utilising machinery more effectively. The specialised nature of this work resulted in many of the cutting tools used by the machines being designed in-house. The *Railway Gazette* reported that Lemon 'personally devised many of the jigs and other special appliances necessary for the carrying out of the work'.[18] He displayed his pride in this work when he stated: 'I well remember the putting together of the first corridor sliding door, the parts of which were machine made, and both Mr Reid and myself were convinced that this was the commencement of a new era in rolling stock construction'.[19]

In December 1924, *The Locomotive* magazine carried an inadvertently amusing misprint in an advertisement for a new form of plywood for railway carriages, which may well have been used at Derby. It was called 'Armour-ply' and was faced on both sides with metal, giving it a much-increased rigidity. The magazine announced that this material was now available in sheets up to 8in. x 3in. – which would seem to preclude it from much practical use![20]

Lemon was Works Manager at Derby for six years, and it is interesting to note the variety and width of his interests at this time. For example, on 27 October 1922, the Derby Society of Engineers awarded him the 'Price Abell' prize for the best paper presented during the previous season. The subject was 'Machine Forging' – not a subject that one readily associates with him but, as already noted, one in which Reid had taken an especial interest during his 1919 visit to America. The prize was presented by the retiring Chairman of the Committee: Bob Reid! There were also social functions at which his presence was required, such as the Annual Dinner of the Derby (LMS) Railway Engineering Club. In 1924, the management contingent included J.H. Follows (Vice-President), Sir Henry Fowler (CME) and Bob Reid, among others. They were regaled by a tenor and baritone singing songs to piano accompaniment.[21]

Lemon *(right)* receives a presentation of a silver tea service from Bob Reid on leaving Derby Works, February 1925.
Derby Daily Express

Meanwhile, on 28 June 1922, a second child was born: David John Lemon. As babies were born at home in those days, Amy decided that she didn't want his inquisitive elder brother around. Richard, who was approaching seven years old, was therefore packed off, in the middle of the summer term, to the preparatory school which he was due to attend from the following September. It was an early age to be sent away to boarding school, but the attitude in those days, especially among people who had not themselves come from a privileged background, was that this was the best education they could give their children.

An anecdote has been handed down in the family about an incident while they were living in Derby, which must originate from around this time. Lemon owned a car, and his wife Amy took it to Nottingham to do some shopping. She parked in a prohibited place and when she returned a police constable was writing her a parking ticket. As she approached, she expressed surprise because she didn't know about the parking restriction. He asked her name – to which she replied 'Mrs Lemon'. To her amazement he snapped his book shut, apologised for bothering her and strode off. When she got home she told her husband and asked him why he thought this had happened. He told her that the Chief Constable of Nottinghamshire was also called Lemon (Col. F.J. Lemon, appointed in 1923), which caused much amusement.

The LMS

WHEN the Midland Railway was amalgamated into the LMS at grouping in 1923, Lemon was appointed Divisional Carriage & Wagon Superintendent, Derby, at an increased salary of £1,800 p.a. Reid was still his boss, being appointed Carriage & Wagon Superintendent for the whole of the LMS at the same time. The reorganisation of the Carriage & Wagon works at Derby, just described, had been completed by 1922, and what happened there became a major plank of LMS engineering practice. According to Lemon, Reid 'realised the economical possibilities of the grouping system',[22] and set about reorganising the whole enlarged Carriage and Wagon Department, and adapting it to cope with the 19,700 passenger carriages and 300,000 wagons that now composed the LMS stock.

A review of the workshops of the other constituent companies that made up the new Company revealed a variety of age, efficiency and level of plant. Thus at the inception of the LMS the decision was taken to concentrate rolling stock production in four workshops: Derby, Earlestown, Newton Heath and Wolverton; whilst the Scottish works at Barassie, St Rollox and Inverness concentrated on repairs.[23] In all cases every attempt was made to play to the local strengths: hence where a factory had been equipped with new machinery prior to merger, this was assessed and where possible the capacity used to supply all the other plants in the group.

Earlestown, near Newton-le-Willows in Lancashire, was an early candidate for attention. It had been the wagon workshops for the former London & North Western Railway and Lemon was put in charge of its reorganisation in 1925. On 1 January, he moved from Derby to become Divisional C&W Superintendent, responsible for both Earlestown and Newton Heath (in Manchester). This was accompanied by a further increase of salary to £2,200, and he left Osmaston Road with his family to move to Lancashire.[24] A 'smoking concert' was held in the County Hotel, Derby on 28 February, by way of a leaving party, at which Lemon was the principal guest (he was a life-long cigarette smoker!). The local paper congratulated the C&W Department on exhibiting the same good taste in their leisure as in their work, for they had decorated the platform in the same style as when the King attended the Royal Show a few years previously! Lemon was presented with a silver tea-service as 'a parting token of friendship from officials, foremen and staff' by his boss, Bob Reid. In making the presentation, Reid said he was extremely sorry that Lemon was leaving Derby, but the change had to be made. He continued: 'After all, he deserved a big job – he had, in fact, rather outgrown Derby, and when Mr Lemon began threatening to build bridges, locomotives and things as well as carriages and wagons, he thought that for safety's sake it would be better for him to have a new pitch where there was some work to do'. Some idea of how Lemon was viewed by his staff and subordinates can be gained from other speeches made at the presentation. The Superintendent of Works, W.J. Smith, said: 'Although at times they thought Mr Lemon was very hard and that he used too much "stick" (laughter), they all realised later how much they owed to his energies and pushfulness [*sic*]'. Lemon, in reply, acknowledged that perhaps he did use the 'stick' pretty often at one time, but whatever had been done had been with the object of getting on with the job. The atmosphere conveyed by the newspaper report of the other speeches was that it was a jovial occasion – one of the foremen announced to laughter that they had guided Lemon though his apprenticeship, and could congratulate themselves on so good a result. If there had been problems along the way, there appeared to be no lasting ill-feelings, and Lemon, in turn, paid tribute to the loyal service and support given to him by all the staff.[25]

In February 1925, there were also family matters to attend to when Thomas Hornbuckle married Margaret Clayton. Margaret (or Pat as she was known) was the youngest sister of Lemon's wife Amy. Hornbuckle, at the time,

Thomas Hornbuckle, Lemon's brother-in-law.

Railway Gazette

was Assistant Works Manager in the Chief Mechanical Engineer's Department at Derby and undoubtedly met his wife through his friendship and professional association with Lemon. As the bride's father had died in 1912 (before even Lemon's wedding), it was Lemon who gave her away on 4 February 1925 at Chesterfield parish church. The reception was held at the Station Hotel and, possibly mindful that Hornbuckle and many of the guests worked for the railway, the local newspaper reported (rather pedantically?) that the happy couple left on the 4.04pm train *en route* for Cheltenham, Bournemouth and London.[26] It is strange that this relationship is not generally known among railway enthusiasts. No mention of it has been found in any source consulted for this book. Even E.S. Cox, who worked for Lemon when he was CME in 1931, rather limply only described Hornbuckle as 'a personal friend' of Lemon's.[27] Perhaps it was necessary, so that charges of nepotism could never be levelled, that their relationship remained generally unknown, even to colleagues.

When Lemon turned his attention to reforming operations at Earlestown, he found that, whilst space had not been a great problem at Derby, the Earlestown shops were on a particularly cramped site of only 36 acres, which was a major barrier to efficient production. Given the constrained nature of the site, it was decided to produce the, by now, standard 12-ton mineral wagons at this works. One improvement that Lemon had made by the time the refurbishment was completed in 1927 was to refine wagon building to just eight operations. However, not only were two of the stages removed, but more was incorporated into the process. Previously, at Derby, wagons had left the assembly line to go to the Paint Shop as raw wood. It was obviously more advantageous if they could leave with a base-coat of primer applied, and space was found

Highfield House, 403 Burton Road, Derby, c.1930. Lemon bought the house on his return to Derby in 1927. Family

to incorporate this into the layout. All that was then needed in the Paint Shop was top-coating. Reorganisation at Earlestown was so significant that the *Railway Engineer* ran an in-depth article in 1928 which stated: 'Every effort has been made to ensure the proper balancing of the work, so that progress in one section shall not be hampered by less rapid methods in another. Considerable ingenuity and forethought have been necessary in bringing about this condition of affairs and those responsible for the work are constantly on the look-out for further improvements aiming at still greater economy of time and labour'.[28]

On 1 January 1927, and with his work in Lancashire complete, Lemon was promoted to Carriage & Wagon Superintendent for the whole LMS, while Reid moved on upwards to become Vice-President for Works and Ancillary undertakings. Lemon's salary was increased to £3,000 p.a. and he returned to Derby: not however to Osmaston Road – a house which he had probably rented from the LMS – but to a property which he purchased called 'Highfield' in Burton Road, on the edge of town.[29]

The promotion meant that Lemon had to attend monthly meetings of the Carriage & Wagon Committee at Euston, one of the sub-committees of the Board, and the Minutes are full of the routine work this position involved.

At the C&W Committee meeting on 28 March 1928, he was specifically asked whether the economies in staff, which had been promised as a result of the greater use of machinery, had actually been realised.[30] He replied that there were now 838 fewer men working for the Department than in 1913. This was going back fifteen years, and not a comparison with the period covered by his reforms. One senses that Lemon was possibly being somewhat economical with the truth, and his reforms in working methods had not led to a brutal reduction in the numbers of workers employed! He qualified his answer, however, by saying that, as the Company had decided that 65 should be the compulsory retirement age, the figure would increase considerably in the near future, as he proposed to dispense with all staff who would soon exceed that age.

One factor not mentioned in contemporary reports describing these reforms is whether there had been any opposition from the workforce or Unions. Lemon's time at Earlestown, for example,

would have coincided with the General Strike of 1926. The speeches at Derby, when he left to take up this appointment (mentioned previously), only refer to the 'stick' that he had wielded – no mention of strikes or major opposition. All the magazine articles describing the changes were written after the changes had been implemented, when any problems had been satisfactorily resolved. Lemon was quizzed on this specific issue at the Traffic Committee Meeting on 28 November 1928, when he announced a further scheme for progressive repairs to wagons at Derby. In response to a question about the views of the staff to such changes, he replied that his experience had shown that they were enthusiastically in favour of such schemes, as they were able to complete the work with much less effort, and invariably obtained more wages.[31]

This factor was a point that was also made in the discussion that followed Lemon's paper at the 1930 Institute of Transport Congress in Glasgow. One delegate said: 'The one important factor which he should have expected the author to have encountered (and he had probably been diplomatic enough to have overcome it) was the personal element', and concluded, 'Perhaps

Carriage repairs at Newton Heath c.1927. View across shop, showing Time Indication and Work Allocation Boards. *Railway Gazette*

the author would explain how he had managed to get the different works to accept his ideas, which were novel, and to which, he should imagine, there had been a good deal of resistance'. Lemon replied:

What they had tried to do in the LMS carriage and wagon department had been to give people a sense of pride and achievement. He well remembered going to Newton Heath and Earlestown to carry out the reorganisation scheme there. He realised that he was not going to impose Derby methods on Newton Heath or on Earlestown, and that [they] had to work out their own salvation, and that he had to show them how to do it. Newton Heath had started the new scheme for progressive carriage repairs. It made Derby go to Newton Heath to see what they were doing there. Derby then had to go back and do it at Derby. What the LMS had been trying to do was to make their people realise that they belonged to an organisation which was really the best in the world, and thus they had got a sense of pride and achievement which formed the motive power for further achievement.[32]

Not a complete answer by any means, and he didn't explain how the Unions were persuaded to agree to the elimination of long-established craft practices.

On 22 February 1928, the Prince of Wales (later Edward VIII) visited the Derby Works. He was accompanied on his tour by Sir Josiah Stamp, Bob Reid, Sir Henry Fowler (the CME) and Lemon. He visited both the Locomotive Works and the Carriage & Wagon Works, where Lemon explained the details of how a carriage was constructed. The *Railway Gazette* described the C&W works as covering an area of 128 acres, of which 36 acres were under cover. 5,250 males and 330 females were employed. The article triumphantly concluded: 'In these shops wagons are assembled in 30 minutes and carriages in 20 minutes'.[33] It is difficult to believe, even with Lemon's reforms, that carriages were ever turned out quite that fast!

Visit to Germany 1928 (?)

THE so-called Derby Registers of the Midland Railway contain five photos relating to 'Mr Lemon's German Report 1928'. The index describes them as showing photographs of such items as a coal wharf and coal wagons, a paint sprayer and a twin-tank wagon.[34] There is no evidence, therefore, of the text of a report – and no such document has been found in all the archives consulted. The photographs have not been available to view while this book was written, because of the closure of facilities at the National Railway Museum in York. However, in 1928, the Institution of Locomotive Engineers arranged a visit to Germany. It was a week-long visit, from 9 till 16 June, and was attended by many delegates as the group photographs show. The Institution's archives do not include Lemon's name as one of the delegates. Indeed, he was not a member of the Institution. Nevertheless it is a remarkable coincidence, and it is hard to believe that he also happened to make an independent

trip to Germany the same year. There is, however, a possibility that the list of participants is incomplete. The *Railway Gazette* reported that: 'Unfortunately Mr H.N. Gresley, President, Mr R.E.L. Maunsell, President-Elect and Sir Henry Fowler [Chief Mechanical Engineer at the LMS] were not able to be with the party, though all three intended to accompany the members up to the last moment.[35] Could Lemon have taken Sir Henry Fowler's place?

Inventions by Company's Officers and Servants

THE C&W Committee Minutes of 26 June 1929[36] show that the Carriage & Wagon Superintendent (i.e. Lemon) applied for permission to patent two devices that he had developed. These were a 'ball-bearing side friction block' and a ventilator for dining and luxury cars designated the 'Dewel'. The Board approved the application a day later.[37] Side friction blocks were an integral part of the suspension fitted between the body of a carriage and the bogies/wheels. It is not known what specific improvements Lemon might have made, but they were presumably the result of an empirical series of experiments he had carried out, and which were reported in the August issue of *Modern Transport* magazine.[38] The Patent Office, however, has been unable to trace the award of either of these patents, although it is well known that the 'Dewel' ventilator was later fitted to LMS coaching stock.

It is worth setting out the Company's policy towards such inventions. This was defined in the Board Minutes of 26 February 1925:

Resolved, That in the case of inventions by Officers and Servants employed by the Company, the following regulations be applicable as from this date, viz:-

No officer or servant shall without permission, (which shall not unreasonably be withheld), patent any invention made in the course of his employment or with the aid of facilities or assistance enjoyed by his employment.

The Board reserve to themselves the right to adopt and use any improvement, whether

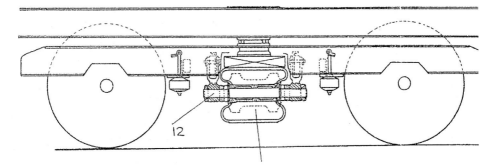

Diagram showing one of the possible layouts for Pneumatic Suspension of Vehicles in the 1929 Patent granted to Lemon. Such an arrangement is commonplace today.
Patent Office

patent or otherwise, invented by any Officer or servant, subject only to such payment in the form of a gratuity as in the opinion of the Board shall be justified by the particular circumstances of the case.

No officer or servant shall dispose of his invention or patent rights without reserving to the Company the right of user of such invention upon their system free of any payment whatsoever, but subject to this condition he shall be at liberty to dispose of or otherwise use his invention or patent rights.

In the case of an invention approved by the Board, the Directors will be prepared, on request, to assist the Inventor to obtain patent rights.

If in any case an officer or servant does not wish to patent any invention then the Board may, if they think fit, require such officer or servant to patent such invention at the Company's expense.[39]

This was a very enlightened approach – especially the final clause – and the Index to the Board Minutes show how a large number of employees were given approval to submit applications. Tommy Hornbuckle, for example, applied for permission to patent a 'change gear device' in 1939, and many other

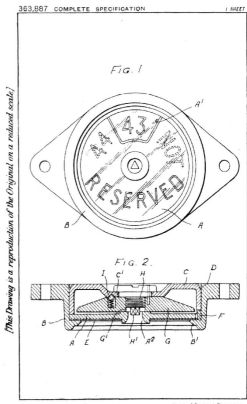

Detail of the Reserved Seat Indicator patented by Lemon and George Lenthall in 1931. Patent Office

senior officials had at least one patent application to their name.

The Patent Office records show that Lemon *was* granted two patents – and the first was also concerned with the suspension of carriages. The method now envisaged used a pneumatic system, and the application was made in association with the Dunlop Rubber Company. The provisional specification described the system thus: 'This invention relates to pneumatic suspension of vehicles and in principle contemplates the provision, or substitution for the usual springs in a vehicle, of inflatable members in the form of rubber tyres, bolsters or the like. The object of the invention is a maximum of efficiency in the suspension of a vehicle whereby all shocks or vibrations are completely damped out.'

The application was made on 13 January 1928, and patent no.311,437 was granted on 13 May 1929. The final complete specification envisaged a variety of layouts, illustrated by appropriate technical drawings. As far as is known, Lemon never built a prototype incorporating any of the ideas in the patent, which therefore, presumably, lapsed. One of the schematic diagrams, however, shows a layout which appears to be identical to the system developed by Bombadier and incorporated in the diesel-mechanical units which they built in the 1980s – over 50 years later!

In 1931, while he was CME, Lemon was also involved in helping Mr George Lenthall to patent a Reserved Seat Indicator.[40] Lenthall was the Chief Foreman of the C&W Department at Euston and, as the Board Minutes show, Lemon's name appeared solely on the application on behalf of the LMS.[41] This was obviously an instance of the penultimate clause of the Company's policy being invoked – and Lemon was merely assisting the inventor to gain the patent rights. A contract was drawn up on 21 July describing Benthall and Lemon as 'servants' of the Company and granting permission to make the patent application.[42] The contract stated that the LMS had free use of the invention, but Lenthall could make any arrangements with other companies in the UK and take out foreign patents.

This is at variance with Divall's assertion that the LMS had 'no real incentive to seek patents'

because they only built locomotives and rolling stock for their own purposes, and were not in competition with other manufacturers.[43] Lemon had developed the pneumatic suspension system in association with Dunlop, the friction block with Spencer Moulton & Co. and the 'Dewel' ventilator with J. Stone & Co. It is, perhaps, curious that the LMS did not themselves seek to patent the devices, but merely ensured that they had an irrevocable licence to use the invention.

Engineer and Railway Staff Corps

AN interesting side-light to Lemon's advancement up the LMS hierarchy came on 27 November 1929, when he was appointed a Major in the Engineer and Railway Staff Corps.[44] This curious branch of the British Army, which was affiliated to the Royal Engineers, was founded in 1865 with the principal objective of ensuring 'the combined action among all the railways when the country is in danger'. One of the main duties was 'the preparation, during peace, of schemes for drawing troops from given distant parts and for concentrating them within given areas in the shortest possible time'. The duties during peace-time, therefore, were purely nominal and the only on-going activity seems to have been an annual dinner! The Corps was also unique in that all its members were *officers*. The history of the Corps sums this up neatly in its title: 'All Rank and No File'![45] Unfortunately, the records of the Corps, which are theoretically in the archives of the Royal Engineers, are now missing.

Institute of Transport Congress in Glasgow, 1930

A FEW years after the reforms had been carried out in the C&W department, Lemon gave a paper entitled 'Railway Amalgamation and its effect on the LMS Workshops' at the 1930 Institute of Transport Congress in Glasgow. Sir Josiah Stamp joined in the discussion and, referring to the principles on which the reforms at the Carriage & Wagon works had been based, noted that he had recently spoken to American manufacturers who 'had been carrying out these

**Robert (Bob) Whyte Reid, who died
28 March 1929 aged 44.** *Railway Gazette*

processes on a wide scale and who had been visiting Europe to see whether they could learn anything there'. Stamp had referred them to the Derby workshops and their verdict had been 'that the best principles that America could suggest had been carried as far or further in those works than anywhere else in Europe'. Another contributor to this discussion was C.E.R. Sherrington, Secretary of the Railway Research Service and a widely-travelled and respected figure in the industry who will feature prominently later in this narrative. He commented that: 'The Railway workshops seemed to have led by at least ten years most of the other industries in the country', and thought that Lemon and Reid could be looked on as 'the joint fathers of rationalisation in this country'.[46] It is unfortunate that, when these tributes were paid, Bob Reid was dead. Unexpectedly, and tragically, he died on 28 March 1929 following an operation, aged only 44, and his early death was a great loss to the LMS.

His achievements received full acknowledgment in the obituary notice in the *Railway Gazette* on 5 April 1929. However, it is a sad fact that the importance of his role in the reforms which he and Lemon instigated has been gradually eroded by history. Sir Henry Fowler, in the discussion following Lemon's 1930 paper, gave Lemon alone the credit – describing him as simply 'following out what was a very sound principle, namely, to detach one's mind from one's own work and go out and see what somebody else was doing in an entirely different direction. In his case, Mr Lemon had gone with that imaginative mind which so few engineers possessed and which still fewer were able to use.' This seems to give all the credit to Lemon, although Fowler knew of Reid's involvement, as he also said: 'The late Mr Reid had seemingly discovered an unshrinkable wood. Afterwards it had been found that this was not the case, but that he had given the wood no time to shrink before placing it in a position where it could not shrink . . . That was the reason for the wonderful results which had been obtained by the Carriage & Wagon Department.'

Canadian production engineering consultant Lewis C. Ord, who was briefly referred to earlier in this chapter and later became closely associated with Lemon, also gave him all the credit in his book *Secrets of Industry*:

About this time [referring to the early 1920s] Mr. E.J.H. Lemon, later to become Sir Ernest Lemon and Vice-President of the LMS Railway, was in charge of the former Midland Railway Carriage and Wagon works at Derby. Although British wagons are less suited by design to mass-production arrangements, he laid out their works to produce wooden railway wagons by this method. The economies he produced were remarkable. While it was a later development, it was undoubtedly superior to any American wooden railway wagon building in technique and detail. This was followed by an even more remarkable development. He undertook to produce first wooden and then composite (steel and wood) railway carriages on mass-production methods. The novelty of this arrangement was unquestionably the improvement in accuracy

Midland Railway Wage Card for E.J.H. Lemon, showing his appointments and salaries before becoming Vice-President National Archives

and quality which he accomplished at the same time. Tools and machine tools were improved in accuracy and in design in order to turn out parts made to the closer limits on which he insisted. The results – in cost, in accuracy, and particularly in output rate per unit of floor area – set new standards for the production of wooden and wooden-framed railway passenger coaches. The greater economy in the use of floor area he extended to the repair of passenger carriage stock, and this one change, by itself, enabled him to effect important economies for the company all stemming from these early developments. Sir Ernest Lemon's work, particularly on passenger-carriage building was much admired in the United States and many details copied there. It was an outstanding performance. Because he thoroughly understood the principles on which mass production was based he made many notable

improvements, of which these were representative examples.[47]

In truth, the professional relationship between Lemon and Reid was very much the meeting of two like minds – no matter who was technically the senior or the subordinate. Reid appears to have had the original idea – and Lemon was the facilitator and 'workshop genius' who gave it reality. As with all joint projects, it is impossible to tell exactly who did what. However, as Works Manager, it is likely that Lemon was the man who actually produced the practical plans for the redesign of the workshops and the new assembly-line procedure. What is certain is that he vigorously promoted this new approach to industrial, managerial and production problems henceforward for the rest of his career. Lemon was fortunate to find in Reid a second person, after Malcolm Laurie, to act as an influential mentor and guide.

THREE

LMS,
1930–1931

AS already mentioned, in March 1929, R.W. Reid suddenly and unexpectedly died, but it was fully ten months before an appointment was made to replace him as Vice-President. In the interim, there were other changes: on 19 December 1929, J. Quirey moved to become Vice-President (Operating & Commercial) and William Wood replaced Quirey as Vice-President (Finance & Service). Wood's appointment heralded the start of a complete clean sweep of senior management at the LMS, eventually leading to the 'unholy trinity' – as they were sometimes called – of Vice-Presidents: Wood, Hartley and Lemon.

Sir Harold Hartley

The unexpected choice to replace Reid as Vice-President was Sir Harold Hartley who was appointed on 1 Feb 1930. Hartley was a distinguished chemist, who had served on many Government commissions and committees but, since 1901, had primarily been a Fellow and Tutor at Balliol College, Oxford. It was a surprising career move for him to have made, and occasioned much comment in the Press and railway journals. He was not a railway man and most of the interest centred on his title of Director of Research. It was in 1928 that Stamp had set up a small committee, under Reid's chairmanship, to report on the need for more intensive scientific research on the LMS, and on the type of organisation necessary to carry out this policy.[48] This committee recommended the appointment of a Director of Research and of a permanent Advisory Committee to assist him. Stamp described the thinking behind the creation of this new post when he said at the 1930 AGM

Sir Harold Hartley on his appointment as Vice-President. *Railway Gazette*

'in every department and business there should be some minds set aside for considering change and improvement, and for experiment'.

The *Railway Gazette* commented: 'The largest British railway organisation is, for the first time in history, to have a guide of the highest scientific standing to co-ordinate and direct the efforts made towards improving railway transport in all its phases.[49]

It is ironic that the man chosen to fill this post should, at the same time, be appointed successor to Reid as Vice-President for Works & Ancillary Undertakings – responsible for all LMS workshops amongst which, of course, were Lemon's carriage and wagon works. Both Hartley and the Board seem to have been cautious about his suitability for this office, and the Special Minutes of the LMS[50] show that both sides kept open the option to revert to the single position of Director of Scientific Research after one year if so desired. (The Special Minutes contain information that was withheld because of its confidential nature. Such information was recorded in a separate ledger with a built-in lock.)

At the 1930 AGM one questioner took issue with Hartley's appointment, stating that in the Press 'there was an indication that Sir Harold Hartley was going to be something besides a research officer' and that 'he very much regretted to hear that he was to be imposed, without, so far as he knew, any specific knowledge of civil engineering, locomotive construction, carriage building or signalling, over the departments which were headed by men who, as the Chairman had told them, were most able'. The questioner provocatively ended by saying that, as there were 'far too many public calls on the Chairman's time . . . he could not help believing that the appointment was made to meet the great need the Chairman must have of finding out what his departments were doing'.[51] Stamp did not deign to respond to this allegation, but directed his reply to a defence of Hartley's appointment. He strongly disagreed with the questioner that the manager of an engineering department must himself be an engineer. The Vice-President was in charge of the technical departments as an administrator – not to do the engineer's jobs over again. He concluded: 'The Board are thoroughly satisfied that with the great experience which Sir Harold Hartley has had in dealing with industrial matters, the reorganisation of factories, and all kinds of industrial experience in addition to his very high scientific attainments, they have made a very wise choice'.

In truth, Hartley was not simply an Oxford

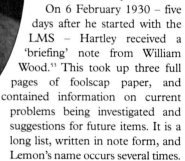
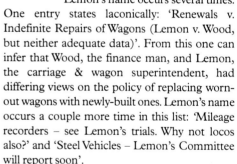

Sir William Wood.
Railway Gazette

academic but had considerable practical experience of industrial matters, as the *curriculum vitae* he supplied to Stamp – and which is now among the collection of Hartley's papers in the Archives of Churchill College, Cambridge – testifies.[52] This archive of papers not only gives a fascinating insight into the changes made at the LMS at this time, but also challenges many long-held assumptions. As will be explained, they indicate that it was Hartley, and not Stamp, who was primarily responsible for the subsequent rapid promotion of Lemon up the LMS hierarchy.

On 6 February 1930 – five days after he started with the LMS – Hartley received a 'briefing' note from William Wood.[53] This took up three full pages of foolscap paper, and contained information on current problems being investigated and suggestions for future items. It is a long list, written in note form, and Lemon's name occurs several times. One entry states laconically: 'Renewals v. Indefinite Repairs of Wagons (Lemon v. Wood, but neither adequate data)'. From this one can infer that Wood, the finance man, and Lemon, the carriage & wagon superintendent, had differing views on the policy of replacing worn-out wagons with newly-built ones. Lemon's name occurs a couple more time in this list: 'Mileage recorders – see Lemon's trials. Why not locos also?' and 'Steel Vehicles – Lemon's Committee will report soon'.

Lemon was, indeed, finalising a report on Steel Rolling Stock. This was dated 3 April 1930, and an expanded version was also scheduled for submission and discussion at the International Railway Conference to be held in Madrid later that year. It was for this reason, one assumes, that he did not go with his wife on a holiday cruise to the Canary Isles. Amy left for Las Palmas on the 30 March, accompanied by her sister and brother-in-law: Margaret and Thomas Hornbuckle.

The Steel Rolling Stock Report

ONE OF the members of the Committee who drew up this report[54] under Lemon's chairmanship was C.E.R. Sherrington, whose name has already been briefly mentioned in the previous chapter. Charles Ely Rose Sherrington was the only son of Sir Charles Sherrington, the distinguished physiologist, but had not followed his father into a medical career. He is listed in the Report as the Secretary of the Railway Research Service (RRS), but this was very much his own personal brainchild, which he founded and ran. The RRS was funded by the four major railway groups and based at the London School of Economics where Sherrington lectured on railway affairs. The RRS issued a monthly journal[55] listing developments on the railways both in this country and abroad, which was a fund of information about current practices on the world's railways. Sherrington also produced an annual assessment of the world's railways covering the passenger, freight and track miles in use, and other key economic indicators, for private circulation. The only copy of such a document discovered while researching this book, is a draft in Sherrington's own handwriting of the assessment for 1938.[56] He also lectured at Cornell University, published many books on transport economics, and served on the Council of the Institute of Transport. With his knowledge and huge sphere of influence, it is not surprising that the LMS invited him to join the Steel Rolling Stock Committee, where his knowledge of current developments outside the LMS would be of great value. Sherrington supplied all the statistics on the French and American use of steel carriages and wagons that are incorporated as Appendices to this Report. It is worth commenting that his knowledge and archive of German and other Continental railway layouts was of great use to RAF Bomber Command in the Second World War.

C.E.R. Sherrington.
Railway Gazette

The LMS members of the Committee were Mr J. Ballantyne (Chief Goods Manager), Mr E. Taylor (Chief Accountant), Mr Murray (Assistant Chief General Superintendent) and Mr H.J. Moore (Personal Assistant to the Vice-President), who acted as Secretary. Naturally, as at the time he was the Carriage and Wagon Superintendent, Lemon took the chair. The other 'outsider' – apart from Sherrington – and, perhaps, a surprising participant was Douglas Knoop, Professor of Economics at Sheffield University.

Although the Committee was charged with investigating the possible benefits to the LMS of the use of all-steel carriages and wagons, there was also pressure from the Government for this action, and the inclusion of Knoop on the Committee indicates one of the reasons for its formation. There had already been concern that the huge use of timber by the railways would eventually denude the forests of fresh supplies. The Government was also keen to protect employment figures in the steel industry. Knoop would bring specific knowledge of the economics of the steel industry, in whose capital he had spent his academic life, to their deliberations.

Given Lemon's organisational brilliance, the report of the Committee is characteristically clear, statistically based and certain in its conclusions. However, considering that it was not intended for a popular journal, but was prepared by railwaymen for railwaymen, the report starts at a remarkably elementary level. It begins by looking at the history and developments in carriage design, describing how the railway carriage had evolved from the stage coach, and how the original all-wooden construction had been modified over time; firstly by using steel components to strengthen the structure, and gradually standardising on steel underframes upon which a wooden body, braced with steel, was mounted. In fact steel already accounted for 75% of the weight of so-called 'wooden' coaches. The use of wood, however, meant the body had better thermal properties, maintaining a more even temperature in compartments during variations in outside conditions. 50% more heating capacity was needed to maintain an even temperature in steel-bodied coaches, although this could be reduced by extensive insulation. The problem with such lagging was that it hid any corrosion, and had to be removed for inspection during maintenance.

The report then reviewed American and Continental practice, based on the statistics supplied by Sherrington. In 1929, steel coaches made up just 8% of the national stock in France, 9% in Italy, whilst Germany had 12% of its larger stock, some 10,000 coaches, made of steel.[57] American railways had been building all-steel coaches since 1902 and these now comprised 50% of their total stock. Their enthusiasm to embrace this method of construction was motivated by the desire to make the coaches as fire-proof as possible while running through the tunnels into New York.

British practice was laid out – including the current position on the LMS. The LMS had actually ordered 535 steel carriages from external manufacturers in 1924 and, at the time of writing the report, had another 110 on order. In 1926 the LMS publicity department had made capital out of this: the *Railway Gazette* printed a piece which began: 'The London Midland and Scottish Railway Company, in continuance of its policy of assisting British and Imperial industries, last year placed with British manufacturers a large order for steel passenger coaches to be built throughout using British material, with the exception of the interior finish, which is of mahogany imported from our colonies'.[58] The political imperative to increase British order books in order to reduce unemployment was almost certainly the reason behind such rhetoric.

Steel bodies were, not surprisingly, found to be safer in an accident, having nearly three times the resistance to telescoping.[59] This was an important safety consideration, and the Committee conducted a review of accidents on the Company's network since 1923, and the amount of compensation paid to the injured, and predicted the financial savings that might thus be made. They noted the worries about deforestation and admitted that the world timber stock was being reduced, but stated that the LMS had no difficulty in obtaining their current £40,000 stocks of teak, deal and mahogany. The only disadvantage with wood was that it could not be used immediately, but had to be allowed to season. Considerable capital expenditure was thus tied up. They acknowledged there was certainly less risk of fire with steel coaches, but the Company was already replacing gas-lights with electric in its existing stock.

They calculated that the cost of steel coaches was 6% more expensive than the equivalent type with wooden body and steel underframe; and that such coaches were on the whole some 10% heavier than comparable wooden vehicles which increased the costs of hauling them. Although painting, maintenance and repairs were less costly than those of wooden carriages, having taken all the factors into consideration, they could not recommend, on financial grounds alone, that the Company build all its coaching stock in steel. They concluded that the net cost to the company would be £94,000 per annum.[60]

However, national financial implications were also a consideration, and these were considered in a further Appendix, entitled 'Economic Aspects of Giving Orders for Rolling Stock to Private Manufacturers'. Although the authorship is ascribed to Sherrington it is hard to believe that Knoop had no influence on these pages. Two problems had been raised, affecting national prosperity and international trade: (1) That the granting of rolling-stock construction to private industry would assist that industry to obtain foreign contracts and (2) that the use of steel, a home product, would decrease unemployment by replacing imported timber.

Having assessed the production figures from private rolling-stock manufacturers, the Appendix concluded that they had 'little cause to be regarded as a depressed industry', as they had witnessed a greater expansion than many other similar-sized industrial groups. It also did not accept that steel was necessarily a 'home product'. Large quantities of ore and pig-iron were imported from Europe. The shipping

LMS Derby Railway Engineering Club Annual Dinner, January 1930. *Back row standing:* Lemon (6th from left). Also includes Sir Henry Fowler *(extreme left)* and J.H. Follows *(5th from left)*. *Railway Gazette*

industry bringing in timber from the Colonies, Sherrington observed, had equal, if not more, right to be regarded as a depressed industry, and concludes: 'In short it would appear that the replacement of timber by steel may be regarded as of a very doubtful national advantage'.[61]

The overall impression one might gain from reading the report, is that it did little more than justify the *status quo*, and was not forward-looking in its approach. As the Carriage & Wagon workshops had only recently been reorganised by Lemon, one might also be tempted to look for bias in the recommendations. However, the advantages and disadvantages of all-steel construction were considered in turn, and the conclusions drawn were scrupulous in their fairness. Whilst the Committee may have been obsessed with the financial consequences of change, this was an important consideration for a commercial enterprise like the LMS. Of course, it can be seen now that the LMS was only delaying the inevitable, and the days of wooden construction were already numbered. The report does allow, that if the company wished to provide steel coaches, then 'suitable plant, estimated

to cost £20,000, be provided at one of the Company's factories to enable the LMS to build such steel stock themselves'. Lemon, knowing from the Committee's investigations that the plant and machinery at Wolverton was at the end of its life, may have seen a production opportunity. A later Report to the Board stated that 'since 1930' the standard design for carriages on the LMS consisted of a wooden body frame fitted with steel side and end panels, a steel roof and floor (underneath the floor boards), and by 1932 it was general policy to fit a steel carriage at the front of each express passenger train, to lessen damage from fire and accident.[62]

The Committee then continued by reviewing steel freight stock. One major aspect of their review concerned the well-known problem with the steel components of coal wagons. These showed an alarming amount of corrosion – 3cwt of rust was removed from one two-year-old all-steel wagon during routine maintenance.[63] Even open 'wooden' wagons with steel underframes suffered badly from corrosion, having a life expectancy of only 20 years. Having surveyed the evidence the committee recommended an expansion of the use of copper-bearing steel underframes, which seemed to corrode less quickly; and noted that more research into corrosion, and its amelioration by the use of alloys, should be undertaken. These problems were not so great with covered wagons, and they concluded that the current policy of building covered wagons with steel underframes and wooden bodies was the correct one for the future – especially as wooden bodies showed greater thermal insulation (an important consideration when transporting margarine in summer!). The Committee then recommended that a total of 10,000 wagons should be built with copper-bearing steel underframes over the following four years. A full record of costs would then be kept for the next seven years in order to obtain reliable information on which to base a definite policy. Further, it suggested the building of 3,000 wagons, the repair and maintenance costs of which should be carefully surveyed by restricting them to LMS lines only, and used solely for locomotive coal. 1,000 of these should be of wood/steel construction, 1,000 should be all-steel wagons (made from copper-bearing steel) and the final 1,000 all wood. The relative merits of each type could then be directly compared.

The 11th International Railway Congress, Madrid, 1930

THE 11th Session of the International Railway Congress was held in Madrid 5–15 May 1930, and three papers on Steel Coaching Stock were given. Two of these were French, submitted by Messieurs Lancrenon from the Nord, and Vallencien of the OCEM.[64] The third paper was submitted by Lemon, and was a revised and expanded version of the LMS Report completed a month earlier. For Madrid, Lemon included detailed statistics of all the steel rolling stock in use on railways worldwide – information undoubtedly supplied by Sherrington. Although Lemon was a delegate attending the Congress, he is not recorded as having contributed anything to the discussions when the three papers were considered. These were dominated by the French contributors, whose country had made the decision to standardise on steel coaches because of the increased safety they afforded, their better

riding qualities and increased life expectancy.

Although these claims had been analysed by Sherrington in an Appendix to the original LMS report,[65] he was somewhat dismissive of the need to follow the French example in the UK. French railways, he wrote, had a lower degree of safety – the standard of track maintenance was not as high as in Britain, hence there was a greater risk of derailment. The 'absolute block' system of signalling was not enforced, leading to a greater risk of collision. Cooking and heating in restaurant cars was by coal, rendering an element of fire danger; and the greater length of French coaches made the construction of a wooden body of sufficient strength very heavy. As a final nail in the coffin, he stated that the coach builders' art in France had never been as good as in Britain, with the result that coaches needed complete rebuilding after five years use!

Institute of Transport Congress, Glasgow, 1930

SHORTLY after returning from Madrid, Lemon attended another conference. At the Institute of Transport Congress in Glasgow he presented a paper entitled: 'Amalgamation & its effect on the workshops'.[66] This has been referred to earlier in connection with his reforms at the Derby Carriage & Wagon works, but the paper also describes the effects and changes these had subsequently provoked across the whole LMS. Each workshop had developed their own schemes for progressive construction of the types of carriage or wagon allotted to them. Lemon also reported that amalgamation had enabled a considerable amount of standardisation to be carried out. A standard width for passenger coaches had been established, and only four different lengths were now allowed. There were also now only three different types of goods brake vans, whereas previously there had been as many as 18. The smaller capacity wagons were gradually being eliminated in favour of a standard 12-ton wagon, the numbers of which had increased from 31,200 to 116,798. Successful schemes for the repair and maintenance of wagons and coaches had been developed along the same progressive lines as construction was carried out. Indeed, a rigorous protocol had been established for this routine maintenance. Carriages would now pass through one of the main factories for general repairs every six years, and for intermediate attention every eighteen months. A similar system also applied to wagons. The consequence of all this was a reduction in costs to the Company allied with a saving in floor-space. However, this was not the only consideration – Lemon reported that: 'The labour-saving appliances which have been installed to reduce manual labour have enabled the workmen to go home less fatigued after a day's work under the new system than they did under the old'.

This was the final act of Lemon's active management of the carriage and wagon department. By the end of the year, he was in charge of the locomotives that pulled them. However, research carried out for this book challenges many long-held beliefs about the accepted order of events and the reasons which motivated them. The source of this new information is Sir Harold Hartley's papers at Churchill College Cambridge, which give a very different view of the changes in the top personnel in the LMS – who was responsible and why.

Sir Henry Fowler.
Derby Railway
Engineering Club

Sir Henry Fowler – Chief Mechanical Engineer

THE 'briefing' note that Sir Harold Hartley received from William Wood when he started at the LMS (referred to earlier) also includes the blunt statement 'Should C.M.E. and C.&W. be amalgamated on Fowler's departure?' [67] – indicating that there were already moves afoot, in February 1930, to replace Sir Henry Fowler as Chief Mechanical Engineer.

The legacy of Sir Henry Fowler as CME is still, to this day, a cause of controversy. There are those who denigrate his work, and others who, just as strongly, defend him. For example, Hamilton Ellis [68] states that it is doubtful whether

Fowler ever designed a locomotive: E.S. Cox [69] writes that he was not very interested in loco-motive design, his prime interests being adminis-tration, workshops and metallurgy. A current website states 'Sir Henry Fowler was certainly a man of very considerable ability, but unfortunately his many strengths did not include the ability – crucial for a Chief Mechanical Engineer in steam days – to design good locomotives (or, acknowledging his own weakness, to surround himself with others who could)'. [70] This allegation is countered by another website which, while acknowledging these remarks, rebuts them with: 'it is obvious that Fowler has been grossly maligned by history and by E.S. Cox and Hamilton Ellis'. [71] Every writer on the subject has an individual view, and this book is not the place to defend Fowler or denigrate him. What is clear, however, from Wood's 'briefing' note is that Fowler's tenure of this office was a cause for concern in the senior management of the LMS by 1930.

The problems of amalgamation of the LNWR and the Midland Railway (ignoring the separate traditions stemming from, for example, the Scottish railways, and the old Lancashire & Yorkshire Railway) seem to have been most acute when it came to locomotive design. The entrenched traditions of Crewe and Derby were not going to be given up lightly. However, as three of the current four Vice-Presidents were men from the Midland Railway, there was an increasing tendency towards 'Midlandisation'. And the Midland traditionally built small locomotives. The reasons for this seem to be that (a) it was cheaper – an important consideration when economic constraints were a major factor in railway expenditure, (b) they were reliable and easy to maintain, and (c) there was less weight on the tracks and lower grade rails and weaker bridges could be used. Neither of these seem to be overwhelmingly convincing reasons

14, North Court,
Wood Street,
Westminster, S.W.1.

7.8.30

Dear Sir Josiah,

An extract of a private letter from Sir Harold Hartley to Sir Josiah Stamp, August 1930, concerning the replacement of Sir Henry Fowler as CME.
Churchill College, Cambridge

been made on the advice and suggestions from subordinate officers. This is what the Vice-Presidents and the Executive Committee were for. As research for this book progressed, it has become apparent that Hartley was much more important than generally realised. Stamp's contribution was to offer encouragement or, conversely, to urge restraint, as appropriate – and to act as a facilitator. In the case of double-heading, Stamp had ample opportunity in the preceding years to have done something about it, but action was only taken after Hartley's appointment.

Now that he had overall responsibility for the CME's department, Hartley very soon came to appreciate that, if attitudes were finally to change with regard to locomotive policy, radical reforms were necessary – and his papers show how he attacked the problem. The first thing he had to do was replace Fowler as CME; and to do so in a dignified way as befitted a man with his reputation and position within the Company. On 7 August 1930 – and just over a week before he led a group of LMS officers, including Lemon, to America – Hartley wrote a private letter (in his truly appalling handwriting) to Stamp:

for sticking with tradition for tradition's sake; and this policy had led to a greater reliance on double-heading than any of the other railway companies.

This use of double-heading was immediately queried by Hartley,[72] but the remark has also been attributed to Stamp – which is confusing. However, while researching this book, the phrase: 'Stamp did this' or 'Stamp did that', is often encountered when describing some new policy. This is especially prevalent in the snippets of news printed in the railway magazines, and Stamp's name is here usually no more than journalese shorthand for 'the management of the LMS'. The phrase, though, also creeps into many books written on LMS history, and here it is a lazy form of scholarship, usually indicating that the author did not know where the original idea came from. Unless one is careful, a general assumption is engendered that Stamp was some omnipotent being, responsible for every new idea and initiative in the Company. In fact, while some may have originated from him, most would have

Dear Sir Josiah

I have had another talk to Fowler about the future of his Dept., and he made things easy for me by saying that he realised that I was in a difficult position and that he was ready to go whenever I said he must, altho' he would like to keep some active connection for two or three years to come for various reasons.
He told me of his suggestions to you last year viz. Anderson C.M.E., Beames, Motive Power

Supt., Symes, Crewe. I told him that this seemed to me a makeshift, and that I must have a younger C.M.E. when the time came for a change, who could look forward to at least ten years activity. He then suggested Stanier of the G.W.R. (who is I believe a brilliant designer) but added that the only younger man in the LMS who was capable of doing the job was Lemon, if we thought of combining C.M.E. and C & W again. I had spoken of the need for certain reorganisations . . . and the need for bringing Derby Crewe and Horwich into a more homogenous system, and he said that he thought Lemon was the man. By this time I had mentioned the possibility of his acting for a time as Consulting M.E. and I felt that he would really welcome relief from Executive responsibility, and he realises that there are big problems immediately ahead which must be tackled. He is worried now about the position at Derby and is coming to see me on Monday when he has last month's figures. I have thought it over carefully and Lemon seems to me to have just the qualities we need. He is a genius at organisation and he has the necessary decision and firmness. Now that I know Fowler's attitude the thing is much simpler, and if you agree I propose to give Lemon a broad hint of what is passing through my own mind – without committing anybody else – and ask him to keep an eye on both sides of the works organisation while he is in America. In view of the position of the Company we ought not to delay tackling our problems, and I am holding up several as I am anxious not to queer the pitch for the new man. We might be making plans during the autumn and change over at Christmas, leaving Fowler to look after design and development while Lemon is reorganising and fusing the two Depts.

Forgive the long letter in my own writing, as it is too confidential to dictate. I hope you are getting a good holiday and building great schemes for the future. Please give my respects to Lady Stamp.

Yours sincerely
Harold Hartley

In a postscript, Hartley added:

From one or two hints he has dropped I fancy Follows would back Anderson for C.M.E. This doesn't affect my opinion, but I think you should know.

Now, Hartley had only been in office a matter of months before he wrote this letter, hence perhaps the acknowledgment that he was in a 'difficult position' when dealing with someone with so many years service, and in such a senior position, as Fowler. Nevertheless, the impression one immediately gathers is that he had assumed the authority to sort out the problem as he thought fit; and he was prepared to challenge the recommendations of longer-serving officers, such as his fellow Vice-President, J.H. Follows. He does not seem to be following any preconceived plan that Stamp had given him.

The letter also gives the impression that Hartley was leading the conversation with Fowler in the directions he wanted. Fowler's suggestion that Lemon was the best man for the job, looks very much the result of judicious prompting. It is interesting that Stanier's name came up at this early stage and, of course, his work for the GWR would have been well known to Hartley from his experiences travelling between Oxford and London. One immediately is inclined to ask the question: why was an approach therefore not made to poach Stanier from the GWR immediately? It was not for another year – October 1931 – that the approach was made. Hartley also stated in his letter that Fowler's earlier recommendations seemed to him to be 'makeshift' and he wanted to make an appointment that would last 'ten years'. Now, as we know that Lemon subsequently only held the title of CME for just over ten *months*, this would appear at first sight to be exactly the type of makeshift appointment that Hartley wished to avoid. So we are forced to consider two possibilities – either Hartley rapidly changed his mind after Lemon's appointment, or he was playing a devious game. The first suggestion does not seem to be borne out in the light of Lemon's subsequent elevation to Vice-President. If he had proved inadequate to the job of CME, he would surely have been quietly moved sideways. And so we are drawn to the second suggestion as the more likely scenario. In view of Sherrington's later comments, it seems therefore that Hartley already had in mind a longer-term strategy – that he had no intention whatsoever of immediately replacing Fowler with someone who would hold the post for ten years. Lemon was the obvious choice to carry out the required changes in departmental organisation and, as a Derby man, would be acceptable to Fowler. After Lemon had carried out the rationalisation and administrative changes, he would move on and be replaced by a specialist in locomotive design. It seems clear that Hartley had quickly realised Lemon's capabilities. His biographer in the DNB notes that 'As a judge of character Hartley was quick to distinguish the efficient from the inefficient'. At this moment in time, therefore, Lemon was very much Hartley's protégé, which flies in the face of the generally accepted idea that it was Stamp who had 'marked him out for promotion', quoted in virtually every book about the LMS.

The Advisory Committee on Scientific Research (1)

ONE of R.W. Reid's recommendations was that the Director of Research should be assisted by an Advisory Committee and, following Hartley's appointment this was duly formed. The inaugural meeting of this 12-strong committee was held on 2 July 1930, and the members included Sir Henry Fowler, Lemon and the heads of other relevant departments. Stamp addressed the first meeting, and had a few choice words to set them on their way. Though primarily an LMS Committee, he said, the results of its work would affect the science of transportation in general, and thus become a matter of national interest.[74] Five initial memoranda had been circulated detailing the topics that the Committee might consider, and it was agreed that they would not necessarily attempt to set up their own research departments to solve their problems, but would work in conjunction with external research facilities. The minutes show that the first item on the agenda was the use of timber – which was used not only in the building

of carriages, but also for railway sleepers and general construction work. Lemon asked that the figures for purchases of timber should be divided into separate totals, according to the use to which it was put. The discussion moved on to the next item, the durability of paint – another topic with which Lemon was involved. He later explained the reasons for his concerns: 'The question arose in this way. It was absolutely essential for us to make certain savings on our carriage maintenance. An analysis as to the reasons why the carriages were sent into the shops, revealed two varying factors – painting and wheel tyres. Make the paint last longer – say twice as long, and the wheel-tyres stand up without requiring turning so often, and we could make a considerable cut in our carriage maintenance.'[75] It was agreed that Lemon and three others would confer on this subject – and its associated problem, the cleaning of paintwork – and seek help from the research unit at ICI. The next topic was the preservation of textiles, and Lemon pointed out that, so far, no accelerated-wear tests of upholstery appeared to be of any great value. Once again, it was decided to seek help from outside research associations. Lest one thinks that this was developing into a forum dominated by Lemon, it should be pointed out that the next twenty-or-so items on the agenda did not involve him to any great extent! The subjects discussed ranged from the welding of boilers, the prevention of fractures in locomotive tyres and adhesion between metals, to the problems of signalling in fog and the removal of ice from conductor rails – to pick out only a few. Lemon was actively involved in the discussions about improvement in carriage painting, and anti-corrosive steel for coal wagon underframes (which had been such a concern in his report a couple of months earlier).

The final item on the agenda was the 'Visit of Officers to America', and Hartley asked the members if they could suggest any specific research institutions they should visit while they were in the country.

The Minutes show that this Committee met four or five times a year. Lemon remained a member after he became Vice-President, and Stanier joined when he was appointed CME.

Five of the LMS
party on their
return from
America.
Left to right:
Newlands,
Fowler, Bound,
Cortez-Leigh
and Lemon.
Railway Gazette

Visit to America, 1930

ON 16 August 1930, Hartley and five fellow officers of the LMS set sail from Southampton on the 'Empress of France' bound for Quebec. Hartley had indicated to Stamp, in correspondence before he was appointed Vice-President, that 'in order to learn his ABC' one of his first tasks would be to visit America and Germany and see how they tackled problems there. Before they left, Stamp stressed to Hartley 'the desirability of your purview being as wide as possible'.[76] He did not want a report to be confined to the special interests of the Chief Officers who were accompanying him, but one that included observations upon all they had observed, covering every kind of railway question.

The other members of the party were Fowler, Lemon, F.A. Cortez-Leigh (Chief Electrical Engineer), A.F. Bound (Chief Signals Engineer) and A. Newlands (Chief Engineer) – all members of the Scientific Research Committee. The practical arrangements for the trip were made by C.E.R. Sherrington, and Hartley reported back to Stamp on 4 September 1930 from Chicago:[77]

So far everything has gone well with us and we have carried out most of our programme. That we have done so much is due largely to Sherrington who prepared the way for us and has saved us an immense amount of time by

putting us in touch with the right people. Everyone loves him over here and I am most grateful to you for suggesting that he should be with us for part of the time. It remains to be seen how we shall fare without him.

He will give you a much better account of our doings than I can – I think we are getting a lot out of the trip even if conditions here are so different to our own. S. will tell you that I have been spending a good deal of time looking into the organisation of budget systems on different roads, which I hope you will approve. It's very interesting to see how the budget system enables them to deal with problems of falling revenue from month to month. In that respect their position is even worse than ours.

One can therefore see that the concept of 'budgetary control', which the LMS subsequently introduced, stemmed from Hartley's observation of American practice on this trip. Many published sources give the credit for this policy to Stamp. Divall, for example, writes that Stamp 'imposed from 1931 a comprehensive scheme of strict budgetary controls'.[78] Hartley ends his letter by listing the hospitality and banquets that had been laid on for them, and how the other members of the party must be getting tired of listening to his speeches. He concludes that they 'will soon be getting up a sweep on the recurrence of my stories and points'.

The group spent about six weeks in Canada and the USA and arrived back in this country on 5 October. Hartley must have travelled back independently, as he does not appear in the group photograph of their arrival that was printed in the *Railway Gazette*. Indeed one can now look at this photograph in a slightly different light. Sir Henry Fowler with tie askew *(back left)* looks cheerful and composed, although he must have known that he was shortly to be replaced. On the extreme right, a confident dapper-looking Lemon, with a cigarette between his fingers, is not even deigning to look at the camera, and seemingly in a rush to get away and on to more important things.

As soon as Hartley had returned from the States, he officially submitted his proposals for changes to the CME's department in a (typed!) memorandum to Stamp.[79] As it seems that this has never before appeared in print, and cannot be found in the LMS papers at the National Archives, it is included here in its virtual entirety:

Memorandum to the President
23rd October, 1930
Organisation of Mechanical Engineer's and Carriage and Wagon Departments

I have reported to you from time to time that there are several important problems connected with the Chief Mechanical Engineer's Department which, I think, need taking in hand, but I have refrained hitherto from doing so because it seemed to me that they were so closely linked that they should be dealt with together.

The problems are, briefly :-

(1) The need for closer co-ordination of the Locomotive Shops at Derby, Crewe and Horwich.
(2) The adjustment of the building and repair capacity of all Locomotive Shops to the present needs of the Company.
(3) The consideration of such manufacturing processes as the Crewe Steel Works, Rolling Mill and Foundry, and the Foundries at Derby and Horwich.

(4) The re-consideration of the present organisation and activities of the Outdoor Machinery Department.

In view of the present emergency I think these problems need to be faced at once, particularly as considerable economies may accrue from them.

This raises immediately the question of a successor to Sir Henry Fowler, who is now over 60 years of age. The reorganisation which I have in mind must take some years to carry through, and I think it should be in the hands of a younger man who is likely to remain long enough in the Service to see the effects of his work.

I do not think it fair to impose such a heavy task on Sir Henry, either in the interests of the Company, or himself. He agrees with me that there is no suitable successor to be found in his Department, nor is there anyone of suitable age and experience in the Motive Power Department.

After making enquiries as to possible Engineers outside the Company, I have come to the conclusion that Mr. Lemon (who will be 46 in December next) is the best selection the Company can make for their future Chief Mechanical Engineer. Mr. Lemon is a genius at Workshop organisation; he was trained as Locomotive Engineer for six years at The North British Locomotive Company, and he had experience in Running Sheds on the Highland Railway. While I was in America I had many opportunities of comparing his organisation with that of other Workshops and of observing the respect with which his views were treated by the Chief Mechanical Engineers of some of the largest systems, and my experience during those weeks with him strongly confirmed my view that he is the best appointment we can make.

Another reason which weighs with me is the great economies which have been effected on American Railways from improvements in locomotive working, and, at this juncture, it is important that this problem should be reviewed by a fresh mind, and there could be no-one better for this purpose than Mr. Lemon.

The proposal to appoint Mr. Lemon raises the question as to the future of the Carriage & Wagon Department. I can see the personal and physical reasons for the separation of this Department from the Locomotive Department on Amalgamation, when there was the heavy problem of a complete reorganisation of the Shops of the constituent Companies to be faced. This work is now practically complete, and the main problem left in connection with the Shops is the adjustment of their capacity to the present needs of the Company. I believe that it is an invariable custom elsewhere for both Departments to come under the Chief Mechanical Engineer, and in view of the state of our organisation, and Mr. Lemon's energy and exceptional powers of delegating authority, I see no reason why the two Departments should not be brought under one head. There is no doubt that certain economies would come from the fusion of the two Departments, and I think Mr. Lemon would be in a stronger position to deal with the following points consequent on the reorganisation, which should yield considerable financial benefits to the Company :-

(1) The closer co-ordination, where possible, of the Locomotive and Carriage & Wagon Shops and Repair Depots.
(2) The adjustment of the building and repair capacity at the Carriage & Wagon Shops to the present needs of the Company.
(3) The centralisation of the manufacturing and reconditioning requirements of the two departments.
(4) The establishment, in conjunction with the Stores Department, of a central reclamation depot for ferrous and non-ferrous material for all Departments of the LMS.
(5) The centralisation and simplification of specifications for stores, for both Departments.

Hartley then included tables of figures assessing the probable financial effects of the reorganisation, and concluded that these reforms could lead to savings of, at least, £500,000 – and possibly even more.

The Memorandum then continues:

I have discussed the whole situation with Sir Henry Fowler, and although he would, naturally, like to retain his present position for some little time to come, he is in agreement with me that the decision proposed in this memorandum is the right one for the Company, in view of the present circumstances, which admit of no delay.

As regards Sir Henry Fowler's position, I think the Company should continue to get the full benefit of his wide knowledge and experience, and I foresee many ways in which he can be of great assistance to Mr. Lemon in the immediate future when the Department is in process of reorganisation, as it must be some little time before he will be able to gather up all the threads into his own hands.

I recommend that Sir Henry's services should be retained as Assistant to Vice-President, for Research and Development, for two years from 1st January, 1931, and that his duties should be :-

(1) To act as Consultant on all matters referred to him from the Mechanical Engineer's Department.
(2) To be in charge of the Chemical Laboratories and Central Testing Bureau of the Company.
(3) To assist the Vice-President in all matters arising from the work of the Scientific Research Committee.
(4) To keep in touch with mechanical developments in this country and abroad, and to report on those likely to have a bearing on the Company's activities.

The suggested changes are bound to throw a considerable amount of additional work on me for a time, and it would be a great relief to me to know that I could leave, for the time being, a good deal of work connected to our Research developments to Sir Henry; otherwise, I feel that part of the work might be seriously prejudiced.

LMS Board Room at Euston 1930. Members of the Board seated, with Sir Josiah Stamp centre. Senior Officers are standing behind with Sir Harold Hartley at extreme right.
National Archives

In recognition of Sir Henry's great services to the Company, and of the fact that we are asking him to retire from the position of Chief Mechanical Engineer at an early date, I suggest that he should be given a pension and a capital sum calculated on the assumption that he had completed his service to 65 years of age.
This would give an annuity of £2,250, and a capital sum of £6,000, and would represent a supplement by the Company to the payments due from the Superannuation Fund of :-

	£	s	d
Annuity	281	5	0
Capital Sum	750	0	0

I recommend that, in addition, he be given a fee of £2,250 for each of the two years he is retained, which would have the effect of giving Sir Henry his full salary for the two years.

It is essential that Mr. Lemon should live in London, and that his Headquarters should be at Euston, as it is an unsatisfactory arrangement for the Chief Mechanical Engineer to be directly associated with one of the Company's Workshops, and also it will be necessary for Mr. Lemon and myself to be near together, so that we can settle things from day to day by conversation instead of by correspondence.

These proposals were considered, a week later, at the Board Meeting on 30 October 1930. The Special Minutes [80] show that, on the recommendation of the Chairman, all of Hartley's proposals, including the terms of the financial pay-off, were agreed without alteration of any kind. Fowler was to retire on 31 December 1930, when Lemon would take over as CME in charge of both Locomotive and Carriage & Wagon Departments. If Hartley's fellow Vice-President, J.H. Follows, had still championed J.E. Anderson, the Motive Power Superintendent, for the job, his opinion did not prevail.

On 31 December 1930, the five-year agreement with Sir Josiah Stamp as President of the Executive also expired. The Board of Directors drew up a new agreement – the terms of which are recorded in the Special Minutes of 18 December 1930. One clause stated that although Stamp could retain his Directorship of the Bank of England, otherwise he was to give his whole time to affairs of the Company – with the option to modify the restriction after 18 months. Stamp had added the Bank of England Directorship to his portfolio of interests in 1928 and, while it may not be entirely unexpected to find that the terms and conditions specified the appointment was to be full-time, nevertheless it does appear that the accusation he was not spending sufficient time on LMS matters, and did not know what was going on in his departments, made at the AGM a few months earlier, may have struck a chord.

The Lightning Committee

MEANWHILE, as a consequence of the American trip, Lemon was appointed Chairman of a Committee to consider what lessons could be learned from practices on the other side of the Atlantic. Sir Harold Hartley later wrote in his obituary of Lemon: 'On our return Stamp appointed a committee with Lemon as chairman to garner the fruits of our visit. It was known as "The Lightning Committee" because it reported so quickly, and its findings foreshadowed many of the changes that were made by the LMS in the thirties, under Lemon's forceful personality'.[81] The 1930 trip can thus be seen to have been a pivotal point in the history of the LMS and a crucial influence on the direction the Management was to take.

It is fortunate that many of the recommendations of this Committee were put into practice while Lemon was Vice-President, as a record of their progress was kept by his Personal Assistant, H.G. Smith. Herbert Grant Smith worked for Lemon from his appointment as Vice-President in November 1931 until Lemon retired from the LMS in 1943. In 1941, Smith itemised all the projects that Lemon had inspired, collating such original copies of memos as he still possessed, and retyping others. These hitherto unknown documents, which have remained in Lemon's personal papers, shed an important light on his career, and will be extensively used as a primary source in the ensuing chapters of this book. Smith's archive starts with several reports that date from November 1930 and, although he does not refer to the 'Lightning Committee' by this name, one can see from their content and date that they all derive from the reports of this Committee. Many of the documents still bear their original LMS reference numbers, which gives them added authority, and they have been an invaluable reference source as duplicate copies have not been found in any other archive.

The Lightning Committee reports are all dated around 12 November 1930 – and this is the date on a report entitled 'Detailed Analysis of Work Performed' which is concerned with the principles of Scientific Management. As we have seen, Lemon embodied these principles in his redesign of the Carriage & Wagon Works at Derby and, in this memo, he urged the LMS management to apply them to every department of the Company.

EUSTON   12th November 1930

Memorandum to the President

Detailed Analysis of Work Performed

The delegation who visited America were frequently informed that 'studies' had been made of this or that operation, and these were found, on enquiry, to be detailed analyses of work performed.

Your Committee feel that a field for economy exists on the LMS by a more intensive application of this principle of scientific management than is the case today; in other words, all phases of Railway activities should be examined.

Occasional analyses of operations are done by all departments. There is, however, no systematic application of the principle.

'Job analysis' can be applied equally to clerical work, workshops staff, depots, yards, and to artisan staff working on the line, and your Committee consider a 'drive' should be made in this direction, so that -

(1) Comparisons may be made between similar operations at A and B.

(2) The best practice at A and B may be ascertained and a standard practice adopted for application to the Line as a whole.
(3) Waste of money and effort may be eliminated.

Detailed analyses of all operations have been carried out in certain Workshops which have resulted in very considerable savings and improvements in methods. The work done by the staff in the Road Motor, Electrical and Civil Engineering Workshops can be investigated on these lines immediately by utilising the experience gained in the other workshops. The principle, however, is one which can be applied to all operations, whether in workshops or elsewhere.

We recommend that Heads of Departments should be instructed to detail an officer on their staff to draw up forms and submit them to the Chief Officer for Labour and Establishment, who would arrange for the matter to be proceeded with.

Amy and David in the garden at 'Highfield', Derby c.1930. Family

This memo was followed in quick succession by other reports, amongst which were 'Coal silos – provision of mechanical handling plant', 'Flood-lighting at marshalling yards' and 'Modernisation of Motive Power Depots'. The consequences of each of these will be dealt with later in this book, as it took several years before the recommen-dations were put into effect. Other reports, however, were acted upon immediately. One such was 'Signalling economies and improved methods', [82] and the Chairman reported to the Board on 27 November 1930 that the recent USA visit had focussed attention on the subject, and a number of fresh ideas had been obtained. Stamp quoted figures showing the benefits that had already been obtained from the modern-isation of signalling arrangements: schemes completed up to 1 January 1929 showed an annual saving of 50% on the costs incurred. However, each scheme was submitted separately for approval and there was too great a time-lag between their authorisation and completion. Stamp proposed to the Board that full-time officers should be appointed from the offices of the Chief General Superintendent and the Signal

& Telegraph Engineer to deal exclusively with these matters; and that the scope of the investigations into possible economies should be widened to include:
1) Amalgamation of signal boxes by the introduction of electrical control of points
2) Application of Centralised Traffic Control
3) Application of Automatic Signalling
4) Power operation of points in Shunting Yards
   He then proposed that any scheme up to a value of £5,000 which showed a net annual saving over 10% could be authorised immediately by the Vice-Presidents without referral to the Board.

Reports to the appropriate Directors' Com-mittees would be made in bulk, and in retrospect, every three months. This was approved by the Board [83] and one can see from the later Minutes how such submissions were regularly approved. H.G. Smith records that by the outbreak of war in 1939, 324 such schemes had been completed at a cost of around £355,000 with annual savings of just over £75,000 giving a return on the investment of 21%.

A month after producing these reports and recommendations, Lemon took over as Chief Mechanical Engineer.

FOUR

Chief Mechanical Engineer, 1931

PREVIOUS writers have always referred to Lemon's CME appointment as temporary. And it undoubtedly was – but not for the reasons that are generally given. Most writers have assumed that Sir Henry Fowler resigned from the post of his own volition. Sir Harold Hartley's papers demonstrate that this was not so. They have also then assumed that Lemon's appointment was merely a stop-gap: a temporary solution to an unforeseen predicament. Denis Griffiths, for example, wrote: 'and it is certain that this was looked upon by all parties as purely a temporary affair whilst Stamp searched for a more permanent replacement for Fowler'.[84] (Note, again, the generic use of Stamp's name as the prime mover in this matter). The evidence is that Lemon's appointment was actually one stage in a carefully-orchestrated plan devised by Sir Harold Hartley.

The implication behind the statement that Lemon's appointment was only temporary is that nothing important actually happened during the next 12 months. Everything one can learn about Lemon indicates that this is a most unlikely scenario. The man was a workaholic, and certainly would not have sat on his hands for the best part of a year, doing nothing. It is certainly true that no locomotives of new design were built during the year – which is the over-riding concern of most railway enthusiasts – but construction and

modifications continued on existing models. Other information as to what he achieved, however, is hard to come by. Most writers have been happy to gloss over this period and move on immediately to Stanier's appointment. Lemon's name was even omitted from a list of previous CMEs in the Centenary Supplement to the *Railway Gazette* in September 1938.[85] However, as will be explained, it was in these ten months that the whole organisation of the use, maintenance and repair of locomotives was changed.

In order to maintain the balance between the Crewe and Derby factions, Lemon's Deputy CME was H.P.M. Beames – a Crewe man (who was repeatedly passed over for the top job). Beames, however, was to be based at Derby, presumably in an attempt to neutralise any untoward problems from the Crewe faction. S.J. Symes, a Derby man, was in charge of (steam) locomotive affairs, whilst Tommy Hornbuckle looked after the diesels that were just beginning to be developed. Both of the latter moved, with Lemon, to offices at Euston as Hartley had demanded. Hartley obviously intended to maintain a close eye on Lemon's progress. It is worth commenting here that Lemon did not sell his house in Derby until 1932, and so must have had to find temporary accommodation in London.

So, what did he do? As Hartley indicated in his original memo to Stamp proposing that the

CHIEF MECHANICAL ENGINEERS OF THE L.M.S.R.	
George Hughes	1923–1925
Sir Henry Fowler	1925–1931
William Arthur Stanier	1932–

The forgotten CME!
Supplement to the Railway Gazette, 16 Sept. 1938 to celebrate the LMS Centenary

Locomotive and Carriage & Wagon works should be combined, Lemon had to carry this through to fruition. Not only would this involve setting up a whole new departmental structure, but would also involve, for instance, physical changes in the allocation and use of buildings. A.E. Langridge, for example, described the office reorganisation that took place at Derby, lamenting the move of his drawing office which meant that he and his colleagues finished up half-a-mile from the dining rooms, library and station.[86] Similar changes must have been made throughout the system. The Locomotive & Electrical Committee minutes record the changes that were made at the Crewe, Derby and Horwich workshops, and later the decision to suspend locomotive construction at Horwich.[87] In fact, Lemon now had to attend both this Committee and the Carriage & Wagon Committee – although he was amalgamating the Departments, the responsible Committees were not unified until Stanier's time in 1932. At the very first meeting of the Locomotive & Electrical Committee that he attended as CME on 28 January 1931, he submitted and explained a proposed new Return Form which would give details of expenditure, staff statistics and work carried out in the Locomotive Department. This was presumably similar in content to the one that he had introduced into the Carriage & Wagon Department on 30 April 1930.[88] This was indicative of the thorough shake-up that Lemon was to give to the working of the Department. Indeed, it is remarkable to discover how many of the initiatives that he set in motion started in the first two months that he was CME. Lemon did not take time to ease himself into the role, and a new vigour swept through the Department.

When Lemon turned his attention specifically to locomotives, he carried out his appraisal in characteristic fashion. Before starting to make changes to the system, he had to understand it thoroughly, and this was the type of task that suited him down to the ground. Accordingly, he set about a comprehensive review of the Company's entire locomotive stock. This was a motley collection of around 9,000 locomotives made up of 261 different types – some of new design, but the majority inherited from the constituent companies that had formed the LMS

in 1923. Many had seen better days and, as a result of this review, were destined for the scrapheap. It was obviously totally uneconomic to have such a wide diversity of types, and in his speech to the 1932 Institute of Transport Congress at Buxton a year later, Lemon expressed the hope that: 'Eventually, the number of types may reach the low figure of 20, for obviously the fewer the number adequate to the task to be performed, the more steady, uniform, and economic the flow of repairs. Unnecessary diversity of types is very uneconomical in repair work.'[89]

[At the outbreak of War in 1939, the LMS had just over 7,500 locomotives of 148 types].

E.S. Cox, who was summoned to Euston and told he was now working for Lemon, recounted how he and a colleague 'stumped the country, examining repair cards, and seeing with our own eyes the results in service of all kinds of design matters from leaky smokebox doors all the way through to defective tender pump sieves'.[90] He describes how the details of every type of locomotive were collected for analysis: their reliability and their weaknesses were all then comprehensively assessed. For example, in describing problems with the Claughton class of locomotive, Cox writes: 'Putting to sea in a sieve was as nothing compared to the problem of how to put these engines to rights!' This was probably the first time that one class of locomotive had been compared directly with another and, in this instance, showed that the Claughtons required ten times more maintenance than the Royal Scot class.

The problem was that engine design was largely empirical, and unsatisfactory locomotives were subject to continual tinkering in order to try and improve their performance. There was also no truly accurate way of assessing a locomotive's efficiency, other than to try it out on the track. And the only method then available was to run the locomotive with a dynamometer coach attached and observers perched uncomfortably and dangerously on the front of the engine. Gresley of the LNER had also been able to demonstrate, in 1928, that the dynamometer car belonging to the LMS gave wildly inaccurate results, having never been recalibrated since it was built in 1913. The first static running shed in this country where such measurements could be made in laboratory conditions was not completed until after the Second World War. So one modification was tried, and then another – leading to a rail-spotter's paradise. But this is missing the point: to the commercial railway companies all this was time-consuming, inefficient and costly. What they required was a fleet of standard well-designed, efficient and reliable engines.

Lemon later summed up what a railway company needed in his paper praising the virtues of the 'Jones Goods' class of 4-6-0 locomotives on the old Highland Railway. Reference has already been made to this paper which is undated, but must have been written soon after 1936. Lemon's words are as true today as they were then:

The action of several of the British Railway Companies during recent years in deciding to preserve, for their historic and sentimental value, examples of outstanding locomotive types now passing into obsolescence, has attracted considerable interest and appreciation from large numbers of people who are interested, both professionally and otherwise, in the steam locomotive.

It cannot fail to escape the observation of the technical man, however, that the interest so aroused has been directed mainly towards the feats of these engine on the running road during the heyday of their performance, and while this tendency is a natural one, it must not be overlooked that, from the viewpoint of those who actually have to maintain and repair the locomotive, there are other considerations more important than its actual performance in running. Sometimes these other considerations, including ease and cost of maintenance and repair, may in the long run be more important to the railway company as an economic factor than the capacity of the engine to haul heavy loads or to maintain high speeds; moreover some types of engine which have gained reputations for performance on the road have been both costly to maintain in the running shed and difficult to work upon in the shop.

The ideal locomotive from the net revenue

viewpoint is thus one which combines efficiency of performance with a low costing factor in maintenance and repairs.[91]

The results of Lemon's analysis of the locomotive situation in 1931 can be found in the March Report to the Board.[92] Although this is credited as being 'from the Executive', the information it contains was obviously supplied by his investigations. The report listed the stocks of locomotives at December 1930, and showed how the numbers had been reduced by 1,077 since amalgamation. Not only had the policy of building larger locomotives reduced the stock requirement, but there had been further savings because of the improved output of repairs. Further questions were being examined, the report states, relating to the greater mileage and hours in service now being achieved by locomotives; and further work was being carried out towards the policy of building locomotives of standard design. All this was accompanied by tables of statistics showing in great detail the savings that could be made by more modern, and efficient engines.[93] The report concludes that the analysis showed that a close scrutiny of older types was warranted, with a view to their elimination. This was being undertaken, and a long-term replacement programme would follow. Cox then writes that: 'When Lemon passed on to higher office, after only 12 months' tenure of the post of C.M.E., proposals had already been evolved as to what to do in each case'.[94] The decisions varied according to the severity or regularity of the problems. Cox describes how, for example, the decision was made that many of the Claughtons should be 'rebuilt'. He continues 'In other words they should be scrapped and replaced. Thus was pronounced the death knell of this controversial class.' Beames, however, was able to argue for a reprieve of the Prince of Wales class. Although it had a worse record than the Claughtons, he persuaded Lemon that the present difficulties could be overcome. All the other classes of locomotives were subject to this dispassionate assessment, and decisions made on their future.

The appraisal established that none of the classes of heavy freight locomotives warranted further construction. Three alternative proposals were developed by the different workshops, which are described in detail by Cox. He then writes 'Lemon was quite unable to make a selection between these alternatives'. This is a harsh judgment. Lemon was a brilliant organiser and production engineer, but he was not a locomotive designer. It is quite understandable that he could not assess the merits of rival proposals from a set of paper drawings. As has been described above, this was often beyond the capabilities of the designers and draughtsmen themselves, who frequently found that, in reality, their designs did not match expectations. If there is any truth in Hartley's original statement to Fowler that he wanted a CME who could last for 10 years, this is when the crunch came. However, it is the author's contention that the next step was never in doubt, and Lemon's whole rôle was to reorganise the Department, and prepare the way for his successor. He may well have deliberately shied away from a decision about these freight locomotives, preferring to leave it to a more competent successor.

Meanwhile, following the regime he had established for the routine maintenance of carriages and wagons, Lemon also categorised a new scheme for the maintenance of locomotives under one central control (the Locomotive Maintenance and Mechanical Efficiency Scheme). In this case, though, he did not set a rigid time-scale for such work, as he had done for rolling-stock. The general maintenance of carriages and wagons could quite conveniently be linked to a simple time-scale, when the deterioration from weathering, together with that from hours in service, could be checked and overhauled simultaneously. This *was* the system that was already used for locomotives, which were called in for a complete overhaul at fixed intervals. However, this was an unsatisfactory compromise, and led to unnecessary maintenance being carried out on parts still in a satisfactory condition.

R.C. Bond, who was appointed by Lemon to be Assistant Works Superintendent at Horwich locomotive works explained the disadvantages of the old system:

Except in the comparatively few cases of engines being sent into the Works for some specific defect – for example to change the boiler after a lead plug failure or to repair collision damage, repairs of a kind which do nothing to liquidate mileage run – it had been the general practice for all locomotives sent in to LMS mainworks to be given a complete general overhaul, irrespective of whether the condition of the firebox or wear of tyres and axleboxes was the determining factor in calling the engine into shops. Whereas in the case of the boiler and firebox wear and tear are related to hours in steam, it is mileage run which is the dominant factor for the rest of the locomotive – the frames, wheels, axleboxes and motion. The relationship between hours in steam and mileage run naturally varied widely depending upon the class of locomotive and the services upon which they were engaged. The rates of accumulation of wear and tear for the boiler and mechanical parts by no means always conveniently coincided to the extent that both were fully rundown at the same time. It follows that neither time nor mileage, by themselves are satisfactory bases for deciding when steam locomotives need to be sent into Shops. [95]

Bond concluded:

Actual physical condition, ascertained by a thorough examination after a pre-determined period in service is the only satisfactory criterion on which to base decisions.

This was precisely the regime that Lemon instigated – as he explained in his paper to the Institute of Transport Congress at Buxton in 1932:

The responsibility for proposing each engine for the shops rests with the district locomotive superintendent, to whom the engine is allocated for running, and two months before the agreed period a report giving particulars of the condition of the engine, i.e. wheels, frames, cylinders, motion, brakework etc., is sent from the shed to the divisional motive power superintendent. This form is then forwarded to the boiler inspector who, as soon as possible after receipt, examines the boiler of the engine proposed and forwards boiler report with proposal form to the central shopping bureau. [96]

Lemon's official passes giving free travel on the Midland Railway and London Transport. Family

A decision was then made centrally as to whether the engine should be put on the list agreed for the shops. In this way, not only was unnecessary work eliminated, but the uniformity of decisions ensured that all engines were maintained to the same standard.

Lemon quoted some further statistics in this Buxton paper. By adopting a 'progressive system for repairs' (i.e. on a conveyor-belt system), the time in shops for one type of engine had been reduced from 5½ weeks in 1925 to six days in 1930. Whereas in 1928 it took 28 days to repair a boiler, this was now done in 11 – materially reducing the stock of replacements the Company had to keep in store. Lemon was a great believer in setting his Works' standards to achieve rather better than current performance. In his 1932 Buxton speech he said:

In my experience of running factories, I have always found it of great assistance to give people something to aim at which is a little better than what is now being done. The aim should be to fix a standard output, or goal, sufficiently high that it requires striving to reach, and yet not so high as to make it incapable of attainment . . . For example, in locomotive practice last year [i.e. 1931] we set ourselves the standard of '100,000 miles between general repairs'. We did not reach it,

but we increased our mileage from 50,000 to about 60,000 . . . This year [1932] we hope to reach that standard; people may scoff at slogans, if this may be regarded as a slogan, but I can assure them that they are powerful instruments for getting things done.

Water Softening

THE hardness of water, and the consequent 'furring up' of boiler tubes with calcium deposits was one of the major factors which governed the length of time a locomotive could remain in service before extensive maintenance was necessary. It was thus an important factor in Lemon's desire to extend the period between locomotive overhauls. Engines in Scotland were able to achieve his goal of 100,000 miles between general repairs owing to the purity of the water whereas in some areas of England only half this mileage could be achieved.[97]

On 27 July 1931, Lemon submitted a memo to the Locomotive & Electrical Committee on the subject of water softening for locomotive purposes.[98] The Minutes record that this already had the approval of the Executive Committee and the memo embodied the conclusions of a specialised committee set up in November 1930 to consider the matter. They recommended that a policy of water softening embracing both of the Company's routes to Carlisle should be given serious attention, and proposed that 28 softening plants should be installed: 16 on the route from Euston and 12 on the route from St Pancras. The majority of these were situated towards the southern end of each line where water quality was the poorest. The committee considered an alternative, cheaper, proposal – namely, to treat the water in the actual locomotive boiler with various compounds, but dismissed the idea because of doubts about its effectiveness. The quantity of water to be dealt with on the two main lines was large, and could more easily be monitored in individually tailored softening plants. The capital cost of the scheme was estimated at £150,000, with annual running costs of £25,000. Nevertheless, it was predicted that the savings in the first year would at least equal the running costs; and in five years it was predicted that the full (net) savings of £136,000 p.a. would be realised after the deleterious effects of the present inferior water had been removed by repairs or renewals of the firebox and tubes. The plan was approved.

As the date on which the investigation started suggests, this was a direct consequence of another of Lemon's 'Lightning' reports. This report was entitled 'Use of Engines'.[99] It was a brief memo to the President, but was to have far-reaching effects. Crucially, it introduced the concept of 'garages'.

Use of Engines

THE memo starts: 'The Deputation of LMS Officers who visited America found that the American Railroads placed very great importance on the question of the utilisation of engines, and their policy in recent years has been to reduce to the lowest possible number the Locomotive units in hand'. It continues: 'The steps which have been taken as a result of the close investigation into the matter have resulted in a considerable increase in the miles and hours per active locomotive day by making engines perform longer runs without going to the Shed'; and then states that: 'It has been found also, contrary to expectations, that maintenance costs have diminished by the institution of longer runs owing to increased boiler life, in that this part of the machine, which is the determining factor

in the life of a locomotive, is subjected less frequently to variations in temperature, and, therefore, does not require such frequent overhaul as was previously the case'.

This was another avenue to explore in Lemon's quest to make the most profitable use of engines. He arranged for an investigation into further changes to operating practices, and the memo notes that Mr Byrom [Chief General Superintendent] was actively pursuing the matter. He then considers the benefits that would accrue from such a policy, and describes how the longer runs made by engines in America had reduced the work in many sheds, and some had been reduced to the status of 'garages' where the only work done was stabling, coaling and watering. As far as the author is aware, this is the first use of the term 'garage' in this country to describe such sheds. The memo recommended that a full analysis of the facilities at each LMS shed be made, and proposed a remit for a Running Shed Committee to enquire what mechanisation could be justified.

Proposed Remit – Running Shed Committee

To enquire into and report the ways and extent to which further mechanisation of work in the Running Sheds can be justified, with particular reference to the following questions:-

1. In view of the large increase of wages between 1913 and the present date, whether the installation of Mechanical Appliances such as Portable Electric Cranes for handling of coupling rods, buffer beams, etc., and other heavy parts of locomotives can be justified.
2. Whether electric or petrol tractors would be of use in Running Sheds for quicker handling in transport of material.
3. Whether economy can be made also, in alteration of coaling plants, or any improvements in this direction in order to save engine power, and what economy could be made in ash handling plants, keeping in mind the position of pits for dropping of fires.
4. Whether further development in the way of cleaning arrangements could be installed, similar to those in use in America, for engine cleaning.

5. Whether any economy can be made in the way of direct steaming of engine boilers from a stationary plant to get engines ready for use instead of raising steam on each engine.

6. Whether sand should be dried in a central place and then distributed, or whether we should continue to have separate drying plants at each Shed.

7. Whether methods of removing smoke box char by use of Vacuum Exhauster and Dust Extractor are feasible.

8. To standardise the practice of boiler repairs in the various Sheds in the group, and to standardise all tools and equipment used, with a view to getting the longest possible times out of the boilers between shopping.

9. Improvement in watering engines, position of water columns, etc.

10. Improvement in or extensions of repairing equipment, drop pits, sheer legs, gantries, machines, tools, etc., and weighing facilities for engines.

11. To what extent are existing turntables satisfactory from the point of view of capacity, type, and position, and would any advantage be obtained by the application of power for turning?

12. Recommendations for the type or types of shed roofs and provision of adequate lighting both general and localised.

13. Recommendations for the improvement of any shed or shed yard lay-out so as to improve the facilities for disposing of engines.

14. What can be done in the way of closing up some of our running sheds or reducing them to the status of a garage.

GENERAL NOTE -

In considering these questions regard should be had to the desirability of moving engines to the men and appliances, rather than the men and appliances to the engines.

The memo noted that the question of coaling plants was already being investigated, but suggested that a field for economy existed in other directions, such as boiler washing and steam raising and considered that these last two matters could be referred to Hartley's Committee for Scientific Research.

The proposed remit for the Committee, printed above, was primarily concerned with the mechanisation of facilities at sheds. It is only Clause 14 that introduces the possibility of a complete reorganisation of the status of sheds and the work that was to be carried out in them. However, this would have been an important consideration – if not the most important. There was little point in the committee recommending new facilities for a shed if it was then downgraded in status and such facilities not needed. It seems, therefore, that before any proposals could be made about individual sheds, the overall organisational structure of repairs and maintenance across the whole of the LMS needed to be established. And this must have been the content of an elusive report entitled 'Area Locomotive Supply, Repair Concentration and Garage Scheme'.

'Area Locomotive Supply, Repair Concentration and Garage Scheme'

NO COPY of a document with this title has been found in any of the archives consulted during the research for this book. With a title this long, one would have expected it to be a report of substantial size! It does occur as a passing reference in a later LMS document from 1934,[100] proving the veracity of the report's existence and title, and showing that it was not a new concept. However, this is the only precise instance thus far found in the LMS records. It was also alluded to in the 1934 report on locomotive construction policy,[101] which concludes: 'It may be stated briefly that the improvement in locomotive operating and efficiency has been due to the introduction of the Garage Scheme and the concentration of running repairs at specified main sheds'.

H.G. Smith merely records that the Running Shed Committee was formed to enquire into, and report upon, the mechanisation of all locomotive running sheds. This small committee, he states, consisting of representatives of the Motive Power and CME departments, was set up in February 1931 – i.e. soon after Lemon became CME – in order to look into the matter further.[102] However, in his description of the subsequent progress of

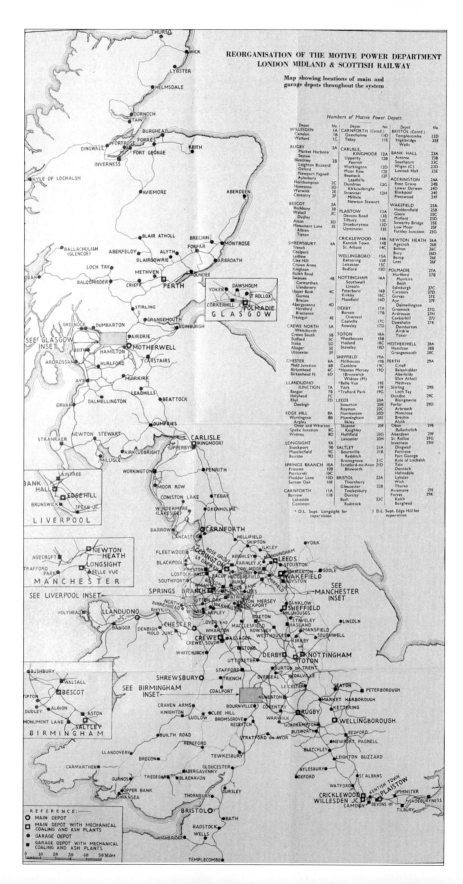

REORGANISATION OF THE MOTIVE POWER DEPARTMENT
LONDON MIDLAND & SCOTTISH RAILWAY

Map showing locations of main and garage depots throughout the system

the scheme after 1933, Smith never once uses this long and somewhat clumsy title.

In 1937, the *Railway Gazette* carried a series of articles on the Reorganisation of the Motive Power Department motivated by this scheme. These state: 'The principles underlying the modernisation scheme adopted, and to which practical effect was given in 1933, were formulated by Mr E.J.H. Lemon'.[103] No plan is conceived at the time of its implementation; and, clearly, the scheme existed in principle well before 1933. Previous writers, for the sake of convenience, have conflated the two separate issues – concept and implemen-

Map showing location of all motive power depots and garages with the complicated industrial area shown enlarged below.
Railway Gazette

tation. The Running Shed Committee's 1933 report was concerned with the latter, and set out plans for the modernisation of the first 14 depots, which was an important adjunct to the successful implementation of the concept. The magazine articles (with one exception) also quote the title as 'Motive Power Area Locomotive Supply, Repair, Concentration and Garage Scheme' – this punctuation is also used by Hawkins & Reeve, in their series of books *LMS Engine Sheds*.[104] The comma between Repair and Concentration is clearly incorrect (and does not appear in the LMS document referred to above), as these are not separate issues. The scheme is specifically concerned with the concentration of repairs at major sheds, and the down-grading of others to the status of garages.

At some time, therefore, Lemon expanded his 1930 appraisal of US practice into a system-wide

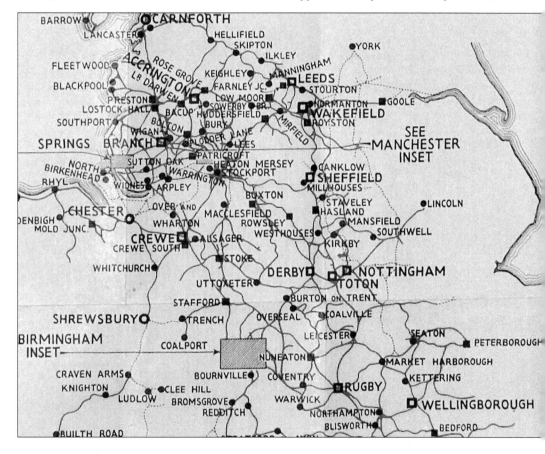

plan for the LMS. This is when the hierarchy of sheds throughout the company's network would have been established, identifying which were to be responsible for major work and repairs (parent depots), and which were to be merely garages. It is curious that this important document should have totally disappeared. The *Railway Gazette* articles quoted specific criteria from the scheme's concept, indicating that the writer had access to a copy of the master-plan, and included a map of all the depots on the LMS, identifying the status accorded to them under the new regime. The network was divided up into 29 areas, 26 in England and Wales and three in Scotland, each with one main or concentration depot, and a number of subsidiary 'garage' depots. The original proposals must have been considered at Executive level, as the scheme was never the subject of a Report to the Board. This is not altogether surprising. Board decisions were generally only concerned with the financial costs of implementing projects, not with the spirit that inspired them. If the Executive approved in principle, then work could start on considering what was necessary to fit the sheds for their new role. This would involve massive expense, and that was when the approval of the Board was sought. Further indications that the reorganisation started while Lemon was CME, and years before Byrom's committee reported in 1933, can be found in the Minutes of the Locomotive & Electrical Committee.[105] For example, on 25 February 1931, it was recorded that both the locomotive repair shop and the carriage & wagon repair shop at Barrow were to be closed. Barrow became a garage in the new plan.

Diesel Shunting Locomotives (1)

ONE OF the items on William Wood's 1930 'briefing list' to Sir Harold Hartley was the laconic comment: 'Diesel Engines – Last experiment bound to fail and did'. This list is signed and dated 6 February 1930, and so it must be assumed Wood was referring to the diesel-electric train-set that was trialled on the Blackpool–Lytham service in 1928. Various operational difficulties were experienced, and after nine months the set was withdrawn from service.

On 20 May 1931, the Traffic Committee received the final report from the CME (Lemon) and other relevant officers of the costs of the experiment. These were actually less than the authorised expenditure, but the Minutes record that the vehicles concerned had already been broken up.[106]

Nevertheless, following Stamp's stricture to the Executive in December 1930[107] that cost savings should be sought wherever possible, the subject was obviously still ripe for further consideration – especially as rapid strides in the use of Diesels were being made in Europe and America. Indeed, Britain was lagging far behind its continental neighbours in developing this alternative technology, which may be partly explained by the seemingly inexhaustible supplies of coal.

One area where the use of diesel locomotives could be considered appropriate was in connection with the perennial problem of shunting. This had been particularly singled out by Stamp in 1930 as an area where further economies were necessary, and an *ad hoc* committee had been formed to investigate the matter. The steam locomotives that were currently used for shunting – like all such locomotives – needed two men on the footplate, even though much of the time in the marshalling yard might be spent stationary. Valuable coal was still being consumed whether the engines were standing idle or working, and they then required hours for maintenance at the depot. Diesel locomotives on the other hand could be single-manned, carried enough relatively cheap fuel for a week and could be stopped and started at the turn of a key. Indeed the only area where they were more expensive was in the capital cost of construction.

Diesel shunting engines embody the logical efficiency that would immediately appeal to Lemon, and the first prototype was authorised during his period as CME. Shortly after his appointment he visited Denmark with Sir Harold Hartley and other officers to investigate the possibilities of diesel-electric locomotives. The precise date of the visit is not known, but it was referred to in the Locomotive Committee minutes on 25 February 1931.[108] Presumably one of the other members of the party was Tommy Hornbuckle, Lemon's brother-in-law, who, as

Chief Technical Assistant to the CME, was responsible for the development of all non-steam locomotives. Hornbuckle's enthusiasm for the technology stemmed from his days as an apprentice with Hornsby's of Grantham when they were developing the revolutionary principle of the compression-ignition engine, from which the diesel evolved. It is Hornbuckle who has since been described as the 'father' of the diesel on the LMS.[109]

After this initial appraisal, Lemon and the Chief General Superintendent (C.R. Byrom) recommended to the Traffic Committee on 28 October 1931 that an old 0-6-0 tank engine (No.1831) should be converted into a diesel-*hydraulic* shunting locomotive for experimental purposes. The Chairman authorised the order, in anticipation of the Directors' approval, with the proviso that the sub-contractors guaranteed to take back the engine, and refund any money paid, if it was not satisfactory. The cost of the conversion was estimated at £5,660. The locomotive was assembled at Derby, and the *Railway Gazette* described it in a two-page article on 2 December 1932.[110]

Sources generally agree that the engine was not a success, with its hydraulic transmission being the major problem. Five years later, on 25 November 1936,[111] it was reported that the actual outlay on this locomotive had now reached £7,514 15s 5d. The locomotive had proved very unreliable in service, and it was not considered desirable to incur any further expenditure. The

Diesel Hydraulic Shunting Locomotive No.1831 built at Derby in 1931.
J.B. Radford Collection

Traffic Committee Minutes state that the locomotive was to be stored but would be available, if required, for any further experiments. There appears to be no memory of the earlier condition that the LMS would get their money back if the engine proved unsatisfactory. Perhaps too long had elapsed! The engine remained in store well into British Rail days, its only use being that of an emergency generator.[112]

Italian State Railways: Visit of Inspection, 6–14 June 1931

IN June 1931, Lemon made another trip abroad with Sir Harold Hartley. They were accompanied by F.A. Cortez-Leigh (Chief Electrical Engineer) and went to inspect the electrification of main-lines on Italian State Railways.

The report[113] on the visit to Italy was written by Cortez-Leigh, and is a neutral affair, merely recording what they saw – they were all much impressed with the new Terminus in Milan, for example. In the relatively short time they spent in Italy, they covered a wide area – from Milan in the north to Foggia in the south – and assessed the relative merits of the different electrical systems in use. The Italians had not committed themselves to one particular standard, and parts of the system used Direct Current and others

Alternating Current. They reported that the Italians' interest in electrification was because of the country's lack of coal, whereas there was a ready supply of hydro-electric power from the Alps and Apennines. This was not the situation in this country, which still had vast supplies of coal (much of which was transported by the LMS!). If their visit came to any conclusions, it was that the LMS did not need to go down this path.

Their visit was probably prompted by the report from a Ministry of Transport Committee on the electrification of main-line railways in Britain published in the Autumn of 1930.[114] One of the mainlines that this committee investigated was the LMS route from Crewe to Carlisle. Electrification was something that Sir Harold Hartley had also investigated while his party were in America in 1930, and he produced a memo on the subject, dated 26 January 1931.[115] The Americans acknowledged electrification was certainly worthwhile on suburban lines, but concurred with the accepted view that it was only worth considering on mainlines where there were exceptional gradients (as is the case through the Lake District). The economics of electrification, and its possible benefits were calculated in great detail by the Ministry of Transport. The net cost of the Crewe–Carlisle scheme was over £5m, taking into account the savings in steam locomotives and their associated maintenance and services. The benefits to the Company were an operating saving of just £127,766 per year which represented a 2.5% return on their investment – less than the interest charged on the capital the Company would need to borrow to finance the scheme. It was therefore not an economic proposition. This surprised the Ministry – the route seemed an ideal choice for electrification with its steep

gradients and heavy weight of traffic. On closer analysis, it turned out that a piece-meal electrification of a section of the main-line could not produce the expected benefits, as the electric locomotives would not be used efficiently. Traffic arriving and departing from the section would still use steam power. The official reaction by the LMS to all this was to set up their own committee to look into the matter. The matter was not treated with a great deal of urgency, and it was not until November 1934 that Lemon wrote a memo to the Chief Accountant assessing the enormous costs of such projects.[116]

Lemon's year as CME was, therefore, not a blank page in the history of the Department. It was a time for reassessment – for a dispassionate appraisal of the locomotives in service on the LMS and the way they were used: and for a complete overhaul of the Department's administration. The ground was prepared for the next incumbent of the post.

Diagram from *A Handbook for Steam Railway Locomotive Enginemen*, (LMS Ref. ERO 52130, produced by the General Superintendent's Department, Motive Power Section, Derby, December 1931). Keith Harcourt

POSITION OF ENGINE HEAD LAMPS.

All LMS engines, whether working over the LMS or other companies' lines, and the engines of other companies working over the LMS line, must, unless instructions are issued to the contrary, carry while head lights as under:

No.

1. Express passenger train, or breakdown van train going to clear the line, or light engine going to assist disabled train, or fire brigade train.

2. Ordinary passenger train, or breakdown van train not going to clear the line.

3. Parcels, newspaper, fish, meat, fruit, milk, horse, or perishable train, composed of coaching stock.

4. Empty coaching stock train, or express freight, or cattle train with the continuous brake in use on NOT less than half the vehicles.

5. Fish, meat, or fruit train composed of freight stock, or express freight, or express cattle train, not fitted with the continuous brake, or with the continuous brake in use on LESS than half the vehicles.

6. Through freight train, or ballast train conveying workmen, and running not less than 15 miles without stopping.

7. Light engine or light engines coupled together, or engine with one or two brakes.

8. Through mineral or empty wagon train.

9. Freight train stopping at intermediate stations, or ballast train running short distance.

Shunting engines working exclusively in station yards and sidings must, whilst in these sidings, carry one red head light and one red tail light. The lamps must be carried in position day and night.
When a train running on the LMS Railway is worked by two engines attached in front of the train, the second engine must not carry head lamps.

FIVE

Vice-President, 1932–1933

O N 4 November 1931, J. Quirey resigned as Vice-President to take up an appointment at the Railway Rates Tribunal. J.H. Follows was given the role of Vice-President (Operating & Commercial) in his place but, as the LMS Special Minutes show, within three weeks Follows had indicated to the Board that he wished to retire, which suggests that other machinations were still going on behind the scenes. On 26 November 1931, the Special Minutes[117] record that Follows would retire on 1 March 1932, although he would stay on the Boards of the various road transport companies on behalf of the LMS. Lemon was appointed in his place as Vice-President (Railway Traffic Operating & Commercial Section) with immediate effect, and William Arthur Stanier was appointed CME from 1 January 1932. Finally, it was resolved that, on the retirement of Follows, the Executive Committee would be reconstituted with three Vice-Presidents rather than four – Wood, Hartley and Lemon – all at 'level salaries' of £5,000 p.a.

Stanier's appointment was a final response to the antipathy that still existed between the rival factions of Derby and Crewe. The policy of balancing the two sides by appointing the CME from one, and the deputy from the other, would no longer apply. As an outsider, Stanier was not beholden to the traditions of either.

The circumstances surrounding his appointment as CME have been discussed in many railway histories – and each author has their own version of the events. Many of these can now be shown to contain errors and assumptions. For example, H.C.B. Rogers writes: 'It was only in 1968 that Riddles learned how it had happened. Lemon had discussed the problem with an outside business acquaintance, who made the revolutionary statement that the LMS should approach the Great Western and try to secure Stanier for the appointment. In due course Stanier was lunching with Lemon at the Athenaeum.'[118] Other accounts[119] also state that it was Lemon who arranged to meet Stanier at the club. What none of these writers seems to appreciate is that neither Lemon nor Stanier were members of the Athenaeum at the time. Lemon became a member in 1936 and Stanier in 1943. It was Sir Harold Hartley who arranged to meet Stanier there in October 1931, as J.E. Chacksfield correctly notes.[120] However it would have been a courtesy to invite Lemon also to the meeting. Indeed, his presence could disguise the true purpose, as we know that the ostensible subject for discussion was water-softening. This was very much a current topic at the LMS and, as described in the last chapter, a massive scheme for the construction of water-softening plants had been authorised a couple of months earlier.

All previous writers also seem to have assumed that the LMS was in a predicament, and desperately casting around for someone to take over as CME. The LMS management were not this incompetent. Everything points to the fact that Hartley was carrying out a well-conceived plan. As has already been explained, Hartley, who knew all about the reputation of GWR locomotives from travelling between his Oxford college and London, had suggested Stanier as a candidate for the post at least a year before. He may have asked Lemon to try and find out, quietly behind the scenes, whether Stanier would be receptive to an offer, but it was he, not Lemon, who was the architect of the plan. This is confirmed by a letter in his personal papers: a day after the Board meeting at which all these decisions were made, C.E.R. Sherrington wrote to him (and one wonders how he found out about these changes quite so quickly):

27th November 1931

My dear Hartley
This morning's news is splendid, I confess I did not believe you could have pulled it off but I shall never entertain such fears in the future. I was hoping against hope that you would make use of Quirey's retirement and Lemon would succeed him as V.P. Transportation as Clements acts on the Penn [Pennsylvania Railroad], and Patterson on the ICRR [Illinois Central Railroad] but naturally I did not know of this new opening which would give you a chance.
Being 25% G.W. I have to be sorry in a way for the G.W. but the work they could have given Stanier could never have equalled the Herculean task you have allotted him.
You will get fireworks from some of the old gang but being a chemical expert you are specially well equipped to deal with them. I have always believed in the organisation which placed under one head the operating and commercial branches (see chapter in my book on organisation) and the S.R. adopted it to some extent last year. But such a policy should start from the top & not the bottom and you have now the opening to carry it to its logical conclusion and save thousands a year. It is fine work and I hope Lemon realises how much he owes to you and the way you have backed him. No-one is worthier of backing than he is and I think the new LMS organisation is leading still further than you have visualised yourself. That I will explain when we meet next.
Ever yours and heartiest congratulations.

'Sherry'

[Postscript added down the margin]

I rather doubt if Stanier will want to build a lot of Class 2 engines, but that remains a little joke between the two of us.[121]

The final barb in the postscript was a reference, of course, to the Midland Railway's tradition of building small locomotives! There is nothing in this letter to suggest that Lemon's tenure of the post of CME had been in any way inconsequential. It implies that he had achieved everything that had been required of him, otherwise promotion to Vice-President would hardly have followed. It also contradicts the common assumption that 'Stamp had marked him out for promotion'. The letter shows that it was Hartley who fiercely championed Lemon's cause. Indeed the phrase that the 'new LMS organisation is leading still further than you have visualised yourself' implies that that all these changes embodied Hartley's, rather than Stamp's, vision for the future of the Company.

O.S. Nock recounts Stamp's jocular explanation to Stanier of why he was chosen – that it was purely to stop the antagonism between Derby and Crewe.[122] But he fails to say why the choice specifically fell on Stanier – and that does appear to be Hartley's decision. However, Rogers makes a curious assertion in his description of Stanier's arrival. He wrote that: 'Stanier's appointment had not received the unqualified blessing of all executive members over which Sir Josiah Stamp presided. There was one member in particular who had felt that a down-to-earth steam locomotive practitioner was not the ideal man for the job, and that a man of more scientific leanings and academic attainments would have been preferable'.[123] As is so often the way with popular railway histories, there are no footnotes or sources to substantiate this assertion. If it is true, then all one can do is look at the list of Vice-Presidents and try to eliminate those to whom this remark cannot apply (or find the original source for the allegation!).

It is worth noting here that J.E. Anderson, the Superintendent of Motive Power at Derby, did not remain in his post for long after Stanier's arrival. He was summarily 'relieved of his duties with immediate effect', on 31 October 1932 'as it was desirable his successor should take office concurrently with pending changes'.[124] Anderson had been the first choice of Sir Henry Fowler for the post of CME in 1930, and was also backed by J.H. Follows, Vice-President at the time. He was a vigorous defender of Derby practices, and it may be an indication, from the peremptory wording of this Minute, that Stanier and his superiors were not prepared to stand any more inter-departmental strife that he might have caused.

On 4 December 1931, the *Railway Gazette* announced the new LMS appointments and, with regard to Stanier's appoint-ment as CME commented 'It may be rather frightening for anyone to have to follow in the footsteps of a man whom Sir Josiah Stamp has described as one of the greatest theorists he had ever met, but who, unlike most great theorists, had the ability to carry out his theories in practice and to see his wildest dreams come true'. Stamp could always be relied upon to come out with some appropriate sound-bite to suit the occasion, but this is high praise – and his choice of words is meaningful and significant. He did not merely congratulate Lemon on a job well done. Lemon was not just someone who had temporarily held the reins as CME in a competent manner. Stamp described him as a great 'theorist'. Moreover, a theorist who had put his ideas into practice. The remark lends added weight to the allegation made in the previous chapter that Lemon had devised the whole scheme for the reorganisation of the motive power department, and the use of engines, while he was CME – further confirm-ation that Lemon's period of office was not the insignificant period that is commonly thought, but one of fundamental and revolutionary change.

The article continued: 'No doubt Sir Josiah considers that Mr Lemon, of whom these things were said, will have in the traffic operating and commercial side of the undertaking . . . even greater scope for evolving not only *money-saving*, but *money-making* schemes. The latter involves to a far greater degree the qualities of imagination, determination and able persuasion of doubting colleagues and directors in translating from theory to practice. Mr. Lemon is an engineer,

William Stanier appointed CME in 1932.
Railway Gazette

and it must be very gratifying to engineers to see so high an administrative post in his hands.'

The hope that Lemon would now be able to devise money-making schemes, as opposed to money-saving schemes, was probably printed in all innocence. After all, he was best known, at this date, for the reorganisation schemes he had carried out. Nevertheless, it was a curiously appropriate com-ment for the *Railway Gazette* to have made. Money-*saving* schemes were, and remained, Lemon's preoccupation throughout his career with the LMS. There are very few, if any, of his major initiatives that directly generated a greater revenue for the Company, whether from commercial or private customers. All of his schemes were primarily inspired by the desire to achieve greater efficiency, and reduce costs.

With Lemon's appointment, the 'unholy trinity' of Vice-Presidents was now complete. With Stamp as their President, they were to run the LMS until the Second World War. They also embodied a totally new approach to management. Decisions were now governed by statistics, costs, efficiency and budgetary control. Before continuing, it will be profitable to describe the management structure of the LMS in some detail – and consider the records that either do or do not exist.

The Management structure of the LMS and the role of Vice-President

AS WITH any public Company, the ultimate responsibility for protecting the shareholders' interests lay with the Board of Directors. However, day-to-day management of the LMS lay with the Executive Committee, presided over by the President. The LMS used the American style of titles: 'President' and 'Vice-President', rather than the more usual 'Managing Director'. The constitution and members of this Committee from 1932 onwards – i.e. from Lemon's appointment – can be found in various sources. One such is a document submitted during WW2 to the national Railway Executive Committee, which assumed responsibility for running the entire country's rail network during the war.

'The whole of the railway [LMS] is administered through an executive committee consisting of the president, three vice-presidents, the chief officer for labour and establishment, chief officer for new works, chief legal adviser, and the secretary of the company.'[125]

When Sir Josiah Stamp became President in 1926, he issued a memorandum on the proposed workings of his new Executive Committee, and the duties and functions of a Vice-President. A copy can be found in Sir Harold Hartley's papers at Churchill College, Cambridge, which carries a note dated 30 January 1946: 'The attached was written by Lord Stamp many years ago for the benefit of his Vice-Presidents and Senior Executives, and is circulated at Sir Harold Hartley's request as a guide to the executives of BEA'.[126] Hartley was the first Chairman of British European Airways, which was formed at the end of the Second World War, and he obviously felt that Stamp's method of working was worth emulating at the new airline.

A section of this memo entitled 'Spirit of Committee' states that:

the spirit and proceedings of the Executive Committee, while businesslike and to the point, shall be informal, conversational, and as easy as possible for the mutual exchange of views. We want no set speeches and no spirit of 'face saving', or 'climbing down', to be prevalent. We shall keep a minute of our proceedings, but not a detailed record of all our cross talk. In short, we want the proceedings to be such as are possible with a small group of three or four, and impossible for a large committee of twelve or more where strict order and rules must prevail if the committee is not to become a bear garden.'

In conclusion, Stamp wrote:

The Vice-President must never forget that the essence of this scheme is that he has no

departmental executive responsibilities; he is primarily a thinker and a reviewer; an authoriser, an adviser and consultant, and not a man who takes the responsibility daily for a hundred executive decisions in letters and commands.

[*The full text of this memo is given in Appendix A*]

The Executive Committee was thus the powerhouse behind the LMS – a think-tank where new ideas were promulgated, and new initiatives formulated. These were then passed down to the relevant officers for implementation. Importantly, Stamp's memo also shows that it was a Committee that *kept Minutes*. Now the records at the National Archives contain all the Minutes of the meetings of the Board of Directors and its various sub-committees: Locomotive, Hotels & Catering, Traffic, Finance etc. However, there are no records of the Executive Committee. It is a surprising absence, and certainly one to be regretted, that no copies of these appear to exist any more. Indeed, several people who have been asked for guidance in the research for this book have expressed doubt that the Executive Committee did keep any records. Stamp's memo shows that it did, but the matter can be quickly and easily verified from other sources. Lemon's personal papers contain many references to the Minutes – often giving precise details and dates. He refers to Executive Minute No. 6543 of 31 May 1936, for instance, in his memo to Stamp about the mechanisation of Toton Marshalling Yard.[127] There is even an isolated page from the Executive Minutes dated 6 June 1941, where Minute 8500 details the reallocation of Vice-Presidential duties following the appointment of Sir William Wood as President. On the reverse, Minute 8501 records arrangements made for canteens on troop trains. The earliest Minute so far discovered at the National Archives is No. 4695 dated 18 December 1933 which is concerned with the naming of Euston House.[128] Copies of later individual Minutes can also be found in Sir William Wood's papers after he became President in 1941.[129]

Wood's papers also refer to a file of *Reports* to the Executive Committee. There are no such files now at the National Archives. It seems purely fortuitous that a copy of the report Lemon and his Lightning Committee submitted to the President in November 1930 following the American trip (see Chapter 3) entitled 'Use of Engines' does still exist in a subsidiary series of LMS papers.[130] No others have been found. Copies of all the other Lightning Committee reports that were submitted at the same time to the Executive only exist in Lemon's personal records. The reason is that these were simply reports on operating practices elsewhere – admittedly with the implied suggestion that the LMS should consider whether to adopt them or not. Until they were developed into practical plans for consideration by the Board, they remained within the confines of the Executive as consultative and advisory documents – and now seem to have gone the same way as all the other Executive records. However, when it was necessary to seek the Board's approval for a major project, a 'Report to the Board' was submitted.

If we consider what other records are available, there is also a surprising dearth of general correspondence emanating from Stamp or any of his three Vice-Presidents. There is nothing in the LMS files, for example, concerning Lemon's secondment to the Air Ministry in 1938 apart from a reference in the Minutes to the re-allocation of his duties. Lemon's personal papers, however, include copies of Stamp's official correspondence with the Prime Minister, Neville Chamberlain, and other Government Ministers in the matter.

This 'black hole' in the official archives has, therefore, hindered research into Lemon's activities as Vice-President. Indeed, the complete absence of any concrete record of the Executive Committee has led many previous railway historians and enthusiasts to overlook its relevance and importance. Lemon's personal papers clearly demonstrate how the origins and inspiration for many of the major initiatives carried out by the Company lay with him. Indeed, many of these were first proposed by his Lightning Committee reports of 1930, and now that he was Vice-President he could actively push for, and promote, their implementation.

Lemon's Duties as a Vice-President

ONCE again, it is Sir Harold Hartley's papers in Cambridge, which contain a copy of an official memo written by Stamp describing Lemon's functions and responsibilities as Vice-President.[131]

Vice-President
Functions
The Operating and Commercial administration of the Railway will now be combined under one Vice President whose functions will be as follows –
Commercial
To direct the passenger and freight (including mineral traffic) commercial activities of the Company in all respects, viz:
(i) The relations between the railway users and the Company including -
– Freight and Passenger rates, charges and conditions.
– Carriage accounts, claims, rebates, refunds, etc.
– Solicitation of traffic by rail, road and water.
(ii) Publicity and Advertising in all its phases including "trade" advertising.
(iii) The management of the Company's property including the selling and leasing of land and premises – in other words, the present functions of the Land & Estate Department.
Operating
To administer all movement of traffic by rail, road and water, viz:
(i) Operation of Passenger, Freight and Mineral trains.
(ii) Motive Power.
(iii) Handling of passenger, freight and mineral traffic at Stations, Depots and Docks.
The Vice-President (Railway Traffic Operating and Commercial) will be assisted by the following principal officers:-
(i) Commercial Manager.
(ii) Operating Manager.
(iii) Estate Manager.
(iv) Commercial and Operating Manager (Scotland).

The memo then continues to describe the functions of these subordinate officers:

Ashton Davies, Chief Commercial Manager *(left)*, **and C.R. Byrom, Chief Operating Manager** *(right)*, **at a trial run on the newly electrified Barking–Upminster route, September 1932.**
Railway Gazette

(i) *Commercial Manager.*
The solicitation of all traffic by rail, road, and water: the maintenance of close contact with the trading and travelling public: freight and passenger rates and fares: carriage accounts, claims, rebates, etc: the responsibilities now vested in the Mineral Manager and Overseas and Continental Traffic Manager: publicity and advertising in all its phases including trade advertising.
The Commercial Manager will be assisted by a Passenger Manager and a Freight Manager, a Publicity Manager, and such Assistants as may be required.

(ii) *Operating Manager.*
The administration and control of all movement of traffic by rail and road: the handling of passengers, freight, and mineral traffic at Stations, depots and docks: motive power: cartage and road transport generally.
The Operating Manager will be assisted by an Operating Superintendent and a Superintendent of Motive Power, and Cartage and Station working Assistants as required.

(iii) *Estate Manager.*
The administration and control of all the Company's land and premises, including sales, purchases and leases: in fact the present functions of the Land & Estate Agent with the added responsibility now vested in the Chief Goods Manager and Mineral Manager of private sidings negotiations and agreements.

(iv) *Commercial and Operating Manager (Scotland)*
The responsibilities of the Commercial Manager and the Operating Manager will not include Scotland; the functions shown under them will so far as Scotland is concerned be combined under a Commercial and Operating Manager for Scotland.
This Officer will be assisted by Freight and Passenger Commercial, and Operating Assistants as required.

This memo is not dated, but the same information can be found in a longer memo from Stamp, dated 21 June 1932, which is also in Hartley's papers. This second memo contains some subtle variations in the responsibilities of the Managers, and continues to list a whole number of further organisational changes that would be made.[132] This memo was obviously intended for circulation throughout the Company, and Stamp starts by describing how the process of amalgamation of the separate companies into one homogenous whole passed through three phases. In the first phase, all practices and methods were reviewed and dealt with centrally in order to enable different conditions on the different sections to be understood. In the second phase, comparative examinations of practices and methods could be made, so that standards for the whole railway could be laid down. When it was felt that the first two stages had been achieved, decisions could then be made as to which sections of the organisation were to continue to be centrally managed, and which could be decentralised. Stamp decreed, in this 1932 memo, that it was now possible to implement the third stage, and that he proposed to follow up the appointment of Lemon as Vice-President by a complete reorganisation of the Operating and Commercial Departments. This involved instituting the concept of Area Management. Now, at a first glance, this may look like a complete 'volte face', and the LMS had abandoned their efforts to run the railway as a unified network. However, the Areas now envisaged were not simply defined by the boundaries of the old constituent Companies, although, for geographical reasons, many areas must have been almost identical. The change would have been most marked around those large conurbations where two or more of the old constituent Companies had previously had a presence. Lemon later described the situation that had existed around Manchester.[133] Here, for example, there had previously been many district officers in different departments of various railways. The whole region was a mass of overlapping areas and functions, of different practices and methods, of different traditions and upbringing. Under the new scheme, one Regional Officer would now be responsible for everything connected with the movement of trains in the area. This Officer had authority over all commercial business, rolling stock, operating, locomotives, signals and track, and was empowered to give orders concerning everything connected with the movement of traffic and maintenance of rolling stock, plant, buildings and permanent way.

The Chief Mechanical Engineer and the Chief Engineer remained responsible as Headquarters Officers for design, works practice and research, and laid down the standards to which maintenance of plant and structures was carried out. Similarly, through [i.e. long-distance] freight and passenger services were still arranged, Stamp decreed, by the Chief General Superintendent; but the Regional Officer could alter, withdraw or institute services local to his area. Stamp appears, in this memo to have momentarily forgotten that the title of Chief General Superintendent would

no longer exist, as it had been superseded by Chief Operating Manager – an easy mistake to have made! There was no change of personnel in this position however: C.R. Byrom merely changing his official title from one to the other.

Stamp ended this memo by envisaging further organisational changes, so that every railway Department worked to the same area boundaries. In this way, greater budgetary control could be achieved. In conclusion, he wrote:

To sum up, in all amalgamations, it is necessary in the initial stages to centralise on a considerable scale in order that standard principles and practices may be adopted. The time has now arrived, however, when decentralisation can, with advantage, be effected so as to enable questions to be settled with a minimum of delay, and so that Headquarters may be relieved of as much detail as possible, thus enabling concentration to be given to major problems and research.[134]

[*The full text of this memo is given in Appendix B*]

★ ★ ★ ★ ★ ★

ONE OF Lemon's first duties in relinquishing the post of CME was to introduce his successor to the various workshops that now became his responsibility. R.C. Bond tells of his first encounter with Stanier at Horwich works thus: 'without any preliminary warning, the door of my room opened – Lemon and Stanier peered in, but came no further than the threshold. "That's Bond" was Lemon's remark – a curt nod from Stanier, and they were gone'.[135]

As an outsider with no previous experience of LMS procedures and methods, it would have taken Stanier some time to familiarise himself with all the different facets of his appointment. He must have relied heavily on Lemon – and Sir Harold Hartley – for guidance. The management hierarchy, of course, meant that Stanier was directly responsible to Hartley in his position as Vice-President for Works & Ancillary Undertakings. Nevertheless, Lemon would also be deeply involved in advising Stanier as to what he needed in order to run the services efficiently and would, undoubtedly, have briefed him on the

Northchurch Hall, Berkhamsted, which Lemon bought in 1932. Hertfordshire Archives & Local Studies

assessment he had carried out in 1931 and which engines should be his earliest priorities. There may have been a time in the past when the CME was such a powerful figure in a railway company that he could dictate which engines were to be built – but Stanier was not in that position.

As a Vice-President, Lemon was not only a member of the Executive Committee, but would now be required to attend the monthly Board Meetings, and one can see that his presence was first recorded at the meeting on 17 December 1931. At the Board Meeting a month later in January 1932, it was minuted that the LMS would purchase his house in Derby for £4,750.[136] One can only suppose that the market was stagnant, and Lemon had been unable to achieve a sale throughout 1931 while he was based at Euston as CME. He was thus able to buy a property closer to London, and alighted on Northchurch Hall in Berkhamsted, Hertfordshire. This was described by the Estate Agents as 'a delightful residence, standing in a Well-timbered Park containing 4 Reception Rooms, 11 Bed Rooms, 2 Bath Rooms and charming Grounds. Eight Cottages, Garage and Stabling, Model Home Farm with extensive Frontages to Main Roads. It is built of brick with a tiled roof, is creeper clad and particularly restful in appearance. The House has all the modern conveniences of central heating, electric light, gas, water and is connected to the main sewer. The brick and tiled stabling has nine loose boxes, two stalls and a garage for 5 cars and a single garage'.

The property had been on the market for some time, with an original asking price of £16,500. But handwritten deletions on the sale particulars show that various associated cottages and land were sold off separately, and the asking price was reduced to £8,000, then £6,500 and finally to £4,950. At that price it was undoubtedly a bargain! Berkhamsted was also within reasonably easy commuting distance from London, standing on the mainline from Euston, north of Watford. Amy and Lemon moved into the house but, by now, both sons were away at boarding school. The eldest, Richard, had progressed from his Preparatory School and was now at Malvern College; whilst David had progressed from Derby School for Girls (!), which he attended until he was seven, and was now at Maidwell Hall in Northampton.

Life must have become lonely for Amy with her husband undoubtedly away for long hours at work and family life restricted to school holidays. For her own reasons, she was not interested in socialising with her husband in London, and preferred to find her interests in Berkhamsted. One of these was her interest in golf – she was a member of Berkhamsted Golf Club, and Lady Captain there in 1935. David, apparently, hated accompanying his mother and her unmarried sisters round the local golf course during school holidays but, probably, had nothing better to do as he can have had few friends in the immediate area. Lemon shared Amy's interest in golf but it is not known how often he was able to play. Unlike

III (a). ENGINEER AND RAILWAY STAFF CORPS.
9, Victoria Street, Westminster, S.W.1.

Hon. Colonel.

✗*Montagu-Stuart-Wortley*, Lt.-Gen. Hon. Sir *A. Richard*, K.C.B., K.C.M.G., D.S.O. (*Col. Comdt. K.R.R.C.*) ret. pay (*Res. of Off.*) *p.s.c.* [L]   12/4/24

Colonels.

Walker, *Sir* Herbert A., K.C.B., *T.D.*   13/12/24
Palmer, *Sir* Frederick, K.C.M.G., *C.I.E., T.D., M.Inst.C.E.*   4/3/25
Ashfield, *The Lord,* P.C.   4/3/25
Trench, E. F. C., *C.B.E., T.D., M.Inst.C.E.*   4/3/25
Ellis, *Sir* William H., *G.B.E., M.Inst.C.E.*   4/3/25
✗Wedgwood, *Sir* Ralph L., *Knt., C.B., C.M.G.*   4/3/25
Kirkpatrick, *Sir* Cyril R. S., *Knt., M.Inst.C.E.*   4/3/25
Stamp, *Sir* Josiah C., *G.B.E., D.Sc.*   25/5/27
Milne, *Sir* James, *Knt., C.S.I.*   10/8/29
Wilson, M. FitzG., *T.D., M.Inst. C.E.*   23/3/32

Lt.-Colonels.

✗Barry, A. J., *C.B.E., T.D., M.Inst.C.E.*   11/8/97
Matheson, D. A., *M.V.O., T.D., M.Inst.C.E.*   1/10/10
Calder, J.   7/5/18

Lt.-Colonels—contd.

Humphreys, *Sir* George W., *K.B.E., M.Inst.C.E.*   11/4/23
Cox, E. C., *C.B.E., M.V.O., T.D.*   4/3/25
Brown, C. J., *C.B.E., T.D., M. Inst.C.E.*   4/3/25
✗Maunsell, R. E. L., *C.B.E. M.I.Mech.E.*   4/3/25
Nicholls, R. H., *C.B.E.*   4/3/25
Gresley, H. N., *C.B.E., M.Inst. C.E., M.I.Mech.E.*   4/3/25
Mitchell, H. H. G., *O.B.E., V.D., M.Inst.C.E.*   14/3/25
Bell, R. S. C. M., *C.B.E.*   18/3/25
✗Fowler, *Sir* Henry, *K.B.E., M.Inst.C.E., M.I.Mech.E.*   30/9/25
Owen, *Sir* David, J., *Knt.*   30/6/26
McAlpine, R., *T.D.*   1/5/27
Szlumper, G. S., *C.B.E., T.D., A.M.Inst.C.E.*   18/8/28
Norfolk, T. L., *M.Inst.C.E., M.I.Mech.E., A.M.I.E.E.*   16/11/29
Ellson, G., *O.B.E., M.Inst.C.E.*   18/12/29
✗Anderson, J. S.   23/5/31
Carpmael, R., *M.Inst.C.E.,*   2/4/32
Lemon, E. J. H., *O.B.E., M.I.Mech.E.*   23/4/32

Majors.

Burt, E. J., *T.D.*   24/12/14
Stemp, C. H., *C.B.E.*   16/6/17
Selway, C. J., *C.B.E.*   21/2/21
Eaglesome, *Sir* John E., *K.C.M.G., M.Inst.C.E.*   22/6/23
Wentworth-Sheilds, F.E., *O.B.E., M.Inst.C.E.*   28/3/25
Hawkins, E. L.   28/3/25
Byrom, C. R., *O.B.E.*   23/3/25
Jenkin-Jones, C. M.   3/4/25
Bushrod, F., *O.B.E.*   14/4/25
Wilkinson, H. L.   20/7/25
Binns, A., *M.Inst.C.E.*   25/7/25
Stamer, A. C., *C.B.E., M.I. Mech.E.*   1/10/25
✗Lomas, K.T., *D.S.O., M.Inst.C.E.*   6/3/26
Shawcross, G. N., *M.B.E., M.I.Mech.E.*   8/4/26
✗Beames, H. P. M., *M.Inst.C.E., M.I.Mech.E.*   15/4/26
Urie, D. C., *M.Inst.C.E.*   15/4/26
Davis, F. W. D., *M.Inst.C.E.*   1/5/26
Hindmarsh, R. F., *M.Inst.C.E.*   17/5/26
Newcombe, G. R.   27/11/29
Leighton, L., *M.Inst.C.E., M.I. Mech.E., A.M.I.E.E.*   27/11/29
Tyler, J. F. S., *M.Inst.C.E.*   25/1/30

[Uniform—*Blue*. Facings—*Scarlet*]

Amy, his name does not appear on any of the trophy boards at the Golf Club. According to the *Evening Standard*, he played off a handicap of five, and at some time won the 'Stamp' cup organised by the LMS Golfing Society.[137] He did attend the Annual Dinner of the London section of the LMS Golfing Society when work permitted;[138] and there are a couple of letters in his personal papers from golfing friends after he received his knighthood expressing the hope that they would soon meet up for a round. He also represented the LMS in a golfing match in 1935 against an army team, as is mentioned in the following chapter, but work undoubtedly came first!

As a Vice-President, Lemon acquired further responsibilities. He was nominated by the LMS to serve on the Board of two of its associated companies. In 1932 he became a Director of Wordie & Co., a Scottish firm of general carriers; and also a Director of Joseph Nall & Co., a bus company in the Midlands which later became part of the Midland General Omnibus Company.

'All Rank and No File'. Full list of members of the Railway Staff Corps, 1932, with dates of appointment.
June 1932 Army List, National Archives

At the same time he became the Company's representative on the LMS Superannuation Fund Committee. He was also expected to represent the Company at other social events. For example, on 12 November 1932, he presided at the Family Dinner of the Railway Convalescent Homes held at the Wharncliffe Rooms, in the Marylebone Grand Central Hotel.[139] Another consequence of his elevation to Vice-President followed a few months later – he was promoted to the rank of Lieutenant-Colonel in the Railway Staff Corps on 23 April 1932.[140]

On 16 July 1932, the man who took Lemon away from Okeford Fitzpaine and to an apprenticeship in Glasgow died. Professor Malcolm Laurie, his first benefactor, thus lived to see his erstwhile protégé rise from those humble beginnings to the exalted position of Vice-President.

Rationalisation on the LMS

Paper read at the Institute of Transport Congress, Buxton, 1 June 1932

THE National Archives contain a book entitled *Modern Developments on LMS Railway* with the name of Sir Josiah Stamp conspicuously printed on the cover.[141] Stamp definitely wrote an introduction to the book, but the contents are transcripts of three papers given by the Vice-Presidents, Lemon, Hartley and Wood, to the Institute of Transport Congress at Buxton in 1932.

Lemon's paper was entitled: 'Rationalisation on the LMSR, Principles of Management and Control',[142] and was an overall view of measures taken since amalgamation in 1923. Considering that he had only been a Vice-President a few months, his paper is remarkably forthright and authoritative. One does not get the opinion that he was still feeling his way into the rôle.

He started his paper by putting the creation of the LMS into its historical perspective. Quoting a Board of Trade report from 1845 reporting on the general principles in which railway amalgamations should be allowed, he suggested that 'amalgamations should not be generally or precipitately conceded; that they should not be allowed where the companies had an independent existence, or where the object of the amalgamation was to put an end to competition'. It was assumed, Lemon continued, that the effect of monopoly was looked upon as something to be dreaded and guarded against. This had led to favour being shown by Parliament in the late 19th century for competing schemes, one result of which had been to encourage a large number of speculative enterprises, and duplication of routes. In 1854 a House of Commons Select Committee deplored a proposed amalgamation because 'it would render the existence of independent rival trunk lines impossible'. By 1921 however, attitudes had completely changed, and the Government's statement of intent for the 'big four' was that 'The groups will be determined on the basis of operating economy and all direct competition between the groups will, as far as possible, be eliminated'. These facts are only quoted here to demonstrate how the railways have always been subject to political doctrine – as we are only too well aware, having passed through nationalisation and back to privatisation.

Lemon then considered the difficulties that the railways had faced at amalgamation, which he suggested were not fully appreciated. Many of these were not caused by amalgamation *per se*, but were a legacy from the War. There were arrears of maintenance in all sections of the railway – track, buildings and rolling stock; and engines, carriages and wagons had all been depleted in numbers. To this had been added an unprecedented trade depression, still persisting, and increased competition from a new and formidable competitor – road transport.

Reference has already been made earlier in this book, to some of the issues that Lemon covered in this paper – notably in the maintenance and repairs of locomotives; but he considered much

Derby Railway Engineering Society Annual Dinner 1932. *Left to right:* **W.A. Stanier, E.J.H. Lemon, Alderman W.H. Salisbury (Mayor), Sir Henry Fowler.** Derby Railway Engineering Society

more, describing what changes had been made in every department of the company. There were sections dealing with improvements that had been made in signalling, permanent way, accounting, new materials – to pick out a few at random. He touched on the concept of Budgetary Control, recently introduced by the LMS, which was an idea that he and his fellow officers had brought back from America in 1930. This must now have been the province of Wood, the Finance Director, yet it was Lemon who explained the workings of the idea in his paper. 'Money talks', he said, 'was an old phrase, and to give a man in charge of, say, a small out-station shop a definite goal for his weekly expenditure of labour and materials had a very good effect. Financial responsibility was thus pushed as far down the line of responsibility as possible'.

However, it is always more interesting to pick out specific examples rather than generalisations, and Lemon gave several instances of the type of seemingly trivial problems that the policy of Rationalisation had to contend with. In order to achieve a greater standardisation of products throughout the company, a committee had been formed to look at the 30,000 or so individual items purchased by the constituent companies. One of the difficulties they encountered was the variety of names used for the same article. For example, the list included: glass frame rests, door light frame pads, glass rests, frame pads, doorlight rest pads. Upon investigation, these were all found to be identical. By comparative analysis, the number of items was thus immediately reduced to about 7,000; and a further attack on this number reduced the figure still further to around 4,400. Then again, a great deal of work had to be done in breaking down old traditions in such simple things as, for example, shovels. The previous constituent companies used handles set at different angles, and whilst the adopted, or standard, shovel was in use at most depots, a large number of workmen in other sections complained that the difference in the setting of the handle interfered with their work, and they could not get through it in the same time. Similarly, there were complaints from some workers that a wheelbarrow with handles raised slightly higher than those previously fitted was more difficult to use, although precisely the same barrows were being used in other divisions for identical work. We always like to moan about changes! Nevertheless, Lemon acknowledged that tradition played a great part in British life, and that the railway companies, many of whom had been in existence for nearly a century, possessed strong and sincere traditions and to have these rudely uprooted could not but cause some dissatisfaction, even if this was only the height of a barrow handle.

Lemon's review of the progress of the company since amalgamation was so comprehensive in its analysis – and went so far beyond the bounds of his responsibilities for the operational side of the business – that a listener might have envisaged it as being delivered by the President himself at an AGM.

The Advisory Committee on Scientific Research (2)

THE three Buxton papers were published as *Modern Developments on the LMS Railway* and the Advisory Committee on Scientific Research asked its members for suggestions as to its wider circulation among Research Institutes and the like.[143] Lemon remained a member of this Committee after he became Vice-President, and occasionally chaired its meetings in the absence of Sir Harold Hartley. At the meeting on 11 October 1932, there was a discussion on the possible use of rubber tyres – as are famously still used on the Paris Metro and other underground railways built by the French. In 1932, the LMS carried out experiments with a Michelin pneumatic-tyred railcar.[144] This first model was hardly a thing of beauty, resembling the cab of an articulated lorry pulling a charabanc. It was called the 'Micheline', and was tried out on the line between Bletchley and Oxford. (The whole subject of diesel rail-cars will be considered in the next chapter). Lemon raised the wider question: that of noise on train journeys, and a sub-committee was set up to examine what came to be called 'Amenities of Travel'.[145] This sub-committee was given the widest remit, and was charged with investigating lighting, air conditioning and heating as well as noise. Lemon himself was never a member of any of these sub-

Lapel badge given to delegates attending the Institute of Transport Conference at Buxton in 1932.
Chartered Institute of Logistics & Transport

committees and his contribution to discussions was not only to suggest new areas for research, but to ginger everybody up so that they actually made some progress! At this meeting he particularly queried what had been achieved by the sub-committee investigating problems with paint, and cautioned everyone to establish the costs of any recommendations they might make.

Work as Vice-President until 1933

ALTHOUGH we can see that Lemon regularly attended both the Board and Traffic Committee meetings, there is nothing in their Minutes to tell us exactly what he, personally, did as Vice-President. For that, one has to look behind the scenes and here his Personal Assistant H.G. Smith's account of the projects he inspired has been a major source of information. Smith lists 23 different projects, and one assumes these were merely a selection of those he considered had the most impact on the workings of the LMS. They were inspired by a variety of sources. There were those which dated back to the 1930 Lightning Committee reports, and which he was now able to implement. There were others that had already been introduced by other railways in this country and abroad, and seemed worthy to emulate. Some became evident on line-visits with senior officers, or through day-to-day operating problems, and here Lemon was not so much concerned with the individual problem – that could be passed on immediately to a subordinate officer

for action. His interest was to establish whether it was an isolated case, or symptomatic of a more general problem across the whole network. Finally there were those that came from his own fertile imagination. Smith's record is a starting-point, and confirmation of Lemon's involvement can usually be found somewhere in LMS records. The documents that Smith collated generally show it was Lemon's practice to start proceedings by sending a memo to a subordinate officer – and, more often than not, this was Byrom, Chief Operating Manager – asking him to investigate a particular matter and then draw up plans for improvements. When this had been done, the plans were submitted for formal approval and authorisation – on the recommendation of the relevant officer. If the project had been developed by Byrom's department, then the formal recommendation was made in his name. If it had been handled by the CME's department, then the recommendation was officially submitted by Stanier. One might therefore conclude from the Minutes of the Board or its Sub-Committees that the whole concept of the projects lay with the officers making the recommendations. This was a strict adherence to the policy laid down by Stamp that the Vice-Presidents had no 'departmental executive responsibilities'. Lemon's name is therefore not necessarily mentioned as the true instigator when the project was submitted for authorisation, a fact that he must have been happy enough to accept. However, this has meant that other writers have often failed to appreciate Lemon's involvement.

The list of Lemon's major initiatives can therefore now be considered in turn. They are arranged in roughly chronological order, according to the date that H.G. Smith gives for the genesis of the idea. Some, however, were not implemented immediately; and others, of course set in motion an ongoing scheme that occupied several years.

Acceleration of (Fitted) Freight Trains [146]

ACCORDING to Smith, one of Lemon's first acts as Vice-President in 1932 was to direct his special attention to the acceleration of freight train services. With main lines being heavily occupied by passenger services during the day,

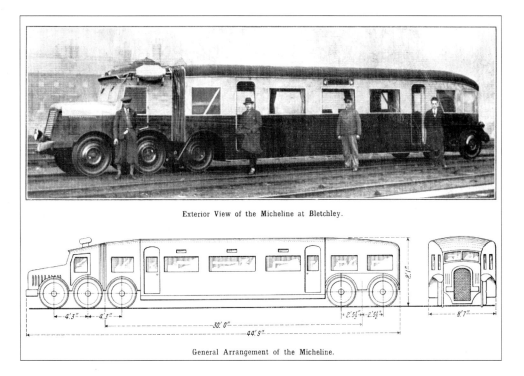

Exterior View of the Micheline at Bletchley.

General Arrangement of the Micheline.

the ability to offer a fast overnight goods service was of paramount importance. Later departure times and earlier arrivals would enable goods, especially perishable goods, to be delivered to urban centres at first light. There were other economic advantages for the rail company however: faster timings could mean that only one crew would be needed for the journey. Most freight trains at the time were limited in speed because the wagons had no brakes of their own, but relied totally on the locomotive and guard's van to control them. Smith wrote his account of the improvements many years later, and his 1941 memo contains only a brief résumé of the improvements that were carried out. This is a complex subject and undoubtedly many changes were made between 1932 and 1941.

At the outset, Smith records, three grades of fitted freight train were defined. A Fitted Freight No.1 (FF1) contained a maximum load of 45 wagons. All were fitted with a brake pipe, and vacuum brakes operated on not less than half of them. The maximum operating speed was 55mph. A Fitted Freight No.2 (FF2) contained

The Micheline Railbus. Its design meant the whole unit had to be turned at the end of a run. *Railway Gazette*

a maximum load of 50 wagons, with vacuum brakes on not less than one third of them, and limited to a maximum speed of 50mph. With the advent of more powerful engines in succeeding years, Smith records that these limits had been raised to 50 wagons for FF1 trains and 55 for FF2 by the outbreak of war in 1939. There was then a class of Express Freight, designated 'Maltese Cross', with four wagons fully fitted with automatic brakes next to the engine. Smith states that this could contain a load of 60 wagons, but does not give a figure for the maximum speed allowed. It was presumably less than 50mph.

Considerably more information can be found in the July 1932 edition of the *Railway Gazette* which carried an article describing the new fast goods services on the LMS. The magazine cited in considerable detail the types of wagons allowed, and the positioning of those with brakes within the overall layout of the train. It also stated that in the six months up to June 1932 (i.e. since Lemon became V-P), the number of FF2 trains had more than doubled, from 21 to 45. The number of FF1 trains however had only increased by one, to 26, in the same period.

The article includes a diagram showing all the routes and timings of the fitted freight trains, and the places where stops were made for traffic purposes. These intermediate stops, sometimes lasting a matter of a few minutes, were to allow faster passenger services to pass through and were not a requirement of the freight train itself. One can therefore see that the FF1 train which left Glasgow (Buchanan Street) at 6.50pm, was scheduled to stop at Carstairs for eight minutes, and at Carlisle for ten, for traffic reasons. It left Carlisle at 10.10pm and then travelled via Leeds and Sheffield down the Midland main line to London, with no further stops, arriving at St Pancras at 6.15 the following morning – a total distance of 418¾ miles in 11 hours 25 minutes (an average speed of just under 37mph).

However, this is not the whole story – the train did make further stops. The LMS publicity department (and the *Railway Gazette*) were primarily concerned with advertising the faster service. There was no mention of the intermediate stops that were made for operating purposes, as opposed to traffic purposes. It is easy to appreciate that the engine needed to stop *en route* to take on water. For example, the diagram shows an FF2 train that left Birmingham at 4.30pm and travelled the 225 miles 'non-stop' to Carlisle, via Chesterfield and Leeds, arriving at 12.28am, worked by the same engine and crew throughout. It is known that this train stopped for water and inspection at Masborough (Rotherham) and Skipton, although this is not shown on the route plan.

Inspection of the wagons was an important consideration – especially the axle boxes, which had not been specifically designed for long continuous runs at these higher speeds. Smith described the progress that was made in this department: 'Another investigation was made into the possibilities of increasing the distances which freight trains were allowed to run without stopping for examination, which had an important effect upon schedules'. He states that, 'At the outbreak of war in 1939, the position in this

respect had been considerably improved: a Fitted Freight No.1, for example, was permitted to travel a maximum of 160 miles between examinations. Fitted Freight No.2 and Express Freight trains with oil axle-boxes were allowed 125 miles, but those with grease axle-boxes were limited to 85 miles before examination'.

However, this statement appears to be contradicted by other sources. The *Railway Gazette* in 1932 quotes the claim made by the LMS to have a fitted freight train making the longest non-stop run in the country. This was the 7.45pm FF1 from London (Camden) to Liverpool (Edge Hill) which arrived at 1.45am – a distance of 191 miles. This was achieved without any stop for traffic purposes or examination, as the engine was fitted with a water scoop, and water taken from troughs while travelling. This is considerably further than Smith's limit of 160 miles. It is clear that it would be necessary to consult the working timetables and other regulations governing freight trains, in order to understand all elements of this subject fully – which is beyond the scope of this book.

Smith notes that a scheme was worked out, just prior to the war, for providing an even faster freight service in each direction between London and Glasgow, by utilising specially converted vehicles and running the trains at express passenger train speeds. However these plans were curtailed by the outbreak of war, when it was also necessary to withdraw the majority of the 350 fitted freight trains in service. They were gradually reintroduced, and Smith tells us that by 1941 nearly one half had been reinstated.

Wasted time

ON 16 November 1932 Lemon sent a letter to C.R. Byrom entitled 'Unproductive Time of Enginemen', asking for information to help him prepare the LMS case for the proceedings of the National Wages Board.[147] One factor that concerned him was the time that was paid for, but not worked, in order to make up the guaranteed working day or week. He asked Byrom to supply details of the portion of the engineman's day that was actually occupied in train running time, and what portion was unproductive. The only information he could deduce from the weekly Operating Statements, was the hours that locomotives spent in preparation and disposal, and did not fully cover unproductive time in the body of the working. He continued: 'I can realise the importance to the Company of any such unproductive time being reduced to a minimum through the process of scheduling the engines and enginemen's workings' and concluded: 'This work must be a valuable feature of your organisation and I should appreciate some information as to how it functions in the routine of your Trains Offices, and the indications you have that such work is energetically pursued and tested to find the weak points in the booked arrangements'. Although this memo is couched in polite and business-like terms, there is, nevertheless, an implied message that 'if you haven't been doing this, then I suggest you start to do it straightway'!

Smith records that as a result of this letter, and further correspondence and discussions, in July 1934 a Committee of Headquarters and Divisional representatives of the Chief Operating Manager was established as 'the medium of a further and sustained effort to achieve a more intensive and economical use of engines'. The results of this work over the next twelve months to June 1935 led to a saving equivalent to 362 engines, and 230 had actually been withdrawn from service. The difference between these two figures was broadly accounted for by the retention of some locomotives to meet unexpected demand. In the second year of the campaign, further savings enabled another 185 engines to be permanently withdrawn.

This led to a progressive reduction in the stock of locomotives from 8,226 in 1933 to 7,546 in 1940. This was not the only action that was taken towards the more efficient use of locomotives, and, in March 1933, Byrom and his Running Shed Committee produced the first proposals for the mechanisation of certain running sheds.

Mechanisation of Running Sheds & Utilisation of Locomotives

THE Running Shed Committee had been investigating the modernisation of locomotive sheds ever since February 1931 when Lemon was CME – as described in the last chapter. In their 1933 report, they told him they had

investigated 43 sheds, and submitted plans and detailed estimates for improvement work at fourteen of them on the Western Division (the mainline out of Euston).[148] This first report was purely concerned with improvements to these fourteen specific depots and not an overall view of a radical new policy for the whole of the LMS system. It was the first practical manifestation, however, of the 'Area Locomotive Supply, Repair Concentration and Garage Scheme', which occupied the LMS up to the outbreak of war in 1939.

On 24 March 1933, Lemon submitted a memo to the Executive, informing them that he had received the recommendations from the Running Shed Committee, and followed this up a few days later with a more substantial memo to Stamp, incorporating extra details about the costs and benefits.[149] Once again, no mention is made of operating practice, which suggests that the classification of sheds into parent depots and garages was a separate issue. The memo starts:

You will remember that in the early part of 1931 a special Committee was appointed to investigate and report upon the manner and extent to which further mechanisation of work in the Locomotive Running Sheds could be justified, particular emphasis being laid on:-
(1) Mechanical Coaling Plants
(2)   -do-   Ash-lifting Plants
(3)   -do-   removal of smoke-box char
(4) Washing-out arrangements
(5) Extended use of portable appliances, cranes, etc.
(6) Sand-drying facilities and central sand supply
(7) Improved layout for Sheds and Shed Yards
(8) Facilities for repairs
(9) Steam-raising methods
It was felt that there were considerable economies to be made by mechanisation and overhaul of our general arrangements at the Sheds.

The real problem to be attacked is not so much the saving in money by mechanisation schemes but the greater use which can be made of engines. We have, as you know, locomotive stock to the value of roughly

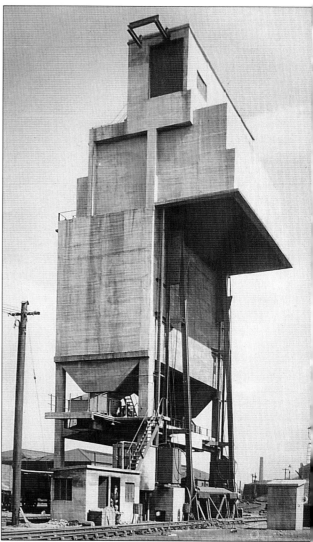

Coaling towers for refuelling locomotives became a commonplace sight in LMS depots. Lemon found it an insuperable problem to extend this technology to the distribution of household coal (see Chapter 10). *Railway Gazette*

£31,000,000 and, as I was concerned to know what was really happening to engines at typical Sheds on what might be called the 'motion study', I arranged for an analysis to be made of the actual operations over a period of 24 hours. The result is contained in the attached statement, which should, however, be used with a certain amount of reserve but it does clearly show that there is a field for economy here through the process of reducing the time occupied by engines in coaling, watering, turning and the usual Shed operations.

A good deal of the trouble today is due to the Sheds having been in use for a great number of years; they were, of course, designed for smaller engines and at the time the layout provided was not prepared for future developments in locomotive progress.

It is curious that Lemon starts this Memo to Stamp with the words 'you will remember'. It implies that Stamp had given no thought to the matter since the Committee was formed in 1931. However, this must have been merely a formality – setting the proposals in context for the Directors who, one assumes, were also given copies.

The total cost of improvements to these 14 sheds, Lemon reported, was estimated to be just over £200,000 leading to savings of around £15,800 – an overall return on expenditure of 7.86%. However, the analysis showed wild variations in the predicted savings at individual sheds, ranging from 45.9% at Lancaster to 0.9% at Walsall. There was also great variance in what the money was spent on, clearly demonstrating that the improvements were specific to the role the sheds would perform: at Rugby, the bulk of the costs (82%) went on mechanical plant for coaling and ash-lifting; at Farnley 75% of the costs were for track improvements; and at Monument Lane 25% of the costs were for a new turntable.

Lemon stated that the scheme would be remunerative from the point of view of mechanisation, but there would be other advantages as well. He particularly singled out the reduction in wasted engine time, or 'standing time', and quoted three examples. He predicted that the time occupied in cleaning fires and replenishing coal, water and sand would be reduced at Patricroft from three hours to 45 minutes, and at Farnley from six hours down to one.

Lemon recommended that 'block' approval for the whole scheme of 14 sheds should be sought from the Board, on the understanding that each would be considered separately by the Accountant in order to verify the savings before work commenced. This simplified the official procedure and gave quicker authority for the implementation of the work. This was approved and the first schemes were immediately put in hand. Lemon visited the sites around Birmingham on his first tour of inspection on 29/30 November 1933. The report on this visit states that he was disappointed with the slow progress of the construction work.[150]

H.G. Smith records that similar schemes for the remaining Divisions (Midland, Central & Scotland) followed, and that by 1941 more than a third of the 150 main depots/garages (i.e. all the mainline depots) had been modernised at a cost of £1,100,000. The benefits were greater than predicted, and the first seven depots showed savings of approximately 20%. The *Railway Gazette* however, in its announcement of Lemon's secondment to the Air Ministry, reported on 1 July 1938 that £2,000,000 had been spent on this scheme.[151]

Not every piece of modernisation went according to plan, however, and to a certain extent some of the mechanisation that was being installed was still experimental. This can be illustrated by the problems at Willesden Steam Shed. Authority had been given in July 1931 for the installation of a pneumatic smokebox ash extractor. On 22 June 1934, the Traffic Committee heard how the appliance was a failure.[152] It had only operated intermittently, under the supervision of the contractors, since completion on 28 January 1933. There were frequent stoppages, some lasting four to six weeks, due to excessive erosion of valves and other components. Although defective parts were replaced at the contractor's expense, it had still gone over budget. The only real observable benefit in the working of the plant was that little dust or grit was blown about when the smokeboxes were being emptied. The appliance was dismantled and removed.

SIX

Vice-President
1933–1938, part 1

A S has already been stated, many of the projects that occupied Lemon through these six years continued over a period of time. This chapter deals in the main with projects that were carried out, or at least started, in the years 1933 to 1935; Chapter 7 then takes the story on to 1938. Each project is described in

**Brochure advertising the visit
of the *Royal Scot* to America, 1933.**
Keith Harcourt

turn, and its progress generally described through to the outbreak of war in 1939. However these dates are approximate only, and greater consideration has been given to clarity in dealing with each subject. As will become apparent, most of the early projects were concerned with improvements to freight operations. However, it was a passenger train that occupied Lemon's attention throughout May 1933.

Century of Progress Exposition, Chicago, 1933

IN 1933, the LMS exhibited a 'Royal Scot' train at the Chicago World Fair. The Chairman had been approached in 1932 by the American Ambassador with the suggestion that the English railways should send a complete modern train to the exposition. At the Board Meeting in September he stated that the other railway companies felt it would not be desirable to send out a mixed train composed of separate units, and thus it was left to the LMS itself, if so desired, to exhibit a complete 'Royal Scot' train.[153]

Stamp informed the Board that, from personal investigation, he was satisfied that participation was highly desirable from the point of view of publicity . He also stated that no charge would be made by the World Fair, and that the costs involved (between £7,000 and £8,000) could be a charge on the Company's advertising budget. Some revenue would also accrue because the Pennsylvania Company were prepared to run the 'Royal Scot' over their system as a revenue-earning train.

The plan was agreed and, after due preparation, the train left for Montreal on the s.s. *Beaverdale*

The LMS party departing for America, 1933. *Left to right:* S.H. Fisher (Operating Superintendent, Euston); G.L. Darbyshire (Chief Officer for Labour & Establishment), Amy and Lemon, T.C. Byrom (Assistant, Commercial Manager's Dept); Ashton Davies (Chief Commercial Manager).
Railway Gazette

on 11 April, ahead of the official party who were to accompany it on its journey through Canada and the USA. Ten days later, on 21 April 1933, Lemon's party embarked on the *Duchess of Bedford* at Liverpool bound for Montreal. For this trip he was accompanied by his wife, Amy. The other members of the party were Ashton Davies, S.H. Fisher, T.C. Byrom and G.L. Darbyshire.[154] A photograph of their departure was printed in the *Railway Gazette*. One always expects official records to be reasonably accurate, and so it is surprising to find that the ship's passenger list described Ashton Davies, Chief Commercial Manager, as a clerk aged 44 (he was 58). Fisher, Byrrom and Derbyshire [*sic*] were, at least, given the appellation 'Manager', but the accuracy of their ages has not been checked! Even more surprising, though, is that Lemon, the leader of the party, is entered as Edward Lemon, clerk, aged 36, accompanied by his wife, Mary, aged 34. This is wrong on five points – he was, actually Ernest, Vice-President, aged 48, and his wife was Amy aged 46! To use a current slang expression, the purser must had a really 'bad hair day'.

The *Railway Gazette* reported that: among the practices and problems to be investigated during this visit were:

sales organisation; passenger terminal operations and facilities; goods sheds and freight terminals; traffic yards; electrification; passenger train workings; intensified use of locomotives; divisional or district control office organisation for both passenger and freight trains; method of analysing the various phases of traffic operations; coal silos; rates for passenger and merchandise traffic; claims compensation and prevention methods; railway advertising and publicity and its relation to railway commercial activities; accommodation schemes and [finally!] road competition.

One wonders why the magazine bothered to use the word 'among' to describe this list – there does not seem to have been any aspect of railway management omitted! Lemon obviously did not intend this to be an easy jaunt. The party were also scheduled to travel 5,000 miles on the train.

The tour started on 1 May, when the train left Montreal for Ottawa. An official reception was held at Ottawa the following day when Lemon gave a conducted tour of the train to the Governor-General, the Earl of Bessborough and his wife, the Prime Minister of Canada and members of his Cabinet. The train then crossed into the USA, travelling through New England until it arrived in New York.

Lemon's wife recalled an anecdote from this trip in a somewhat disjointed letter she wrote to Sir Harold Hartley after her husband's death in 1954 to thank him for attending the funeral:

Did W Ashton Davies ever tell you of our New York visit – the time of the Royal Train.

The Americans had all been most kind and hospitable & so I suggested to my husband that surely by now it was our turn to be host and hostess, so we were.

That day I had decided to have a quiet time beforehand – so just went into The Canadian National Office & collected literature dealing with a trip across the Rockies & to the Pacific Coast. I collected a host of phamlets [*sic*] from a most luxurious office – nobody came forward or spoke one word – so just waving them to the distant attendants, I said, Do you mind if I take these? No answer. Then when we get to our dinner party – to a place where my American relatives were horrified that we had been – one Dottie Long – of the Murphy party started to run down the attention she had been given at the LMS office in The French Building – cutting under the loyalty of – shall I say our Staff – I mean LMS. Perhaps as hostess I should not have said a word but I said, You were lucky Miss Long to be given all that information & attention & told my tale – to this day I can see Ashton Davies holding his sides with laughter – & I didn't know that the LMS party had been taken there by W. Murphy – as a set piece – that very morning.[155]

The train left New York on 13 May, and one assumes this dinner party was therefore held a day or so earlier. The tour continued on via Washington and St Louis, finally reaching Chicago on 31 May, where the train was exhibited until

September. However, if Lemon and Amy had time for a visit through Canada to the Pacific Coast, it seems likely that they must have left the official party after New York as they were certainly on their way home by 27 May. Even this scenario seems to leave little time to accomplish the trip; but Stamp, who had travelled separately to Chicago, sent Lemon a telegram from the exhibition site on 27 May. This reached Lemon on the St Lawrence estuary as his ship returned home. The telegram read:

Highly gratified to find what lasting impression created by your personality on all ranks railway officials and public Stop Our railway greatly indebted to you as always Stop Wish you good voyage and complete rest Stop At Toronto gave press interviews talkie camera and also expressed appreciation of Canadian reception of Royal Scot in broadcast address from university. Stamp.[156]

Lemon and Amy arrived back in Southampton on 2 June 1933.[157] Other members of the party who had accompanied Lemon arrived back later,[158] indicating that they had stayed longer with the train on its procession through America. On the return voyage, the ship's passenger list was accurate (!) describing Lemon as a Vice-President and giving his address as Northchurch Hall, Berkhamsted, Herts. News came through soon after their arrival home that their elder son, Richard, had passed the entrance exam for Oxford University. He chose to go to Balliol College to read PPE – Politics, Philosophy and Economics. This was Sir Harold Hartley's old college, which probably influenced his decision.

LMS Film Propaganda

A FILM was made of the Royal Scot's trip to America, which was shown at various centres around this country. Members of staff received the film with such enthusiasm that it indicated more could be done along these lines. On 21 November 1933, Lemon sent a memo to the President that starts:

Whilst our publicity for public purposes has developed in step more or less with modern conditions, I am afraid that publicity or propaganda for staff purposes has not kept pace with the times. This has been forcibly brought home to me by the reception which has been given to the 'Royal Scot' film presentations at various centres recently, e.g. at Crewe the enthusiasm of the audience composed of railwaymen was simply astonishing.

It seems to me, therefore, that we shall have to pursue a policy which will awaken the interest of and develop the esprit de corps of our staff by bringing before their notice phases of railway working with which they, in their particular occupations, do not come into contact.
In other words, we must let them see what the railway really means in all its workings.[159]

Lemon considered that film presentations were a very effective medium in this direction, and he informed Stamp that he had asked Mr Loftus Allen, the Advertising and Publicity Manager, to look at the matter from the point of view of establishing a stock of films, which could be used for the purpose of lectures amongst the staff. He suggested an immediate list of twelve subjects that he thought would be suitable:

(1) Assembly of locomotives
(2)   -do-   carriages
(3)   -do-   wagons
(4) A day's work in a railway hotel
(5) The turn-round of a steamer at, say, Holyhead or Heysham
(6) A railway laundry
(7) How a railway handles the mails
(8) Shunting operations at a marshalling depot
(9) Handling operations at a goods depot
(10) How a locomotive depot prepares its engines for traffic.
(11) The marvels of modern signalling
(12) Passenger traffic and how crowds are handled.

He also considered that gramophone records might also be made, conveying a personal message from Stamp or other Chief Officers in regard to particular phases of railway work.

He concluded the memo:

With regard to cost, it would appear that a sum not exceeding £2,000 would require to be sanctioned in order to get the matter going as a practical job, and I shall be pleased if you will let me know whether you are in sympathy with the idea and agree to the experiment being made. It is a line of action which is somewhat new so far as the Railways are concerned, although other public bodies, such as the Post Office and probably big industrial concerns, have done and are doing something of a similar nature. I think there is a lot in it.

Stamp endorsed the idea, and replied that the idea had been well received by the Directors who, like himself, would also like a periodical newsreel of domestic events developed. The first two films to be ready for exhibition, *Corridor Third* and *Euston House* were shown at Euston in March 1934 and then at Crewe, Liverpool, Manchester, Birmingham, Derby and Glasgow. The whole tour produced a total audience of approximately 10,000 and from the enthusiastic way in which the films were received, the popularity of further films was assured. Accordingly, screenings at 41 centres were arranged for the winter of 1934, by which time six more films were ready for presentation. The films were advertised by posters and handbills, and there were nearly 40,000 attendances, demonstrating that large numbers of staff could be reached through the medium, and that the message conveyed would 'get home' more certainly and permanently than by any other means. These first films were 'silent', but in 1935 synchronised sound started to be used.

For the first two or three years, the films were limited to educational and travel interest but, by March 1934, Lemon was also using film as an internal aid in the analysis of work methods and practices. Lewis Ord, who was carrying out an investigation into the workings of Goods Terminals wrote: 'Mr Lemon has made use of the Movie Camera – both to analyse the work in more detail and to enable the very great amount of instructional work to be carried out cheaply, quickly and effectively'.[160] Lemon had seen that it was possibly less intrusive and more effective to film work in progress, rather than using men in

Interior of the carriage converted for use as a mobile projection unit. *Railway Gazette*

white coats with clip-boards and stop watches. The film footage was then used for analysis, and could be replayed to the workers together with suggestions as to how the same task might be achieved more easily.

In February 1936 Lemon wrote to the Chairman outlining modifications in the organisation of the Advertising & Publicity Department necessary to put the Company's film production on a sure basis. He also proposed that an old carriage should be converted for use as a mobile projection unit; this unit being absolutely self-contained and capable of exhibiting films anywhere on the system. This was approved, and in May 1936, as H.G. Smith bluntly puts it, 'it was proposed to use the film medium to instruct the staff in the correct [!] method of carrying out their work, and it was felt that, particularly with this type of film, the mobile unit, which would enable the staff to be reached in places where no facilities for showing films existed, would be particularly useful.'

In December 1936 it was necessary to construct a second Mobile Film Unit to cope with the increasing number of films being produced, and to cover the extensive programme of exhibitions. When war broke out in 1939, activity in this direction had to be curtailed – with the result that only one Mobile Unit was kept in service, engaged in showing the *Salvage* film.

Loudspeakers at passenger stations and traffic yards

H.G. SMITH recounts that in October 1933, Lord Knutsford, one of the Directors, suggested to Lemon that more staff should be appointed for the purpose of directing passengers at stations.[161] Lemon considered a better solution would be to utilise more mechanical devices, e.g. loudspeakers. This would give the desired result without increasing staff expense, and he requested the Chief Operating Manager, C.R. Byrom to institute a review of the stations where loud-speakers might be used. This was not a new idea: the LNER had been using such equipment since at least 1928 at Liverpool Street station.[162]

It is difficult to establish the sequence of events which then followed, and when stations were fitted with the apparatus. One would imagine that Euston was the first to be equipped, and *Modern Transport* magazine announced on 26 May 1934 that loudspeakers were to be fitted there, which would 'be used only for communication between staff and not for directing the public'.[163] Smith alleges that, on 18 October 1934, Byrom reported that loudspeaker apparatus had been installed at six of the larger stations and that both from the Company's and the public point of view the assistance provided was unquestionable. However, the earliest authorisation for any scheme in the Traffic Committee minutes is not until 17 April 1935, when it was agreed that £604 should be allocated for the installation of loudspeakers at Euston.[164] This was followed, on 24 July 1935, by the authorisation of £585 for a similar system at Birmingham New Street. It is clear that Lemon was able to give his own personal authority for schemes without reference to the Traffic Committee, and this is confirmed by the Minutes for 27 October 1937. At this meeting, Byrom reported that loudspeaker apparatus had now been installed with successful results at 23 passenger stations and 18 traffic yards (where they had proved most useful for broadcasting information when telephone communication was not possible). The Minutes record that he submitted a schedule of the loudspeaker installations authorised (a) by the Traffic Committee and (b) by the Vice-President in anticipation of a comprehensive report covering the whole of such schemes. A new Works Order was issued to cover the whole project, and previous Minutes on the subject were deleted. The locations of the 41 sites where installations were in place are not given, and it is thus impossible to tell from these records exactly where and when they were made.

However, slightly more information can be found in the *Railway Gazette*. On 5 February 1937 the magazine reported:

So successful have been the loudspeakers installed at various stations on the LMSR for directing crowds and for conveying information to passengers, that the company is to extend the system during 1937. Installations are to be provided at Holyhead, Fleetwood, and

Llandudno Junction, and consideration is being given to the provision of similar equipment at numerous other stations including Chester, Crewe, Leicester, Manchester (London Road and Victoria), Preston, Sheffield, Wembley, and Longsight. The loudspeakers at Euston, St Pancras, Birmingham, Derby, and a number of seaside stations including Blackpool, Morecambe, Southport, Rhyl, and Southend-on-Sea have proved most useful, especially at holiday times.[165]

Willesden sidings

PART OF Lord Knutsford's problem may well have been that he could never find his train at Euston station! Although sections such as the Doric Arch and the Great Hall may have displayed their grandeur, the overall layout, which had grown piece-meal over the years, was now an unsatisfactory hotchpotch, with the Great Hall inconveniently dividing the station into two distinct halves. One description of the layout of the platforms concluded: 'As for platform 9, used mainly for bank-holiday extras, it was tucked down another passageway and probably many intending passengers never actually found it at all!'[166] Proposals for the complete rebuilding of the station had been in hand for many years, and intrinsic to the plans was a scheme for the redesign and expansion of the carriage sidings at Willesden. However H.G. Smith recounts that the plans for both projects had been deferred in 1930 because of the expenditure involved.

In December 1933, it was found necessary to increase the number of carriages on main-line services to cater for the growing number of passengers. Lemon pointed out that at Euston, the most important station on the line, the facilities for fitting out these express trains with dining and sleeping equipment, and for marshalling them to the best advantage were unsatisfactory. At holiday times, in particular, the existing arrangements were inadequate to deal with the additional traffic. This obviously gave rise to dissatisfaction from passengers and Smith states that, as these had been secured in opposition to road competition, the company did not wish to alienate or lose them.[167] Lemon expressed the opinion that the scheme for additional facilities at Willesden should be looked at again, and Byrom was asked to consider the problem. This review took time, and there were further problems over the summer of 1934 but, by the Autumn, Byrom had finished his assessment and plans had been drawn up. No work had therefore been done as Christmas 1934 approached. The extra traffic engendered by the holiday, coupled with the bad weather conditions, caused massive disruption to the service. Lemon explained the reasons for this in a memo to the Chairman on 19 January 1935 – 'we have all been made aware of the circumstances which arose at Euston in connection with the working of the passenger traffic on the Saturday before Christmas Day, and you are aware of the complaints and adverse comments which have been made upon our organisation at Euston'.[168]

Lemon reports that he had thoroughly probed the arrangements that were scheduled for dealing with the anticipated traffic. One problem was that the existing layout at Willesden meant that coaches had to be split over various different sidings before they could be marshalled and taken up to Euston. On this occasion, problems had been exacerbated by fog which had brought marshalling operations almost to a complete standstill. Diplomatically, Lemon reported that: 'There is no question of the Euston situation at Christmas being used as a weapon to force the Management to undertake the proposals for additional accommodation at Willesden' – but he asks Stamp to 'ventilate the matter' with the Directors at the forthcoming Dinner, and get them to agree to immediate expenditure on improvements. Lemon argued that these would show year-long benefits. This was done, and formal approval for the work was recommended by the Traffic Committee on 27 February 1935.[169] The sidings were lengthened, fitted with electric lighting, and all equipped with washing, gas and water facilities by late summer 1935.

In response to Stamp's enquiry at the Traffic Committee meeting, Lemon reported that these actions were not a complete remedy for the defects at Willesden, and further proposals would be submitted. In May 1936, approval was given for further improvements.[170] Whereas the first work had cost just under £12,000, these new proposals were estimated at a massive £382,400. A large proportion of this cost was due to the amount of excavation and removal of soil that was necessary. The scheme involved the provision of a new shed to give additional covered accommodation for 192 carriages on twelve roads, and two groups of uncovered sidings, eight roads in each, holding a total of 320 coaches. No longer would carriage working be carried out in separate sheds on opposite sides of the main line, and crossing movements would be cut to a minimum. The covered accommodation would also mean that carriages would be kept in a dry and warm environment, which was particularly appropriate for sleeping and dining cars. In 1937, Lemon revised his ideas on the layout of the covered accommodation, and devised a system on 'progressive' lines. This was actually cheaper than the original plan, and the Board accepted the revised scheme in July 1938.[171]

The progressive shed was planned in four stages: Inspection; Exterior cleaning and inside maintenance; Interior cleaning and outside maintenance; Equipping with linen, towels, etc. Four coaches would stand in each stage at a time, and after a suitable interval for the work to be completed, would be moved forward into the next stage. All subsequent movements within the shed would be carried out by mechanical means, controlled by a signalling device operated by a member of the shed staff. This afforded greater safety, as all movements would be made at pre-determined times, thus eliminating the need for the men to be kept clear while shunting took place. H.G. Smith described at length the benefits these ideas would bring both for the staff and the company – and they were, of course, a development of the assembly line techniques that Lemon had introduced for the construction of rolling stock. However, war interrupted proceedings. In October 1939, the Executive Committee allowed certain of the work at Willesden to continue when it postponed the scheme for remodelling Euston Station. Smith reported than in July 1941, the greater part of the siding accommodation had been completed – but work on the carriage shed was 'in abeyance'.[172]

Line Inspections

In November 1933, Lemon inaugurated a new regime of regular line inspections by Head-quarters staff. Leading these visits whenever possible, he was usually accompanied by C.R. Byrom, the Chief Operating Manager and Ashton Davies, the Chief Commercial Manager together with other subordinate officers. The inspections lasted two days and took place at intervals of six weeks or so. Every section of the network was visited in turn, and the first such tour took place on 29/30 November 1933. One assumes from the report that clearly labels it as Tour No.1, that such a practice had not existed on a regular basis before.[173] This first tour visited Motive Power depots in Birmingham and the surrounding area, and, as has been previously mentioned, the conclusions drawn were that the progress on modernisation schemes was disappointing. Once again the report records the principle of establishing parent depots in each area, with other sheds within a radius of 30/40 miles being merely garages. In this area, Rugby had been designated the parent depot, with garages at Nuneaton, Warwick, Bletchley and Coventry.

These tours were an opportunity to meet local management staff on their own patch, explain Company policy and hear their current problems at first-hand. Every aspect of operating practice came under Lemon's close scrutiny and questioning eye. On the first tour, for example, he asked why two men were pumping water out of a turntable pit by hand, and suggested that either the drainage should be improved or a mechanical pump acquired. However, his excessive zeal for rooting out inefficiency and sloppy practices seems to have got out of hand occasionally, as the following incident shows. At one yard on this tour he reprimanded the staff for using the telephone for trivial matters. Apparently, they had phoned Derby for a replacement glass eye for one of the fitters! (presumably this was a prosthetic, and not some obscure locomotive component?). Why was it necessary to make an issue of this particular incident? The cost of the call was hardly likely to destabilise the company's finances. It also does not demonstrate a warm-hearted compassion for

the poor fellow's distress. Perhaps the secretary who compiled the report may have been deliver-ing a mild reproof to his boss for making such a big deal of it. In fairness to Lemon, he did show his empathy for the workforce at other times on this tour. At Nuneaton he emphasised the undesirability of getting rid of men rendered surplus by machinery, and urged the local management to find work for them elsewhere. Similar attention to what might be considered inconsequential details can be found in the reports of later tours. As an example, at Rowsley Depot in 1937 he recommended that the partitions between toilets should be heightened and doors fitted.

There were other, more general, comments. Whilst touring the Manchester area, he drew attention to the necessity for improving working conditions in goods yards and engine sheds by brightening up the interiors and by better lighting. On another occasion, he noted that a glass roof was excessively dirty and artificial light was being used during the day (how often nowadays are lights left on all day on railway platforms!). All these points were immediately passed on to the appropriate officer for action. However, from time to time a specific problem at one location led to a general review over the whole network. H.G. Smith recounts several specific occasions when this happened, and one such instance occurred during the tour of the Tilbury line in November 1934. Lemon observed that the Parcels Office accommodation had not kept pace with the development of traffic, and facilities were consequently seriously inadequate. Ashton Smith, the Chief Commercial Manager, was asked to review the position throughout the whole of the LMS and prepare a priority list so that the matter could be dealt with systematically.[174] As a result, certain small schemes were authorised, and in April 1937 a special Department was set up to carry out time-and-motion studies on the handling of parcel traffic. Lemon kept a close eye on progress and suggested various forms of mechanical devices, such as conveyor belts and wheeled containers, that they should try out. Such equipment was fitted at Euston, and a comprehensive scheme for handling parcels was incorporated into the plans for the rebuilding of the station. Another specific scheme for conveyors was agreed in April 1938 to deal with the transfer of mail and newspapers to steamers at Holyhead.[175] Smith cites several other problems that were discovered on these trips, and which led to a general review of practices throughout the company.

Large distances were covered on these tours, and one wonders how the official party managed to fit all the visits into the two days allowed. As they also presumably travelled everywhere by train, it is a marvel that their itinerary could be shoehorned into the day-to-day normal traffic working. On 5/6 June 1934, for example, Tour No.5 made the following journey:

Starting from Paddington at 8.55am [i.e. by GWR] the party arrived at Bristol at 11.20am inspected certain properties there, and then proceeded as follows: Bath – Gloucester – Cheltenham – Worcester – Stoke Works – Bromsgrove – Blackwell – Birmingham New St. The next day, after visiting further sites in Birmingham such as Lawley St. Goods Station, Saltley Control Office & Motive Power Depot, and Washwood Heath sidings, the party left for Burton, Beeston sidings and Nottingham before returning to St. Pancras.

Lemon led the vast majority of these Tours until he was seconded to the Air Ministry in 1938. The tours continued thereafter until July 1939, but were discontinued on the outbreak of war. However, Lemon did *not* go on the second tour to Lancashire on 10/11 January 1934. As he had only just inaugurated this regime of line visits, his absence was surely unexpected. He also cancelled a scheduled lecture at the Institute of Transport on 12 January, when the *Royal Scot in the USA* film was shown. One might reasonably suppose that he was ill – he was actually on a boat to the Caribbean.

E.J.H. Lemon
(date unknown).
National Portrait Gallery

Marriage problems

LEMON left Avonmouth on a ship of the Elders & Fyffes Line, the s.s. *Ariguani* on 8 January bound for Kingston, Jamaica. The ship was not a cruise liner, although it carried 54 passengers on the outward trip, but a working ship bringing back bananas from the West Indies. The shipping records show that he travelled alone and did not disembark in Jamaica in order to spend a few days lying on a tropical beach. Surprisingly, he merely made the round trip and arrived back in Avonmouth on 12 February.[176]

It does not appear therefore that the trip was planned well in advance, and timed to fit in with work commitments. As his later life was blighted by periodic bouts of a depressive illness – undoubtedly caused by a highly-strung temperament and overwork – this may have been a reason for his absence. He was obviously a man who lived on his nerves and subject to extremes of mood. Sir Harold Hartley acknowledged this in the obituary he wrote in *The Times* following Lemon's death: 'He had a mercurial temperament . . . Often he would bounce into my room saying: "I have had one of my good days" and tell me the results, but at other times he could be argumentative and difficult'.[177] However, in the light of subsequent events, there may well have been other reasons for the trip. Lemon needed to think seriously about his private life – and what better way to do this than on the high seas where he could be alone, away from the distractions and pressures of work. Although this trip was only six months after his tour to the USA with Amy, his subsequent actions are the first indications of problems in his marriage.

After his return, Lemon took an apartment in Marylebone at 3 Bank Chambers, 13 Dorset Street, W1. He is recorded there in the Electoral Roll dated 15 October 1934. Crucially he does not qualify the entry, as is customary practice for people with a London *pied-à-terre*, by giving his 'abode' as Northchurch Hall. This implies that, as far as Lemon was concerned, Dorset Street was now his main residence. He did remain, however, on the Electoral Roll at Berkhamsted – qualifying him to vote in two locations! Presumably his wife continued to supply the information for Northchurch Hall. Of course, the apartment in London could simply have been a means to avoid the daily commute from Berkhamsted, and not necessarily an indication that the marriage had broken down, were it not for one other fact. At the same time that Lemon moved into Dorset Street, Miss Hermione Mervyn took rooms just around the corner at 117 Gloucester Place and is listed at this address for the first time in the 1934–5 Electoral Roll.

Hermione Mervyn MBE

ON moving to London in 1931, following his appointment as Chief Mechanical Engineer, Lemon would eventually have met the Chief Lady Welfare Supervisor of the LMS, Miss Hermione Mervyn. She entered LMS service as Welfare Supervisor for the London area in 1923 and, prior to her railway appointment, had spent some years in the office of the Director-General of Transport and Coal Controller for Ireland. Later she was transferred to the Ministry of Transport in London, and was awarded the MBE for her work in Government service during the First World War. In 1926, she became Assistant to the Chief Lady Welfare Supervisor at Euston, upon whose retirement in 1930 she was promoted to the top job.

Muriel Hermione Marion Mervyn – to list her full Christian names – was born on 6 October 1897 in Dublin, the daughter of the Rector of Clontarf, Reverend Frederick William Mervyn. By 1923 Mervyn's church career had also taken him from Ireland to London, where he died, at 54 Redcliffe Square, Kensington on 23 February 1933. His widow, Marion, and daughter,

Miss Hermione Mervyn.
Railway Gazette

Hermione, were joint executors of his Will, and the probate records show that, at the time, Hermione was living at 39 Dorset Square, Marylebone. This address is listed in the London Directories as 'The Ladies' National Club', and, as its title indicates, the two dozen or so residents were all women – most of them unmarried.

Lemon's granddaughters were aware of Hermione, her relationship with Lemon, and how he eventually left his wife to live with her. However, all they knew was her Christian name – it appears, for instance, in correspondence following Lemon's death – now in their possession (see later). Her surname, background and position at the LMS have only become apparent during research for this book. What nobody knows now is when the relationship started. Without any first-hand knowledge, it is impossible to arrive at an incontrovertible sequence of events. All that can be done is to try and interpret the circumstantial evidence. The close proximity of these two addresses in 1934 is the earliest evidence so far discovered for the relationship. The fact that Lemon's name continues in the registers at Northchurch Hall demonstrates that he had not left his wife at this stage, and one assumes that he lived happily with Hermione during the week and returned home to his wife at weekends. For the sake of propriety and secrecy, they maintained two addresses. He would not be the first man to do this!

Other duties of a Vice-President

AS HAS been indicated earlier, the second film to be made by the LMS was called *Euston House*. Both Hartley and Lemon had been much involved in arguing the case for this new building. Hartley's archive housed at Churchill College, Cambridge, includes a hand-written note to Stamp dated 27 July 1932 which starts: 'I have asked Lemon to hand over to you the drawings of the Office Building and the memorandum

I am writing with Hamlyn [the LMS architect, W.H. Hamlyn] so that you can deal with it at the Dinner tonight'.[178] He continues with details about changes to the front elevation, and concludes: 'With our new organisation the case for the building is very strong. Lemon will enlarge on this – but the Board may say that the cost is too high'. Approval was granted nevertheless, and the building went up rapidly.

The opening ceremony held on 16 February 1934, was attended by a host of dignitaries from the LMS. Surprisingly, as he had been so involved in its creation, Lemon's name is absent from the list of those attending the opening ceremony. He arrived back from his round-trip to the West Indies on 12 February, and would surely have been able to attend the occasion. Maybe the official list of those present was prepared in advance before his whereabouts could be known with certainty? The reason for his absence, if such it was, is unexplained – especially as the building was to house his Operating Department, which was thereby relocated from the motley collection of offices it had previously occupied.

Lemon was certainly back at work by 9 March 1934, as he attended the Annual Dinner of the LMS (London) Golfing Society.[179] Attendance at such events was normally part and parcel of the duties of senior management, and similar occasions can be found recorded in issues of the *Railway Gazette* or local newspapers throughout this period.

He was also called upon to attend other events on behalf of the company. In the Autumn of 1933 he made a speech at the Commercial Motor Exhibition. No contemporary account of this has been found, but Lemon referred to it in a similar speech at the Exhibition held at Olympia in 1935.[180] On the latter occasion, he was a guest at a luncheon given by the Society of Motor Manufacturers and Traders. After the usual pleasantries, Lemon delivered a few forthright comments (as one might expect!) on what the motor trade should, or should not, be doing. Although he congratulated them on the initiative, ingenuity, and variety put into the design of commercial vehicles, he commented that they were now introducing the idea of streamlining them. He wondered whether, in following an absurd fashion adopted in the United States, where they were even streamlining refrigerators, they were not working on the wrong lines. He could see no advantage in streamlining a commercial vehicle that was limited to a speed of 30mph since no great benefits could be obtained until speeds of over 60mph were reached. He also suggested that the chassis should be designed so that it would be a simple matter to replace any component fitted to it. In this way, a vehicle would not be rendered obsolete because of improvements in any one part. Finally he referred to the speech he had made two years earlier at the Exhibition in 1933, when he pointed out to the manufacturers that they had gone wrong with regard to the development of the 'mechanical horse' (a simple motorised cab unit, that could be attached to a dray or cart). They had started with a unit to replace the horse, he said, but had lost sight of their objectives and developed it into a unit to replace two-ton or three-ton lorries. So far, he said, the manufacturers had made no progress in the directions he had outlined – an omission he obviously thought they should have done something about!

In conclusion, he urged that there should be more co-operation between road and rail transport. Both were providing essential public services, and so far as the railways were concerned, they would not complain – provided they were working under conditions of equality as to public regulation. The railways were prepared to play fair, he said, but it had got to be fair. He wished to emphasise that the railways were the motor manufacturers' biggest customers, and they, in turn, were important customers of the railways. There ought, therefore, to be no real enmity between them. This was a crucial issue, and the railways were acutely aware that they were losing customers to the road hauliers, who by their very nature could offer greater flexibility to their customers in door-to-door service. In an effort to combat this, some years earlier in 1926 the LMS had begun an experiment that was eventually to change freight practice across all four railway groups. It began with a report from the Goods Department entitled 'Freight Transportation in Container Trucks' and a number of containers were built to test their

Euston House under construction. Note the shop on the corner which continued trading as the new building engulfed it!
Hurst, Peirce & Malcolm

efficacy.[181] In the first experimental year of 1926/7 the claims for lost, stolen or damaged goods was a third of those for ordinary goods traffic. The experiment was deemed a success, expanded, and efforts made to involve the other railways via discussions at the Railway Clearing House. The development of containers also influenced the design, use and efficiency of Goods Depots.

The Modernisation of Goods Terminals and Analysis of Handling and Cartage Costs

H.G. SMITH records that early in 1930, the LMS had set up a small committee to look into proposals 'for mechanisation and modernisation with consequent economy and improvement in efficiency' of Goods Depots. The committee consisted of a range of officers from various departments, the Chief Operating Manager, Chief Mechanical Engineer, the Electrical Engineer and the Chief Civil Engineer. In 1933, Lemon took an active interest in their progress and achievements, and reported to Stamp in a memo dated 23 March 1933 that they had decided upon and implemented a number of schemes,

some of which 'have been successful and others not'.[182] Lemon continued in this memo: 'We spent last year in wages for the handling of goods traffic just over £1,500,000, and I have for some time felt that we should secure the services of an expert to devote his whole time for a period on studying ways and means of improving our methods with a view to –

(1) reducing labour costs
(2) improving conditions for the staff
(3) expediting the handling of goods.'

Goods traffic – as opposed to bulk traffic, such as coal – was an important part of the freight delivered by the railway, but it was difficult to handle, labour intensive and open to pilferage. Items could, and did, get stuck at transhipment points, simply because they were one amongst so many. This was one area where door-to-door transport by road had a positive advantage, and a challenge the railways had to meet. William Cunningham, Assistant Professor of Transportation at Harvard University detailed differences between British and American experience in his 1912 article on freight handling.[183] He noted that 'the most striking dissimilarity is seen in the character of the freight itself and in the design and capacity of their freight cars. The freight traffic of England is said to be decidedly *retail* [his emphasis] in character, while that of America is *wholesale*. The British merchant, because of his nearness to sources of supply and the expeditious service of the railways, is not accustomed to carry large stocks of goods. The service of the railways is such that goods ordered one day from the wholesale dealer are delivered at the merchant's door early the next day . . . the English retailers find that they can rely upon the railways for good service which equals the service of the express companies of this country, and it has had the effect of forcing the railways to handle a large volume of small packages and a relatively small number of car-load shipments. [i.e. fully loaded wagons all going to one destination]'.[184]

The retail analogy and the description of the traffic is accurate and useful. It stesses the importance, as Lemon noted, of next-day delivery and accurately describes the fragmentation of the traffic into small, but numerous, consignments. Retailers did depend on the efficiency of the railways and, as the cost of freight was factored into their pricing structure, the public generally perceived the railways to be the main culprits when costs increased.

Freight operations were thus an important political issue, and the railways had been under criticism about the cost and handling of freight since the end of the First World War. Roy Horniman, in his 1919 book on how to make the railways pay for the war, wrote that 'the mobility of a goods wagon on the track is three percent of its entire existence, and of this three percent mobility half a percent is laden mobility and two and a half percent is unladen mobility'.[185] This means that for 97% of the time a goods wagon was unprofitably stuck in sidings and marshalling yards. It was, obviously, a horrendous uneconomic use of resources. Horniman includes a description of a goods station from *The World* magazine.[186] 'A typical goods station is a wilderness of sidings, perhaps a mile or more long, and a quarter to half a mile broad. It is furnished with a loosely congregated jumble of sheds, which are dotted over it higgledy-piggledy from one end to the other. It has no design, and is too unwieldy and scattered to admit of the rapid intercommunication of parts, which is essential to a building designed for a place of exchange. It is devoid of any equipment other than a primitive crane.'

Although Cunningham and Horniman were writing many years before Lemon's 1933 memorandum, the situation had not radically improved in the intervening years and was still relatively accurate. Large numbers of labourers were still walking long distances, often pushing carts or barrows full of goods; the level of shunting was high and goods wagons, as

Lemon and Sir Josiah Stamp at the billiard table (October 1935?). Derby Engineering Society

Horniman described, were still detained in the goods depots for long periods. Horses and carts were extensively used, both for local delivery, as well as to move goods round the depot, and horses were still used for wagon shunting operations. In 1932, the LMS owned 8,950 horses, 17,000 carts and nearly 2,000 motor vehicles.[187]

H.G. Smith recorded that the object of Goods Shed Mechanisation was to analyse 'the causes of the greatly varying working results at stations dealing with traffic similar in volume and type, and ascertaining the best methods of handling in order that they might be adopted generally – one main principle being the bringing of the work to the man instead of vice versa.' Here again Lemon, with his love of efficiency, was seeking to apply the principle of the production line methods he had established in the carriage and wagon works.

In order to impose order on chaos, the first step was to study the problems in depth. Mechanical handling methods could then be designed to take the place of the old inefficient labour-intensive ways. Perhaps a measure of Lemon's power at this time can be glimpsed from his memorandum to Stamp which states: 'I have therefore engaged the services of Mr Lewis C. Ord, who has wide experience in works and other re-organisation schemes on a monthly contract at a fee of £550 per month, to include out-of-pocket expenses. Mr Ord is at the present time engaged on a study of the position at Crewe Tranship Shed, which is one of the largest and most difficult cases of its kind.'

£550 measured against the retail price index, one of the possible indicators, is at the time of writing the equivalent of around £27,000. Ord submitted a report in March 1934, showing that he worked for the LMS for at least a year, hence the contract was worth, at least, £6,600 – in modern values £325,000. To put this sum in the perspective of the time: Lemon, Wood and Hartley as Vice-Presidents of the LMS were each earning £5,000 p.a. and Lemon had just purchased Northchurch Hall, Berkhamstead, a substantial house with grounds and outbuildings, for £4,950. Lemon could apparently authorise expenditure of substantial sums.

Lewis C. Ord, who was briefly mentioned in

the last chapter, was an experienced railwayman as well as an industrial consultant. He was a Canadian and had entered the service of the Canadian Pacific Railway aged 13, rising to become superintendent of the company's car shops. During this period he spent some time being taught by Henry Gantt, who from 1887 to 1893 had worked with the originator of Scientific Management, Frederick Taylor. Gantt's ideas were a great influence on Ord, particularly those expressed in his book *Organising for Work* and Ord became an expert in both Scientific Management and Mass Production. Ord himself picks up the story, 'In 1919 some British industrial leaders visited the USA and Canada to study industrial developments and particularly mass production. As a result of what they saw it was decided to invite some experts, with practical experience of mass production, to come to Britain to introduce the new method. I was one of those who were brought over at that time.' Once in this country he began practicing as a consulting engineer and was engaged by such firms as Cammell Laird, AEC, the London Underground and the Rootes Group prior to his work for the LMS.

Ord was set to work with C.R. Byrom, the Chief Operating Officer and, having studied the Crewe operation, spread out his analysis to a number of comparable sites to see what could be learnt. Data was collected from all the Company's Goods' Depots, and statistics were drawn up showing the tonnage of goods dealt with and, from this, the cost per ton and the man-hours per ton at each depot. Ord submitted an interim report in October 1933, and Lemon notified the Chairman that, with his agreement, steps would be taken to test Ord's theories of ways to reduce costs at selected stations.[188]

A year after starting work, on 3 March 1934, Ord submitted his report, 'Mechanisation of Goods Sheds'. This is the only such report from the period that that still exists in its entirety amongst Lemon's personal papers and, because of this, it can be considered in greater detail than is possible with others of Lemon's initiatives.

The report starts:

At my first long interview with Mr Lemon he asked me to make written notes of the following points where he thought improvements could be made and in the accomplishment of which he thought mechanisation would assist:

1. The entire elimination of trucking.
2. A reduction in the amount of handling, and therefore of damage claims.
3. A quicker clearing of traffic; in the morning to get a greater percentage delivered each day; in the afternoon to compensate for the tendency to later collection and to assist in speeding up transit.
4. Attention to the speeding up and cheaper handling of container traffic; extensions of the container principle.
5. Reduction in shunting by locomotive by the use of other cheaper mechanical means.
6. To make sure that reductions in shed handling costs were not lost in increased cartage costs.
7. To try to obtain quicker release of wagons under load.
8. To concentrate the work as much as possible in order to reduce walking time of the men and horses and to aid supervision.
9. To bring the work to the men in every case that was possible and not having the men moving all over the place to their work.

Ord also records that Lemon placed two important restrictions on the investigation. There should be no criticism of past results so long as a man did all that was possible in the future; and that, for the same reason, there should be no attempt to split the economies due to physical change or mechanisation from those that might have been made without. Lemon obviously did not wish this investigation to be a witch-hunt, merely seeking out and replacing inefficient employees, but a scientific appraisal of the best methods that could be used to achieve greater efficiency. It is interesting to see these concerns – especially after the lack of any such details in the descriptions of the remodelling in the Carriage & Wagon works.

At the end of his year long investigation Ord concluded: 'It is really surprising the accuracy of Mr Lemon's forecast as to the possibilities, apparent then only to himself . . . every one of Mr Lemon's points (with the exception of the first

part of number 3) can be accomplished, and I believe on further investigation that something can be done in that direction also'. However, it has to be said that this does not seem to be the conclusion of the report at all, as will become apparent! The report itself is surprisingly impenetrable, with seeming contradictions and ambiguities, and the undoubted conclusion – unequivocally stated by Ord – was that remodelling work undertaken had *not* been a success.

It is tantalising that this is the only report of Ord's known to survive, as it gives a glimpse of the economic and industrial conditions at the time in this important area of rail operations. It also provides a fascinating – and unique – insight into the attempts to address the problem; and the working and the politics of the LMS Goods Department where, as Ord says, there was great prejudice against mechanisation.

Goods Depots handled three classes of traffic, *Received* i.e. goods received by rail, *Forwarded* or traffic sent to other destinations via another railway company's lines and finally *Tranships*, goods that had to be moved into a different wagon to get to their destination. Ord's preliminary work established that the difficulty in handling goods at different sheds varied little from one to another. This was a crucial factor: it wasn't that depots handled a similar volume of traffic – obviously they didn't – it was that the *difficulty* in handling that traffic was similar. Ord expected, therefore, that if the [local] management, working practices and pace remained the same, all depots should return similar improved results, in man hours per ton, after remodelling.

Ord states that very early in his investigations 'it became clear that many stations were not being worked efficiently'. As an example he quotes the different statistics from Kettering and Halifax: operating conditions were, if anything, slightly more favourable at Halifax, yet Halifax operated at nearly double the costs of Kettering. Despite the fact that at Halifax the men were on bonus after 16cwt, they earned very little extra by this means. At Kettering, however, the men were only on bonus after 26cwt but were often taking home an additional 12/- per week per man. Conclusive evidence, one might assume, that Kettering was being worked much more

Inaugural trip of LMS steamer *Princess Maud* on the Larne–Stranraer service, March 1934. Lemon in centre of group. *Railway Gazette*

efficiently than Halifax. However, despite investigations carried out very carefully by a District Representative and a Headquarters Inspector, spread over two months, the District Manager for Halifax had not been convinced that the two stations could be compared. Even evidence that the Halifax shed operated most efficiently between midnight and 5am (when one might expect a certain amount of lethargy to prevail) did not convince him. There was stiff opposition to change, and it was doubtless galling for local managers to have an outsider watching their men, questioning their methods and asking awkward questions.

Initially five stations, Lancaster, Chesterfield, Kettering, Preston Butler Street and Blackburn were selected for detailed assessment; and then three depots, namely Blackburn, Preston Butler Street and Kettering, were chosen for experimental remodelling, which was duly authorised by the Board. At the time of the report, only one of these – Blackburn – had been completed, and the report concentrates on the results thus obtained. Indeed, Preston gets no further mention at all, and Kettering, it seems, was a 'good' example and included for purposes of comparison.

Blackburn depot was selected because it had the worst performance of any station on the line that Ord had seen, and the deep-rooted objections of both local management and men to mechanisation led to Ord suggesting, and Lemon approving, the simplest possible layout with the minimum of machine handling. Further mech-

anisation 'would then be carried out step by step, where there was an obvious need. Only then would it be possible to prove, not only that mechanisation pays, but that the best results could not be obtained without it.'

However, Ord reported that:

One of the factors that will prevent the full achievement of the figures the Company has a right to expect at Blackburn is the age of the men. They are much older than average, their physique is not good and they and their foreman are set in their ways and it will be a difficult thing indeed to speed them up [from the methods] they have been working for the last 30 years. If analysis and mechanisation be proceeded with and all the economies that are possible with and without mechanisation are made, the average age of the men on the Shed Dock is bound to increase in the next few tears. This handicap will therefore become worse. The importance of Mr Lemon's suggestion of mechanisation and the reduction of physical effort and walking becomes increasingly apparent for this reason alone.

Ord then reports that after the improvements at Blackburn had been made, and the District Goods Manager and Agent officially thanked for their good work, 'the shed was actually worse run than at any time before in view of the better facilities'. He comments that this had made it 'more difficult than ever to get them to agree to the remaining economies which should be made'. The economies made in staff due to the improved layout were, apparently, practically wiped out by quite unnecessary increases in cartage expenditure, and the working costs at the depot were still twice those of comparable sites with older and poorer layouts. He notes that there were only two reasonable assumptions to be made: 'The District Managers, Agents and foremen either did the best they knew, their failure being due to lack of knowledge; or on the other hand, they knew what was wrong and how to put it right, but were too lazy or indifferent to do so. The former assumption is the only possible one for many obvious reasons'. Blackburn was one of the stations visited by the management team from Euston on the second of their Tours on 10/11 January 1934. As previously mentioned, Lemon was unwell for this tour, but Ord was a member of the party. As his report was dated 3 March 1934, one has to conclude that the improvement work was at an advanced stage, if not completed. Was this the occasion when the local officers were officially thanked for their good work? The report of the January visit particularly noted that partially-disabled men were being employed to sweep out the shed and yard. This would appear to have been a compassionate and charitable thing to do, and yet the report also states that Byrom was asked to check out the cost of compensating them and employing part-time able-bodied men instead.

Ord concludes – and puts it quite bluntly – that the Blackburn experiment proved 'conclusively that it is unwise for the Company to spend more money on remodelling Goods Sheds unless steps can be taken that will ensure that, in future, they get the whole of the economies which are possible and for which they have paid'. This seems a veiled allusion to the opposition he had met from all the parties involved, which he attributes to 'lack of knowledge and experience . . . and the ability to plan and educate and, if necessary, to enforce results to which the Company are entitled'. However, Lemon's stricture that this should not be a witch-hunt led him to go no further down this path. Rather, he acknowledged that it was 'wrong to expect a man without technical experience, especially where both seniors [i.e. management] and men were

putting up the worst performance we could find, to suddenly put up the best that was possible'.

Despite these major reservations, Ord maintained that the physical remodelling at Blackburn had been a success. The new facilities had been much admired and he recommended that the programme should continue. This does seem rather to be a case of putting on a brave face when expected benefits failed to materialise; but he defended the situation:

It is necessary to realise that this planning of Goods Sheds and Goods Handling is a really stiff technical job. With its infinite variety of goods, its hour to hour and day to day variations, it is more difficult to plan than many workshops and still more difficult to operate . . . It is essential, if the work is to be successful in the future, that the analysis, the design and the operation of that design until it is working satisfactorily be under the same effective control.

The investigation into mechanisation was not complete, he wrote, and a great deal more needed to be done by way of analysis of present and future working. Perhaps as a reference to Lemon's original assertion that a number of previous schemes 'have been successful and others not', he wrote that, if accurate analysis had been available in the past, earlier layouts such as Ancoats (Manchester), Heysham and Huddersfield would never have been attempted. It would have been apparent, even on paper, that they could not succeed.

Ord also notes that a number of the company's staff were now gaining training in Scientific Management; and that they should be used throughout the LMS to train Goods staff in the new methods of working. It was undoubtedly important to make a start on the modernisation of Goods Depots, but the reluctance of personnel to accept change was a major stumbling block. Nevertheless, and despite these unpromising beginnings, the Scheme continued and was in full swing until the outbreak of war. H.G. Smith, ever Lemon's faithful secretary and chronicler, notes that up to 1939: 'some 50 schemes had been authorised involving structural alterations . . . at an estimated outlay of £500,000, with anticipated

	Blackburn was	Blackburn is	Other Stations	Blackburn will be
(Received	1.85	1.65	.85(Kettering)	1.35
SHED(Forwarded	2.0	1.1	.41(Lancaster)	.85
(New Warehouse	–	.75	–	.65
YARD	.95	.95	.33(Lancaster)	.75

net savings approximating to £30,000 per annum; 80% of these schemes were actually in operation, and back-checking of a number of them showed that anticipated staff savings had been obtained'. Smith also notes that between 1933 and 1939 the total staff savings as a result of the modernisation schemes were some £113,500 per annum and that in 1939 a further 30 schemes 'were in various stages of completion, in order that they may be introduced as and when circumstances permit'.

In Smith's view, Lemon's Modernisation Scheme had been a real success. 'This modernisation campaign has successfully introduced an entirely new outlook and technique into goods shed working which was previously a somewhat haphazard job and, apart from the actual economies, the all-round improvement in working has of course enabled us to provide better services for the traders'.

Diesel Shunting Locomotives (2)

DESPITE the setbacks with the original converted diesel-hydraulic shunting engine, development continued. Lemon was now no longer directly involved, although he would have retained a keen interest in the progress. Hornbuckle remained in control of the developments and, according to E.S. Cox, it was apparently his idea to 'obtain samples of everything then available on the market, and after a suitable period of trials, to choose the best for future purchase'.[189] The problem facing the designers of these diesel locomotives was the transmission of power to the driving wheels, and the development now concentrated on the rival merits of mechanical and electrical transmission.

On 25 January 1933, The Traffic Committee Minutes record that:

The Chief Operating Manager and Chief Mechanical Engineer recommended, with the

One of the tables in Ord's Report, showing comparative costs for Blackburn goods depot. Lemon's personal papers

approval of the Executive, that authority be given to an outlay of £40,000 in the purchase of ten 150/200 H.P. Diesel locomotives and one 250 H.P. Diesel-Electric locomotive to enable a thorough investigation to be made of the utility of Diesel shunting engines of different capacities, and embodying various forms of transmission, and to accelerate the development of the most efficient types of economical shunting units to meet general requirements.[190]

In the event, only eight of the small locomotives were ordered, of which one appears to have been acquired in 1932, after exhibition at the British Industries Fair, before authority was officially sanctioned. These were all diesel-mechanical in operation and came from a variety of manufacturers. With one exception they had an 0-6-0 wheel arrangement, and each carried a different combination of engine and transmission. The 250hp diesel-electric locomotive came from Armstrong-Whitworth, and all nine locomotives had been delivered by the end of 1934. A full break-down of their characteristics, numbers and specifications can be found in one of the regular Diesel Supplements of the *Railway Gazette*.[191]

H.G. Smith then tells us that early in 1934 Lemon wished to expedite the investigations. He obviously did not want a leisurely appraisal of the respective merits of these prototypes, but a competent locomotive that could be put to use as soon as possible. In April, a further diesel-electric, rated at 350hp, was obtained on loan from English Electric, and on 14 June 1934, comparative tests were carried out at Beeston between this locomotive and the 250hp diesel-electric from Armstrong-Whitworth. Perhaps not surprisingly, the conclusion reached was that for general working in adverse weather conditions, the more powerful unit was the preferred option.

At the AGM on 1 March 1935, Stamp reported: 'The tests made indicate that the development of the diesel locomotive with electric transmission has sufficiently advanced to justify us acquiring more units of this type'.[192] A further order was placed for twenty 350hp locomotives – ten each from English Electric and Armstrong-Whitworth – at a cost of £132,000.[193] The diesel-electric that had been loaned to the company by English Electric was also purchased and given the LMS No. 7079.[194] The Company endeavoured to get this last locomotive at a knock-down price, arguing that it was no longer brand new. English Electric would have none of this and took the engine back for a complete overhaul, and sold it to them at the same price as agreed for the other

Hunslet Yard, Leeds, with five of the first diesel shunting locomotives ordered by the LMS in line abreast. *Railway Gazette*

ten on order![195] Further development of diesel-mechanical units was dropped. Smith states that unless there was a reasonable prospect of successfully applying the principles of mechanical transmission to diesels rated in excess of 250hp, there was no point in continuing to build any more lower-rated engines because of the difficulties in finding suitable work for them to do.

Hornbuckle does not seem to have resented abandoning further research into mechanical transmission, as suggested by E.S. Cox.[196] He later wrote in his 1936 paper to the Diesel Engine Users Association:

In any application of Diesel engines to railway work, the method of transmission is of primary importance. Many varying types have been employed with a greater or lesser degree of success. The most successful method adopted has been electrical transmission, a result to be anticipated from the fact that it has been well tried out over many years on electric railways and practically all the detail parts have been standardised to a large extent and are in production. This method of

transmission has marked advantages from the point of view of elasticity in application . . . in the driving of auxiliary apparatus and in the method of control.[197]

However, he did consider that there was still a future for mechanical transmission and continued:

Mechanical transmission had no comparable advantages derived from previous use as was the case with electric transmission. Change gears as developed for use on road transport were generally much below the capacity required for rail work. As a result much exploratory work has had to be undertaken. Successful applications of mechanical transmission are now being made in which 300/400 H.P. is developed. The hydraulic coupling has proved a useful adjunct in connection with change speed gears, assisting starting from rest and giving protection against severe shock. The type of gear to be adopted is largely determined by the working conditions but, in view of modern developments, it appears probable that there is a wide field of usefulness for transmission of the mechanical type which will be increased by the use of high speed engines. An outstanding advantage of mechanical transmission is that its maintenance is more readily undertaken by the steam locomotive maintenance organisation than is the case with electrical equipment.

He was later proved correct. E.S. Cox notes that though the mechanically-driven units were not proceeded with at the time, they were perfect for lesser shunting applications and thus over 500 were subsequently ordered post-nationalisation of the railways in 1948.

Despite the decision to concentrate on the more powerful diesel-electric units, Smith reports that a back-check on the performance of smaller engines, which had been working in the Willesden

**C.E. Fairburn,
Chief Electrical Engineer.**
Railway Gazette

yards shunting empty wagons, did show that a considerable saving would accrue provided that two or three turns of duty per day were guaranteed. If the locomotive was only used for one turn (i.e. 8-hour shift), then there was no benefit, but savings of up to £1,000 per year could be attained from three turns of duty. However, he acknowledges that the engines were 'slightly slower' in use, and they were of limited value because of their lesser capabilities. In fact, not only was their tractive power around half that of a 250hp unit, but the maximum speeds of these original prototypes also varied widely from model to model, which was an important consideration when assessing their capabilities. Two of them could only achieve 9mph. Although a slow operational speed would certainly be required whilst shunting, this limitation was a disadvantage when the locomotive needed to be moved to a different location.

A couple of months after the comparative tests had been carried out at Beeston, C.E. Fairburn joined the LMS as Chief Electrical Engineer in July 1934. Fairburn had previously worked for English Electric and must have been fully aware of the ongoing diesel trials. It has also been generally assumed that he was firmly committed to his former company's designs with regard to diesel-electrics. He immediately took over the electrical side of proceedings from the CME's department; and E.S. Cox has interpreted the continuing development of diesels as a conflict between Fairburn and Hornbuckle – with the views of Fairburn, the superior officer, prevailing over Hornbuckle's, and preference given to English Electric methods rather than Armstrong-Whitworth's. Memories can be notoriously fickle – Cox's memoirs were not published until 1965 – and, although he was working in the CME's department at the time, he was not necessarily privy to all the reasons for decisions. Primary sources from contemporary reports give no indication of any conflict on the subject of diesels between the two men, and there is no evidence that either Fairburn or Hornbuckle had entrenched opinions on the way forward. Both were pragmatic enough as engineers to appreciate the merits of the different elements of the designs, and select the best for future use. What influenced their decisions – and this is a fact unappreciated by Cox and other writers – was the problem of overheating. Fairburn's paper to the Institute of Locomotive Engineers in 1941 makes this clear. It was a problem, he wrote, that had been overlooked before. The Armstrong-Whitworth engine had a *forced ventilated* motor with a double reduction gear driving a jackshaft, whereas the English Electric had two single reduction nose-mounted self-ventilated motors.* It was not the difference between single or double reduction gearing that was crucial, or whether the final drive used a jackshaft or not, as many previous writers seem to think, but the ventilation and cooling of the motor. Fairburn wrote: 'When the locomotives were used regularly for hump shunting and certain other duties which required a heavy drawbar pull at a very low speed for considerable periods, it was found that the self-ventilated motors tended to overheat, as the self-contained fan was practically inoperative at the slow speed of revolution of the traction motors'.[197] He continued later in this paper: 'it was obvious from all points of view that double reduction gearing with forced ventilation for the traction motor was the correct arrangement. As the jackshaft drive with this arrangement of the motor had proved satisfactory it was adopted pending further investigation into the axle hung motor design.'[198] Fairburn was therefore totally prepared to accept those elements of the Armstrong-Whitworth design that had proved superior to those of his old Company, English Electric. There was no conflict between him and Hornbuckle over this.

---

* A jackshaft was a subsidiary drive shaft to which the wheels were connected by connecting rods. The 'nose-mounted' motors drove one of the wheel axles directly. The jackshaft introduced another intermediate stage between the motor and the wheels, and was eventually superseded by the direct axle hung design.

Fairburn appears to have been cast in a similar mould to Lemon – a man obsessed with the minutiae of detail in his work. Other evidence indicates that the two men struck up an immediate rapport – and not only at work: they became golf partners! On 15 November 1935, they were part of the team representing the officers of the LMS in a match against the (Army) officers of Eastern Command which was played at the West Herts Golf Club. They lost.[199]

The 350hp locomotives were an immediate success and the *Railway Gazette* reported in July 1935 that the original model loaned by English Electric had generally been in 24-hour service on the LMS for six and a half days per week since it was acquired.[200] In that time, it had achieved a total of 4,000 working hours: it had shunted yards at Crewe, Beeston, Salford and Rugby amongst others and proved economical to operate. The general inspection pattern that had been established was very favourable – two or three hours' weekly maintenance was adequate to keep it in first-class condition. Heavy maintenance was only required every 5,000 to 6,000 hours, which effectively meant annually. The diesel locomotives did indeed seem to fit the bill, though curiously no mention is made in either Smith's digest or any of the standard histories as to how the issue of single-manning was resolved. It is possible that the hugely improved working conditions, enclosed cabs and heating weighed heavily in the balance with enginemen – although, it should be noted, these were *not* features of the earliest diesel-mechanical units.

In March 1936 the *Railway Gazette* was almost prescient in its comment that: 'It is possible that the 20 oil electric shunting locomotives now being delivered to the LMSR may form the beginning of an extensive vogue for such units in this country, and it may be that very few steam shunting engines will be built in future for use on the lines of the four British mainline companies'.[201] Indeed, the last steam shunting engine to be built for the LMS had already been delivered: Sentinel 0-4-0 No.7192, which was put into service in 1934. However, most locomotives that were used for shunting work were not specially built, but had simply been downgraded from other duties as they were reaching the end of their lives. They had been depreciated to zero value for accounting purposes which, as far as the financial department was concerned, meant they had been acquired for shunting duties at no cost. This made any brand-new engine, whether steam or diesel, appear even more of a drain on resources.

If the accusation is now levelled that the LMS were slow to take advantage of the benefits of diesel traction, then it can only be said that they led the way in this country. Other countries, however, such as Germany with *The Flying Hamburger*, and America with *The Burlington Zephyr* and the Union Pacific *Fliers*, had already by 1936 put diesels to use for express, long-distance, passenger trains. Diesel-operated passenger train sets were also widely used in Europe, and the Russians had even built a 2,500hp goods locomotive. This makes the tentative steps in this country seems small-fry in comparison. The reasons for this cautious approach – what Hornbuckle called 'feeling the way' – were discussed in a paper that he presented to the Diesel Engine Users' Association in 1936.[202] The two prime considerations were reliability and cost. Reliability had to be proved by experience, Hornbuckle claimed, although, as one contributor to the discussion pointed out, diesels had proved perfectly reliable in other applications. The costs were a separate factor. The railways in this country had an enormous capital investment in steam engines and the associated plant for supplying and servicing them. Diesels had yet to prove that they could out-perform these locomotives in general service, and the LMS had therefore looked for a niche where there *would* be immediate benefits. Nevertheless, the LMS did sanction a number of trials with diesel railcars and train-sets on their lines. Various manufacturers were involved, as are detailed by Hornbuckle in his paper.

Diesel Railcars

AS HAS already been mentioned, in 1932 experiments were carried out with a pneumatic-tyred railcar on the line between Bletchley and Oxford.[203] In 1933, during the British Industries Fair in Birmingham, Armstrong-Whitworth and Shell Mex ran a daily service from Euston to Castle Bromwich with a diesel-electric railcar fitted out as a dining car. This was timed to run at express schedule, and no difficulties were experienced in maintaining this even in bad weather. English Electric ran a similar vehicle on several cross-country routes while, in 1934, Leyland Motors also carried out trials on three light railcars. A later design of a Michelin pneumatic-tyred railcar was trialled in 1935. A demonstration run was made from Euston to Leighton Buzzard, after which a luncheon was held at the Euston Hotel, hosted by Lemon. He was reported as saying that although railcars had been widely adopted in France and elsewhere on the Continent, conditions here were not strictly comparable.[204] Because of the dense population in this country, there was a correspondingly dense train service over the principal routes. Nevertheless, he said, the British railways were determined to try out every likely experiment with a view to improving services, and the LMS was going to try the railcar on the cross-country service between Oxford and Cambridge, to see whether it would increase traffic. This route, connecting the country's two great universities, was a convenient guinea-pig for all these trials. As none of the academics from one end of the line had any great desire to visit colleagues at the other end, it basically served the sparsely populated rural area in-between. None of these trials led to any permanent change of policy by the LMS.

Toton Hump Shunting Yard

ONE SUBJECT that was completely absent from discussions within Sir Harold Hartley's Scientific Research Committee was Diesel Engines. As this was not only a new technology but something which came under his overall responsibility, the absence is surprising. One would have expected the rival merits of hydraulic, mechanical and electric transmissions to have been a subject for deliberation – especially, as has just been described, these were assessed through a series of practical trials. However, at the meeting of this Committee on 10 April 1934 chaired by Lemon, C.R. Byrom, the Chief Operating Manager, attended to discuss certain other problems associated with shunting in goods yards and, in particular, operating problems at the Toton hump-shunting yard. These had been under active consideration for at least a year. H.G. Smith tells us that in March 1933 Lemon alerted Byrom to the way in which the LNER were using the eddy current rail brake to control hump shunting at their Whitemoor yard in March, Cambridgeshire. The *Railway Gazette* correspondent had visited the yard on 22 February 1933 and was very impressed:

The gentle treatment each wagon receives from these eddy current retarders is remarkable, there being no shock or tendency of the wagon to jump the rails nor for its contents to be shaken up and damaged . . . A very small percentage only of the braking is due to mechanical friction, practically the whole of the controlling influence on the moving wagons being due to the strong magnetic field – augmented by eddy currents set up in the wagon tyres and braking rails★ – the strength of which is regulated according to the weight and speed of the wagons by control handles in the central tower.[205]

Shunting wagons over a hump and letting gravity do the work of sorting them out into a fan of sidings was a very convenient method of operation. However its basic simplicity meant that it was also very inexact. It might seem incongruous that, having pushed the wagons over the top of an incline, the most difficult problem then was how to stop them! But not all wagons were capable of rolling exactly the same distance and, whereas at the start of operations a wagon might have to roll to the far end of an empty siding, later ones would have to travel less distance as the siding filled up. For this reason the hump had to be set high enough to cope with all eventualities, but it was obviously essential to keep control of the wagons and slow them down as necessary, so that they did not crash at speed

★ As a wagon passes through the magnetic field generated by an electromagnet alongside the tracks, eddy currents are created in its metal wheels. These eddy currents then generate an opposing magnetic field, which resists the rotation of the wheels, providing a braking force. The faster the wheels are turning, the stronger the effect, meaning that as the train slows the braking force is reduced producing a smooth stopping motion.

into those already in the siding, causing damage to the contents. A sophisticated braking system was therefore essential. Current practice on the LMS was to employ men to 'steady' the wagons by applying the hand brakes on the side of the wagons as they passed. The points were also set manually from small elevated cabins. The work was labour-intensive and ripe for modernisation.

Lemon, as ever with an eye on greater efficiency, pointed out to Byrom in 1933 that, whilst the LMS had reviewed a number of schemes for similar purposes in the past, as yet all had been deemed too expensive to implement, because of the extensive modifications which would be required. As the LNER had obviously reached a different conclusion with this particular method Lemon wondered whether there might be 'something worthwhile in the arrangement for LMS purposes'.[206]

Soon after contacting Byrom in this matter, Lemon and party set off for the USA tour with the *Royal Scot*, as described earlier. The report on their visit was written by S.H. Fisher, and he records how they had seen several mechanised hump shunting yards there, operated by various railroads, and comments:

I am satisfied that with the evidence at present in my possession that if at any future date the LMS Company decide to install car-retarders they should be constructed on the lines of either the Froelich or the Eddy-current brake. Both the all-electric and electro-pneumatic retarders I saw in America would be liable to lift the wagons off the rails owing to frictional force.[207]

UK wagons were much lighter than American ones, hence the concern about the all-electric and electro-pneumatic retarders. Froelich retarders had however been used as early as 1929 by the LNER at Whitemoor. A disability of this system was that wagons whose wheels were fitted with bolted or riveted tyres could not be retarded because the projecting heads were sheared off. Fisher concluded his report on American practice by writing: 'The experience gained by the L.&N.E. Company in their new yards at Whitemoor should enable a decision to be arrived at after a sufficient lapse of time as to which type of brake is the more suitable for the conditions encountered in this country'.[208]

An examination of the LNER scheme by Byrom and his assistants followed, but the words 'a sufficient lapse of time' were ominous. It was obviously going to be some time before any comprehensive changes were made by the LMS, and so the first specific item that Byrom put to the Scientific Research Committee in April 1934 was a temporary compromise, and more of a statement of intent than a problem they could solve. It concerned his request to erect wooden screens at Toton to protect against the prevailing wind, which was slowing the wagons so that they did not run the required distance. The second item was something the Committee probably could address: the effect of cold weather on grease-lubricated wagons. Toton was an exposed site and once again, in these conditions, wagons were adversely affected and not rolling as far as needed. The third problem he put to the Committee was more intractable. He asked whether anything could be done to improve the general illumination of yards in fog. This request, therefore, pre-dates the chaos that was caused just before Christmas 1934 at Willesden marshalling yard, which has already been considered in this chapter. One might therefore argue that the Company were slow to deal with the problems caused by such conditions but, in fairness, there is no easy solution. We are all aware, to this day, how fog can bring transport – and especially airports – to a complete grinding halt! Lemon had actually addressed the problem of lighting at marshalling yards in one of his 'Lightning Committee' reports of 1930, following his first visit to the USA. At the time, it was felt that there was not a large field for economy in this matter (the over-riding concern!), but where new facilities or extensive alterations were planned, then flood-lighting was, in principle, considered desirable as part of the scheme. Little action had therefore been taken – and, indeed, flood-lighting is of itself not an enormous benefit in fog.

As a result of Byrom's submissions, a new Research sub-committee, called the Traffic & Operating Group, was established which looked into the whole question of lighting of marshalling yards, including whether any provision could be made to enable work to be carried out in fog to a greater extent than formerly possible. Lemon commented on their 1935 report on this matter: 'I think the Research Department might be pressed more strongly to see what can be done to obtain some relief by using coloured lights or solenium [sic] cell rays'.[209] It is not at all clear what he had in mind with these suggestions! A selenium cell 'wheel counting apparatus' had been experimented with in 1933, but abandoned as unsuccessful.[210] The lighting at specific points of Toton yard was improved as a result of this investigation; and H.G. Smith records that 'investigations into lighting conditions at other marshalling yards were pressed forward'.

No further progress was made towards the redesign and mechanisation of major marshalling yards, however, until 1936. In February of that year Lemon visited Toton, and then contacted the General Railway Signal Company to ask them to carry out an enquiry into the matter. Toton had previously been assessed by this company in 1930 when their proposals had been considered an uneconomic proposition. Mr Kubale, who had carried out the original report, was dispatched again to the yard to re-examine it in the light of current conditions.[211]

Kubale's proposals were examined, Smith reports, by a small Committee of LMS Operating and Technical Officers. A scheme was produced for consideration by the Executive Committee embracing five major changes. The hump would be raised, thus increasing the distances that wagons could roll. A centrally controlled, electro-mechanical set of rail brakes or retarders would be fitted, together with power-worked points similarly controlled – thus saving on brakesmen and pointsmen. These alterations would necessitate a realignment of the track layout on the hump and at the entry to the fan of sidings, as well as the installation of track circuits, lighting, communication equipment, buildings and other facilities. Ancillary equipment was also needed for the compilation of a 'cut list' showing in consecutive order the siding for which each wagon was destined. This was made out while the train was standing in the reception sidings preparatory to humping and communicated by teletype to the central control.

The Executive considered the proposals which, it was acknowledged by Lemon, would not increase revenue, but would save on staff and engine hours. The cost of the scheme was given as just under £60,000 with estimated additional annual costs of £725. It was considered, however, that this additional cost would be fully covered by economies in the use of engines, reduction in damage to wagons and other indirect ways. The Executive approved the scheme in Executive Minute 6543 on 31 May 1937, which asked Stamp to present the scheme informally to the Board. Stamp, as President, would have been party to this decision but, in the somewhat convoluted way that the LMS conducted its business, Lemon then wrote an official briefing memo to him as Chairman which amplified the reasons for the proposals for the benefit of the Board members who would ultimately sanction the expenditure.[212]

In this memo, Lemon briefly summarised what progress had been made in reducing the costs of shunting – which he called 'a necessary evil' – since 1930, when Stamp had stressed the necessity for further economy in this respect. He reported that between 1931 and 1935 the saving in wages by the elimination of staff positions was approximately £100,000 a year. There were further savings made in engine hours, but these were difficult to evaluate financially. However, in his view, increasing traffic was now eating into those savings as it had been necessary to reinstate staff to cope, and he considered that the Shunting Analysis Committee had exhausted the scope for any further economies by current methods.

He gave specific information for the Chairman's use. In 1936 alone, the volume of shunting had occupied just under 8 million hours with movements totalling nearly 40 million miles. He also noted that Toton had in the four weeks ending on 20 February 1937 'handled 187,000 wagons or 7,000 per day on both the Up and the Down sides'. In Lemon's view:

Whilst the Toton scheme will not produce additional revenue, the time has arrived when we are justified in adopting such a scheme from the point of view of bringing our equipment up to date. Ever since railways were constructed

shunting has been carried out on the present lines and no one will say that this is the last word. Other railways both at home and abroad, have adopted mechanised arrangements and I consider that in the case of Toton which is our largest marshalling yard and also the key yard in connection with the Midland Division coal traffic, the adoption of the scheme will provide additional capacity for future utilisation . . . It will be an experiment with permanent benefit and it is also possible that the lessons we shall learn from it will be capable of adaptation elsewhere.

Both the briefing memorandum and Sir Josiah's canvassing of the Board were effective as the scheme was approved in October 1937. It was also probably no coincidence that approval was given to the Toton scheme soon after Lemon and other officers had attended the 13th International Railway Congress in Paris which ran from 31 May to 11 June. At the same time, the Paris International Exhibition was in full swing. The site of this exhibition ran from the new Palais Chaillot, across the Seine and past the Eiffel tower, to Les Invalides, where the station had been converted into the Palais des Chemins de Fer, exhibiting the very best of French and European railway practices. One of the sites the French were keen to show off was the État hump-shunting yard at Trappes, near Paris. Photographs show that this yard embodied all the latest developments, including Fröhlich retarders, and bear a striking resemblance to the plans for Toton.[213] The French example could have been just the spur that was needed to gain authority for the remodelling at Toton.

On 30 May 1939 the Toton scheme was completed and brought into operation. All the work had been carried out without interrupting traffic operation at the yard. It was five years since Lemon had alerted Byrom to the LNER's use of eddy-current braking in Cambridgeshire.

Before moving on to the next chapter and the projects that Lemon inaugurated after 1935 it is worth noting that, on 27 June 1935, his salary was increased to £6,000 per year. He was thereby earning more than Sir Harold Hartley who had championed his appointment as Vice-President.

SEVEN

Vice-President
1933–1938, part 2

O N 25 April 1936, Lemon and his fellow Vice-President, William Wood, travelled to New York on a month-long visit to the USA. No report on their visit has been found, but it was undoubtedly an opportunity to exchange ideas and information with American railroad officers. They returned on the *Queen Mary*, landing at Southampton on 10 June, and the passenger list gives Lemon's address as 13 Dorset Street, W.1.[214] This was the source of the information, already discussed in the last chapter, that he had started his affair with Hermione Mervyn. The Electoral Rolls showed how he had moved to this address two years earlier – sometime between February and October 1934. The address, *per se*, cannot therefore have been a secret to those in the LMS who had to know and be able to contact him. What is not clear is whether senior officers in the Company were yet aware of the relationship with Hermione. Within a few months, however, Lemon had left Dorset Street – he is not recorded there in the Electoral Roll dated 15 October 1936. At the same time Hermione disappears from the register in Gloucester Place. It is not known where either of them went. It could be that they simply moved to another location, or that Lemon returned to live at Northchurch Hall. He is still listed there in 1936 and 1937.

At this time, Lemon also acquired another *pied-à-terre* where he might conveniently spend the night if he did not wish to return home. In 1936, he was elected a member of the Athenaeum Club in London, and increasingly used this as his contact address. It appears in his entry in *Who's Who*, for example, and this has added to the difficulty of establishing exactly where he was living in succeeding years.

Evidence also seems to suggest that Lemon had been caught up in socialising with the 'smart set' in London. His granddaughters remember hearing about allegations of wild parties and drug-taking in the LMS from their parents, and a curious letter that Lady Amy wrote to Sir Harold Hartley after Lemon's death appears to confirm this. A section of this letter, relating an anecdote of the 1933 American trip, was quoted in the previous chapter. However, the mention of those earlier, happier, times causes Lady Amy to continue:

That was one of the pleasanter encounters under the regime of those people. The others had far reaching effects on my husband & myself – it became so abhorrent to me I said, You may bring them here as often as you like, I'll see they have as good a dinner as they would be given at 'The Savoy' but I will not sit down with them. Years after I was told there nearly was a police court case – but I never knew more than that & I can't remember was it Podsnap or Pecksniff who said, I don't know & don't want to.[215]

As is the way with such letters, we are left wondering: who exactly were 'those people'? Why was there 'nearly a police court case'? What *had* been going on which became so abhorrent to her? The answers will probably never be known, but it does show that Amy did not approve of Lemon's associates, and the life-style he was following. This is not the sort of information that one can readily verify in the archives or histories of the LMS. However, there is one example, which may be indicative of a similar type of behaviour, quoted by Whitehouse and Thomas.

They present the story as a merry jape, and recount how:

Two rising sparks in the management once had a night out in the West End of London, accompanied by two lively nurses from a big hospital. Midnight passed and the quartet had nowhere to stay. No problem; they descended on Euston, pulled rank with the night relief stationmaster and ordered out a first-class sleeping car from the sidings, in which the rest of the night was passed. Early morning tea was ordered from the refreshment room. Not the sort of escapade that would have amused Lord Stamp![216]

The LMS records show that Hermione abruptly resigned her position with the Company on 31 March 1937.[217] The reason for her resignation remains a mystery. Perhaps it indicates that it was necessary in order for the relationship to remain a secret; or, alternatively, maybe the relationship had become known to Lord Stamp and the Board who strongly disapproved. It is certain that such a relationship would not have been condoned by Stamp, who had strong moral and religious convictions. However, there is no direct evidence of any cooling in his relationship with Lemon, although the latter's absence from the ceremony to lay the foundation stone at Derby School of Transport in September 1937 is still unexplained.

Whilst it may be discourteous to make this suggestion: could there also have been another reason for Hermione's sudden departure – one that was going to get more obvious with time? Lemon's Will made in December 1950 contains a curious clause. This states: 'My trustees may at their discretion apply all or any part of the income to which any son of mine shall be entitled in expectancy and would if of the full age of twenty-five years be entitled in possession under the trusts hereinbefore contained for his maintenance education or benefit in such manner as they may think fit'. Why did this clause include the words '*any* son of mine'? Lemon had two sons, and the more appropriate choice of words would surely have been '*either* son of mine'. Why also the phrase 'if of the full age of twenty-five years'? In 1950, both his sons were well over this age – Richard was 35 and David 28. They were both married and established in their professions. Why was Lemon, therefore, still making this provision? It would seem somewhat careless if this clause had merely been left unnoticed, and unaltered, from an earlier Will. So one has to assume it was there for a reason. To the author, it implies that Lemon could have had another son. Did Hermione become pregnant and return

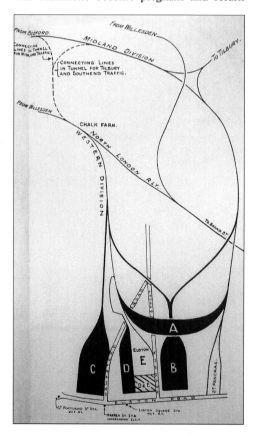

Proposed new layouts for Euston and St Pancras.
A – New high-level through station serving both termini
B – New high-level terminus serving both stations
C – Euston rebuilt further west
D – Euston enlargement
E – Euston rebuilt on two levels.
National Archives

discreetly to Ireland for the birth? She still had family in Ireland – her mother did not remain in Redcliffe Square after 1933 when her husband died. The answer is still unknown, and there is no other evidence whatsoever for this supposition.

According to Lemon's grand-daughters, the final break-down of the marriage was actually caused by a photograph in a daily newspaper which purported to show Lemon and 'his wife' dancing together in a London night-spot – a picture that eventually came to the notice of Amy in Berkhamsted.

Family affairs can now be temporarily put aside, and consideration given to the ongoing work at the LMS.

Rebuilding of Euston Station

IN 1936, active consideration was given again to the proposed rebuilding of Euston Station. This project, as previously mentioned, had been on hold since 1930, but was revived at the end of 1935. Lemon was Chairman of a committee investigating a proposal to electrify the suburban routes into St Pancras and divert them to Euston through a tunnel. This would necessitate the complete rebuilding of the station, and schemes were considered for re-siting the station elsewhere on the Euston Road, or building a new through station further north replacing both Euston and St Pancras.[218] These plans came to nothing, but a meeting of senior officers, chaired by Hartley and Lemon, was held on 19 December 1935 to discuss what elements should be incorporated into a new design for the station. A large dossier of suggestions was collated and one of the more far-fetched suggestions (not made by Lemon!) was that a landing strip for aircraft could be built on the roof. This takes us somewhat into the realms of science fiction and, as this was in the days before helicopters, a runway of considerable length must have been envisaged! Sir Harold Hartley's Advisory Committee decided to give this proposal 'careful consideration'. At the same time, the Committee agreed that there were very few scientific considerations for them to consider in the rebuilding plans other than the ventilation for underground parking.

The President of the Royal Institute of British Architects, Percy Thomas, was appointed as a

---

TRIALS OF RAILWAY CHAIRMAN

◆

SIR J. STAMP AND EUSTON ARCHITECTURE

Sir Josiah Stamp, speaking at the dinner of the Royal Institute of British Architects at Claridge's Hotel, last night, said that, as the head of a great railway, his contacts with the architects' profession were numerous, responsible and astonishingly wide.

He had, at the risk of being thought a faddist, saved Stratford House—one of the few remaining sixteenth century houses in the Birmingham area, from being " butchered to make room for a siding," but now he was told he must on no account touch " the noble proportions of the great hall at Euston." (Laughter.)

With regard to the Euston arch, " or may I be correct and call it the propylæum?"—it is one of the grandest specimens of the Greek style in this country, but an advertising expert had advised him to cover it with luminous paint so as to make it a striking object at night. (Laughter.) He dreaded the cost of having it removed, but could not say what its ultimate fate would be.

" I understand," he said, " that I am the last remaining man with mid-Victorian spirit, who is sufficiently Philistine and bourgeois and altogether out of the running to be an unashamed admirer of the Albert Memorial, but now I am responsible for the St. Pancras Hotel—once described as one of the wonders of London. (Laughter.)

The Chairman's views on the Euston Arch. *Daily Telegraph* (Lemon papers)

---

consultant to advise the in-house team of architects in January 1936, and planning continued over the following years until war put a stop to proceedings. The station was not therefore redeveloped until the 1960s when the destruction of the Doric Arch was considered (by some) to be an act of cultural and historical vandalism. It may, therefore, come as a surprise to know that in 1936 the Company agreed that it would be 'impossible to incorporate the existing portico in the design', as the plans should be 'based on the best features of modern architecture'. Questions were asked in Parliament about this decision on 29 March 1938, as the

money for rebuilding was to be borrowed under Treasury guarantee. A spokesman for the Ministry of Transport replied that architects for the LMS had given very careful consideration to the possibility of embodying the Doric Arch in the new design, but it had not been feasible to do so. The Company was willing to consult the Royal Fine Arts Commission with regard to the re-erection of the portico on another site, and would gladly give permission for its removal if those interested in its preservation were willing to bear the expense. If the war had not intervened, the Arch might have disappeared a whole lot sooner.

It is therefore interesting to see what the station could have looked like if the earlier scheme had progressed. It is surprisingly difficult to find any definitive architectural plans or drawings. Two schematic diagrams of the site are included in the relevant file at the National Archives: the first envisages the station fronting directly on to the Euston Road, the second shows the main building set further back with two side wings stretching forwards to the main road – one containing a new Euston hotel and the other containing offices. Within the central area were the entrance and exit to an underground car park. The passenger concourse, however, was not particularly large and the only benefit of this repositioning was that the platforms could be considerably extended. The records also include an artist's impression of the second design, showing the front elevation of the building, as it would appear from the Euston Road. This is remarkably bland and (in the author's opinion) of little architectural interest – the central section being merely a brutal ten-storey office block.

Artist's impression of the new Euston Station frontage. National Archives

Advisory Committee on Scientific Research: Shock-absorbing wagons etc.

AT THE Advisory Committee Meeting on 12 October 1937, Lemon reported on the introduction of shock-absorbing wagons.[219] He had been aware of the problem of breakages with ceramic goods since at least 1932, and on 2 June of that year had sent a memo to J. Ballantyne, the Goods manager, telling him that a manufacturer of pipes in Swadlincote, Derbyshire was increasingly using road transport for deliveries because of excessive breakages on the railway despite the large quantities of straw used for packaging.[220] Lemon asked Ballantyne for the full facts, and told him that he would be writing to the Chief Mechanical Engineer to ask about the practicality of suspending a false body or container within the ordinary wagon by means of springs. The matter was presumably investigated, but it took another four years for Lemon's idea to come to fruition. After a period of research and experiments, on 26 November 1936 the Board gave formal approval for the construction of 100 shock-absorbing wagons on the recommendation of the Traffic Committee.[221] In June 1937, the first of these was demonstrated in a sequence of tests at St Pancras Goods Depot. The press release announced that a standard wagon and a shock-absorbing wagon would both be loaded with gravel: a semi-fluid substance which would give an easily visible reaction to various shocks.[222] The wagons would then be run into buffers at low speed, made to collide with each other and put through a sequence of stops and starts by a shunting engine. The company claimed that this wagon was the first of its kind in the world, and was the result of an idea formulated by Lemon to give 'passenger comfort' and protection to freight consignments, by insulating them from shocks due to impact, or to the snatching of couplings, during conveyance or shunting operations.

Lemon later reported to the Advisory Committee that 'wagons of this type, in which the body was allowed a certain movement relative to the underframe, under the control of rubber springs, had undoubtedly helped to regain some of the pipe traffic which was being lost owing to excessive breakages. A film prepared by the Research Department had been most valuable in enabling the behaviour of the wagon to be demonstrated and analysed.' H.G. Smith's papers then contain a long report dated 7 November 1938 from Byrom to Ashton Davies, the Commercial Manager, listing the loads carried by the new wagons, and the reactions of the consignees.[223] Apart from sanitary tubes and conduits, which formed the bulk of the traffic, the company had been able to carry fragile machinery without the need for protective packaging, as well as sheet glass and carboys of acid. Breakages had been dramatically reduced. Ashton Davies stated that the LMS had been

able to demonstrate to a number of important traders that they were successfully tackling a problem that had always been a source of complaint and annoyance; and recommended that the Company should rapidly expand the use of this type of wagon. Smith records that, up to May 1939, the construction of 500 such wagons had been authorised.

It is interesting to look at some of the other subjects that were discussed by the Advisory Committee, as they throw light on the thinking that was prevalent in the company at the time – and include projects that never got beyond the discussion phase. Thus we can see that, in April 1934, there were the first discussions about building a wind-tunnel to help with the streamlining of engines and carriages. The LMS had been carrying out experiments, in conjunction with the LNER, at the National Physical Laboratory since 1932. These had measured for the first time the proportion of drag caused by the engine and coaches. The Advisory Committee proposed that the LMS should consider building its own wind tunnel at Stonebridge Park, between Willesden and Wembley. This idea was later revised, and the wind tunnel was incorporated into the plans for the new Research Centre at Derby. This opened in December 1935 and was equipped with a small wind tunnel whose cross-section was 4½ft by 3½ft. The streamlining tests for the Coronation Scot express were subsequently carried out there.[224]

The shock-absorbing wagon.
National Archives

High Speed Passenger Services

ALL THE projects that have so far been considered were motivated by one requirement – to improve efficiency and save money. Lemon's prime consideration was to reduce costs and eliminate the unprofitable use of personnel and resources – although, as a result, the service offered by the railway to its customers undoubtedly improved.

It is also indicative of the relevant importance of passenger and freight traffic that all of Lemon's major innovations so far described had been directed towards the freight side of the business, which generated the greater revenue and profits. The one exception to this philosophy was the action taken from 1936 onwards to speed up passenger train services. There were no immediate financial benefits – other than the hope and belief that more customers might be attracted to use the faster services that became available. The LMS was not the only company to speed up its services, and was acutely aware of what its competitor, the LNER, was doing on its service to Edinburgh. This culminated eventually in the rivalry between the 'Coronation Scot' on the LMS and the 'Coronation' express on the LNER, both of which entered service in 1937. In fact, the timings of passenger services had shown an increase in speed over the years as Stanier's new and more powerful engines became available, but dramatic improvements were put in hand in 1936. H.G. Smith records that, at a meeting of the Executive Committee on 2 November 1936, the question of high-speed long-distance passenger trains was discussed. The current daily service between Euston and Glasgow on the Western Division mainline from Euston, performed by the 'Royal Scot' trains, took 8¼ hours for the distance of 401½ miles – an overall average speed of just under 49mph. Although the Executive Minutes are no longer available, Smith cites Minute 6232 as follows:

Mr. Lemon stated he had been considering the matter, and was definitely of the opinion that the LMS Company should run a high speed train. The line capacity had been examined, and a train could be scheduled to leave Euston at 4.0 p.m., arriving at Glasgow at 10.0 to 10.30 p.m., performing the journey in 6 or 6½ hours, at an average speed of over 61 miles per hour. This would cause little interference with the evening freight express goods services to the North. The train should be streamlined and be worked by an engine of the 'Princess' class, and, with a load of about 250 tons, a substantial time saving could be secured over the rising gradients, thus avoiding uncomfortable speeds elsewhere.[225]

The Vice-President further said he proposed to run a high speed train experimentally on Monday, the 16th November, returning the following day.

Following discussion, the Executive agreed that a high speed train as outlined by Mr. Lemon should be run.

At the Executive Committee on 9 November the matter was again discussed, and Minute 6246 reads:

Mr. Lemon referred to the arrangements which he had made in connection with the trial run of a high speed train leaving Euston at 9.50 am on Monday, the 16th November, arriving at Glasgow at 3.50 pm. The train will be drawn by a 'Princess Royal' class engine and the weight limited to 202 tons; a speed of 81 miles per hour is expected to be reached in the Lancaster District, 70 miles per hour being maintained over most of the journey, although, of course, this will be considerably reduced at certain places. He said he intends to supply the President with a 'passing' schedule, and will arrange for him to be advised of progress during the trip.

On the general question of high speed travel, Mr. Lemon said that while the aim of this Company was for a uniform speed-up of all trains with comfort, it was necessary to make one or two high speed trips in order to judge what alterations and improvements to the stock could be made to give comfort at the speed reached.

This trip was actually the culmination of a series of trials carried out by the new 'Princess' class of locomotives to test their capabilities. As with all

The arrival of the experimental high-speed run to Glasgow on 16 November 1936 with Lemon *(top left)* leaning out of cab.
Glasgow Herald

new designs, these showed up problems that necessitated modifications to the engines. On an earlier demonstration trial run to Crewe, Lemon travelled on the footplate while R.A. Riddles, Stanier's Chief Assistant, leant out of a carriage window. Riddles gives no date for this run in his Memoirs but describes how, a few miles south of Stafford, the train came to a halt with the left-hand driving box aflame. Riddles records that the driver had sensed it was running hot and had climbed through the cab window and crept forward to pour oil on it. He did this while the train was moving – a very dangerous act but, presumably, with the consent (or encouragement?) of Lemon who was on the footplate. Unfortunately the box was so hot that the oil immediately caught fire. The train had to limp slowly to Crewe, where it arrived 45 minutes late. The engine was so badly damaged that it had to be withdrawn from service for repairs, and the return trip was made behind a substitute 'Royal Scot'.[226]

The experimental high-speed runs from Euston to Glasgow and back were duly made on 16 and 17 November 1936, and on the outward journey the 401½ miles was covered in 5 hours 53½ minutes at an overall speed of 68.11mph with a maximum of 95.75mph. Lemon declared to the Press in Glasgow that the trial was not simply a stunt, but had been carried out by ordinary rolling stock and an engine built in 1933 in order to find out the conditions necessary for a regular high-speed service. Lemon contradicted a published statement that all speed restrictions had been withdrawn for the run. Recordings of the speeds, the riding of the carriages and the jolts that took place would be analysed to see what alterations would be required – particularly on the 'difficult' sections of the line. As Lemon said: 'It is no use giving speed to passengers if they feel at the end of a journey that they have been so shaken about that they are dead tired'.[227]

The return run to Euston took 5 hours 44 minutes at an overall average speed of 70mph. Smith's sober record of the times and speeds, which he describes as 'highly satisfactory', tells us nothing of the activity behind the scenes that was necessary to obtain these results. The technology of the day was pushed to its absolute limits in order to achieve these times, and the runs were not as incident free as Smith's report might suggest – or, indeed, as Lemon might have appreciated at the time! A description of the frenetic activity that was necessary to prepare and maintain the locomotive for these runs can be found in Riddles' account of the two days. On this occasion, roles were reversed: Riddles rode on the footplate while Lemon travelled in one of the carriages. Riddles recounts how the locomotive, *Princess Elizabeth*, was carefully prepared and then 'gone over with the proverbial toothcomb' on the day before the trials – a Sunday. However, at 5.15pm, it was discovered that a special stainless-steel pipe joint had failed and the only replacement part was at Crewe. Fortunately the part was discovered in the (closed) stores in time to be sent to Euston on the last train of the day. It was fitted by 2.30am on the morning of departure. The train was able to leave Euston on time and arrived at Glasgow 6½ minutes ahead of the scheduled six hours. The passengers, LMS officials and Press retired to the Central Hotel for a celebratory tea. Flushed with success, Lemon apparently suggested to Riddles that they ought to try and run even faster on the return to London. Riddles was opposed to this, and suggested that they add an extra coach instead, to which Lemon agreed.

A dinner was held to celebrate the run, at which Lemon presided. On his right were the driver and guard; on his left the fireman and reserve fireman. These were the sole occupants of the top table. The health of the crew was drunk, and Driver Clarke, in reply, said: 'I was asked on Friday if I could do this job. I said I could. I was asked on Saturday if I would do it. I said I would. Today I have done it'.[228]

All seemed set for a similarly successful return trip to London the following day. However, at dinner, Riddles received a telephone call telling him the examining fitter had discovered that one of the slide blocks of the locomotive had worn out on the journey to Glasgow. He arranged for the engine to be taken to the sheds at St Rollox for emergency repairs, and said he would get there as soon as he could. Sitting among the happy and oblivious company, Riddles recounts

how Lemon looked at him and said: 'You look tired; you had better get to bed; a big day tomorrow'. He made his excuses, and hurried to St Rollox. The repairs took until 5.30 in the morning, at which time the engine had to be prepared for the return journey. As the journey back started, Riddles was understandably nervous that the engine – with its new slide block and extra coach – would even make it to the Beattock summit. However, despite bad weather, all went well and the train made even faster time, arriving back at Euston 16 minutes inside the six hours.

Lemon was unaware of any of this. When they arrived back at Euston, his comment was merely: 'Riddles, why did you lose a minute to Beattock?' To which Riddles says there was no appropriate answer. One assumes that Lemon was later told the full events of the two days, and how close they came to failure.

At the Board Meeting on 26 November, the 'Chairman was requested to convey to the Vice-President (Mr. Lemon) an expression of the Board's appreciation of the success of the trials'. At this meeting Stamp outlined the proposed new train policy and the considerations reached. The trial had been carried out under unique circumstances – for example, the timings of some 200 scheduled trains had to be adjusted for each journey, in order to give the high-speed train a clear track. It was also apparent that track realignment and improvements needed to be carried out to remove some speed restrictions. The data obtained on the test runs was analysed for the purpose of preparing the schedule for a daily high-speed service between Euston and Glasgow, and in February 1937 it was agreed that the trains should leave at 1.30pm and be timed to make the run in 6½ hours – an overall average speed of 61.8mph. An announcement to this effect was made by the Chairman at the Annual Meeting on 27 February, and on 26 May 1937, the streamlined 'Coronation Scot' was inspected by the press 'under the guidance of Mr E.J.H. Lemon' at Crewe. The train entered scheduled service on 5 July 1937.

A week before this service actually started, another record was broken. It was, apparently, a fairly open secret that, during a final demonstration run to Crewe on 29 June 1937 an

Arrived at Euston at 3.54 p.m.

Mr. F. A. Lemon, vice-president of the L.M.S., toasts the train's crew on arrival at Euston. Left to right: John Lewis (fireman), F. F. Brockbank (guard), Tom Clark (driver) and footplate inspector S. E. Miller.

attempt would be made on the world speed record of 119.8mph recently achieved by a German train. The crew were asked to try to get to 120mph. Once again, things did not go entirely according to plan. The attempt was made on the incline down the Madeley Bank into Crewe – in other words, in the final seven or eight miles of the journey. It was perilously close to the destination and, as a consequence, braking was left dangerously late. There was chaos in the dining cars as the train lurched at excessive speed through a series of low-speed crossovers before arriving – fortunately safely – at Crewe. Frank Norris, the dining car attendant, described the mayhem thus:

It was impossible to hold the pot of coffee I was carrying, and it fell with a crash to the corridor floor . . . On my return to the dining car I found the other attendants had been less fortunate. Cutlery and plates had slid off the tables lying everywhere. Some half-empty coffee cups had been spilled over, staining the white cloths. Glasses and crockery had been smashed in the pantry due to some of the small sliding cupboard doors being left open. One unlucky traveller had even received a

Lemon congratulates the crew on their arrival back at Euston after claiming the British speed record of 114mph on the outward trip to Crewe, 29 June 1937. *Daily Sketch*

silver dish full of hot vegetables over him. With apologies from the attendant and a clean down, all was taken in good part.[229]

The time taken over the final 1.1 miles to a complete stop in the station was 1min. 19sec., i.e. an *average* speed for this distance of just over 50mph! If the braking was uniform, the train was still travelling at around 100mph one mile out of the station. The independent observers on board all agreed that a maximum speed of 112½mph had been reached – just short of the existing British record of 113mph held by the LNER. One of the four stop-watch timers on the train was O.S. Nock, and he records what happened next:

The large party of guests was entertained to lunch at the Crewe Arms Hotel; E.J.H. Lemon presided, and very wittily and successfully made light of the somewhat precipitate entry into Crewe, which as one correspondent afterwards wrote 'strewed the floor of the dining car with a mosaic of broken crockery'. In the course of his speech, however, he was handed a slip of paper; it was the result of a scrutiny of the speed-recorder chart taken off the locomotive. Up to that point he had quoted the 112½mph agreed among the four of us, but as he read the paper a broad smile spread over his face, and he said, 'I have not been bribed, but I can now tell you that the maximum speed was 114mph'. It is, I am afraid, no exaggeration to say that those of us who had been taking so detailed an account of the running regarded this claim with some scepticism. We would all have readily agreed that a peak of 113mph could have occurred, although it had eluded four independent stopwatches; but 114 took some stomaching, particularly as by this the British railway speed record was snatched by one mile per hour from the LNER. We had, however, little time to reflect on the ethics of the situation. The LMS had now officially claimed 114mph and we all made for the return special to Euston.[230]

[*Unlike land speed records, which are taken over a measured mile, and then repeated again in the opposite direction, the railway record was simply the maximum speed attained – possibly only momentarily. It was therefore also a benefit to make the run on a downhill gradient, which would have been of no advantage if a run then had to be made in the reverse direction.*]

The occasion had been closely followed by the newspapers, and a report of the event occupied the whole of the front page of the *Daily Sketch*. One of the pictures shows Lemon congratulating the driver and fireman after they all arrived back in London. The caption reads: 'Mr F.A. Lemon, vice-president of the LMS, toasts the train's crew on arrival at Euston'. The picture is clearly 'E.J.H.' Lemon – so why the mistake with his initials? There *was* a Mr F.A. Lemon who worked for the LMS. He was the long-serving Works Manager at Crewe, and therefore in charge of the locomotive works that built the 'Princess' class of engines, such as used in the record-breaking

run. They were in no way related, and it is unsurprising that there was confusion between the two men who bore an uncommon, yet distinctive, surname.

Both men appear in an anecdote recounted in Riddles' biography.[231] In 1936/7, Stanier was in India, and so it was to Riddles that F.A. Lemon reported a defect with the boiler of a Class 5 engine. Within 24 hours, the same problem had been found with seven other locomotives, and Riddles, who was acting as CME, gave orders that no more Class 5s were to leave the sheds until they had been checked. A monumental flap ensued and Riddles found Vice-Presidents Lemon and Hartley waiting for him at Euston demanding he justify his actions. A casual reader of this anecdote might not immediately register that two different men with the same surname were involved!

H.G. Smith, in conclusion, records that the high-speed trains were well patronised right from the start and their introduction secured very good publicity for the Company. They even attracted royal attention! On 5 November 1937, at the invitation of the LMS, King Boris of Bulgaria took to the footplate for a special trip from Euston to Bletchley and back. He had apparently used his regal privilege to become a fully qualified engine driver (every schoolboy's dream!) and been driving trains for 27 years. He was presented with a model of the locomotive on his return by Sir Josiah Stamp.[232] The trains continued to run regularly until the outbreak of the war when the Railway Executive Committee (REC) decided that such facilities should be withdrawn.

Meanwhile, at the same time as the improvements to the Western Division were set in hand, Lemon turned his attention to the services from St Pancras, which were a source of major concern. In November 1936 he wrote to C.R. Byrom, the Chief Operating Manager, about the matter. The letter is long, but is interesting in that it embraces a number of issues and shows the complexity and 'knock-on' effects of radical operating changes. In particular it highlights the difficulties faced by the Company where it was in competition with itself, as was the case with the Manchester and Scottish routes from Euston (Western Division) and St Pancras (Midland Division):

C.R. Byrom Esq.,
EUSTON.

19th November 1936.

PASSENGER TRAIN SERVICES
Midland Division

With further reference to your letter of the 23rd October; I have been thinking over the circumstances connected with the Midland Division working, and whilst the points you mention certainly have a bearing, I do not think they go sufficiently deep to be the dominating factors.

We are today losing prestige with the travelling public from the point of view of punctuality and also improvement in the running times of our express trains on the Midland Division. Whilst accelerations have been carried out to a substantial degree on the Western Division, acceleration on the Midland Division has been much less, for reasons which have been advanced from time to time and which relate mainly to the trading and geographical features of the intermediate towns.

I think what is wanted if we are to bring satisfaction to ourselves and passengers alike is a general re-modelling of the whole of the passenger and freight services on the Midland Division, as I presume such has not yet been attempted since, say, the amalgamation or since the 1926 General Strike. Some patchwork has been done with the services and it seems to me that such re-modelling would have enormous benefit to us in many ways. As you know, the division has been supplied with improved tractive effort and this ought to be reflected more noticeably than at present appears to be the case. Out of the re-modelling we ought to get quicker services between London and the important provincial towns such as Leicester, Nottingham, Sheffield, Leeds and Manchester, whilst the Scottish services also should be capable of improvement and, moreover, on balance there would certainly be an addition to line capacity and probably a saving in mileage.

One lamentable feature of the acceleration on the Western Division has been that the trains have become so popular as to attract to them much traffic that is quite capable of being accommodated on the Midland Division, say, Manchester and London. Only the other day Mr. Towle [Catering Superintendent] drew my attention to the fact that so far as Manchester is concerned, the 6.0 pm. train from Euston and the 5.45 pm. from London Road [now renamed: Manchester Piccadilly] are getting so full that his staff cannot serve sufficient meals, whilst on the Midland trains the lack of business is having a very bad effect on the staff employed on the cars.

So far as Glasgow is concerned, he would like to get more business on the Midland cars, but the services compared with the Western Division provide no alternative from the point of view of attraction to the public. Then again in this morning's 'Times' there is reference to the 9.40 am. Bradford to St. Pancras picking up fifteen minutes on its journey from Leicester yesterday which – whilst a good piece of work so far as the driver was concerned – raises in my mind the question as to how it was possible for the driver to make up such an appreciable amount of time. Presumably he had clear signals which makes me wonder whether many of the delays which arise today are due, not so much to the engine performance, but to having distant signals against express trains en route, which in turn brings me to the point I made in the early part of this letter as to the present timings requiring to be re-modelled.

You no doubt have, currently, particulars of the time regained, and whilst we must give credit to drivers for being able to recover time lost for various reasons, if the figure is a substantial one there must be other reasons why it is possible for such a figure to be regained.

Your weekly statement of the express trains arriving punctually or not more than five minutes late for the eight weeks ended 31st October reveals a position far from satisfactory.

Watercolour of Wordsworth's home at Dove Cottage, Grasmere, by Norman Wilkinson RA with dedication to E.J.H.L. Wilkinson painted many similar pictures for the LMS which were used in publicity posters. Family

All this leads me to the view that a complete re-modelling of the Midland Division timetable can justifiably be undertaken. It will be a long job before completion and I doubt if it can be carried out within the day to day work of the staff concerned. Some relief from such daily duties will therefore be required and additional staff may be necessary.

Unless you have very good reasons against the wisdom of my suggestion I shall be pleased to hear how you propose to tackle the problem.

E. J. H. LEMON.[233]

There were several other reasons for the poor performance of this Division. Firstly, the route from Manchester over the Pennines to Derby had many more severe gradients than the Western Division route. Secondly, the line from Nottinghamshire into London carried an enormous amount of coal freight brought down

from Toton to the Brent yard on the northern outskirts of the city. Nevertheless, discussions were held and a programme of test runs was carried out early in 1937 so that data could be collected for the preparation of an accelerated service. This came into effect in the winter timetable of 1937. The in-house magazine *On Time* proudly announced:

One of the biggest tasks of timetable revision ever carried out by the L M S Operating Department will be brought into fruition with the introduction of the Winter Time Table on Monday, September 27th. On this date there will be introduced greatly accelerated services over the principal main lines of the Midland Division, south of Leeds and between Derby and Manchester, involving faster schedules, additional mileage, and better connectional services on a very large scale.

The article listed the improved timings that were

incorporated in the timetable, the most important of which, it stated, were the alterations to the St Pancras–Manchester service. All the principal day expresses had been accelerated by up to 42 minutes. There were other notable gains; particularly in the cross-country routes, with the timing between Leeds and Bristol, for example, reduced by 83 minutes. The number of trains scheduled to run at 60mph or over, start-to-stop, was increased to 34 per day. However, no substantial improvements were possible on the northern section through Nottinghamshire and on to Sheffield and Leeds because of the large number of speed restrictions caused by mining operations. Although the problem had been addressed, it was never fully resolved, and the LMS eventually sought to combat the slower timings in this Division by promoting the greater attractiveness of the route through the Pennines to Manchester and beyond.

It was also at this time that speed indicators started to be fitted to mainline locomotives. Experiments were carried out in the early part of 1936 to ascertain which method to use, as Smith reports:

In January 1936 Mr. Lemon expressed the opinion that it was desirable to fit locomotives with speed indicators to enable drivers to see exactly the speeds run from point to point, with a view to effecting a greater percentage of punctuality and enabling the drivers to make up lost time. They would also be able more easily to observe strictly the speed restrictions which were laid down over certain parts of the line and so minimise the possibilities of accidents. The question of the advisability of fitting speed indicators which afforded a visual indication to the drivers, or speed recorders which recorded on a roll the speed of the engine throughout its journey, was one which needed to be solved by experiment.

It was decided in February 1936 that 20 engines should be fitted with speed indicators as an experiment. The Board approved the proposal to equip 12 'Princess Royal' Class engines with an electrical speed indicator and 8 'Royal Scot' Class engines with a mechanical speed recorder, as an experiment.

Comparisons were to be made of both types of instruments as regards maintenance, reliability and accuracy.[234]

As a result of this experiment it was decided that no further action should be taken to fit engines with speed recorders owing to the possible margin of error due to wear of tyres and rails, etc., and the difficulty and cost of checking such records, but that an electrical type of speed indicator which had proved to be the most efficient should be used when fitting any further locomotives.

In March 1937 when Mr. Lemon took up the question of accelerating express passenger trains, he urged the fitting of speed indicators on all engines of fast express trains in order to afford the drivers the maximum of assistance. It was estimated that 998 engines would need to be fitted for the accelerated services and this was approved by the Traffic Committee.[235]

At the beginning of the war when 180 engines had been fitted out of the 998 authorised, the work was stopped, but in May 1940 it was decided to go on with the work of fitting the indicators as the engines went through the shops, and up to the end of June 1941, 315 engines had been dealt with.

Improvement in lineside locomotive water supplies and a Model Control Office

ON THE twenty-third tour of inspection made by Lemon and other officers from headquarters during January 1937, two specific issues were raised which led to a review of such problems throughout the network.

The report of their visit to Codnor Park records: 'During the visit to this station it was stated that the pressure of water in the column was not satisfactory and that the matter had been duly reported and was under consideration'.[236]

Lemon wrote to Byrom asking for an official report into whether the appliances for taking water had been the subject of a general review, and what action was being taken to improve appliances that were known to be defective.[237]

A general investigation of the watering facilities throughout the line was made. On 25 October 1937 Lemon submitted a report to the Chairman enclosing a preliminary list of the more important cases where improvements were desirable and explaining the delays occurring, and the serious occupation of main lines, owing to engines having to run considerable distances for water at the nearest column.

H.G. Smith recounts that the Chairman approved Lemon's suggestion that an immediate effort should be made to bring the water facilities up-to-date and to a higher standard. At the Traffic Committee on 27 November 1937 two schemes, typical of the improvements in mind, were approved by the Directors, and authority given to Lemon to arrange for similar schemes to be taken in hand, reports to be submitted to the Committee at six-monthly intervals.[238]

The first scheme was for the provision of a 6,000 gallon tank at Cardigan sidings, Sheffield costing £856; and the second for a 12,000 gallon tank at Washwood Heath costing £819. The Traffic Committee Minutes describe the expected benefits of these two schemes; and it is the second scheme at Washwood Heath which shows the most dramatic changes: 'At least double the number of engines able to take water, avoiding light running to the extent of 13 mins for each additional engine using the supply. Time occupied in taking water reduced from 35/45 mins to 5 mins for tender engines and from 45/55 mins to 6 mins for Garratt engines.'

Smith quotes several other schemes which were subsequently carried out. One of these, at Mirfield cost just £40. Yet the improvements which were made reduced the time taken to fill a 3,500 gallon tender from 24 minutes to six!

These time savings are quite remarkable, and one wonders why this had not been done before. Water, after all, was one of the basic requirements for a steam engine, and the cost of these improvements was not high. It is therefore strange that these problems should have taken so long to come to light, and were not, for example, one of Lemon's earliest projects. Presumably, enginemen and all ranks of officials who were actively involved in watering the engines had never questioned the time it took. That was the

way it was. Even Lemon who had been a Vice-President for nearly six years, and had inspected the line on a regular basis, had not picked up the deficiencies in the system in all that time. Smith concludes his report by stating that up to the end of April 1940 the outlay on schemes sanctioned under this arrangement reached a figure of £14,602; and the total savings in wasted time, whilst difficult to quantify, were considerable.

The other issue that came to light on this tour concerned the layout of equipment in Control Offices. Lemon observed the situation at three offices: Toton, Westhouses and Rowsley, and found the accommodation was very unsatisfactory and that the staff had to work under considerable difficulties. Once again, Byrom was asked to investigate the general question of the layout and equipment of such offices, making a comprehensive review of the facilities so that standards could be established. In addition, Lemon decided that a 'theoretically' ideal Control Office should be built, incorporating all the latest technology. In designing the layout and equipment for this model, every effort was made to eliminate the operating and electrical difficulties experienced with existing Control Office layouts. The prototype was installed at one of the Company's houses at 19 Euston Square and inspected by Lemon on 22 December 1937. Subject to minor alterations, the equipment and design were approved for general application. The first office to be modernised was Wellingborough, and part of the equipment from the Euston Square model office was transferred there. Schemes of improvement were also carried out at Westhouses and Kirkby district control offices, but the War interrupted proceedings. However, Smith wrote in August 1941, that it remained the intention to carry out modernisation schemes based on the model office at many places, particularly on the Midland Division.[239]

Diesel power

THE introduction of diesels, both for shunting purposes and in light railcars, was described in the previous chapter but, although time had passed, the subject was still contentious. On 14 April 1937, the Diesel Engine Users' Association, whose President was now Tommy Hornbuckle, devoted an evening to a general review of the whole subject. Lemon attended this meeting, and his contribution to the discussion may be thought to sum up LMS thinking at the time:

In my opinion, the field for the employment of the diesel engine on railway work is fairly limited. The experience of the LMS Company has been that, whilst the diesel engine is suitable for light rail units, the main difficulty is in the scope of selection of areas in which it can be profitably employed under the conditions existing in this country. Experiments have proved that the diesel engine is also very suitable for shunting work but, even here, there is no economy unless the unit is working for more than twelve hours per day. The maximum economy arises, of course, where the diesel shunting unit is rostered on 24-hour shifts, but the economy is in the main a saving of man power – one man being employed instead of two – and not so much a saving in fuel or in other phases of operation.

We commenced with ten diesel units with a variety of types of mechanical drive, but, generally speaking, they have not been very successful; the electric drive holds out more promise.

Looking to the future it would appear that on the LMS system there is scope for not more than one hundred diesel locomotives, the economy being, as I have said, largely the halving of labour costs.

The steam engine has still a low initial cost and its simplicity – which pre-supposes reliability – is such that we experience comparatively few failures.

I wish to dispel the idea that the railway field is a very rich one to attack from the point of view of diesel engine development; moreover, the steam engine is constantly being improved, and a good deal of the actual economy even in shunting comes from the greater availability of the unit. The diesel engine has a much higher thermal efficiency than the steam engine, but the capital cost per h.p. of the diesel engine is higher and the only advantage rests on the availability and the saving in man power. However, in spite of what I have said, the LMS Company has ordered another twenty diesel engines in order to give them a fair trial, but the application of the diesel engine to main line trains is, I think, a long way off. After all, British Railways have to be run on an economic basis and not for political or other reasons, and this may perhaps account for the cautionary attitude towards the development of the diesel locomotive in this country.[240]

Despite their lack of interest in diesels for passenger traffic, Lemon acknowledged that the LMS had continued to investigate their use for shunting. The twenty 350hp engines to which he referred were the first batch of diesel-electric locomotives ordered from English Electric and Armstrong-Whitworth and which were delivered during 1935/36. A specification based on the best features of this first batch was then drawn up, and the *Railway Gazette* tells us that a further order for twenty locomotives was placed in August 1938.[241] Surprisingly, no specific authorisation for the construction of these locomotives can be found in either the Traffic Committee Minutes or the Board Minutes. They were built in the Derby workshops with engines and transmission supplied by English Electric. As previously mentioned, the forced ventilation and double reduction gears of the Armstrong-Whitworth design were adopted for this specification in order to avoid overheating at low speeds. The specification also retained the use of a jackshaft for the final drive to the wheels – another Armstrong-Whitworth feature. Yet Armstrong-Whitworth were not involved in their construction. The reason being simple: Armstrong-Whitworth withdrew from all railway construction work at this time, in order to concentrate on other Government work.[242] This makes a nonsense of Cox's remark about 'Blood being thicker than water' when describing why the order was placed with Fairburn's old firm of English Electric.[243] Armstrong-Whitworth were simply not an available option.

In 1938, discussions were held at the Institution of Locomotive Engineers, following a paper on diesel traction by a Frenchman, M. Dumas. One of the speakers accused the railways in this country of 'philandering' in their approach to the subject. He was specifically referring to the attitudes towards the latest three-car diesel-hydraulic train set which was being tested by the LMS on its favourite test-bed between Oxford and Cambridge. The speaker making this allegation, surprisingly, was W.A. Stanier – the CME and someone who one might expect to have been a committed champion of the steam locomotive. The *Railway Gazette* reported that, so exactly did the word describe English efforts with railcars, that it became almost a catchword at the meeting, and 'all that need be asked is – who is holding up the application of one of the most successful traffic units ever evolved?' The magazine answered its own question, and stated: 'To judge by the discussion at the Locomotive Engineers' meeting, the traffic departments are the culprits'.[244] This accusation should be compared with Lemon's own thoughts on the subject – because, of course, it was Lemon who was ultimately responsible for the workings of the Traffic Department at the LMS.

In 1939, Hornbuckle reported on the experiments with this three-car train in a paper delivered to the Institution of Locomotive Engineers.[245] E.S. Cox was in the audience and provocatively asked what use the train could actually serve, which indicates the innate predilection for steam power and apathy to the subject of diesels. Hornbuckle replied that the LMS used a large number of 2-coach, 60-ton trains hauled by a 110-ton steam locomotive, and this was an ideal replacement. Photographs of the construction of this trainset, which were published in the *Railway Gazette*, proudly show the interiors of the carriages being generously sprayed with asbestos.[246] How attitudes change! The train did go into main-line service on the St Pancras–Nottingham route on 24 March 1939, but the war put paid to any further experiments of

this kind. Once again, Hornbuckle was ahead of his time, as is demonstrated by the almost ubiquitous presence of such trains on the present-day rail network.

The School of Transport

THE last major project to occupy Lemon during the final years of this decade was the establishment of the School of Transport at Derby. Indeed it could be argued that this was his final major contribution to the LMS as Vice-President. By the time the School officially opened in 1938 he was on loan to the Government as Director-General of Aircraft Production; and, as will be shown later, when he returned to the company in 1940, the railway was operating under war conditions, the balance of power had shifted and his presence, from the evidence of his secretary H.G. Smith, was tolerated rather than valued.

Col. Lionel Manton, Principal of the School of Transport.
Railway Gazette

On 18 November 1935, Lemon submitted a memorandum to the Executive Committee, entitled: 'Commercial and General Training of LMS personnel – Proposal to establish School of Transport'. This started:

From time to time I have felt that it was very important we should, by some means or other, be able to train our staff in the best practices that exist throughout the railway as, for one reason and another, there is today no general uniformity of practice; indeed, it is often obvious, particularly on occasions of inspection of the line, that certain sections are much more efficient than others. How to disseminate the best practices rapidly has, therefore, been much in my mind of late.

The Executive Committee will be aware that during the [First World] War the development of the Ministry of Munitions could not have been accomplished without intensive training of the staff concerned and the provision of schools, etc. Similarly, the Army uses the school system to teach its personnel the latest developments in mechanical and other practices; at present there are 40 schools of training and yet the personnel of the British Regular Army is not as large as that of the LMS Railway.

The LMS Railway is a commercial concern working for profit and it is essential, under modern conditions, that all the staff should be given opportunities for acquiring all information which will make them more efficient in the railway service.[247]

In a subsequent summary of the progress of this project, Lemon's secretary H.G. Smith wrote:

Mr. Lemon felt that, although the management had been careful to adopt and standardise those practices which had proved to be the most efficient, it was inevitable that with so large a personnel any individual holding a position of responsibility exercised considerable influence over his juniors in respect of the methods and practices which they learned from him. In many cases these juniors accepted and used these methods for the remainder of their careers until, in turn, it became their responsibility to inculcate into the next generation the same ideas and influence. There was a wastage of ideas and experience when a practised hand retired from the service, leaving behind only that knowledge and skill which his colleagues and subordinates had learned from him in their daily work. The transfer of this knowledge from one generation to another had in the past been left too much to chance, and it was necessary to establish some central medium in which to pass on to promising younger members of the staff the fruits of the best experiences of the past in conjunction with the most advanced theories of the present.

Lemon was inspired to make the proposal following his visit to French railways in 1934. As early as 1928 the French had set up a training school in Rouen whose aims and methods were comparable to the proposals for the new School of Transport. Its courses were a year in length and based on 'practical work, papers, oral examinations and visits to outside stations'. The practical work

Front entrance to the School of Transport. Derby Silk Mill Museum

comprised shadow working with a fellow employee for up to eight hours at a stretch and the areas covered included traffic, permanent way, locomotives and workshop practices. The permanent-way element included the maintenance to a very high standard of a specially-selected stretch of line in the vicinity of the school. By the time of Lemon's visit in 1934, four such schools had been established.[248]

Lemon's 1935 memo, quoted above, shows that he considered – even after 12 years of amalgamation – that there was still no 'uniformity of practice'; and the old company culture of the constituents of the LMS had not been totally eradicated. Education rather than coercion was therefore, in Lemon's view, the only way to change these matters. As we have seen, Lemon had come from the humblest of origins and perhaps this, more than anything else, had shown him the importance of education. He must also have been aware of how his success in life had depended on the influences he had fortuitously received from others along the way. The School of Transport could give others a similar start.

Lemon reported to the Executive, in his proposal, that a suitable site had been found for the School: the Ursuline Convent at Crewe, which had recently been put up for sale at a price of £4,720. He had already taken an option on this, and calculated that the cost of converting it to a railway training centre would be approximately £31,000, with an estimated yearly running cost of £25,000. In March 1936 the Executive Committee decided it would be more satisfactory to erect a new building in preference to con-

verting an old one, and suggested a new building should be erected in Osmaston Park, Derby. The Chief Engineer was instructed to prepare detailed plans, which were approved in principle by the Board in May 1936.

The scheme was then announced to the Press: Stamp called a press conference at Euston on Thursday 5 November 1936 (an interesting date to announce a revolutionary idea) to impart the news that the LMS was to establish the first railway staff college in the British Isles. He announced that the scheme was a serious effort to eliminate the 'luck factor' in promotion, and pleaded 'We don't want cartoons with porters dressed in mortar boards'.[249] The omnipresent *Railway Gazette* was caught out by this announcement, as it was the day the magazine went to press, and only managed a brief mention of it in the editorial.[250] A week later, they were able to redress the balance and apologise for an error in their original editorial 'due to the necessary haste with which that note was prepared', Sir Josiah was reported 'as alluding to a payroll of £250,000, instead of over a quarter of a million employees'.[251]

The editorial on 13 November noted that 'the college will be open to all who are likely to profit by the training, whatever their ranks or grades, . . . It may even be found possible, now and again, to fill the college for a fortnight's course with some of the 4,000 women employees of the company'. The editorial goes on to state: 'Should the scheme prove successful, other colleges may be opened in Scotland and elsewhere. And we may look forward to a flourishing crop of these institutions springing up throughout the LMSR system'. However, if this was the original intention, the War put paid to any further plans and no further institutions of this type were built.

The Derby College was built to accommodate 50 students, and was not

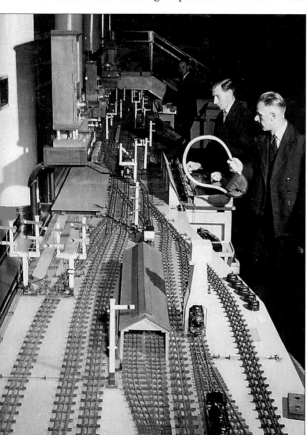

The model railway at the School of Transport, showing how railway working was replicated on the layout. Derby Silk Mill Museum

meant to conflict with such technical training or education as was presently provided. The management did not regard the School as a replacement for the courses attended by staff at technical colleges, universities and other formal learning institutions. It was intended to complement existing forms of education and, as Stamp said, ensure that 'the best shall not be the monopoly of the few but shall be put at the service of many', and that the mix of work and play provided by the college was intended to break down 'departmental, grade and other barriers'.[252]

The *Railway Gazette*'s first Editorial quoted the statement, 'At present a man's success is often due to his chance training under a first-class man, and the college is intended to eliminate the element of chance and secure for all promising candidates an equal opportunity for sound training and not lose through retirement the valuable experience of senior men'.[253] It is impossible to attribute these words with any certainty. They may well have come from Lemon himself, as he was present at the press conference and noted as having answered questions. If one is looking for a succinct description of his advancement in life, then these words sum up his situation perfectly. At pivotal moments, he had fortuitously come under the influence of a 'first-class man'. He had as his early mentor, Professor Malcolm Laurie, and had seized the opportunities he had thus been given. Later, Bob Reid had contributed by fostering his inquisitive and experimental nature, and when he became Vice-President he had always had the full backing of Stamp.

After the initial announcements in the Press, progress – for whatever reason – was slow, and the local papers queried why progress had stalled. On 19 April 1937, the *Derby Evening Telegraph* asked: 'What is happening in connection with the projected LMS staff college at Derby?' The writer reported that no work had yet been done on the building and he had been unable to trace the allocation of any contracts for the work.[254]

In May 1937 the Board approved a total expenditure of £64,036 to cover the cost of the building and equipment, and the work was put in hand. However it was not until 22 September 1937 that Stamp laid the foundation stone. Lemon

was not present at this ceremony. Although he was very much the driving force behind the project, there does not seem to be any obvious reason for his absence, and one can only speculate why this was so. The building was designed to be prestigious: the main façade incorporated sculptures of the different phases of railway industry. Inside, the students were to be treated in a style to which working people had not been accustomed. They were provided with individual bedrooms, each with a bed, wardrobe, desk and wash basin. Within easy reach were an ample supply of bathrooms and toilets. All linen was supplied and there was provision for laundry to be processed. The lounge was decorated with a mural by William Hamlyn entitled 'One Hundred Years', showing the changing face of the LMS, and the final plans included a large Hall of Transport, 118ft long and 47ft wide, which contained a model railway layout (for demonstrating train operations …) sunk below floor level.

The residential nature of the college was intended to complement the curriculum, which was designed to give time for both work and play. The Porter had an important role to play, ensuring that those who were unused to being away from home were as happy as possible.[255] The atmosphere to be engendered was one of team work, and each course appointed their own committee to liaise with the permanent staff. *The Times* noted that 'An essential part of the scheme is considered to be the provision of a boarding college rather than a day college, so that men can work and play together, and by doing so tend to break down any tendency to a "departmental outlook" which is a potential danger in all large organisations'.[256]

The motives of the LMS management were not primarily those of a social reformer. However, if providing better working conditions, education and living spaces allowed workers to work more efficiently, enabled better safety standards to be maintained, and removed causes of sickness, then production rates would rise and profits would accrue for the company. Whatever their higher motives, even such luminaries as Titus Salt and Thomas Cadbury were ultimately engaged in the pursuit of profit. The motives of the LMS management, in founding the School of Transport, were no different. Although the social aspects of the School of Transport could be seen as being as important as the study sessions at the college, the intention was, after 13 years of internecine strife, to give the practices, loyalties and knowledge of the disparate staff of the company a single corporate focus.

Once the foundation stone had been laid, the School was completed in just ten months, and was formally opened on 23 July 1938 by the Rt. Hon. Dr Leslie Burgin MP, Minister of Transport. By this time, Lemon had started work at the Air Ministry (see next chapter), but he was able to attend the ceremony together with Sir Wilfrid Freeman. The philosophy of many of the speeches at the opening ceremony could well have flowed from Lemon's pen, as they certainly encapsulated his ideas. The Minister noted: 'That management should be invested with the dignity of a science was a sign of the times. Knowledge of a science had to be acquired by study, by experience and by experiment. The science of management of one of the great mainline systems was now specially to be taught.'[257] Lord Stamp, as might be expected, also made a speech. In this, he singled out Lemon as having first suggested the idea, but his view of the School was somewhat different. He is quoted as having explained that the purpose was: 'to clarify the knowledge which tended in big institutions to become merely a sort of verbal tradition; to show that, whilst everyone knew that plant must be kept up to date, individual and co-ordinated brains were their greatest asset'. He described the foundation of the school as 'an experiment not only in railway management, but also in education and human contacts' and hoped that it would be a 'source of institutional pride'. The school would induce a new attitude to knowledge on the part of the men who attended, combating what was the worst form of bankruptcy, namely the loss of enthusiasm.[258]

The first Principal of the School was Col. Lionel Manton, who was appointed on 16 August 1937. He had considerable military railway experience and, prior to his appointment, had been Commandant of the Army Railway Training Centre at the Longmoor Military Railway, near Aldershot. Although he was appointed while the buildings were still being constructed, he was not the first member of staff to be engaged. This was Miss Barbara Cramp (later Mrs Armstead), who was appointed Secretary, and remained in that rôle until the early 1960s. She kept a scrapbook, detailing every key event at the School throughout all these years, which has been an invaluable reference source.[259]

In February 1938, before the School was opened, Col. Manton gave a paper on the training of railway staff to a meeting of the Railway Students' Association at the London School of Economics.[260] He regretted that, whilst it was obviously information about the School of Transport that was wanted, the amount of concrete information he could give was small, as progress in preparing the courses had not been so rapid as hoped. However, he told the students that the oral training would augmented by audio-visual techniques, and supported by 'draft textbooks, under preparation' incorporating all the best practices of railway operation. It was envisaged that a panel of practical men would be created and that, from time to time, they would be called to give students the benefit of their experience. In this way, the knowledge that these men imparted should not be lost when they retired. No record of the curriculum, as developed by Manton and his staff, has so far been found and, necessarily, this would have subtly changed from course to course. However, at least five textbooks were completed and published internally by the LMS: *Advertising; Goods Station Working; Passenger Station Working; Cartage* and *Salesmanship* – the last carried the admonition 'for the use of the company's servants only'.[261] Although it may be thought that 'salesmanship' only concerned those whose responsibility was to sell the railway's services to the customer, the topic seems to have formed a backbone to many different courses. A member of a course for Permanent Way Inspectors, held many years later in September 1950 (two years after nationalisation) stated: 'we were given a lecture on Salesmanship and this proved to be very interesting. The lecturer pointed out that even though Permanent Way men were not strictly concerned with the commercial end of the job, they could in no small way expedite the

The lounge at the School of Transport – in a haze of tobacco smoke (!). Part of William Hamlyn's mural, *One Hundred Years*, featuring the Euston Arch at its centre, can be seen on the rear wall. Derby Silk Mill Museum

working of traffic by the removal of speed restrictions as soon as ever possible.'

The first course was held between 5 September and 28 October 1938, and the 50 students were selected from Headquarters and District office staff, Station Masters, Goods Agents and ex-Traffic apprentices. They assembled for a trial course in Salesmanship and Operating. The method of instruction and general organisation met with approval, and the students were unanimous in asking for further demonstrations and discussions. A second course for students drawn from the Wages Staff and junior clerical grades was held from 9 January to 5 April 1939 and, at the conclusion, it was reported that results were most satisfactory and that the students were enthusiastic about the good which their stay had done them. A third course was completed successfully at the end of July 1939, and was attended by 50 students with an average age of 22. However, the immediate benefits to the LMS were limited as, at the outbreak of war, the School was closed and placed at the disposal of the War Office for use as a Military Railway Training Centre.

The School of Transport remained in railway ownership until privatisation. Today it is the Derby Conference Centre – a Grade 2 listed building and a lasting memorial to the foresight of Ernest Lemon.

Canada – 1938

IN MAY 1938, Lemon made a fleeting visit across the Atlantic to Canada. He took with him an introduction to the Governor-General in Ottawa, Lord Tweedsmuir, written by Lord Wigram, one of the Directors of the LMS, dated 27 April 1938.[262] The LMS records show that Lemon attended the Board Meeting on 28 April but, confusingly, the shipping records show that he travelled on the Canadian Pacific liner the *Duchess of Richmond* which left Liverpool, bound for Montreal, the day before (27 April). One can only assume that he may have been able to join the ship at Greenock, after a quick dash up from London – the Railway Air Services had just started flying between London and Glasgow – either that, or the Board records are wrong!

He certainly disembarked at Greenock when he arrived back on 20 May: travelling on the same liner, the *Duchess of Richmond*.[263] This ship – like other Canadian Pacific ships – shuttled back and forth across the Atlantic, sailing at weekly intervals from one country to the other. And so, allowing for the week spent on the crossing in each direction, Lemon can only have spent a fortnight in Canada. At first glance, this looks suspiciously similar to the trip he made to the Caribbean in 1934, at a time when the first problems with his marriage surfaced. The shipping records, as before, show that he travelled on his own and, once again, it appears that the seclusion afforded by a ship on the high seas, where nobody could contact him, was a great solace. Significantly, Wigram wrote in the letter which enclosed the introduction to Tweedsmuir, 'Bon Voyage – & good luck with a complete restoration to health'.

There is also evidence to show that Lemon was acting erratically at this time, and it comes from February 1938 – two months before the trip to Canada. In view of the timing, it could be relevant. Lemon's behaviour resulted in a personal letter of complaint to Sir Harold Hartley and, although this may refer to an isolated incident, is more probably an indication that matters were building to a head. The writer of the letter was Sir Thomas Merton, Professor of Spectroscopy at Oxford University and a fellow of Balliol College like Hartley.[264] It starts:

My dear Harold,
I have been very worried about an unfortunate incident which took place last Thursday night. I had dined with the R.S. [Royal Society] Club and as I was leaving I met Lemon in the hall. I nodded to him and was going out when he came up to me in an excited state and angrily accused me of making very disparaging remarks about him to yourself. I was completely taken aback by this attack, and to avoid a scene I ignored his flagrant breach of good manners and merely told him that I did not know what he was talking about. He calmed down and after some further trivial conversation on other subjects we both left the Club. I need not go into details in this letter, but his attitude was distinctly hostile and at least one remark that he made was offensive.

Merton continues by saying that he therefore felt compelled to resign from his association with Hartley's Research Committee. Although the letter is somewhat pompous, it is clear that Lemon had not acted as a 'gentleman' was expected to behave. The letter had a postscript:

I might mention that amongst other things Lemon said to me 'Don't say anything to Harold about this'. I don't know whether he

seriously thought that I could allow the matter to pass without further action on my part.

All the indications, however, are that it was not just the stresses and strains of his professional work that had affected his health and behaviour, but another crisis point in his emotional relationships. The first indication is that in 1938 Lemon's name finally disappears from the Electoral Rolls at Northchurch Hall. The roll came into effect on 15 October 1938, and must have been collated after the trip to Canada. The only name recorded at Northchurch is that of Amy Lemon. This time Lemon had taken an apartment at No. 17 Dorset Square. (He seems to have had a predilection for locations named after the county of his birth! Dorset Square is about half-a-mile north of Dorset Street, close to Marylebone Station.) At the same time, as shown in the Marylebone register, Hermione also moved back into the Square, returning to 'The Ladies' National Club' at No. 39, where she had lived before 1934.

Also in the Autumn of 1938, Lemon's elder son Richard was married. He and his wife had met at the University Jazz Club, while they were both students at Oxford. Richard's daughter, Christine, told the author that not a single photograph of the wedding exists, nor was it reported in the papers, and it is impossible now to know exactly who attended the ceremony. This also seems significant. If Lemon and Amy did both attend, the situation would hardly have lent itself to a happy group photograph. All this leads one to suppose that it was at some time in 1938 that Amy finally became aware of her husband's infidelity. Of course, she may have known for years and chosen to ignore it, but it is clear that from now on the couple permanently lived apart.

Although the trip to Canada was intended as an opportunity for rest and relaxation, and a time to recover his health both physical and mental, nevertheless his introduction to the Governor-General implies that the journey was not exclusively a rest-cure. The LMS Board Minutes give no hint of any railway business in which he might have been involved, but it seemed prudent to try and seek other reasons for the trip. One possible reason immediately suggested itself. Lord Wigram had been Private Secretary to the Sovereign. He retired from this post in 1936 when King George V died, but continued to serve the Royal household in other capacities. Significantly, Wigram's letter was written from Windsor Castle. Now, in 1939, King George VI and Queen Elizabeth made a Royal Visit to Canada and the USA. This trip certainly started in Canada, and the Royal couple then travelled by train to Washington and visited the 'World's Fair' in New York. Lemon – who had experience of arranging such journeys in this country – may well have been involved in planning the Tour, and given advice to the Governor-General. However, if so, he did not meet on the trip any of the Canadian railway officials who were building a special Royal train for the State Visit. None of the congratulatory messages he received from Canadian railway officials on his secondment to the Air Ministry, one month later in June 1938, makes any reference to a recent meeting or any ongoing business, or the fact that Lemon gave no indication of this surprising move when they met, which they would surely have done if such had occurred.

Lemon disembarked on his return in Scotland, although the boat continued on to Liverpool. In so doing, he may have taken the opportunity to visit the Empire Exhibition in Glasgow. The LMS had been much involved in running special excursion trains to the Exhibition (which included a pavilion devoted to British railways). 1,885 such excursions were run during the period of the Exhibition carrying over 600,000 passengers from all parts of the system. There were even day trips from London every weekend – it must have been a very long day![265]

The records then show that he attended a Board Meeting on 26 May and that this was the last meeting he was to attend for some time. It is a curious coincidence that two days later, after the peace and quiet of this trip, the magazine *Modern Wonder* carried a profile of Lemon and his hectic life-style at the LMS.[266] *Modern Wonder* was a children's magazine which featured articles on the marvels of new inventions and technology. The article, on 28 May 1938, has the headline: 'He Builds the Crack Locos' and, as the title suggests, was written in a popular sensationalist style that would appeal to its young readers. The following extracts demonstrate the point:

At a large desk in his office at Euston Station, telephones ringing incessantly, men and women coming and going, sits Mr E.J.H. Lemon O.B.E., M.I.Mech.E., and Vice-President of the London, Midland and Scottish Railway. He is in charge of the mechanical side of the railway. If a new engine is to be constructed, final responsibility rests with him. A new design of train, and again Mr Lemon is behind it.

The article continues in similar vein:

'Faster! Faster!' goes the cry. 'More trains! Longer trains! More luxurious trains!' And men like Mr Lemon have to see that the demand is met. The chief mechanical engineer gets to work on a new engine . . . Mr Lemon gives the O.K. and work can be started.

This article may very well have been written from material supplied by the LMS Publicity Department without Lemon being personally aware of it. After all, for the previous month, he had been in Canada. What is therefore interesting is that it demonstrates how the CME was perceived – even within the LMS – as the servant of the Operating Department. It forcibly brings home that Stanier was beholden to Lemon's requirements, although the CME was theoretically answerable to Sir Harold Hartley, Vice-President in charge of Works and Ancillary Undertakings. However, by this time, Hartley was taking more interest in the company's air interests and, since 1934, had been Chairman of the Railway Air Services.

There was a moral to the story, intended to inspire young people to follow Lemon's example. The article describes how he climbed from apprentice to the 'top rung' of the management ladder – but 'Mr Lemon does not like to talk about his achievements. He does not want the limelight, but prefers to get on with his job. And he has set an example that any youngster today can follow. Determination, perseverance and intelligence will bring anyone the chances Mr Lemon had.'

Little can anyone have realised, when this article was published, that Lemon would soon move on to other, very different, work.

EIGHT

The Air Ministry, run-up to war, 1938–1940

IN THE Summer of 1938, Lemon's career took a sudden unexpected turn when the LMS agreed to second him to the Air Ministry as the new Director-General of Production. It is no exaggeration to say that the work he subsequently carried out for the Ministry undoubtedly helped to save this country from defeat at the hands of Nazi Germany in the Second World War. Before describing his work for the Ministry, it will be necessary to explain how and why this appointment came about.

To understand the reasons, it is necessary to go back to the beginning of 1938. On 8 January, the *News Chronicle* carried the banner headline 'Air Ministry Indicted in Rearmament Muddle' on its front page. The article by the paper's Air Correspondent started: 'There is a rapidly growing feeling in the aircraft industry that inefficiency at the Air Ministry, and consequent hampering of production of aircraft for the expanded Air Force, will soon cause the greatest storm in the Ministry's history. On all sides there are signs of a coming outburst.' The article, and the leader column on an inside page, then listed all the failures, delays and shortcomings in the re-armament programme for the RAF. One allegation was that: 'Other machines announced over two years ago – the two boasted fighters with speeds of over 300mph – have not been built at all. They

Lemon in 1938 when he was seconded to the Air Ministry.
Modern Transport

exist only as single machines or prototypes'. These, of course were the Hurricane and Spitfire which proved so crucial in the Battle of Britain.

The Government's defence policy in the inter-war years has been the subject of many books. Nevertheless, in view of subsequent events, a short summary is appropriate, although this may necessarily over-simplify some of the issues. The RAF Expansion Programme had been started in 1935 as a response to the news of Germany's re-emergent air force. In March of that year, Germany had publicly admitted the existence of the Luftwaffe, which had been built up clandestinely over the previous years (starting even before Hitler came to power in 1933). At that time, the Luftwaffe already had nearly 1,900 aircraft – greatly in excess of the RAF's strength. However, many years before, in 1923, the Government of the day had accepted the Salisbury Committee's recommendation that this country should have an 'Air Force of sufficient strength adequately to protect us against air attack by the strongest air force within striking distance of this country'.

The Government was therefore in a quandary. On the one hand it wished the RAF to have parity with any potential aggressor, but it also did not want to be seen to be starting an arms race with Germany, which would have been politically disastrous both at home and abroad. Ever since the end of the 'war to end all wars' in 1918, public feeling in this country was one of abhorrence to all things military. For this reason, the armed forces had been drastically reduced in size, and little money committed to development and re-equipment. Nonetheless, and in spite of these misgivings, action had to be taken and a decision was made to expand the RAF in the hope that this would act as a deterrent to Nazi expansionism. And then the arguments, problems and delays started. Plan 'A' was quickly followed by others until, by 1938, the letter 'K' had been reached.

The fact that the Government took the *News Chronicle*'s accusations seriously can be seen from the files at the National Archives which include cuttings from the paper and the proposed response.[267] A week after the article appeared, Clement Attlee from the opposition Labour Party wrote to the Government with a list of 56 questions to which he demanded an answer. The Secretary of State for Air [the 'Minister'] was, at this time Viscount Swinton, and he was advised by the distinguished Scottish industrialist, Viscount Weir. Weir's papers housed at Churchill College, Cambridge, contain a copy of Attlee's 56 demands which was circulated to him on 16 January 1938.[268] It is worth quoting a selection of these as they demonstrate many of the specific concerns that were being voiced about the state of the rearmament programme.

— Is it a fact that no one of the four service members of the Air Council is technically qualified?

— Is it also a fact that the Director of Research is not a technician, and that the Director of Armaments has not taken an armaments course?

— How many members of the Air Council and the Directors and other senior officers have had recent or any experience of flying modern high speed aeroplanes either by day or night?

— How many hours of flying have these officers done in any kind of aircraft in the last two or three years?

— Why is it that despite the vast sums spent on research at Farnborough and elsewhere, all the principal inventions seem to come from abroad, e.g. the retractable undercarriage, variable pitch screw, blind flying apparatus including the artificial horizon, enclosed cockpits, power driven turrets, landing lamps, etc?

— Why is the Air Ministry so slow to adopt these inventions?

— Why, although abroad the biplane was being discarded for the monoplane, did this country continue with the biplane?

— Why was it that when expansion came we had to order the production of experimental planes? What had the large designing staff been doing prior to this period? Why had not the latest designs of other countries been studied and designs made?

— Is it a fact that the aeroplanes being produced are already of less capacity than those being produced in other countries?

— Is it a fact that although the majority of our planes are bombers, they have an effective range insufficient to operate against the aerodromes of a possible opponent, Germany?

— How many squadrons are really ready for instant action? How many are complete with instruments, guns etc? Is it a fact that when the German visitors were over here it was only by borrowing from all over the place that it was possible, and even then with difficulty, to make a show with a few squadrons? When we are given statements about numbers of first line aircraft, does this mean aircraft ready for action, or does the number include a very large proportion of planes that are without instruments and are not fitted with turrets, guns etc.?

— How many pilots are capable of flying to Germany and back? How many do we calculate will be able to do so in six months' time? How many are practised in blind flying? How many planes equipped with blind flying apparatus are available for the purpose?

— Are the types of aeroplane now being manufactured really up to date? Are the shadow factories being equipped with jigs etc., for really up to date planes and apparatus, or are they based on types already obsolescent?

The *News Chronicle* returned to the subject on 1 February, and declared that the Air Ministry had been 'sabotaging the air rearmament programme by its own inertia' and that 'The public waits from a statement from the Government to allay growing disquiet which has been fanned by Ministerial silence and flabby official denials'. However, as the paper goes on to say, four days after the original January article, Sir Charles Bruce-Gardner had been appointed the first ever Chairman of the Society of British Aircraft Constructors with the task of 'interpreting the views and wishes of the Air Ministry and industry to one another'. This new post had been created, the *News Chronicle* believed, as a direct result of Government reaction to their previous article.

Sir Thomas Inskip, Minister for the Co-ordination of Defence discussed the situation with Viscount Swinton, and suggested that maybe they should adopt the idea, put forward in the Press, to bring a planning and production expert into the Air Ministry. Weir's reaction was a dogged belief that the organisation in place at the Air Ministry was perfectly adequate. He repudiated the suggestion in a letter to Inskip on 2 March stating: 'Bruce-Gardner's appointment should result in the Industry pooling its experience and thus broadening and hastening application of the best practices', and he reiterated that the Government should not impose any central Air Ministry production expert on the manufacturers.[269] Inskip replied on 9 March, apologising for having made this suggestion, and writing 'I am, of course, quite satisfied that this particular idea is not one that would work in practice and that in any case having regard to Bruce Gardner's appointment, it need not be considered further. I fully appreciate the reasons that you gave for having come to this conclusion. It was very good of you to take so much trouble to satisfy me.'[270]

Three days after this exchange of correspondence, on 12 March 1938, Hitler's troops marched into Austria, and the country was annexed by the Third Reich. This concentrated people's minds wonderfully, and finally caused many within the Government to wake up to the threat from Germany, and seriously question the ability of the country to defend itself. Bruce-Gardner called it 'the second gypsy's warning – the first being when Germany walked into the Ruhr at a weekend with practically no notice'.[271] On 2 April Sir Warren Fisher, Secretary to the Treasury, sent a Memo. to the Prime Minister simply entitled 'AIR', which read: 'I have prepared the attached table [showing comparative strengths of the RAF and Luftwaffe] from reliable sources, because in this form the appalling facts are self-explanatory. For some years we have had from the Air Ministry soothing-syrup and incompetence in equal measure. For the first time in

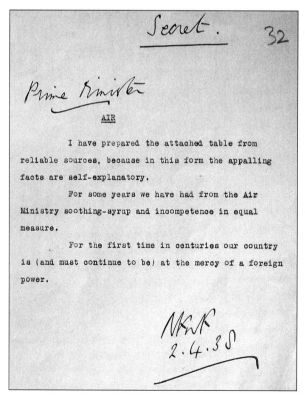

Sir Warren Fisher's letter to Neville Chamberlain.
National Archives

An extract
from the table
comparing
the size of the
Luftwaffe and
RAF which
was attached to
Warren Fisher's
letter
National Archives

```
                    Air comparison 2nd April, 1938.

        GERMANY                              ENGLAND

A. 1st Line Aircraft, including    A. fighter machines - 420 including
                                                        280 obsolete
   100% reserves,                                       and 42 not yet
                                                        mobilisable,
                                                        with reserves
        5,000 to 5,200                                  for 1½ weeks

                                      bomber machines - 804 including
                                                        384 not yet
                                                        mobilisable &
                                                        of the mobilis-
                                                        able balance 120
                                                        are obsolete,
                                                        with reserves
                                                        for 2 to 3 weeks

                                      other aircraft  - 410 including
                                                        200 light naval
                                                        machines, 126
                                                        reconnaissance,
                                                        84 army co-
                                                        operation (? how
                                                        many obsolete)

                                   ⎡for above see report dated 28th
                                    ultimo by Chiefs of Staff - D.P.
                                    (P.) 22.⎦
```

centuries our country is (and must continue to be) at the mercy of a foreign power'. Sir Maurice Hankey, Secretary to the War Cabinet, added this comment to the Memo: 'It is a pity he is so venomous to the Air Ministry. Bruce Gardner's letter suggests that the Treasury also have a heavy responsibility. People in glass houses shouldn't throw stones!'[272]

As this correspondence shows, finance was – as it almost always is – one of the root causes for delays in Government procurement. But it was not the only one, as will be explained later in this chapter. However, the records show that the Government now accepted, albeit privately, that war with Germany was inevitable, and preparations were speeded up accordingly. Although there were urgent discussions between the interested parties as to how this could be achieved, the Air Council's reaction to the crisis was merely to suggest that an RAF officer be placed in each aircraft factory to oversee production.[273] The trade unions, meanwhile, were unhappy at any extra pressures being put on the labour force, and the Prime Minister, Neville Chamberlain, had to intervene personally to allay their fears.[274]

On 5 April, Weir saw the Prime Minister and emphasised the need for a new expansion programme with revised targets and completion dates, and thus Scheme 'L' came to be adopted. The official 'History of the Second World War' describes the new Scheme thus:

Not only did it reflect the heightened sense of urgency in the Government and Air Ministry, but it also signified the end of the purely financial checks on rearmament. The R.A.F, was the first among the Services to enter into what to all intents and purposes were war-time conditions of supply, for from now on expansion in the air was to be subject only to industrial limitations: raw materials, labour and management.[275]

Weir wrote a memo following his meeting with Chamberlain. It is undated, but must have been written immediately afterwards, as he left for America on a Trade Mission a few days later. In this memo, Weir reluctantly set out his proposals for an Air Ministry Supply Organisation headed by a Director-General of Production.[276] He considered two possibilities: the first involved appointing such a person from outside the RAF. He wrote:

Such a man I think we cannot find inside the Service, and he would be almost equally hard to find outside of it. The type of man I have in mind might be one of the chief mechanical engineers of one of our great railways, such as Gresley or Stanier; alternatively from industry a man like Sir Charles Craven, or the Managing Director of one of the great electrical equipment firms.

However, he also suggested an alternative approach, which would keep the responsibility for supply within the RAF – to give these extra duties to Air Marshal Sir Wilfrid Freeman, Air Member for Research & Development, with Bruce-Gardner as his Deputy. He wrote:

To put this additional burden on a serving Officer at the present time would, I think, be unfair unless he was provided with a deputy or chief assistant in the form of the most useful civilian who can be found with administrative, technical and industrial experience. Within the Department you would then have the users' influence and responsibility plus the industrially minded influence as a temporary reinforcement during this acceleration period.

And there the matter rested until 12 May when there was a disastrous debate – for the Government – in both houses of Parliament. The Government's critics rehearsed all the arguments about the chaotic state of the programme and, time and again, the Members suggested a Ministry of Supply should be set up to oversee production. They particularly asked why there were no engineers with manufacturing experience in the Air Ministry. The Irish peer, Earl Winterton, Chancellor of the Duchy of Lancaster, who represented the Ministry in the House of Commons (Swinton sat in the House of Lords), replied that the 'Air Ministry did not design aircraft . . . it was a consumer, not a producer'. He continued: 'there was a contention that it was absurd to order aeroplanes if one was not an engineer. That seemed to be as bad as saying that anybody interested in the industry of house building should himself have a knowledge of the technical details of construction and should be an architect.' [277] One questioner asked if it was true that, in the two years since the orders were placed, only 28 Hurricanes had been delivered and one Spitfire? The Minister replied that the programme was 'well up to schedule' but evaded the issue of

precise numbers – merely reiterating the total numbers that had been ordered. It is worth commenting here that, at the height of the Battle of Britain in 1940, the RAF was losing this number of fighters in a single day!

It was generally agreed that the Government had made a very limp defence of its policy in these debates and, as a result, the Prime Minister, Neville Chamberlain, made a clean sweep of all the Ministers at the Air Ministry. Viscount Swinton, along with his junior ministers, was dismissed and, on 17 May, Sir Kingsley Wood appointed in his place. Chamberlain had concluded that, as a first step, the Secretary of State for Air must be an MP and able to be questioned directly in the House of Commons.

The debate, which had been adjourned, was then continued on 25 May. The fact that the Prime Minister had sacked the responsible Ministers gave the Government's critics even more ammunition to use. It certainly implied that he acknowledged there was a crisis. Although there was a general feeling that Kingsley Wood should be given some time to effect changes and improvements, nevertheless Hugh Dalton, for the Opposition, resumed the attacks. He pointed out that there was still no member of the Air Council with engineering qualifications, and claimed that it was the Directorate of Aeronautical Production which was largely responsible for the whole of the production muddle and bottlenecks.

On 1 June, Kingsley Wood received a letter from Sir Walter Preston. He was Chairman of Platt Brothers of Oldham, who made machinery for the textile industry. He had also been MP for Cheltenham, but had resigned his seat in 1937 in order to devote himself to his hobby of yachting! And it was from his yacht in Cowes harbour that he wrote to Kingsley Wood:

The thing that stands out in my mind as a mistake is the control of civilian technicians by non-technical serving officers. The lower jobs only being available to technicians there is no attraction for the best men who can often obtain bigger pay in private industry than that of the Air Ministry chiefs. The result – you have non-technical, or semi-technical chiefs making decisions on the advice of what are often only second-rate men. The A.M. ought to have and to pay for the very best of technical advice, and the only way to ensure this is to place technicians in charge of technical departments and to make the pay high enough to attract the best brains out of industry. The argument against, viz. that Service control is needed to secure the confidence of the rank and file is, in my opinion, knowing some of them, bunkum.[278]

With the departure of Swinton as Minister, Weir, in solidarity, resigned his position as Adviser. In his place, Kingsley Wood appointed a Panel of Advisers, who first met on 8 June 1938. The Minutes of this meeting record that 'The Secretary of State himself [i.e. Kingsley Wood] thought that a post of Director of Planning and Supply should be created, and he suggested that certain members of the Panel might advise him as to the appointment of a first-class man to fill this post.'[279] Five days later, Sir Charles Bruce-Gardner set out his views on the duties and responsibilities of such a position, and the following day, on 14 June, the Panel of Advisers accepted Bruce-Gardner's recommendations.[280] Within a further week, a decision had been made. Kingsley Wood took on board the recommendation made by Weir and – as suggested – looked to the railways for a suitable candidate. The choice did not fall on Stanier or Gresley though, but on Lemon who, within the railway fraternity, was undoubtedly the most qualified candidate. On 21 June Kingsley Wood reported to the Air Council that he had discussed the proposed appointment of Lemon with the Prime Minister, Neville Chamberlain, and it had been agreed to proceed.[281] The speed of this whole decision process – a mere fortnight – is most surprising, considering the time it had been in gestation. As Kingsley Wood inaugurated a complete change of policy at the Ministry, one would expect to find

Sir Kingsley Wood, Secretary of State for Air (c.1941).

National Portrait Gallery

a large file of relevant documents – recommendations for the appointment, short-lists, the views of other interested parties, interviews etc. – as the wheels of Government ground slowly on. If there is such a file at the National Archives, it is remarkably obscure. No trace of it has yet been found! There is, therefore, no paper trail to tell us exactly how Lemon came to be chosen, who had recommended him, and whether other candidates were considered. Perhaps he was simply chosen in informal discussions within the gentlemen's clubs of Pall Mall? It is tempting to see the hand of Sir Harold Hartley in this. Hartley was well-known in Government circles, and was already advising the Air Ministry on the RAF's requirements for aviation fuel. However, no evidence to support this supposition has been found. What is certain is that Lord Stamp cannot have been actively involved. He was in America at the time and only arrived back at Southampton on the *Normandie* on 20 June, just in time for the final negotiations.[282] When Kingsley Wood informed the Air Council, on 21 June, that it had been decided to proceed with Lemon's appointment, he also told them that he and the Prime Minister were accordingly meeting Lord Stamp that same evening.

Lemon kept a file of papers relating to his work at the Air Ministry which has remained in the family, and is the source for all the correspondence quoted later in this chapter. Although this has proved invaluable in researching this period of his life, the contents shed no light on how he came to be chosen and start from the moment that Stamp put the Government's proposal to him. Stamp did this on 22 June, the day after his meeting with the Prime Minister, and then replied to Kingsley Wood:

I have now had a talk with Mr. Lemon, and he and I both feel that before he comes to a decision he ought to hear from you personally a little more precisely than I was able to give him a) the exact nature of the responsibilities that he is to carry and the duties expected of him, and b) the power or authority for carrying these duties into effect. We are also not clear as to his position in the department vis-à-vis the Permanent Officials, and how far it would be advisory only. It is only after knowing this from you personally that he can judge whether he feels his experience and abilities are adapted to it.

Stamp then continues his letter by querying the proposed financial arrangements. He had agreed at the meeting with Chamberlain that the LMS would continue to pay Lemon's salary of £6,000 but, as the Chairman of a public company with shareholders, asked that the Air Ministry would pay the costs of filling Lemon's post during his absence. He thought that 'probably £2,000 or £3,000 would cover the additional expense'. Kingsley Wood was agreeable to this and, in fact, because of Stamp's generosity, had negotiated a bargain. The actual cost to the Ministry for Lemon's expertise would be half what he was being paid at the LMS. However, it should be borne in mind that the railway did pay its senior staff extremely well – and a Minister's salary at the time was £5,000 pa.

Lemon's caution was understandable. He was to be a civilian working with RAF officers and civil servants. Although he would have the authority of the Government behind him, he might still expect to find resentment from some people at his appointment and the changes this would bring about. He would also have to persuade independent aircraft manufacturers to change their whole attitude to the mass-production of aircraft. It would have been counter-productive merely to try to crack a whip and demand greater efforts – he had to facilitate

**Air Marshal
Sir Wilfrid Freeman.**
National Portrait Gallery

them by helping with raw material supplies, labour problems and so on. As an engineer, though, he would understand the problems and be able to suggest ways to solve them.

Lemon's appointment as Director-General of Production (DGP) was announced in Parliament on 27 June, and his membership of the Air Council was formalised the following day.[283] This was not the only organisational change. The official announcement stated that he would assist Air Marshal Sir Wilfrid Freeman, Air Member for Research & Development, who would now be responsible for production as well. Kingsley Wood had, therefore, followed Weir's recommendations to the letter. Ultimate responsibility for the expansion programme still lay with the RAF, and Lemon thus found himself cast in the rôle of, to use Weir's phrase, 'the most useful civilian who can be found with administrative, technical and industrial experience'. Incidentally, one wonders why Kingsley-Wood – or Weir, for that matter – had not considered looking for a candidate for the post within the car industry. Heavy steam locomotives, carriages and wagons have very little in common with aeroplanes, whereas car manufacturers were accustomed to quantity mass-production and their products used internal combustion engines. Perhaps it was this last fact that excluded them. They were already heavily involved with the 'shadow' factory schemes for the Air Ministry building aero engines, and it might have been invidious to choose one of their number as DGP for fear of later accusations of bias or nepotism.

The appointment was reported in the Press, and most papers generally included a brief summary of Lemon's career. The London *Evening Standard* went that bit further and included details that are not important in themselves, but give a biographer a wealth of trivial information. Lemon's golf handicap, and how he came to join the railway, have already been mentioned; but we also learn that he had no time for gardening and that the top joint on the index finger of his right hand was missing – 'a witness to the close interest he takes in machinery'![284]

Letters of congratulations flooded in. They came from such diverse sources as the Presidents of US railroads and humble employees from the C&W works in Derby: one from 'a shareholder in the LMS', commented: 'If I may say so, this is a round peg in a round hole, so different from the usual selection'.[285] J.H. Follows, whose resignation had opened the way for Lemon's appointment as Vice-President, travelled especially down from Derby to 'shake him by the hand' and offer his congratulations in person. On arrival at Euston, he discovered that Lemon 'had already fled' and so could only leave a note to be forwarded to him which ends 'How proud Bob [Reid] would have been with your selection'. It is a curiously poignant letter and shows that, whatever were the circumstances surrounding his own resignation and Lemon's promotion to Vice-President, there was no ill-feeling between them. Lemon replied to all these letters, and his reply to Follows contains a surprise. It was naturally addressed to him at his home and, in a remarkable coincidence, one can see that Follows was living at 'Highfield', Burton Road, Derby – the house which Lemon owned before he became Vice-President, and which he sold to the LMS in 1932. Sadly, Follows died a few months later on 13 December 1938.

Another rather rueful letter came from R.E.L. Maunsell, who had retired as CME of the Southern Railway the previous year. He offers his congratulations, and says: 'I often wish I was back at work. The so-called "life of leisure" does not suit me'. Amongst all the congratulations, well-wishing and encouragement there were also words of caution from people who could foresee the pressures and enormity of the task ahead.

Lemon started work at the Air Ministry on 28 June 1938, and was welcomed to the meeting of the Air Council held that day.[286] The LMS Board ratified his secondment on 30 June, and appointed Ashton Davies as temporary Vice-President during his absence, which was initially for a minimum period of one year. Lemon's task was to complete the 12,000 aircraft required for Scheme 'L' by the scheduled completion date of March 1940. He may have known nothing about aeroplanes, but he understood full well the principles of production engineering – which are the same whatever the end product might be.

It is a curious coincidence that less than a week after Lemon started at the Air Ministry, the LNER broke the speed record of 114mph claimed by the LMS in such dubious circumstances a year earlier – and did it in emphatic style. It was on 3 July 1938 that *Mallard* achieved 126mph on the East Coast main line south of Grantham, a world record for a steam locomotive that stands to this day. Would the LMS have sought to improve on this, if Lemon had still been there?

**J.H. Follows,
former Vice-President LMS.**
Railway Gazette

Many of Lemon's earliest contributions to the Air Council meetings as DGP were, as one might expect, very much of the 'this is what we do at the LMS' variety. Thus we find that, on 5 July, he told the Council how the LMS had the assistance of a panel of scientists. Periodic meetings were held when the Heads of Departments put problems to them on which they required advice. He suggested that the Air Ministry might adopt a similar procedure. This was agreed, but Lemon did not delay and wait for such a committee to be formed: one week later he reported that he had asked Lord Stamp whether the Air Ministry might refer problems for advice to the LMS Committee. Stamp had readily agreed, and one problem had already been referred.

Similarly, when the Council discussed air-raid protection, which it found a big problem, Lemon advised them that the LMS had some 10 or 20 people, under a naval officer, employed solely on this work. A full scheme had been worked out, booklets prepared showing what every man would be required to do, and already some 20,000 men had been trained. Factories were not going to be camouflaged, he told them, but signal boxes and other vital buildings would be protected with sandbags. He arranged for Council members to have copies of the booklets. The Air Council seemed to be singularly unprepared for war.

These were only incidental matters, however, and Lemon was immediately entrusted with responsibility for major decisions. Thus we see that, in August 1938, additional expenditure at the Cardiff Bomb Factory was agreed 'subject to the approval of the details by the D.G.P.' An order for a further 300 de Havilland 'Moths' had the caveat 'provided the D.G.P. was satisfied with the Company's production proposals'.[287]

So what did Lemon find was the true position with regard to aircraft production when he arrived at the Ministry? The National Archives contain a document dated 18 June 1938 – 10 days before he actually started work – listing all the aircraft delivered and on order.[288] Although this list only identifies the various types of aircraft in each category with an 'x', someone – and this may have been Lemon himself – has added the actual numbers completed in pencil. What is immediately apparent is the great preponderance, of bombers: over 5,300 of different types had been ordered, of which a mere 611 had been delivered – leaving a balance of 4,717 still to be built. Less than half this number of fighters were on order, showing that attack, and not defence, had been the policy of the RAF up to this moment. The heavy bombers already delivered were made up of 77 Whitleys and 100 Harrows. Not a single squadron of Whitley bombers was fit for operations, however, as only one aircraft had gun turrets fitted![289] The other bombers were classified as 'medium bombers' and included 183 single-engine Battles, with a further 1,335 on order. With

hindsight, one can see how inadequate these planes turned out to be in the realities of war. The Battles were a complete failure and were annihilated during the defence of France. They were withdrawn from front-line service after a few months, and used for target-towing. The Harrow also proved unsatisfactory in service, and was downgraded for use as a minelayer. The only type that proved to be moderately successful in use was the Blenheim, of which 251 had so far been delivered. Meanwhile six other types of heavy bomber were on order, but none had yet been built. The existence of this bomber deterrent – complete or incomplete – had clearly not deflected Hitler from his purpose and, on the advice of Sir Thomas Inskip, Minister for Co-ordination of Defence, this was all to change. The priority now was the defence of the country and Kingsley Wood ordered that fighter aircraft should take precedence over all other orders.[290]

If one therefore looks at the figures for fighters, one can see that 200 Gloster Gladiators had been delivered, with a further 378 on order. The Gladiator was a biplane and already largely obsolete, although it was, by necessity, used in some theatres of war after 1939. Of the new generation of fighters, 44 Hurricanes had now been delivered, as a further 16 had been completed in June – a low figure for which a representative of Hawkers 'had no satisfactory explanation to offer'.[291] In fact, the factory had been on strike for the whole of May, and this figure represented two month's output. Freeman reported that the current output was about three aircraft a week – and the most they had ever produced in a month was twelve.[292] The Air Council Minutes also show that the prototype Hurricane was still undergoing trials, but these had been delayed for want of a thermostat. It is somewhat ingenuous, therefore, when we read in histories that 'the Hurricane entered service with the RAF in December 1937' and 'squadrons were rapidly equipped with Hurricanes'. This implies that the aircraft were rolling off the production line in large quantities whereas, in fact, they were still, in the summer of 1938, coming out in penny-numbers. At the existing rate of progress, the 900 still on order would not have been completed until October 1944!

List showing aircraft ordered, with the numbers actually delivered added in pencil, dated three days before Lemon's appointment as DGP. National Archives

Class	Type	Delivered	On Order
	Harrow	x 100	
	Whitley	x 77	271 x
	Wellington		564 x
H.B.	Hampden		380 x
	Halifax		100 x
	Hereford		150 x
	Manchester		200 x
	Short B.12/36		200 x
M.B.	Battle	x 143	1335 x
	Blenheim	x 251	1517 x
	Wellesley	x	
F	Gladiator	x 200	x 278
	Hurricane	x 44	x 980
	Spitfire		x 570
	Defiant		x 450
A.C.	Hector	x	
	Lysander	x 5	x 283
T.B.G.R.	Beaufort		x 350
	Botha		x 442
	Lockheed		x 200
F.B.	Sunderland	x 3	21 x
	Lerwick		21 x
B.T.	Bombay		x 50
Spotter	Swordfish		x 90
	Seafox	x 43	91 x
	Roc		136 x
	Skua		190 x
F.A.A.	Albacore		800 x
	Swordfish	x 404	44 x
	Fairey O.8/36		250 x
	Walrus	x 85	83 x

At the beginning of July 1938 there was still no sign of any Spitfires, although four had been promised for delivery during June. They did not arrive, and Lemon reported that the situation at Supermarines was 'pitiful'. When his inspection team visited the factory, they found the firm had started work on 78 fuselages, but only three sets of wings![293] A lack of jigs was cited as the reason, and workers on the fuselages were being laid off as a result. A week later, after his staff had held a conference with Supermarines and the sub-contractors, Lemon reported that 'he thought it would be possible to get the Spitfire into production. But it would be necessary for him to have a talk with the firm. They were trying to keep as much work in their own hands as possible and they would have to be told that the Air Ministry could not tolerate this.'[294] This is a surprisingly pessimistic assessment at such a late stage of the aircraft's development, and one wonders what might have happened if had *not* been possible to get the aircraft into mass-production.

Why had this situation come about? The problem was that the aircraft manufacturers were not that large in engineering terms and, crucially, wished to keep all aspects of production in their own hands. Hawkers, for instance, who built the Hurricanes, had only one erecting shed at Brooklands in Surrey, and could not expand there because of space restrictions. The Government had recognised these problems some years before, and embarked on a scheme to build 'shadow' factories. The Government financed these, and the original intention was only to build aircraft engines for the different manufacturers. Accordingly they were placed among the car manufacturers where there was already a workforce skilled in the construction of petrol engines. Thus we find Austin, Rootes and Nuffield factories being expanded for use in the 'shadow' scheme. In May 1938, Lord Nuffield had also pledged to build a completely new factory at Castle Bromwich in Birmingham expressly for this purpose. Some of these factories were just becoming available when Lemon was appointed – and the scheme was greatly expanded under his supervision during subsequent years, when the factories were used for the assembly of complete aircraft. Indeed, as time passed, more and more floor-space was needed for the programme and other factory sites were acquired. The disused LMS depot at Newton Heath, where Lemon had previously worked as Carriage & Wagon Superintendent, was just one of many factories and sites that were purchased, or requisitioned, by the Ministry for aircraft production.[295]

It had also been Government policy that aircraft orders should be spread equally around the various 'approved' firms, so as to keep them in full employment. This meant that fairly small numbers of a great variety of aircraft were on order and, in an earlier attempt to speed up the time it took for a totally new design of aircraft to come into service, the policy had also been adopted of placing orders with each manufacturer for a certain number of aircraft 'on spec'. The following recommendation was adopted in 1935: 'The only way of achieving acceleration of delivery is by some departure from the existing system, and by the immediate placing of production orders, before prototypes have been tested, for certain types of aircraft. This entails some risk of failure, but we are satisfied in the special circumstances, and recommend that this should be adopted'.[296]

Orders were therefore placed simply to meet the specifications drawn up by the RAF. Whilst this meant that the RAF could keep their options open, and select the best types for further development and orders, it did mean that a great deal of time, effort and money went into producing redundant aircraft which did not come up to the expected performance. In truth, and with hindsight, we can now see how many of the aircraft that Lemon and his team struggled so diligently to produce fell into this latter category, and proved hopelessly inadequate when war broke out. Examples of this have already been cited, but two further examples worth noting were the Botha bomber and the Lerwick flying-boat. Although the Botha bomber made its first flight on 28 December 1938, deliveries were not

predicted before March 1940. It then proved to be grossly underpowered, and only stayed in operation for a few months. The Lerwick meanwhile was undergoing prototype trials when Lemon started at the Air Ministry and was finally abandoned in August 1939 as a 'complete failure'. It would not take off except in the calmest of seas and after two and a half miles gathering speed![297]

To be fair to the manufacturers, the late 1930s were a period of rapid advances in the design of aircraft – and a design could become obsolete in a couple of years. Planes were becoming more complex as a result of new technology; speeds were increasing as engines became more powerful, and wooden construction was being superseded by the use of metal. All these changes brought their own associated problems which had to be solved. With limited resources and public distaste for rearmament, the manufacturers had been struggling to keep up with all the latest developments in aircraft design – as is apparent from Attlee's list of 56 questions quoted earlier. Nevertheless, now that there was a crisis, instant results were expected; and so, optimistic predictions and glib promises were made, only to be scuppered by unforeseen snags – a situation we are familiar with to this day!

Lemon summed-up the existing situation in a letter he wrote in December 1939 to defend his reforms (see later):

You will recollect that when I came in I found that all the Air Ministry were working on were promises from the various aircraft firms, a large number of which, so far as I could see, were not based on any definite facts as regards man hours, floor space and materials required to produce the aircraft. I found the staff was much too small to carry out efficiently the task that had been set them. I therefore immediately started an analysis of what was required under the three headings of men, material and factories to carry out the programme.[298]

Vague promises and gentlemen's agreements were no longer good enough, and once again, as he had always done on the LMS, Lemon set to work to collect precise figures: to establish exactly how long it took to construct an aircraft, and then – for the first time – to make accurate predictions

Diagram showing the actual deliveries of aircraft in the two years before Lemon's appointment as DGP, with an (optimistic) assessment of the increase necessary to complete the programme on time. National Archives

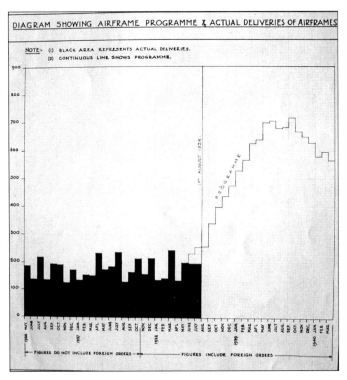

on the delivery schedule that could be realistically achieved. To help him with this analysis, he brought in Lewis Ord, who he had employed in a similar capacity on the LMS some years before. Ord had sent a letter of congratulations to Lemon on 28 June 1938, after hearing about his appointment 'on the wireless' in which he wrote: 'It is the most important and the most difficult job in the country today, and they have selected the best man for the job'. Little did he realise that he would soon be called upon to play a part in this work.

Ord later described the work that he had carried out, in letters to the Ministry's official historian.[299] He stated that 'I joined the Air Ministry at the request of and, as he put it, as a favour to Mr E.J.H. Lemon, as he then was. I agreed to accept a rate which was one-third of what I had been paid on a consulting appointment for him a few years earlier but I stipulated that the period was to be limited to six months. I made it a condition that I should act as a consultant or advisor and that I should not take an executive appointment.'

Ord was under pressure to produce a preliminary assessment as quickly as possible, and his investigations were not as thorough and exhaustive as he would have liked. In his letters he describes how he was restricted by the limited information that was available and the small number of men who could be released to work on the project. Nevertheless, an initial analysis of such basic statistics as floor area, man-hours and raw material requirements for the programme was rapidly produced. Lemon incorporated these, together with recommendations for the way to proceed, in a memo which he presented to the Air Council on 5 September 1938.[300] The copy of this report is subtitled 'Memorandum by D.G.P.' and, on the copy in the National Archives, someone has helpfully added in pencil 'Director-General of Personnel'. How quickly a man's work and status is cast into oblivion!

The recommendations that Lemon made will be considered in detail later, but the progress chart *(above)* illustrates the situation that existed on Lemon's arrival, and graphically shows that the current level of output was totally inadequate to complete Scheme 'L' by the Spring of 1940, as required.

Before the desired reforms could be set in motion, an organisational structure for Lemon's Directorate had to be established, and this was officially adopted on 19 October 1938. He had a single Deputy, under whom were Directors of

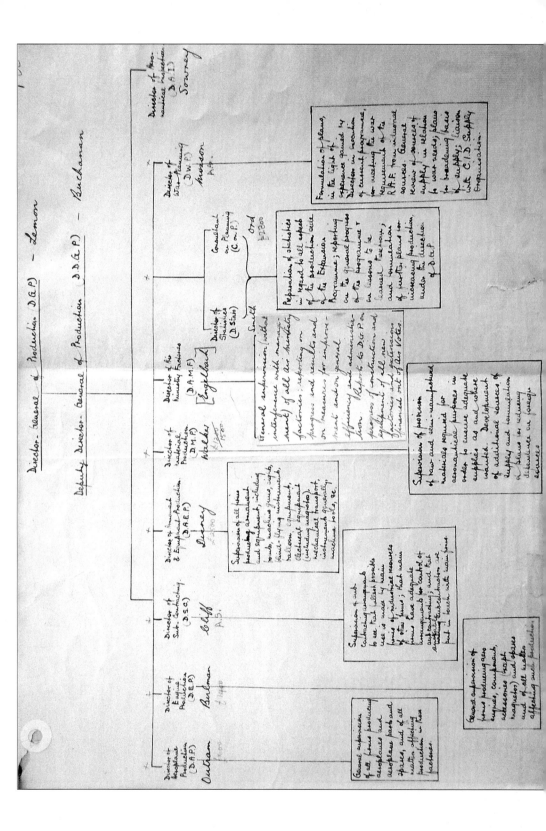

different departments, each responsible for a particular section of the programme.[301] There were departments dealing with airframes, engines, armament & equipment and materials, with further departments dealing with sub-contracting, Air Ministry factories, war-planning and aeronautical inspection. In fact, under the previous system there had already been an officer with the title of Director of Production but, as Henry Self later wrote: 'the production staff was small in number and not of outstanding status'.[302] The position did not hold the status that was now accorded to Lemon, and the incumbent, H.A.P. Disney, was moved to become Director of Aircraft Equipment Production. This does not appear to have caused any resentment or rancour. Disney later wrote to Lemon: 'I am in a better position than anyone else in the Air Ministry to realise what your difficulties were and what a gigantic task with which you were confronted and exactly what you achieved. I learnt a hell of a lot in the 2½ years I was on my own and it was all unreservedly at your disposal'.[303]

With one exception, the Directors were all civilians, although the RAF Lists show that they were, in the custom of the day, still using the military titles they acquired during the First World War. (Lemon could legitimately have called himself Lt-Col. – his rank in the Railway Staff Corps – but didn't). The only RAF officer was the Director of Aeronautical Inspection, Group-Captain J. Sowrey, and he had been brought back from retirement. Inspection had come in for some particularly ribald criticism in the House of Commons debates, when Hugh Dalton claimed that 'many of the Inspectors sent by the Air Ministry were inefficient, and sometimes manufacturers had to tell them what to inspect'.

The establishment of Lemon's Directorate was an opportunity to establish a totally new system of organising and controlling production for the RAF. Professor M.M. Postan, in his book *British War Production*, acknowledges the inadequacies

Organisation of Lemon's Directorate, with duties of subordinate Directors, names and proposed salaries.
National Archives

of the previous regime thus: Lemon and his assistants 'took charge of "planning", or of what stood for planning, in the Air Ministry'.[304]

No official record of Lemon's 'job description' has been found in the relevant files. Bruce-Gardner set out his original proposals in a letter to Kingsley Wood dated 13 June 1938, and these were accepted by the panel of industrial advisers at their second meeting on 14 June 1938 when they agreed that they should appoint a qualified engineer with the following terms of reference:

1. General planning of supplies;
2. Preparation of war-time supply organisation;
3. Supervision of the progress of production;
4. General co-ordination of the requirements of the manufacturing industry;
5. General facilitation of production so far as the Ministry is concerned.

His primary task would be to ensure that everything was being done within the Air Ministry and without to facilitate the achievement of approved programmes of supply. For this purpose he would become a member of the Supply Committee and would be assisted by Air Progress Overseers at the factories and specialised officers in the Ministry. He would also have the task of planning ahead the necessary capacity for further peace-time or war expansions and of securing suitable distribution of orders to the industry having regard to capacity, industrial conditions and readiness for emergency. The supervision of 'shadow' factory arrangements would also fall to him.

Lemon quoted these duties verbatim in the Appendix to a letter of April 1940, when he was in dispute with Sir Samuel Hoare over the erosion of his duties.[305] This job description was clearly drawn up in haste, and the speed – or lack of caution – led to one important factor being unclear. It had been announced in Parliament that Sir Wilfrid Freeman, now designated Air Member for Development and Production (AMDP), had been given the added responsibility for production, and would have the *assistance* of a DGP. Lemon was therefore clearly answerable and subordinate to him – Freeman promptly gave him the nickname of his 'Lemonade'. But it had not been clearly defined as to when the ultimate responsibility for decisions rested with Lemon, and when with Freeman. Freeman's name (and superiority) does not appear, for example, on the official chart showing the organisation of Lemon's new Directorate. This may seem a pernickety point to make, but it did eventually lead to friction between the two men, when Lemon accused Freeman of taking decisions on production without his knowledge.

As we have seen, Lemon immediately became a member of the Air Council, and started to attend the weekly meetings. He also became a member of the Air Council Committee on Supply which had been formed a couple of months earlier, on 30 April.[306] This met twice a week and included the Director of Contracts, Henry Self, and officials from the Treasury. At its meetings, manufacturers were called to attend and grilled on the current state of progress of their orders. He also attended meetings of Kingsley Wood's panel of industrial advisers. This all rather flies in the face of the suggestion expressed before Lemon's appointment that it might be wise 'to relieve him of all Committee work so as to leave him free to visit factories and investigate difficulties on the spot'.[307]

If one now considers Lemon's first report of September 1938 in more detail, it can be seen that he calculated that, if the programme was to meet its target of completion by Spring 1940, the labour force would need to treble in size from 60,000 to 180,000 within four months – an increase of 50% per month. This was manifestly impossible: the current rate of increase was running at 4–5% per month. The only solution was to intensify sub-contracting, and he calculated that 35% of the total man-hours required in the airframe construction needed to be sub-contracted. Sub-contracting had been suggested many times before, and Lemon acknowledged that most firms were already sub-contracting to some extent, but this brings us, once again, to the problem for a biographer of where the credit for a new initiative truly lies. It is the problem that has already been discussed in this book over the attribution of the reforms carried out in the Carriage and Wagon Depart-

ment at Derby. Here the problem is over the importance of Lemon, or his superior, Sir Wilfrid Freeman, to the complete change of emphasis in the air expansion programme that now took place. Anthony Furse, who has written a biography of Freeman, pointed out in correspondence that Freeman proposed the creation of 'a new satellite sub-contracting organisation on 3rd December 1937' – over six months before Lemon's appointment. This is undoubtedly true. The point is that this proposal had remained just that: a proposal. The time for tentative suggestions was over. Lemon's investigations had clearly shown that there was no possibility that the workforce could be expanded fast enough to achieve the intended target. Sub-contracting was the only solution, and he was prepared to push this policy forward ruthlessly. Sir Henry Self's obituary tribute to Lemon's work at the Air Ministry, published in *The Times*, singled this out as one of four major reforms that he instituted:

he broke down the natural hostility of the aircraft industry to large-scale sub-contracting of component parts of aircraft. This was an essential first step to the development of production on a widespread scale, and it was Lemon who laid the foundations on which the large structure of aircraft production was built during the war with the main firms employing tiers of sub-contractors and sub-sub-contractors in a comprehensive flow through to the central assembly sheds.[308]

As has been mentioned several times already in this book, it was one of Lemon's enduring dictums that work should always be taken to the labour, instead of endeavouring to draw labour to the work. In this case, labour was not available within the aircraft industry, so the work had to be taken elsewhere. Naturally, this policy received the backing of Freeman but, as Freeman later acknowledged, he had no experience of production engineering at the time and 'learnt everything he knew from Lemon' (see Chapter 11). It was Lemon's knowledge, experience and hard work that brought the policy to fruition, as Self indicated in his obituary.

Ord's views on subcontracting, however, were not what one might expect. He wrote that subcontracting, however carefully it was done, would raise manufacturing costs. The dispersal of construction to different sites, the building of piecemeal extensions to factories and other moves, would all handicap efficiency and costs.[309] This was also the view of the manufacturers. The Chairman of Supermarines, defending the slow progress of the Spitfires, wrote about their experiences.[310] The Spitfire, of course, was one of the first generation of fighter planes to be constructed totally of metal rather than wood. Sub-contractors who were accustomed to wooden construction, he wrote, had been the cause of great delay owing to their inexperience and a lack of people to train their labour force. Other firms, he continued, which were accustomed to deal with heavy pressings for the motor trade, had found the techniques needed for light alloys so different that the results were still not satisfactory, and correcting these pressings by hand had wasted much time. Overall, he concluded, the dispersal of work to so many places in the country, and to people unaccustomed to it, was the major cause of delay.

Ord then started to look into further aspects of British manufacturing practices – in particular, why did British firms need more than twice as many non-productive staff as American? Why was the amount of paperwork three or four times as great? Why did an American plane take half the number of man-hours to produce? Ord did not conclude his investigations, but they were a consideration that Lemon later addressed in the work he did for the Ministry of Production during 1942. In the Autumn of 1938, they were of lesser importance, and he overruled Ord's caveats – it was too late for them. He had decided the only way to achieve a rapid increase in the output of planes was by subcontracting, and he vigorously promoted the policy. Output was the prime goal, and the consideration of cost and efficiency could come later. As Postan and others have written, the Government had already freed the Air Ministry from purely budgetary limitations.[311]

Lewis Ord, at his own request, was only engaged as a planning consultant for six months. Lemon pressed him to take a permanent post as Director of Statistics and Planning, but he declined in order to take up an appointment in Canada. Ord maintained, in his letters to Postan, that there were men in the Department, who he had trained, that he felt could continue the work he had started. Lemon refused to consider this suggestion and, instead, brought in T.S. Smith of the Bedaux organisation. One can see that Ord did not approve of T.S. Smith's methods. He wrote:

When I was handling planning Mr. Lemon trusted me entirely but did not bother to investigate in detail the methods I had used. When the new man arrived Mr. Lemon was probably unaware that his methods were very different and in many important particulars were exactly opposite to the methods I had used ... The new man, sitting in his office using his slide rule, planned aircraft output without having seen the inside of an aircraft factory and apparently without wishing to do so.

Professional rivalries and jealousy of another man's way of working are not unexpected. The manufacturers were reluctant to co-operate in sub-contracting, but their concerns did not invalidate the policy. There was no need, for example, to build the fuselage in the same place as the wings. All that was needed was to fit these sub-assemblies together at a later stage along with a host of other components. The very fact that aircraft require so many specialised parts makes them ideal subjects for this technique and, of course, it is now normal practice. But this seems to have been beyond the comprehension of most people at the time. The Prime Minister had been dismissive of the calls for the use of assembly-line techniques in the Parliamentary debates. Although this was successfully used by the motor industry, he declared that a car engine only contained about 1,700 components, whereas an aircraft engine contained 11,000. There were then upwards of 70,000 components in the rest of the aircraft. With this massive total to incorporate, in his view, there was no real hope of ever achieving mass production.[312] In this statement, Chamberlain was reiterating the principle rigidly enforced by Viscount Weir 'that modern aircraft were so complex that it would be impossible to sub-contract production'.[313]

Nevertheless, this was the challenge that Lemon and his team were now prepared to face. On his own initiative Lemon reviewed output with complete disregard to Lord Weir's principles. He and his team had to persuade, cajole and bully the manufacturers, because, as Kingsley Wood pointed out, they had no legal power to demand such changes on existing contracts.[314] However, as the firms were dependent on the Air Ministry for future orders, considerable pressure could be brought to bear.

The uncertainty about orders was a cause for concern to the aircraft manufacturers. They were reluctant to make sweeping changes to their methods just to save a temporary crisis. If they invested a great deal of time and effort to expedite the current orders, they might then find themselves with an over-capacity if no further orders were forth-coming – and they would promptly have to downsize again. In the autumn of 1938, it was by no means certain that war was inevitable. These considerations must have been in Lord Rootes' mind when, in October 1938, he is reported as strongly resenting the criticism levelled by the Air Ministry at the results from his 'shadow' factory. He demanded an order for a further 200–300 Blenheims, and Lemon bluntly told him that 'in view of the fact he had only built one Blenheim so far – and that with the help of parts from Bristol's, he was not prepared to recommend an additional order at this time'.[315] This brusque response does not appear to have antagonised or alienated Lord Rootes in any way, as later letters in Lemon's personal papers demonstrate. In fact, Lemon's proposals did not apportion blame for any shortcomings, but were purely intended to make the manufacturers' task easier and actively help them to achieve their targets.

The overall picture nationwide, therefore, was that the aircraft industry would be unable to meet the targets unless drastic action was taken. However, this did not necessarily mean that all constructors faced the same predicament and Lemon, in his first report, then analysed the situation in each of the individual manufacturers. He placed them into three categories. Category A was made up of those firms who could be reasonably relied upon to complete their pro-

grammes by March 1940. Category B contained those firms who could not complete their programmes on their present basis of working, but who could do so if the necessary steps were taken; while Category C contained those firms who could not possibly meet the 1940 target deadline. Half the firms in this last category were new to this type of work, and included several of the 'shadow' factories. For the firms in the last two categories, Lemon made specific recommendations on the actions that should be taken. This involved removing orders, and rescheduling them to firms in Category A. For example, in the case of Armstrong-Whitworth, which he placed in Category B, Lemon wrote:

I regard the present situation of Armstrong-Whitworth as being perhaps one of the worst in the whole industry. Yet it ought to be one of the best since it is in a particularly good labour area and has all the necessary buildings and equipment. The firm are engaged on the production of Whitley aircraft and then they are due to execute a small order for 64 Wellingtons towards the end of the programme. I think that subject to adequate revision of plans and intensification of sub-contracting, which I regard as essential, this firm should have no difficulty in completing the bulk of their programme in time. I think that the most serious difficulty will centre round the Wellington and I suggest that it is for consideration whether the firm could not more profitably be allowed to carry on with Whitley production rather than to endeavour to turn to a new type of which they have had no experience and for which it has not been possible for them to do very much planning up to date.[316]

Similar recommendations were made for all the other firms in Categories B & C and these were discussed at length at the Air Council meeting on 7 September.[317] Many small improvements to the flow of production were made by moving orders, or parts of orders, from one manufacturer to another. There was an immediate improvement on the output figures from September 1938 onwards, but it would be wrong to attribute these solely to Lemon's recommendations. Much of this improvement could be attributed to actions taken before his appointment, and Lemon warned the Air Council that it would take time – up to 18 months – before any of his radical changes would bear fruit. There was no 'quick fix'.

One problem the manufacturers continually faced was a shortage of raw materials. Lemon soon established that, because supplies were limited, the practice had grown up that firms who were first in the field with their orders obtained more than they needed, and then hoarded the surplus so that other manufacturers went short. One firm, he discovered, had been waiting over two years for certain material. He proposed that some order of priority for raw materials would have to be laid down. At the time, of course, the country was not officially on a war-footing, and the economy was not geared solely to war production. The aircraft manufacturers had to compete for raw materials with other industrial firms, and it was pointed out to Lemon that the Air Ministry could not intervene in the allocation of raw materials between the aircraft industry and others.[318] This is in marked contrast to the situation once war had broken out when Lord Beaverbrook, for example, could appeal for pots and pans to be handed in for the war effort. In fact, up to this time, the country had been importing aluminium from Germany, but the Germans stopped this source of supply in September 1938. Supplies were then sought from America.[319]

One of the other perennial complaints voiced by the manufacturers was over the number of technical modifications that the Air Ministry kept demanding. This problem was never totally resolved, and constantly disrupted production throughout the War. Analysis carried out after the end of the War showed that these on-going changes meant that the savings in time, labour and costs that could be achieved by true mass-production methods were never actually achieved in practice.[320] The American solution was to carry out all the preliminary work for a modification and then keep it to one side until a whole bundle could be introduced simultaneously. This meant that the flow of production was not being constantly interrupted, but it did mean that necessary improvements were sidelined while

inferior quality aircraft continued to be produced. British practice, however, was to carry out continual improvements to existing aircraft. This did mean that each aircraft was developed to its maximum potential, and the Spitfire that existed at the end of the War had a performance and capability that was vastly superior to the first version. Although such a policy may have constantly interrupted the flow of production, it did eliminate the major delays that always accompanied the introduction of a totally new design.

However, when a firm *was* building a totally new and original design, it was only to be expected that unforeseen problems would occur. As we have seen, there were problems with the construction of wings for the Spitfire. In his preliminary report Lemon wrote:

I propose to press them [Supermarines] to complete the fuselages even to the installation of the engines in the greatest possible numbers and to store them at Eastleigh until the wings become available. Moreover, I would propose that there should be a few sets of standard wings with which the fuselages can be tried in flight to make sure that those fuselages are in every respect satisfactory and ready for the production wings which I feel sure will flow in adequate quantities a little later in the programme.[321]

The first four Spitfires were eventually delivered on 26 July 1938.[322] Once again, many sources imply that squadrons were rapidly equipped with the aircraft, and chose to ignore the continuing problems.[323] Firstly the undercarriage proved to be under strength and collapsed, then tests on the prototype found that the guns would not operate at high-altitude. Modifications were necessary which again delayed production. At the end of September 1938, Lemon reported that 'he had received so many conflicting statements about the Spitfire situation that he had sent for representatives of all the firms associated in the manufacture, and he intended to find out, round the conference table, precisely what the difficulties were and what action was necessary to overcome them'.[324] It appeared that delays in the construction of wings were caused by a sub-contractor, who was making the ribs and had only one set of tools. To make matters worse, following the modification to sort out the problem with the guns, these tools now needed to be altered. Lemon urged that production should proceed without the modification but other voices pointed out that 'if the guns would not fire at heights at which Spitfires were likely to encounter enemy bombers, the Spitfire would be useless as a fighting aircraft'. Freeman agreed that there was no alternative but to insist on the modification. This difference of opinion neatly demonstrates the different priorities of the customer (i.e. the RAF) and the production engineer (Lemon). To Lemon, the most important factor was quantity and speed. To the RAF, fitness of purpose was of equal importance.

These latest problems coincided with the Munich crisis – on 29 September the Sudetenland was ceded to Hitler which gave a further sense of urgency to the programme. One example of the emergency measures then taken was that all completed Spitfire fuselages (without wings!) were scattered to different factories around the country, so that they would still be available if war broke out and the Supermarine factory was destroyed.[325] Freeman then wrote to Warren Fisher at the Treasury on 30 September saying, 'As you know we have been let down over and over again on the matter of the production of the Spitfire which is not technically clear even yet. The only alternative we have of a modern fighter is the Hurricane. This machine is technically clear, the very best machine we have at the present time and available to go into production forthwith at another works'. He asked Warren Fisher to authorise the purchase of a further 1,000 Hurricanes from the Gloster works.[326] A month later, the Spitfire situation had not altered radically, and Supermarines' response to the Air Ministry's continuing pressure was to issue a bland Memo: 'Our programme of deliveries will be communicated to the Department as soon as a reliable estimate of expected deliveries has been received from our sub-contractors'. Lemon reported that, as soon as wings became available, a large number of Spitfires *would* be delivered, but he did not know what answer the Minister could give if he were again criticised about the output in Parliament. The Meeting accepted that

there was no point in trying to conceal the situation.[327]

It has since been argued that the delays in the production of Spitfires were actually a blessing in disguise. It meant that the country had a 'secret weapon' up its sleeve when war broke out. If the aircraft had entered service earlier, it is suggested, it would have been evaluated by the Germans who might even have been able to purchase one and copy its design. This seems to be a dubious argument. It is often forgotten that the bulk of the defence of this country in the Battle of Britain was carried out by Hurricanes, which greatly outnumbered the Spitfires. The Hurricane was certainly known to the Germans, and some had even been sold to foreign countries, but this did not prevent them being effective in battle. The Germans did also capture at least one Spitfire during the fall of France, and had plenty of time to evaluate it. However, this did not compromise its effectiveness as the War progressed. Delaying their production was certainly not a tactic that ever crossed anyone's mind at the Air Ministry!

The bound volumes containing the Minutes of the weekly meetings of the Air Council do not give the production figures for individual types of aircraft. It was probably an advantage to be suitably vague in this way, as the numbers could include, for example, aircraft which were ordered for other purposes, such as training and communication. The production figures for individual types of aircraft appear in a separate file containing the weekly Reports submitted to the Air Council.[328] One can therefore see that in the first week that Lemon was at the Air Ministry (the week ending 2 July 1938) 41 aircraft were completed – none of them Spitfires: two were Hurricanes, and fifteen were bombers – eight Blenheims and seven Battles. The other completed aircraft were a motley collection; some were destined for the Fleet Air Arm and the Army, others were for training or reconnaissance, whilst three were flying boats.

By 1 November 1938, however, 180 Spitfire *fuselages* had been completed – and 21 of them had wings! Or as the Minutes recorded: 'the 21st Spitfire had flown'.[329] By the end of the month, 29 Spitfires had been completed, and 167 Hurricanes. This was nine months before Britain

Early Spitfire production showing the methods used before Lemon's reforms (photo taken 23 January 1939).
Flight magazine 9 February 1941

declared war. However, this did not mean that all these aircraft were available for immediate service – as has already been stated, the Spitfire's guns were a problem at this time; and a few months later, in March 1939, it was reported that of 252 Hurricanes then delivered, 64 were grounded – 40 for lack of propellers, and 24 for other reasons.[330] There were also continuing concerns on the limitations of the fabric-covered wings fitted to these planes. The early Hurricanes were totally fabric-covered, and it is a moot point whether they were fit for the type of service that would be required in WW2. The Air Council meeting on 1 November 1938 also minuted that 'Hawkers had again broken their promise to fit Hurricanes with metal-covered wings', citing, as the reason, difficulties in obtaining 'Alclad'. The meeting resolved that this situation could not continue indefinitely because 'Hurricanes with

fabric-covered wings were subject to flying restrictions on diving. In wartime, pilots of Hurricanes would be compelled to put their machines into dives, and with fabric-covered wings this would certainly result in accidents'. This is a truly astonishing statement, especially with its use of the euphemism 'accidents'. One can only wonder at the *naïveté* of the Air Council – and the manufacturer – that the original specification of this fighter did not actually require that it could dive in operation! What sort of aerial warfare did they think the planes would be involved in? Did they imagine that pilots would be able to fight with a rule-book in one hand?

If so, the reality of the dog-fights that took place over England must have come as a rude shock.

Lemon had not totally abandoned his work for the LMS, and on 12 October 1938 was called on to react to a wildcat strike at Euston when other members of the Executive were unavailable. He addressed a mass meeting of strikers at Camden Town and the *Daily Express* reported that 'Mr Lemon, trying to make himself heard, pleaded that members of the Executive were spread over three counties, that they had met for the first time at 6.30pm, and that it would be inadvisable to take further action until the company had replied to their letter. He was howled down'.

In November 1938, the LMS ran into an unexpected problem when Ashton Davies went down with typhoid fever. Lemon immediately wrote to Stamp: 'In view of A.D.'s serious illness I am writing to tell you that I am prepared to come back if you so desire, as I feel that my first duty is to you and the Board of the LMS. My work here is by no means complete, but you will be in a better position to say where my services will be of most use'. Stamp replied: 'Badly as we want you, in view of all that has been said to me by the Minister and others of the golden things about your work and its urgent necessity, I do not feel I can press our claims at present'.[331]

Throughout this chapter, first consideration has, so far, been given to describing the progress of the fighter programme, whose importance was so crucial to the immediate defence of the country, and to which priority was being given. However, the bomber programme obviously still continued and the medium bombers that were built at this time, such as the Wellington, and Hampden, were the first backbone of the RAF's attack force and served the country well. The heavy bombers that eventually became the mainstay of Bomber Command later in the war had not even got off the drawing-board at this time. These were aircraft of great complexity and the manufacturers had questioned the need for them, pointing out that Germany was relying solely on medium bombers.[332] On 19 July – at one of the earliest meetings of the Air Council that Lemon attended – he drew attention to the lack of design capacity in many firms, which was delaying progress on these planes. He told the meeting that he had already arranged for Hawker's to transfer men to work on the Manchester heavy bomber being designed by A.V. Roe. He also suggested that Metropolitan-Vickers (Metro-Vick) should be given parts of the Manchester and asked how the design could be improved from the point of view of production. Metro-Vick had a large staff engaged in a variety of undertakings, and Lemon felt they would bring a fresh approach to problems.

These were the first steps towards a greater co-operation between the aircraft manufacturers. These ideas were developed into a scheme, presented to the Air Council on 6 December 1938, for accelerating the production of all new types of aircraft, but in particular the heavy bombers such as the Manchester, Halifax and Stirling.[333] The idea of the Group scheme was (cunningly?) introduced as a subsidiary element of a decision to reduce the number of aircraft in service – thereby reducing the costs and complexity of equipment needed for maintenance. The preamble to this change of policy stated it was hoped to organise the aircraft industry, at the same time, on a basis to provide as rapid production as possible. The proposed solution was to arrange the aircraft manufacturers into Groups, each working on a specific small number of individual types, and each under the overall control of a Group Committee. These Committees, which would be chaired by Lemon in order to maintain impartiality, would advise on the distribution of orders within the Group, particularly with regard to the use of sub-contractors. The Committee would ensure that sub-contracting work was spread around evenly, so that any one firm was not overloaded with orders. In this way, it was predicted that the resources of the companies would be better used, and result in the development of new types with the maximum speed. The scheme was a logical attempt to eliminate many of the reasons for delays that Lemon had identified in his September analysis. Grouping manufacturers together in this way would, it was hoped, reduce bottlenecks in the production of technical drawings, caused by the relatively small number of drawing-office staff an individual company could afford to employ. However, it did mean that one company would

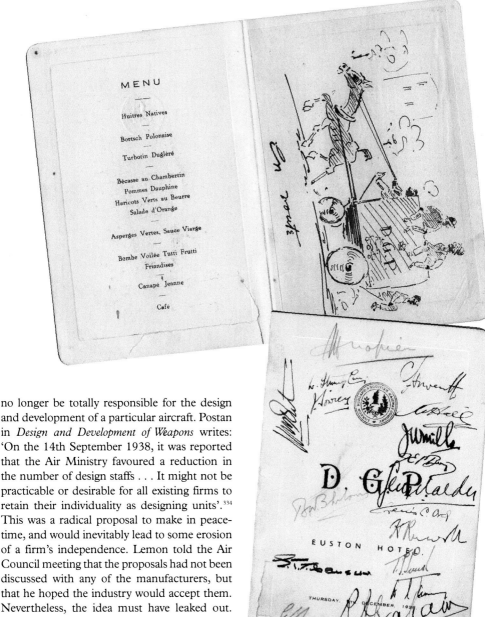

no longer be totally responsible for the design and development of a particular aircraft. Postan in *Design and Development of Weapons* writes: 'On the 14th September 1938, it was reported that the Air Ministry favoured a reduction in the number of design staffs . . . It might not be practicable or desirable for all existing firms to retain their individuality as designing units'.[334] This was a radical proposal to make in peacetime, and would inevitably lead to some erosion of a firm's independence. Lemon told the Air Council meeting that the proposals had not been discussed with any of the manufacturers, but that he hoped the industry would accept them. Nevertheless, the idea must have leaked out. The minutes record how it was known that 'Mr Handley Page and his firm would not cooperate in the production of aircraft by other firms except under duress'.[335] It was not going to be easy to get the manufacturers to accept the proposals. Bruce-Gardner, Chairman of the Society of British Aircraft Constructors, had been present at the meeting when the idea was mooted and was sympathetic, although there had been a difference of opinion about the level of

Menu for the lavish dinner at the Euston Hotel hosted by Lemon in December 1938, attended, and signed, by members of his Directorate at the Air Ministry.
The artist of the sketch is not known.
Lemon's personal papers

control that the Air Ministry would exercise. On 7 January 1939, the Panel of Industrial Advisers were informed that the Air Council had intimated to the various firms that they wished to enter into consultations with them and decide how to proceed in the matter. The first meeting of the 'Manchester' Group was held that month, chaired by Lemon, and it is probably no coincidence that, when the inadequacies of the two-engined Manchester bomber became apparent, it was possible to develop it rapidly into the most well-known bomber of the war – the four-engined Lancaster.[336]

The bottle-neck in the production of airframes was only the first of the problems which Lemon and his team had to address – the airframe itself was only the basic constituent of a fully-equipped fighting aircraft. He listed a selection of some of the other, more abstruse, problems he had dealt with when he was in dispute over the erosion of his duties in 1940 (see later), but the following examples, from the Autumn of 1938 illustrate the point. At the sixth meeting of the panel of Industrial Advisers on 21 November 1938, it was reported that no firm in this country had a large enough capacity to make optical instruments in the quantities now required.[337] Past orders for such specialist equipment had not been large enough to be commercially attractive to firms; and development, which was also very costly, had therefore been undertaken at the Royal Aircraft Establishment at Farnborough. The only way these instruments could now be obtained in large numbers would be to expand, at Government expense, the works of some existing instrument firms. This type of problem existed across a wide spectrum of precision instruments, and it was not only quantities that caused a problem. It was also quality. Only one specialist manufacturer was capable of producing cameras of the required standard for aircraft use, but it was unable to cope with any increase in orders. Lemon instigated an investigation into the production of high-quality optical instruments, and turned to Sir Harold Hartley with his knowledge of academia for suggestions of suitable Oxbridge men who could help.[338] One hopes that his altercation with Sir Thomas Merton earlier in the year did not complicate the situation. Merton had invented a cheap rangefinder that was already used by the RAF – it cost less than a shilling to make – and he would surely have been just the man to help Lemon with this problem.

Another subject that seemed to cause an inordinate problem was the quality, and quantity, of aviation fuel that would be needed in war-time. Hartley, as previously mentioned, was Chairman of a Committee investigating this, and there were discussions amongst the civil servants at the Air Council meetings as to how many storage units would be needed, and how they were to find the labour to build them, and whether this should be 100-octane fuel or a lesser quality and so on. One senses Lemon's growing exasperation at the problems, real or imagined, that dogged all these decisions, and the Minutes of the meeting on 24 January 1939 record him bluntly remarking that welding was not an unusual skill, and the railway and shipping companies could probably supply men to build the tanks if there was a problem.[339]

As the size of the building programme grew, even Lemon became slightly alarmed and reported that he was concerned at the size of future orders that would be necessary to keep this production machine operating. The national workforce involved in aircraft manufacture was increasing at 4,000 a month, and Lemon thought they might have to continue with obsolete designs merely to keep them occupied. There was also a new problem: there were now not enough ferry pilots to fly the completed aircraft away from the manufacturers. Nevertheless, he was able to report, on 31 January 1939, that the tools for the production of Spitfire wings were now ready. The wings would be available soon after production started and could be fitted to the 98 fuselages awaiting completion at Castle Bromwich 'in due course'. However, no-one knew when the new factory would actually start production in its own right. As it turned out, they had good reason to be apprehensive. Six months later, on 14 July 1939, the situation there had not progressed much further. On that date Lemon could only report to the Air Council that he had examined the scheme for the new factory at Castle Bromwich, and was satisfied that it was efficient and economical for the production required . This seems to indicate that the factory had not yet even reached the building stage! Full production finally got under way there in early Summer 1940 – by which time the war had been raging for nine months, and Lemon had left the Ministry.

The Court Circular for 15 February 1939 reported that 'Mr. E.J.H. Lemon (Director-General of Production, Air Council) had the honour of being received by His Majesty'. He was not accompanied by Sir Wilfrid Freeman, any other RAF officers or Government officials. The conversation was obviously private and confidential, and therefore no record of what was discussed is known. One can only assume that the King wished to find out personally from Lemon the true and current situation with regard to the rearmament programme.[340]

A week later, on 22 February and on the recommendation of the Minister for Co-ordination of Defence, the Government formed another Supply Committee, No.VIa, specifically to deal with the ever-growing needs of the air expansion scheme.[341] As has been mentioned, the supply of raw materials was one of Lemon's major concerns. This proliferation of Committees, all with very similar names, can be most confusing and so it is probably wise to point out that this was not the same body as the Air Council Committee on Supply, which was referred to earlier. Supply Committee VIa was a subsidiary of the Supply Board, which was a forum where the needs of all the armed services could be discussed and priorities agreed on a national basis. It came under the aegis of the Ministry of Supply and its members were the Chairmen of all the subsidiary (numbered) Supply Committees, which each represented the interests of different sections of the armed forces, together with officials from the Treasury and Board of Trade. Lemon was appointed Chairman of this new Committee on 22 February 1939, and its terms of reference were to 'be responsible for initiating investigations and making recommendations to the Supply Board as to the plans necessary for meeting the requirements of Airframes and Aero-Engines for the fighting services in the event of war'. Several of Lemon's subordinate Directors, but not Sir Wilfrid Freeman, became members of this committee which also included officials from the War Office, Admiralty, Board of Trade and

Ministry of Labour. In view of his dismissive description of Lemon's career at the Air Ministry in his Memoirs (see later), it is worth noting that the name of G.P. Bulman, Lemon's Director of Aero-Engines, does not appear in the printed list of members, but was written in by hand later. As Chairman of this Committee, Lemon also became a full member of the Supply Board, with Freeman co-opted as an Associate Member.

All this work took its toll on Lemon's health, and on 6 March 1939, he was admitted to a Nursing Home in Devonshire Street to have his appendix removed. A week later he wrote to Stamp, breaking the news and telling him that the operation was completely successful and it was only a question of time before he was fitter than ever.[342] This was not quite the opinion of his doctor, however. He wrote a stern, somewhat flowery, letter to Lemon, which shows how well he understood the nature of his patient:

So glad you will be starting your convalescence proper at the end of this week. There are certain important aspects of your condition which you must have very much to the fore when the stern call of duty knocks on the door of your conscience.

Care must be taken not to allow duty to yourself to be over-ruled by what you consider duty to the nation or to other corporate body.

You have been an ill man for many months and have carried on your work, despite my severe objections – objections based on medical grounds alone.

A state of health undermined by a diseased appendix had not been able to withstand the strain put on it by additional responsibilities.

A successfully performed operation has removed the prime cause of your disability; a successful convalescence will restore you to better health than you have had for a long time.

We doctors have 'done our bit,' it is now up to you to do your bit. Boredom and irritability will be your constant companions for the next few weeks; incisive invectives will probably be hurled at my head for keeping you inactive,

yet inactive – mentally – you will have to
remain for the next six weeks.

If you will come to see me early in May
I will hope to allow you to resume your
responsibilities. Perhaps by that time you will
be so well trained that you will not kick unduly
if I have to impose certain restrictions on you,
even after you have once again 'shouldered
the load'. I will look forward to receiving good
reports from you.

As has already been explained, there had been
earlier indications that Lemon suffered from
periodic bouts of illness brought on by overwork,
and the necessity for this operation was
undoubtedly caused by the stresses to which he
subjected himself. He obviously felt that this
might be an opportune moment to return to the
LMS, and finished his letter to Stamp by saying
that he was looking forward to rejoining his
colleagues at Euston 'with increased energy and
good health'. Stamp wrote back: 'Now I am
rejoicing at your successful operation and steady
recovery. I hope that the enforced rest and quiet
will be good for your nerves too, so that when you
get back to things you will have your usual vim
and inspiration. I assure you we all <u>do</u> value the
great work you are doing for the nation and are
very proud of you. All the same <u>we</u> want you back
at Euston just as much as you want to come!'

It was not to be. On 21 March 1939, Stamp
wrote again to Lemon:

Kingsley Wood asked me to see him today
and you will probably not be surprised that he
pressed me to agree to your remaining until
the end of the year. He said he only did this
because of the new situation that had arisen
last week.

I explained to him that we were most anxious
to have you back as important work was
awaiting you, and that you were equally
anxious to get back, but I agreed that I could
not gainsay the urgency of his request, and
I would not stand in the way of your doing it
provided it was left to your free initiative,
and that I could not be represented as exerting
any kind of pressure upon you. Moreover,

I promised to assure you that through the
extended time you should not suffer at Euston
in any way whatever. This assurance, of course,
I unhesitatingly give you.

There is no question of your being forgotten,
or the waters passing over your place and
obliterating it; that would be impossible, for
you are much too valuable to us for that to
happen. At the same time, I do not want you
to feel that I have prejudiced your refusal by
anything I have said if you feel that you would
prefer to return.

The Minister promised he would facilitate
your training someone to take over your work,
and that he would take every step to make it
simple and natural for you to return to us at
the end of that extended time.

I am sorry to worry you while you are ill, but
I thought it best to let you know straightaway
the result of our talk.

It is interesting to note – in passing – that while
Lemon was away on sick-leave, a meeting of his
subordinate Directors minuted their prediction
that war would be declared before 1 October:
a pretty accurate assessment, as it turned out.[343]
At the beginning of April, Lemon dutifully started
his period of convalescence. Kingsley Wood
wrote to him:

I was very sorry indeed to hear what a bad time
you had been through. I am sure that you were
wise to take a good period of convalescence,
and we shall not expect you back until the
beginning of May. Naturally we miss you, but
I think that things are going very well now,
and you have probably heard the excellent
production figure which was reached in March.

Please do not worry about the future. There
is, I am sure, no urgency, and the great thing
is for you to get completely fit.

Lemon was nevertheless still undecided whether
to stay at the Air Ministry or return to the LMS
and mulled the matter over while convalescing.
By 9 May, however, he was back at the Air Ministry.
On that date, he officially applied to requisition
further factories for the programme. As Chairman

of Supply Committee No.VIa, he submitted the following memo to the Supply Board:

Consequent on the expansion of facilities for the production of airframes and the development of the sub-contracting scheme for the manufacture of airframe components, I am to request that the firms, establishments and works named in the attached list may be allocated to the Air Ministry, to the extent of the capacity indicated. The capacity specified has already been allocated to Supply Committee No.VIa for the product or work stated.[344]

The attached list extended to four pages, and included many of the smaller car and coach manufacturers – including Edinburgh Corporation Transport Department! The bulk of the list, however, was made up of railway workshops whose 100% capacity was required for airframe main assembly. They were: Swindon, Caerphilly and Coventry (GWR); Barassie, Crewe, Derby, Earlestown, St Rollox and Wolverton (LMS); York, Darlington, Shildon, Stratford, Cowlairs, Doncaster, Faverdale and Gorton (LNER); and Ashford, Eastleigh and Lancing (SR). This was the first indication of the great contribution made to the war in the air by the railway workshops.

It was not until a fortnight later, on 22 May, that Lemon officially wrote to Stamp from the Air Ministry to tell him of his decision:

I have delayed my reply to your letter of the 21st March, about the proposal that I should stay at the Air Ministry until the end of the year, because I wanted first to review the position in my Department and then to speak to the Secretary of State. I have now had an opportunity of doing this.

I understand that you leave the decision as to the date of my return to me and I must confess that it is a difficult decision to make. I am most anxious to get back to my own job and my personal choice would be an early return to Euston. On the other hand, we are now in process of launching a new programme of production under which each new type of aircraft will be produced by several firms. A number of committees have been appointed to deal with various aspects of this 'Group' scheme and it would not be easy for my successor to take over at the present stage. I doubt therefore whether it would be advisable for the Air Ministry to change horses in the early future. Six months hence, however, the Group scheme should be well under way and there should not be the same difficulty in making a change.

I have come to the conclusion that I ought to stay at the Air Ministry until the end of the year and I hope that you will feel that I am right in coming to this conclusion which has cost me a good deal of anxious thought. If there is no war, the work here should begin to ease off in the autumn and I should then propose to keep in touch with Euston as much as possible in order to be ready to start work there at the beginning of the New Year.

In June 1939, Lemon completed a year as Director-General, and prepared a report on the progress over the period.

NINE

The Air Ministry, War (1939–1940)

BEFORE Lemon's assessment of his first year in office was officially presented to the Air Council, a draft was circulated to colleagues for comments. Freeman felt the draft was unbalanced, and did not give sufficient credit to the efforts of Lemon's predecessors. Henry Self wrote that he was convinced Lemon would wish him to be a 'candid critic', and thought the draft, as it stood, gave undue weight to Lemon's reforms. 'At present', he wrote, 'it reads very much like propaganda as to the virtues of the Production Department'. The draft was re-written with an acknowledgment of the work started by Lemon's predecessors, and the revised Report was presented in July 1939.[345] It is a mass of detailed statistics from which certain salient facts emerge. The first is the number of sub-contractors now working on the air programme. Ignoring those involved in engine or equipment manufacture, there were over 1,200 working on air-frame production alone. The Directorate of Sub-Contracting had received applications from over 1,600 firms who wished to take part, and there was no indication of any future shortage of capacity. The statistics also clearly showed that it was much cheaper to utilise existing workshops than to build new factories. The cost of using the LMS workshops at Derby, for example, worked out at £0.18 per square foot, compared with £2.38 for Lord Rootes' shadow factory in Liverpool. Airframe production now outstripped the quantities of aero-engines being produced, although these had also increased three-fold in the previous year. Consequently, the whole engine position was under investigation, and the report makes clear that it was not just the number of engines being

produced that was critical. The new generation of heavy bombers needed four engines apiece and as these aircraft increased in size and carrying power, more and more powerful engines were needed in quantity. The situation at each of the engine manufacturers was considered in turn and in great detail. The report further emphasised that the trend towards heavier and more complex aircraft was leading to a situation in which the increase in man-hours required for construction was exceeding the increase of labour. Lemon warned that this could eventually result in a falling off in the numbers produced.

The report then considered the consequences of the current practice of placing quantity orders 'off the drawing board'. The disadvantages were described in the last chapter, and Lemon recommended reverting to the practice of ordering prototypes before quantity production was even considered. He also commented that, in the past, insufficient attention had been paid to the production aspects of a new design. It was obviously beneficial if construction was as simple as possible. Action had therefore been taken to ensure that all plans were carefully scrutinised with this consideration in mind. It was, for instance, unnecessary for one component to call for an extrusion of 1 inch diameter, while another specified a 1¼ inch diameter, if both could be accommodated with one size.

As one might expect, the supply of raw materials, and the tools and jigs to work them, were still an over-riding concern. The situation was so acute that Lemon recommended that non-standard alloy sheets and bars should be bought and used wherever they would serve.[346] However, it was not just the supplies of steel, aluminium and other metallic alloys that were an ever-present worry. There had been a bottleneck in the production of plywood – only one firm in this country was capable of cutting the raw timber into veneer. Three new factories were being developed, and veneer was being imported from Canada. There were similar descriptions of action taken with the supplies of such commodities as perspex, rubber, silk and flax. The overall responsibility for the allocation of raw materials lay with the Government's Supply Board, and Lemon wrote that requirements for a wide range of commodities had been considered at this level 'from pig iron to opium'. It is hard to imagine how any of the country's defence forces could have had a need for opium?

Other unexpected side-avenues show the wide remit of Lemon's responsibilities. The point has already been made that a fighting aircraft is more than an airframe with engines, and Lemon reported on the current position with the supply of bombs – there was, for example, a serious deficiency with the supply of 500lb bombs and questions over the design of the fuses. Similarly there was a shortage of quartz crystals which had hitherto only been required in small quantities. The cutting of these was a specialised trade, and sudden expansion presented difficulties. He also reported on the situation regarding the provision of barrage balloons. 1¼ million yards of fabric had been ordered, but the fabric had not come up to expectations. Lemon had a meeting with the spinners and weavers to explore all avenues for hastening production.[347] There was also a shortage of hydrogen cylinders to hold the gas that inflated them. All these problems were being dealt with. He also stressed that throughout all the intense industrial activity associated with the expansion programme, one aspect commanded precedence. Quality could not be subordinated to quantity. This had taxed the inspectors to the limit, but new training facilities had been opened and the number of new inspectors recruited and trained in the previous twelve months was over 1,000, compared with a figure of less than half this in the year before.

Although only 6,000 of the required total of 12,000 aircraft had been completed by June 1939, Lemon predicted that Scheme L, which had a completion target for the end of March 1940, would be brought in early. He concluded his Report by asking whether the programme should therefore be slowed down or continue at full blast. The decision was made to press on unabated and, of course, such considerations became superfluous the moment war was actually declared, and a massive increase in aircraft numbers was required.

One item of concern that unexpectedly came to light at this time was a problem in starting the Merlin engines fitted to Wellington bombers. When this was investigated, Lemon found that there were similar problems with the engines fitted to Battles, Hurricanes and Spitfires. He was concerned that he had not been informed about this, and that there seemed to be no feedback to his Department when problems like this occurred. The matter was discussed at the 19th regular meeting that Lemon held with his fellow Directors on 10 July 1939, when it was reported that larger starter motors were to be fitted and that Hurricanes and Spitfires would get priority. Lemon also reiterated the concern with engine production, and that the earlier superiority of output had created a false sense of security: expansion had not kept pace with the accelerated aircraft programme.[348]

A week after this meeting, on 17 July 1939, Lemon and Freeman were called to present a six-monthly report to the Prime Minister's Panel of Industrialists. They had been similarly quizzed earlier on 18 January 1939, when they answered questions about the progress of the re-armament programme. Copies of Lemon's report on his first year in office had been circulated and, at this second meeting, the Chairman introduced proceedings by saying to Freeman: 'I think first of all we would like to tell you and Mr. Lemon that we are greatly impressed both with the care with which this memorandum has been prepared, and also with the really outstanding achievement that has been accomplished since we met you last . . . the figures are extraordinarily encouraging with perhaps the exception of the major worry of engine production'.[349]

The range of matters that were dealt with at the various Committee meetings at this time is again indicative of the wide number of issues that Lemon was dealing with as DGP and show how he was actively involved in every sphere of the RAF's requirements. On 14 August 1939 for example, he was asked to investigate whether an order for 800 artificial horizons, which would have to be bought in America at a cost of £93,000, was truly a priority.[350] A continuing topic of concern was the problem of industrial disputes. A strike at Handley Page was still continuing and Lemon stated that he was uneasy at the frequency of recent strikes and felt that, although they were essentially a matter for negotiation between firms and the unions, the position must be watched closely as it indicated that the shop stewards were trying to exert increased power. Strikes were a recurring problem, caused by the need to push the workforce as hard as possible. Their settlement, in turn, led to continuous rumblings of discontent among workers in other industries at the preferential pay-rates given to those engaged in aircraft production.

At the meeting of the Air Council on 4 August 1939, the Chief of Air Staff warned that, although there was now a general spirit of optimism about the air defence problem, this optimism was not well founded.[351] He reported that Germany still had twice as many planes as the RAF. Despite the rapid strides that had been made during Lemon's first year in office, Germany had 1,750 long-range bombers to the RAF's 832, and 1,175 fighters to the RAF's 614. Of course, it was reasonable at this date for the authorities to assume that Britain could rely on France, with its own large air-force, to play a part in thwarting Hitler's aggression if war should break out. However, the Chief of Air Staff concluded that air defence was still the country's greatest problem, and greatest deficiency – and that the RAF must not continue to work to an inadequate programme of expansion a moment longer than necessary. This consideration, of course, was outside Lemon's remit: he was only charged with bringing Scheme L to completion on time. Any further expansion was a matter for the RAF and politicians to decide.

War was declared less than a month later on 1 September 1939. Immediately there was a flurry of letters back and forth concerning Lemon's position. Kingsley Wood wrote to Stamp: 'In view of the outbreak of hostilities there has of course been an intensification of work on the production side and I should find it extremely difficult to find any substitute for Mr. Lemon. I hope very much in these circumstances that you will be willing to agree to his remaining at the Air Ministry for the duration of hostilities'.[352] Stamp agreed – albeit a trifle reluctantly because, as he pointed out to the Minister of Transport, both he and the other Vice-Presidents, Sir Harold Hartley and Sir William Wood, were also now actively involved in Government work. He didn't wish to see the LMS suffer from this loss of leadership, but admitted that it was not 'reasonably possible to refuse the Air Minister's request' as 'his work with the Ministry is so important that I cannot urge anything here as superior to it'.[353]

In line with the Government's emergency plans, Lemon's Directorate was immediately evacuated to Harrogate in North Yorkshire, and based in the Grand Hotel where it was identified as Department ZA. Whilst this move was understandable in the confusion surrounding the outbreak of war, Harrogate was not well-situated for such a Department – it was not even close to any of the aircraft manufacturers. Lemon must have spent a great deal of time shuttling back and forth between Yorkshire and London in addition to the trips he had to make to the various factories around the country. (The move was later seen to be unnecessary and, after the threat of invasion had passed, the Department moved back to London.)

Soon after the outbreak of war, and because of the increase in work, the structure of Lemon's Directorate was revised to give him two Deputies: several departments were also divided, which increased the total to 11. Each Deputy was now responsible for four Departments, while Lemon himself took direct responsibility for the remaining three.[354] Lemon had recommended this rearrangement several months earlier, in May 1939, when he returned from convalescence following his appendix operation. He was concerned that too many Departments were reporting to one man – his single Deputy, J.S. Buchanan – and with the workload that was thereby forced on him. His Chief Administrative Officer, E.F. Cliff wrote to Freeman suggesting

The Grand Hotel,
HARROGATE.

The Grand Hotel Harrogate in the 1930s. The government requisitioned the building, and Lemon's Directorate moved there, on the outbreak of war. Author

that changes should be made to the organisation of the Department, but it was only the outbreak of war that brought them about.[355]

The C-in-C Fighter Command attended the meeting of the Air Council on 26 September, and enquired whether it was possible that the forecast of the output of Hurricanes was too pessimistic. Lemon was able to reply immediately that this was not the case. He knew the position exactly, and informed the C-in-C that the despatch of Hurricane squadrons abroad had depleted the spares' stock, and replenishment would adversely affect the production of completed aircraft. Incidentally, at this meeting, a prediction was also made of the types of aircraft that would still be in service in 1942. It is interesting to see that the Spitfire was scheduled to 'disappear' in 1942.

In October 1939 it was reported that 21 types of aircraft were now unserviceable. Many of these aircraft had not been damaged in combat, or even in flight, but by unnecessary accidents on the ground. All the Harrow bombers, for example, which were now used for training, were immobilised because of a lack of spare parts.[356] The whole question of repairs and maintenance was soon to become a major issue. There were two related

problems. Firstly, the need for a comprehensive supply of spare parts to be built up and maintained; and, secondly, to establish who was responsible for repairs and where they were to be carried out.

The National Archives have an interesting file on the subject.[357] Interesting because it shows that, only a few years after the end of the war, it was already difficult to establish the true facts of the case. The file was collated by an official historian at the Ministry of Supply, and contains personal recollections from senior RAF officers and Civil Servants of the situation that existed when war broke out. One anonymous author starts his damning analysis by quoting from Sir Edward Ellington, Chief of Staff, 'There will be no repair in War'. This allegation is not substantiated but, if true, shows a most curious attitude to the use of resources. Did Ellington really regard all equipment as dispensable – to be discarded as paper tissues are today?

This attitude was obviously totally unrealistic and the RAF did have plans to deal with the situation. There were to be three RAF Repair Depots and, in order to deal with the expected extra work in wartime, three large Civilian Repair Depots. The work would be split so that the RAF carried out 25% of the work while the remaining 75% was done at civilian depots. Once again, however, the building and equipping of the depots was way behind schedule and consequently it was imperative, now that war had been declared, to sort out the problem. Even the responsibility for running the civilian repair depots still had to be resolved. The Repair Department was controlled by the Head of Supply & Organisation, and thus was not within the remit of Lemon's Production Department. However, the problem of repairs could not be divorced from the problems of construction because, of course, repairs needed replacement parts. And these had to be made by the same firms that were building fully-assembled aircraft. The two requirements were inter-related, and priority for one would unavoidably affect the other. Freeman averred that the head of the repair organisation should come under Lemon's control, as he could then co-ordinate the proportion of spares to completed aircraft. He reported to Lemon on 13 July 1939 that he was 'at loggerheads' with the head of Repair & Maintenance and other RAF chiefs on the issue.[358] Their view was that as the civilian depots were primarily for repair, it was better that they were run by RAF personnel who were more 'repair minded' than production experts. Freeman felt that there was no great difference between repair and construction and, even if there was, service personnel lacked the experience of dealing with civilian labour in large numbers. The RAF also had no skills in dealing with labour problems such as rates of pay and hours of work. His reasons for wishing to hand over the running of the depots to a civilian organisation was precisely because it could draw on its own personnel for the higher management posts.

A meeting was held on 10 August 1939 – before war was actually declared – to consider the problem. Air Commodore Sir Christopher Brand, the Director of Repairs, argued the case for RAF control of civilian depots. One of his fears was

that an outside organisation would be motivated by output and profit, rather than service requirements. Lemon thought there was something to be said for this argument, but still felt that an outside organisation would be better able to develop the principles of repair on the large scale required. In a typical British compromise, it was resolved that one civilian repair depot would be run by the Air Ministry, one by an outside industrial organisation, while the management of the third was left in abeyance to be decided in the light of further experience.

At the outbreak of war, however, Kingsley Wood immediately accepted the offer of Lord Nuffield to take upon himself the organisation of the civilian repair depots. He explained the reasons for his decision to Freeman and Lemon at Grantham on 6 October 1939. Grantham is approximately half-way between London and Harrogate, and was, presumably, a convenient place to meet. Kingsley Wood told them that Nuffield had made the offer of his own volition, and stressed that there was no suggestion that he had been pressed to do so. Freeman urged him that Nuffield had no experience in such matters, and that the firm could only undertake this work to the detriment of their control of the Castle Bromwich factory, with a consequent drain on aircraft production there. Any firm that was to be involved in repairs, Freeman said, should come from *outside* the aircraft industry, and be one whose business would otherwise be curtailed or reduced by the war. Kingsley Wood replied that Nuffield had assured him that there would be no reduction in the construction programme, and that his senior executives would co-operate fully with Lemon on the subject.

This may have clarified one part of the problem. The other issue, however, still remained – the supply of spare parts. Time, space and raw materials had to be found for the manufacture of these within the overall construction programme. Lemon's view, according to his son David, was that every new aircraft should be accompanied by a set of spare parts.[359] This is an extreme response which, if carried to its logical conclusion, would have halved the output of planes at a stroke! A more balanced approach had to be achieved, and four days after the Grantham meeting, on

Mass-production of Spitfires at Castle
Bromwich after the factory was finally
operational. This picture should be
compared with the earlier photo of
Spitfire production in the previous
chapter. Birmingham Central Library

10 October, Lemon announced at the Air Council
meeting that 'instructions had been issued to the
industry temporarily to reduce the production
of aircraft by 10% to permit the production of
spares'.[360] He reported that this action had to be
taken, but he had no doubt that the output would
soon be built up again.

Not a lot seems to have happened in the next
weeks, and it was only on 6 December 1939 that
a meeting was held in Harrogate 'to consider
matters relating to the repair organisation'.
In preparation for this meeting Freeman had
discussions with Lemon on 4 December.[361]
The meeting two days later was chaired by Air
Marshal W.L. Welsh, the head of Supply &
Organisation, and he reconfirmed the current
situation with regard to Nuffield, and stated that
work on two of the three civilian depots had
stopped. Freeman reiterated that he was unable
to accept a situation where outside contractors
were under the control of different authorities.
Competition between the interests of production
and repair would be inevitable. He also thought
that, as far as possible, repair and construction
should not even be carried on in the same
factory. However, if a factory engaged upon
production did have spare capacity for repair
work, then this work, obviously, should be
controlled by Lemon. Lemon supported him but

emphasised that the real problem was shortage of
workers. The increased construction programme,
now that the country was at war, meant that a
million more workers were required, and the
needs of both repairs and construction had to be
balanced. Following further discussion, it was
agreed that certain small 'fringe' firms could be
immediately allocated for repair work.

Meanwhile, and not surprisingly, the decision
to build more spares meant that the monthly
production figures dropped. This was not what
the politicians wished to hear. As far as they were
concerned what were needed were planes, planes
and yet more planes. A secret debate was held in
Parliament on 13 December 1939 to discuss the
whole issue of supplies to the Armed Forces. *The
Times* newspaper reported on the unprecedented
arrangements that were made for this sitting – the
first of several that were held during the war:

Special precautions will taken to see that no
unauthorized person is in or near the Chamber

during the secret sitting. Before the House meets police and messengers will make a search of the Chamber and its precincts. During this search certain doors will be locked and the keys will be handed to the Serjeant-at-Arms. When the Press and public galleries of the House are cleared for the secret sitting the members' lobbies will also be cleared of strangers, and after that only members of the House of Commons, peers, and certain specified officers of the House will be allowed in the members' lobbies.

Before the House sits all the employees normally in the vicinity of the Chamber – including those who attend to heating and ventilating arrangements beneath the iron grille in the floor – will be withdrawn. If anything goes wrong with the heating or ventilation during the secret sitting the chief official responsible will have to be summoned by the Serjeant-at-Arms and specially authorized to do what may be necessary. Even the stoking of the open fires in the division lobbies during the secret sitting will have to be done by the Assistant Serjeant-at-Arms.

No record of what was said at this debate was thus ever made, even by parliamentary officials. (Permission was granted after the war so that

Lancaster nose sub-assemblies on the production line at Castle Bromwich in 1942. When war was declared in 1939, a rapid expansion of production was required for the massive number of further aircraft then ordered. Planning for this was one of the specific terms of reference in Lemon's duties as DGP. Birmingham Central Library

participants could publish their recollections of proceedings, and several speeches were 'reconstructed' in retrospect). However it is clear from the list of those who were expected to make speeches, which included Kingsley Wood, that the situation at the Air Ministry was discussed. Later sources allege that the RAF rearmament programme was severely criticised; and if this description of the slow progress over repairs is accurate, justifiably so. Churchill may have famously remarked, on a later occasion, that 'jaw-jaw' was preferable to 'war-war' but, now that war had been declared, the time for talking was over, and the inordinate length of time it took for any Government department to reach a decision needed to be severely questioned. The anonymous author, quoted earlier, alleged in his recollection of the situation that 'The accomplishments of the Repair Organisation prior to the formation of the Ministry of Aircraft Production [in May 1940] were negligible. Not a single aircraft had left a repair factory while the only repaired engines had come from a very scanty organisation at the main engine firms. Lord Beaverbrook's first decision as Minister of Aircraft Production was to clear up the large number of unserviceable aircraft which were littering RAF operational aerodromes'. Despite the apprehensions of those who believed they would be unable to carry out the necessary tasks, workshops throughout the land were pressed into repair work, and eventually fulfilled the rôle admirably.

While this was all going on, we have evidence of a rift developing between Lemon and Sir Wilfrid Freeman. Although the two presented a united front at the meeting on 6 December, four days earlier, on 2 December, Lemon wrote to Freeman:

After thinking over our recent discussion, I have come to the conclusion that we must try to get a clearer understanding as to our respective responsibilities.

Since my illness last March the practice has been steadily growing of sending for my various Directors and discussing with them production questions which are in some cases of a highly involved and industrial character, and of which you cannot, in the nature of things, have as much knowledge as I have.

Whilst I do not object to you seeing the Directors on specific problems, I do feel that I should be present at the discussions, or, if I am not available, informed of any decisions that are made. In a number of cases, I find myself taking an opposite view to you, and it is only after a lapse of time that this is discovered, resulting in a certain amount of muddle. Moreover, if it is a question which concerns outside contractors, we may be issuing contrary instructions, making us look very foolish.

If we tumble down on our production programme, it will be no use my saying to my colleagues and friends that you were in charge of production, because they realise quite well that you cannot have had any industrial experience, whereas they all know my career.

I am sure you will appreciate my point of view and that my only desire is to see that the organisation we have built up during the past eighteen months shall function properly, without divided councils or conflicting orders, and that we shall all work together as a team, but team-work, as I understand it, does not consist of one man playing full back, centre forward, half back, and goal-keeper, all at the same time.

I am sure you will not take this note as a personal criticism, because I know that a number of the things you do are done unthinkingly. Further, you know that I have the highest personal regard for you, and for your ability, otherwise I should not have stayed here as long as I have under existing conditions.[363]

The first part of this letter seems reasonable enough – it is always essential, and a courtesy, to maintain proper communication down the management line. However, Lemon obviously felt that Freeman was meddling in areas that were not his responsibility, and there is quite a sting in the tail when he concludes: 'a number of the things you do are done unthinkingly'. Lemon would never have written to Lord Stamp in such terms. However, there were other reasons for his irritability. On the very same day he wrote a furious letter to Kingsley Wood about a review of his Department by the Treasury.[364] The letter starts: 'I have now received a copy of the report made by Mr. Addison and Mr. Speed of the Treasury on the Production Directorates under my control, together with a copy of the letter Sir Alan Barlow has written to Sir Arthur Street. I was a little distressed to think you considered it necessary to carry out such an investigation'.

Lemon was particularly aggrieved that this report had recommended a reduction of sub-contracting. He continues in his letter to describe the situation he found at the Ministry on his arrival, which was quoted earlier in this chapter, and continues:

The matter [i.e. subcontracting] was discussed at the Air Council and a letter was issued to all contractors giving instructions that this policy was to be carried out and that they were to set up a separate organisation at their works to look after the problem of sub-contracting. You are aware that nearly 18 months after the plan was prepared we are still 583 machines in front of that planned programme in spite of set-backs as regards material, Embodiment Loan equipment, etc. some of which was not under the control of my Directorate. I have set out these facts in detail because of the criticism which Mr. Addison and Mr. Speed have considered it necessary to make, and to point out to you that if there is any relaxation of our present sub-contracting drive together with the further extension of it, you have not the slightest hope of getting the programme that has been planned.

It is perhaps a rather personal matter, but I would like to refer to my career as an engineer, starting at 15 years of age and eventually becoming Vice-President of the largest corporation in the world. Yet with my 40 years experience it is considered appropriate to send an official and a business man who is not an engineer to pass judgment after three days analysis of the work which has been done by this Department, and which has taken me nearly 18 months to build up; an organisation which has to deal with almost every branch of industrial activity in the country, including fine chemicals, textiles, the highest class of instruments and all branches of heavy engineering; an organisation which has to deal with such things as the development of new methods of obtaining the raw material for making magnesium and ensuring supplies of rare metals, including such things as radium.

You will, I am sure, readily understand that I feel that a report made to the Government by this Committee should not pass unchallenged by me. Had you sent two of the foremost industrialists in the country with engineering knowledge to spend, shall we say, a month on the job with me giving them explanations as to why certain things should or should not be done, it would not have been a waste of their time, but might have been a waste of mine. May I, therefore, know whether you agree with the recommendation that subcontracting

should not be extended because if so I must tell you definitely that the programme is impossible of achievement.

One can well understand his anger. For some reason we believe, in this country, that really important decisions should be left to amateurs – whether it be trial by jury or, as in this case, an analysis of complex engineering practices by accountants. Kingsley Wood wrote a placatory reply on 6 December, explaining that the investigation was carried out on the initiative of the Treasury, who felt that it would help to meet uninstructed criticism, which sooner or later was bound to be directed in war-time to every large and expanding Departmental organisation. He then writes: 'I confess that I did not anticipate that the report would deal with such matters as the extension of subcontracting. In this respect, it has gone beyond the scope of an investigation into departmental staff and organisation and invaded the field of policy. I have no doubt that, in making his observations, Mr. Addison thought that he was being helpful to you and your colleagues. I need hardly say, however, that it is to you, and not to Mr. Addison, that I should look for advice on this important matter.'[365]

There was no reduction in the amount of sub-contracting and, as has been previously mentioned, this policy was later generally considered to have been one of Lemon's most important achievements.

Meanwhile the Minutes of Lemon's meetings with his subordinate Directors in early 1940 continue to show the minutiae of details that were discussed – shortages of canvas for portable hangars, use of bakelite for some small components, the employment of aliens in aircraft factories, whether female labour should be used on night shifts, and so on. However, there was one matter which predominated all these meetings, and that was the continuing shortage of raw materials. In fact, the supply of aluminium was about to get significantly worse. The country was importing substantial quantities from France, Norway and Switzerland, and these markets were all to fall into German hands. There was also a problem with heavy machinery – the extrusion presses, for example, were all

Repairs to wing sections and fuselages at Derby LMS works. Nelson Twells

made in Germany. Lemon warned that it would take this country 12 months to build alternatives. A crisis meeting was called on 18 January 1940 to discuss what action to take.[366] Lemon advised his Directors that an increase in output during the next few weeks was essential. It was very much a matter of making the best use of whatever raw materials you could get, so that if, for example, extrusions were unavailable then rolled sections would need to be used instead. The problem was that the Ministry of Supply had now taken over responsibility for the allocation of raw materials, and a formal system of priorities was in operation. Lemon strove to get 'blanket' priority for all RAF construction, but was firmly told that one of the armed services could not receive preferential treatment over the others.[367] On 30 January, Lemon announced that he was requisitioning Earl's Court exhibition centre for the production of barrage balloons. He was aggrieved to report that, although negotiations for the use of Olympia were at an advanced stage for this purpose, the Ministry of Supply had appropriated the site. This may have still been in his mind on 18 March, when he told his fellow Directors that they were not to allow the effects of

Ministry of Supply controls to pass unchallenged if they affected 'our' interests.

One can detect a certain weariness creeping in to Lemon's reply, of 26 March 1940, to questions about the state of Lord Nuffield's new factory at Castle Bromwich for the production of Spitfires. He said that 'Lord Nuffield was prone to resent any outside interference. If Lord Nuffield and Sir Charles Craven of Vickers could work together the position would improve rapidly'.[368] Lemon probably did not realise, when he made this remark, that Sir Charles Craven was very soon to enter the equation and join the Department.

On 4 April, *The Times* reported that Sir Samuel Hoare had been appointed Secretary of State for Air in the place of Kingsley Wood. This was not the only new appointment, and Lemon was astonished to read in the paper that Lord Riverdale had been appointed Vice Chairman of the Air Council Supply Board, taking over many of the responsibilities which he felt were his.

The *Daily Mail* used the banner headline 'Lord Riverdale says – call me a Speed Chaser'

in its announcement of the changes. Riverdale, formerly Sir Arthur Balfour, was Chairman of the Sheffield steel manufacturers of that name. There is no hint in any of the official documents that such a change was on the cards, and the news must have come as a bolt from the blue to Lemon. However, according to Anthony Furse in his biography, Freeman had asked Kingsley Wood at the beginning of 1940 for 'an experienced industrialist' to support him and counter the growing political pressure he was under. The choice of Riverdale had been made by 30 January 1940 – two months before the official announcement. Furse quotes a letter that Freeman wrote to his wife, describing Riverdale as 'a grand old man, and more than a match for Lemon and Nuffield'.[369] Freeman was apprehensive enough to conclude the letter to his wife 'he [Riverdale] will be a great help to me, if he doesn't get rid of me'.

It is revealing that Freeman felt he needed someone to counter Lemon's influence. After all, Lemon *was* an 'experienced industrialist' and this was precisely why he was brought into the Air Ministry in the first place. Freeman's remark also implies that he saw some threat from both

Lemon and Nuffield. Yet, as has just been described, Lemon was as exasperated with Nuffield's failure to deliver on his promises as Freeman must have been, but there was little he could do about it. Nuffield's participation in both the Castle Bromwich scheme and the Repair Organisation had been foisted on them by the politicians – and he had to accept those decisions, and try to make them succeed.[370] Lemon and Nuffield were hardly in league together. One is forced to the conclusion that Freeman wanted to curtail Lemon's importance for other reasons – to protect his own position. He was clearly apprehensive about this, as the remark 'if he doesn't get rid of me' indicates.

Four days after *The Times* announcement, Lemon wrote to Sir Samuel Hoare: 'I noticed with astonishment in *The Times* for the 4th April 1940, the announcement emanating from 10 Downing Street that Lord Riverdale "has been charged with special functions relating to the speeding up of aircraft production". This statement, or a more or less accurate paraphrase of it appeared also in the popular Press and raises in an acute form the question of the delineation of my responsibilities. I find it impossible to avoid the conclusion that the duties which Lord Riverdale is to undertake clash with those laid down in the official statement of my duties, a copy of which I attach hereto.' [371] [Lemon enclosed a copy of the 'job description' which was quoted in the last chapter].

He then detailed how the organisation he had developed had not only produced the 12,000 aircraft required by 1 April 1940 ahead of time, but the total had actually been exceeded by 1,600. He also sent Hoare a copy of the correspondence between Lord Stamp and Kingsley Wood, from the previous September, when it was agreed he should stay at the Air Ministry 'for the duration of hostilities'.

He finished the letter: 'In these circumstances I deem it necessary that I should be accorded an early interview with you or with the Prime Minister in order to clarify what is, prima facie, a confused and confusing situation'.

Now it is not unusual in politics for people to find they have been stabbed in the back, and learnt their fate from the newspapers! It is also not surprising that the Government should keep the workings of its various departments under constant review. It is interesting to see that Lemon's attitude to his job had also changed – a year earlier, when he had his appendix removed, he seriously considered leaving the Air Ministry. Now, with the task that he had been set completed, he was affronted to find he was being moved aside. However, his position was a strange one – he was still technically only on loan to the Air Ministry from the LMS, who were still paying his salary. One wonders if he would have considered breaking all ties with the railway if his post as Director-General of Productions had been confirmed on a permanent basis.

Meanwhile work continued as normal, and Lemon attended the Air Council meeting on 9 April as usual. He was still trying to get priority for materials for the RAF, and told the meeting that he was disturbed about the general position with regard to supplies of steel. He asked two questions – did the Air Ministry have priority on

special steels or not; and why was it not possible to purchase adequate supplies from America. He stated that output of aircraft was generally retarded because of supply problems; that 60% of the drop-stamping capacity of the country was unemployed because of the lack of raw material; that he needed 10,000 tons of steel (14 days consumption) immediately, and that between 500 and 600 aircraft would need to be stored in the open because of the lack of hangars. He had raised the whole question with the Ministry of Supply but was not satisfied with the answers he had been given. Freeman reiterated that the Air Ministry could not expect general priority. It was agreed that Lemon should prepare a statement, which would be forwarded to the Ministry of Supply, showing the need for Air Ministry priorities. In fact, the March figures showed that 976 aircraft were built during the month, although there had been a break for Easter – and this was nearly twice the number built in France during the same time. This was the last meeting that Lemon attended. There were no further meetings until 23 April. [372]

On 18 April, Lemon went to visit Sir Samuel Hoare, who told him of further changes that were to be made. He was going to 'double-bank' [his phrase] Freeman's work and appoint Sir Charles Craven as Civil Member for Production and Development. [373] (Freeman, as an RAF officer, was the Air Member for Production and Development). Craven was another experienced industrialist: he was a Director of Vickers-Armstrong – the parent Company of Supermarines; the Company Lemon had wrestled with in order to get the Spitfire into production. After the catalogue of delays that have been listed in this chapter, Craven's appointment seems to be very much a case of 'poacher turned gamekeeper'! His title also meant that he had been accorded equal status with Freeman, and Hoare stated that he intended Craven to relieve Freeman of responsibility for production matters – leaving him to concentrate on Development. This further eroded Lemon's position, and on 21 April he tendered his resignation. He wrote to Hoare:

I have given the most serious consideration to the matters which you discussed with me on Thursday last and I can only request you to believe the decision I am making is one which I feel to be in the best interests of the Production Department.

From the time that I was seconded from my position on the Railway and was privileged to devote all my energies to the carrying out of the Air Ministry Programme and to the building up of the necessary organisation required for War Potential, I have endeavoured to place all my knowledge and experience of industry at the disposal of your predecessor in Office and of my colleagues in the Air Ministry. I fully appreciate the necessity of further strengthening the present organisation of the Production Department in order to spread the burden of those who are carrying the principal responsibility for the enormous Programme envisaged.

I am convinced, however, that if I were relieved of my post it would facilitate the re-organisation you have in mind. I beg, therefore, to tender to you my resignation from my position as Director-General of Production and as a member of the Air Council.

I can only ask you to appreciate that my decision has not been reached without a considerable degree of reluctance and regret.

In announcing my decision to you I am seriously concerned on behalf of those of my Directors who, at my invitation and not without considerable self-sacrifice, came forward to assist me in establishing the Production machinery. I trust my resignation at this moment will in no way involve a disparagement of their work, particularly in view of the enthusiasm which they have displayed in carrying out the Programme and providing for War Potential.

I feel it my duty to add that should you consider that the immediate cessation of my work in the Air Ministry would jeopardize the work of the Department as a whole, I readily place my services at your disposal.

In fact, the appointment of Craven, and Lemon's resignation, immediately threw a greater workload on Freeman – not the reverse. Craven was not in the best of health, and was often too ill to work.[374] One can only conclude that there were tensions within the Department that made such a change necessary. It is apparent from the blunt, if not rude, letter that Lemon wrote to Freeman in December 1939 that relations between the two of them were strained. G.P. Bulman, who was Director of Engine Production, described the situation as he saw it in his memoirs: 'Poor Lemon, the lemonade from whom Freeman was palpably estranged, used to disappear on long journeys, round the factories ostensibly, so different from his goods wagon shops and finally passed out of our ken about February 1940. He was, however, of great use to us in that as a director of the LMS Railway he was able to lay on a nightly sleeper both ways between London and Leeds. This was an enormous boon and mitigated the worse consequences of our isolation in Harrogate.'[375]

Bulman should not be thought of as a particularly authoritative source, and it is generally unwise to take everything one reads in personal memoirs at face value, as by their very nature they tend to exaggerate the importance of the author to the events around them. But the whole tone of his remarks about Lemon is offensive and patronising. His use of the words 'us' and 'our' also implies a cosy little clique to which Lemon had not been admitted. Bulman makes many factual errors in his narrative, and confuses the sequence of events around this time. For example, Lemon did not leave about February 1940, but at the end of April – and he was not a Director of the LMS. However, if he is vague about precise facts and their order, we cannot easily dismiss his remark that Freeman and Lemon were 'palpably estranged'. There must have been some very good reason for making a radical change in the workings of the department.

Freeman's reply to Lemon's letter telling him of his decision to resign, while being somewhat formal, carries no indication that there had been any estrangement:

My dear Lemonade

It is with great regret that I have received your letter telling me of your decision to give up your post as Director General of Production

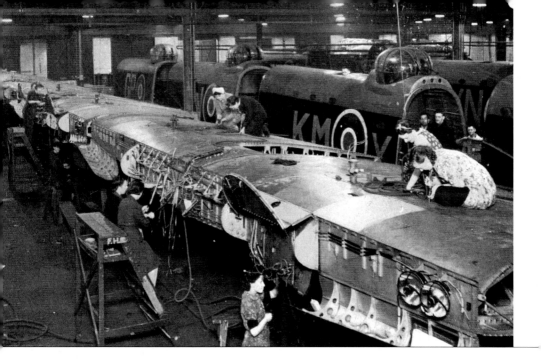

and resume your former appointment as Vice-Chairman [*sic*] of the LMS Railway.

Although I realise that our loss will be the railway's gain, I feel I shall greatly miss the invaluable assistance that you were able to give to the Air Force during the last two years in the field of production.

These two years of anxious preparation, in face of the possibility of that war on which we are now unhappily engaged, may well have been vital, not only to the R.A.F. but to the country.

During all this time I have been supported, if I may say so, both by your great technical knowledge of quantity production, and all that this involves, and by your shrewdness and commonsense, which have contributed so much to the solution of difficulties.

The co-operation between us has been of the closest kind and you have always been able to appreciate the Service point of view, and even to make allowance for the personal idiosyncrasies of individual officers – including my own which I feel must sometimes have been rather trying!

Much as I regret your departure, I cannot question the wisdom of your decision which,

Women employed on aircraft construction, Derby LMS works.
Nelson Twells

as I know, has been made only after the most careful consideration of all the factors involved and the different claims upon your services.

I have also the consolation of knowing that your work has been built on sure foundations and wise precepts and will, therefore, endure after you have gone. I think the Service, and the country as a whole, will have good cause to be grateful for your achievement in organising the production of aviation material on a scale hitherto undreamed of, and that the seeds you have planted will continue to bear invaluable fruit

In a sense, I suppose one might say that the work which you undertook to do for the Air Force has been performed, and that all we have to do now is to ensure that it continues with an impetus similar to that which you supplied.

I feel that this letter is a very inadequate expression of my personal gratitude for all you have done for us.

Yrs, Wilfrid Freeman

Lemon wrote letters to all his colleagues, telling them of his departure and thanking them for the great efforts made under his leadership. The phrase he used to Henry Self was 'The logic of the situation is ineluctable' – a curiously dispassionate way to describe the situation. They all replied in the warmest terms, telling him of their astonishment at his decision to leave. In view of the previous comments about G.P. Bulman it is worth quoting his reply:

Dear Mr Lemon

I much appreciate, as I am sure will all the other Production Directors, the kindly reference you make in your letter of April 22nd to such services as we have been able to render in our common task.

It came as a great shock to-day to know that you were leaving us. One's first feeling, however, was frankly one of envy for an escape from a nightmare! Only those of us who have been privileged in some small way to share in the immense strain of your late responsibilities can understand what has been achieved, and at what difficulty, under your direction; but in coming months you will have the satisfaction of seeing increasingly the harvest of your sowing, including even, I hope, a vigorously accelerating engine production!

You will be relieved at least of my long-winded minutes, but there will not be lacking, I hope, many opportunities of our meeting you again, now, and in happier days when the job is done.

May I offer you very sincere good wishes, and my warm thanks for all the patience and encouragement you gave me.

Yours very sincerely
G.P. Bulman [376]

This seems a warm enough letter. However, if we compare the tone of this letter with his opinion of Lemon as it appears in his memoirs, one gets a very different picture. One passage has already been quoted, but he also describes Lemon's appointment in these terms: 'Lemon was a director of the then London Midland and Scottish Railway. It was understood that he had distinguished himself in laying down a production line in Derby for building goods wagons for his company, which was no doubt highly efficient but hardly a background or breadth of experience calculated to win the confidence and support of the aircraft industry.' [377] Bulman had been Director of Engine Production before Lemon's arrival and it is apparent from his memoirs that he cherished the importance of his previous relationship with Freeman. Under Lemon's regime, however, he came lower down the pecking order, and was one of the nine Directors reporting to Lemon through his Deputy, J.S. Buchanan (who he inaccurately describes as 'my opposite number on aircraft'). It clearly rankled that he was no longer directly answerable to Freeman, and he contemptuously described his working relationship with Lemon thus: 'Lemon, my production boss under Freeman, used to get out new charts for engine deliveries to match similar long-dated forecasts of aircraft deliveries, and we used to argue about them. However, he never really got into the engine side, whatever he did on the airframe programme, and I was fortunate to retain a pretty free hand to prevent other folk mucking about with the engine firms.' [378] The casual remark 'whatever he did on the airframe programme' shows that he had no comprehension of the scale of Lemon's activities, nor does it indicate any appreciation of the complexities of the mass-production of fully-equipped fighting aircraft. The shortage of engines had been a major concern to both Lemon and higher authorities, as has already been noted in this chapter. Bulman was either oblivious to the wider picture or not interested. The words 'sycophant' and 'hypocrite' immediately spring to mind.

Understandably, the official records do not contain any information that could shed further light on the circumstances of Lemon's departure, but it is perhaps relevant to quote an extract from a private letter written to him later in the war. The contents of this letter, and its author, will be considered in greater detail in Chapter 11. It must have been written in the Autumn of 1942 when Freeman had just returned to the

Air Ministry. The writer was trying to get the two of them to work together again, and told Lemon that Freeman 'promised me that he would do everything possible to re-establish the partnership between you. So it's up to you to make it as easy as possible for him to do so, – and it won't be easy for him since he is a proud man'. This suggests that, in the letter writer's opinion, the onus was on Freeman to repair the relationship. The caveat 'it won't be easy since he is a proud man' also implies that Freeman was in some way to blame for the alienation. The inference is that some underhand tactics had been going on – something of which Freeman could *not* be proud. It may therefore be appropriate, at this juncture, to consider again the remark made by Sir Thomas Chegwidden that was quoted in the Introduction to this book: 'Some day the true story will be told, stripped of all the petty jealousies and intrigues'.

Against this has to be set the assertion by Sir Harold Hartley, made in 1955 after Lemon's death, that he 'was an awkward customer and was not at his best personally in those days'.[379] As Lemon's practical achievements at the Air Ministry were considerable, one has to infer that this comment did not refer to his work. Once again, it appears that his state of health was a problem, as can be seen in the response of his Deputy, J.S. Buchanan, to news of his resignation. Buchanan delayed his reply until the end of April, by which time he had the monthly production figures, and wrote to Lemon: 'We have exceeded your expectations or target by 61. I hope this is clear. This is a thing which you can fairly say is the result of your efforts, and no mean result.' However Buchanan's letter continues: 'I do hope you will get back to your normal health very soon'.

Sir Henry Self was abroad in New York with the British Purchasing Commission when Lemon resigned. It was not until 3 September 1940 that he cabled to Lemon:

I know better than anyone how much you have contributed to the effort which has made possible the defence of England and I also know what it cost you in health and peace of mind. I hope sincerely your recent rest has enabled you to recover your strength and energy for fresh activities in the supreme cause. Judging from your past contribution, they will never fail to yield great results whatever direction they may take.

I cannot possibly express how much I appreciated the opportunity of being associated with you in the great enterprise you directed for the creation of our air strength during the years 1938 to 1940.

Once more, Lemon had driven himself to a state of complete nervous exhaustion. The Minutes of the last meeting of the Air Council that he attended on 9 April are couched in the usual businesslike, dispassionate, terms. But one senses that his questions about raw materials were more of an ultimatum than questions. He appears to have been totally exasperated at the restrictions placed upon the expansion plans – and a man reaching the end of his tether. He may have simply become impossible to work with. It was also barely a year since his previous illness in the spring – although that had been a physical condition (undoubtedly stress-related) necessitating the removal of his appendix. But the breakdowns were getting dangerously close together.

Lemon left the lodgings he had found with the Crabtree family at Stonefall Hall, on the outskirts of Harrogate, and returned to London. The warm letters which passed between him and his 'landlords' on his departure show how he had been totally accepted into the family for the six months he was in Yorkshire. These letters were personal and consequently there was no need for discretion. Lemon had obviously discussed his situation with Crabtree, who wrote 'How the H— any man can believe that either Craven or Riverdale can know how to handle such a job is more than I can understand; they are nothing more than names which may carry weight with the public but mean nothing to those who realise what the job is. To make changes at the moment is like dropping grit in the gears'. The letter continues with chit-chat about the Crabtree's children, but there is no mention of Lemon's private life. If they were aware that he had left his wife, they were discreet enough not to mention it. Hermione presumably did not visit him in

David Low produced several cartoons for the *Evening Standard* in which he drew attention to the delays in the RAF expansion programme. Most pre-date Lemon's appointment as DGP, but this one appeared on 26 October 1938. Was this the cartoon that stood on Lemon's desk?
Solo Syndication

TIME THE PACEMAKER

Harrogate. Lemon arranged for all his possessions to be sent to an address in Acacia Road, St John's Wood, and took great pains to ensure that this information was restricted to those with an absolute need to know, and was not disseminated generally around the Air Ministry or RAF. Because it was wartime, it is impossible to establish who else might have been living at the address that would necessitate such secrecy – there are no Electoral Rolls to consult. One assumes it was because Hermione was living there. He also asked that the original cartoon by Low which stood on his desk at the Air Ministry be returned, but it had been lost in the move to Harrogate and was never found.

The circumstances of his actual departure from the Air Ministry were also not without controversy. *The Times* newspaper only made a brief announcement of the changes on 23 April. When this was queried by Sir Harold Hartley – presumably on Lemon's behalf – the paper answered that no slight had been intended. Indeed, it was the paper's policy to print all Government communiqués in full. However, the Air Ministry had not issued the communiqué until late in the evening, after the paper's deadline, so they had printed what information they had received from other sources.

The official communiqué paid tribute to Lemon's work, and stated that he would be a member of the newly-formed Air Supply Board which would replace the existing Supply Committee. The Chairman of this new Board

was Sir Charles Craven, with Lord Riverdale as his Deputy. Privately, one imagines, this must have been hard for Lemon to swallow and, maybe because of this, the Minutes of the Supply Board show that Lemon did not attend any of its subsequent meetings.

On 27 April 1940 Lemon had the honour of being received, for the second time, by King George VI.[380] For this visit he was accompanied by Air Marshal Charles Portal, and one presumes the Monarch wished to thank him personally for his work as DGP.

The appointments of Riverdale and Craven were made in the dying days of Neville Chamberlain's premiership and were, as it turned out, only the prelude to much greater changes at the Air Ministry. Just under three weeks later, on 10 May 1940, Churchill took over as Prime Minister and promptly dismissed Sir Samuel Hoare, Secretary of State for Air, and sent him as Ambassador to Spain. Hoare, therefore, only held the post for just over a month. Churchill then raised the status of Aircraft Production to a Ministry in its own right and, on 17 May 1940, appointed the charismatic Press baron, Lord Beaverbrook, to be the first Minister of Aircraft Production.

Lemon and Freeman's contribution to the rearmament of the RAF went largely unnoticed and unappreciated by the general public. It is Beaverbrook who now receives all the credit in the popular imagination. Lemon and Freeman, as has been described, had to work within the confines of official channels to obtain the raw materials needed, but Beaverbrook could bring a whole new dimension to the problem. It was only a figure such as he who could galvanise the whole country into handing in its unwanted pots and pans for the salvage campaign. One of the letters congratulating Lemon on his knighthood appreciates this: 'The fact that the Beaver has now a complete Ministry to do what you and your Dept. did is a proof of the great effort you made and the solid and unadvertised success that attended your efforts'.[381] The groundwork had been done long before Beaverbrook's appointment. As Lemon had written in his very first report in the Summer of 1938, the reforms would take eighteen months to come to fruition. Perhaps Bruce-Gardner appreciated that the credit would not be apportioned correctly when he wrote to Lemon after his resignation: 'If the country could be told what you have so ably achieved in the last two years, they would be as grateful to you as I am'.

May and June 1940 saw the end of the 'phoney' war as German forces quickly over-ran Western Europe and advanced ever closer to this country. Lord Dowding steadfastly, and wisely as it turned out, refused to allow the bulk of his fighter force to be committed to the defence of France, which capitulated in June. British troops were clawed back from Dunkirk, and the country waited for the inevitable onslaught. A month after his appointment, Beaverbrook reported to the Cabinet: 'On June 18th, one month after taking office, I report that . . . the supply of aircraft is now in excess of the available pilots'. And thus began the Battle of Britain. But for the efforts of Lemon and his team, the RAF would have been totally ill-equipped to fight the aerial battle that ensued. Even so, it was a desperately close-run thing. Nevertheless, the official figures show that the number of aircraft produced while the battle was being fought was unaffected. Despite its losses, the RAF actually had more planes available at the end of the Battle of Britain than at the beginning. It was pilots they lacked.

The organisation that Lemon set up remained basically unchanged throughout the War, although it necessarily grew enormously in size. His erstwhile Deputy, J.S. Buchanan, wrote to Lemon in September 1941, eighteen months after he left:

'Last week we had a record output of aeroplanes – a very substantial improvement over previous figures and we also have had a record monthly output. These figures are not a flash in the pan but represent solid hard engineering production. The object of this letter is to tell you that the machinery you laid down for the production of aeroplanes is working smoothly and efficiently, and I want to say how much I personally understand the enormous contribution you made to the present state of progress'. Lemon has scribbled on the letter 'Agreed lunch, Thursday 11th'. By this time, he was already Sir Ernest Lemon. His knighthood was announced in the 1941 New Year's Honours List, and the investiture took place at Buckingham Palace on 18 February.

The final words can be left with Sir Henry Self who was closely associated with Lemon in all aspects of his work. In his description of Lemon's achievements, published in *The Times* after Lemon's death, he wrote:

In the appreciations already published of the late Sir Ernest Lemon the reference to his work in connexion with production of military aircraft in the period preceding the war was necessarily curtailed. As one who was privileged to be closely associated with him in the years 1938–40, the writer may be permitted to touch upon one or two points which indicate the effectiveness of Lemon's enthusiasm and vision.

He came to the Air Ministry in June, 1938, on loan from the London, Midland, and Scottish Railway Company, where he was serving as vice-president, to assume the post of Director-General of Production – a new post specifically created by the Air Council to mark the urgent need for streamlining the plan for intensive aircraft production. The importance of his appointment was marked by his becoming also a member of the Air Council; in that capacity he played a great part in association with the late Air Chief Marshal Sir Wilfred [sic] Freeman. The two succeeded in organizing aircraft production on a scale which made possible the tremendous expansion achieved during the war, and as one who was very close to the work of both men the writer feels that Freeman would have been the first to stress

Testimonial presented to Lemon on leaving the Air Ministry, April 1940. Family

the vision and initiative shown by Lemon in planning the pure production side.

Lemon somehow succeeded in doing what he had obviously done many times before in his career. He inspired his associates and all those whom he controlled with the conviction that they could achieve results in spite of the handicaps and difficulties that they were encountering. This stimulus came at a time when it was badly needed, because the programme which had already been launched so courageously by Lord Swinton was tending to become bogged down by the inherent difficulties of a developing programme of new types which had not passed sufficiently far through the design stage for their production possibilities to be reasonably estimated.

It was here that Lemon showed his courage and his initiative. These qualities focused themselves in four outstanding achievements directly due to him – namely:

(i) Before he came to the Air Ministry the production staff was small in number and not of outstanding status. He at once set about reorganizing and expanding that staff, creating some six directorates which were staffed partly with people already in the Ministry and partly by new recruits. In all this he was, of course, wonderfully supported by Freeman. This organization provided the nucleus of the wartime organization of the M.A.P., and in fact did not change in any significant way throughout the war, although of course it expanded in size.

(ii) Secondly, he broke down the natural hostility of the aircraft industry to large-scale subcontracting of component parts of aircraft. This was an essential first step to the

development of production on a widespread scale, and it was Lemon who laid the foundations on which the large structure of aircraft production was built during the war with the main firms employing tiers of sub-contractors and sub-sub-contractors in a comprehensive flow through to the central assembly sheds.

(iii) His third contribution was the improvement and development of the central planning system, which became of paramount importance in coordinating the supply of the very large number of individual items of equipment and components which have to be incorporated in the modem military aircraft.

(iv) His wide knowledge of the engineering industry and of its leading personalities was of the utmost value to the Air Ministry in broadening the base of aircraft production. That is indeed particularly evident in the aircraft industry, which had, in the years preceding the start of the war expansion programme in 1934, been a relatively small branch of the engineering industry. This contrasts markedly with the tremendous expansion and improvement in its status which occurred before and during the war.[382]

TEN

Return to the LMS, 1940–1941

WHEN Lemon returned to the LMS in 1940, one familiar face was missing. In the Autumn of 1939 Tommy Hornbuckle unexpectedly resigned from the LMS.[383] Although he was then 59 years of age and not far short of retirement, many previous writers have speculated on the reasons for his departure, which they feel have never been satisfactorily explained. E.S. Cox attributed it to the 'personal contest' between him and Fairburn over diesel engines, and wrote that Hornbuckle was 'no match, either in position or capacity, for his formidable chief, and before long he retired from the fray a somewhat embittered man'.[384] Undoubtedly, there were disagreements between the two men on certain points, but nothing that has been discovered suggests that any of these would have become a resignation issue.

Alternatively, J.E. Chacksfield suggests Fairburn saw Hornbuckle as a rival for the post of CME after Stanier's retirement.[385] In 1937 Fairburn had become Deputy CME when the Electrical Department was amalgamated into the CME's Department. As with any large organisation, there was probably a lot of internal politicking going on for which Hornbuckle may have had no stomach. It is certainly true that Fairburn's star was in the ascendancy, and Hornbuckle may have felt his was waning. Hornbuckle may also have become despondent at the lack of any real interest or commitment to diesels in the LMS – apart from shunting engines – and aware that war had curtailed any further development for the foreseeable future. Neither of these reasons seem completely convincing for his resignation, although they may have been contributory factors.

There may, however, have been another reason for his resignation. One significant factor that was unappreciated by previous writers, was his close relationship with Lemon. Hornbuckle's career had for years been closely linked to Lemon's: in 1924, he was Assistant Works Manager at Derby; in 1928, he was Technical Assistant to the Carriage & Wagon Superintendent (i.e. Lemon); and in 1930 he had gone to Euston as Chief Technical Assistant to the CME – a few months before Lemon was appointed to the post. Crucially, as has already been stated more than once, they were brothers-in-law.

When Lemon left the LMS to work for the Air Ministry in 1938, Hornbuckle would have lost a powerful ally – if indeed he still regarded Lemon as such. Lemon's affair with Hermione might originally have been a closely-guarded secret but if, as seems likely, it was known amongst the family by the early part of 1938 (at the latest), it would have put Hornbuckle in a most awkward situation. He could hardly continue to work with Lemon as if nothing had happened. Indeed, Lemon's secondment to the Air Ministry would have been a welcome, but temporary, relief. Nevertheless, Hornbuckle would have had to decide his reaction to the fact that Lemon and Amy had split up, and it seems to the author that he may well have decided, out of loyalty to his wife and sister-in-law, that it was time to move away. Although Lemon was working for the Air Ministry throughout 1939, the original secondment from the LMS was only intended to be for 12 months. Therefore, he was expected to resume work as Vice-President as early as the summer of 1939. It was only the imminent prospect, and then outbreak, of war that caused his stay at the

Air Ministry to be extended. It seems that a far more convincing reason for Hornbuckle's departure lies within the family relationships and loyalties than at work.

There were other indications that the return to the LMS was not the welcome home-coming that Lemon may have expected. Despite Lord Stamp's protestations that he had not been forgotten, the railway had managed well enough in his absence: Ashton Davies had been confirmed as a full Vice-President, and taken over the responsibilities that Lemon had previously held. Lemon appeared to be unsure of himself, and uncertain how to react. Now we are fortunate that H.G. Smith, Lemon's personal secretary at the LMS, continued to maintain a record of Lemon's career. He collated a substantial quantity of documents covering the period between 1938 and Lemon's retirement from the Company in 1943. To these he added his own version of events in a 'Diary of No Consequence', and all were bound into a volume which is now in the possession of his grand-daughters. Smith was fiercely loyal to his boss and this may have coloured some of his comments about Lemon's return. He described the situation at the LMS, as he saw it, at the start of this Diary. The style is highly idiosyncratic, and Lemon is always referred to as 'The Chief' and Smith himself as 'The Shadow'!

Resuming duty with the LMS in July 1940, he found an unaccountable atmosphere of unwelcome awaiting him; curious it is that memories should be so short and that jealousy should still be able to rear its head. Perhaps the shock of his appointment as Vice-President in 1931, when as an Engineer he was placed in control of operating work – to the dismay of certain officers who considered their claims to be cast-iron, inevitable and as of right – still lingered, tingeing the outlook with feelings that after all it was a shame THE CHIEF had returned to disconcert their hopes, and to upset the conventions surely intended as their birthright. From the top downwards this atmosphere was apparent and colleagues even were lukewarm in extending wholehearted greetings to one, but for whose efforts in providing essential aircraft there would have been no resounding Battle of Britain victory, and consequently no LMS would have remained in existence. Efforts to fob him off with suggestions of other duties, trifling in themselves and not fitting for one who had done such a magnificent job for the country and moreover out of keeping with the extraordinary work put in in previous years for the LMS, naturally caused THE CHIEF furiously to think: ingratitude was it? or place-seeking by others? or intrigue for various reasons? or a dulling of consciences as too often happens as an outcome of war tendencies? Whatever it was, there were the visible evidences. Supported by THE SHADOW who had opened his eyes to the position of affairs with devastating frankness, THE CHIEF swallowed his disappointment and settled down to make the best of things in a bad world. A difficult task when old confidences have lost some of their integrity and what was thought to be gold turns out to be but polished brass.

Smith also wrote a private letter to Lemon, urging him to stand up for a proper restoration of his former title and responsibilities. As he was only Lemon's secretary, this might have been somewhat presumptuous (as he acknowledges), but surely shows the trust and relationship that existed between the two men. It also contains a most unflattering description of the current management of the Company, which clearly shows where Smith's sympathies lay. The letter reads:

Dear Mr. Lemon,

I am typing this myself so that no one else knows anything about it. A little reflection last night leads me to make what might be thought to be presumptuous remarks. You said the Chairman was going to let you take Pickford's and Carter Paterson's jobs under your wing together with certain other extraneous matters. This is the cart before the horse. The Operating and Commercial Departments are the two most important jobs on the LMS. Prior to going to the Air Ministry you were the Vice President for these two Departments

– full-bloodied, *in toto* and absolute. During your absence A.D. [Ashton Davies] was made Acting Vice President, and since then has been made a full Vice President without denomination. He is an additional Vice President and is therefore SECOND to you. As a Vice President you come FIRST – in every way – and must come FIRST in the future, otherwise you lose prestige. Your job on the LMS is therefore Vice President for Operating and Commercial. Extraneous jobs will not fit the picture, and for your own sake will not do, as you would drop in everyone's estimation into second place, no matter what the Chairman might say.

You must without any hesitation come back as Vice President for Operating and Commercial; and extraneous jobs must go to A.D. I have no doubt in my own mind that this is the RIGHT PERSPECTIVE, and in your own interests you must stick to it. It will be quite simple to work out. A.D. is at present Chairman of a Special Committee, originally appointed to work out the policy and principles for implementing the Square Deal legislation, which was side tracked by the outbreak of the War, but the Committee is now working on behalf of the General Managers for defining the policy and principles for the Road Rail interests in readiness for adoption on the termination of the War. A.D. has in this a good job of work. If the Chairman wishes to rid himself of Pickfords and Carter Patersons he can quite easily push these on to A.D., together with any other special items which may arise from time to time.

Always keep this in the forefront. A.D. is hanging on solely for 'SIR ASHTON' to come along, as he is certain will do out of the war. He will hang on until his teeth drop out. He is entirely selfish, and No. 1 comes first every time. He is a skater on the surface, and does not get down to root problems, and since you went there has been no real criticism of the work in the Operating Department. And some real criticism is needed. Royle swallows everything Fisher tells him, and moreover Royle is getting a swelled head, which is not

good. A.D. will not stand up to anything Royle tells him, and a strong captain is wanted to hold the baby now, and the man to do this is YOU. Certain people round here were hoping against hope that you would not come back, and this is not a good sign, and therefore means that all is not well in the state of Denmark.

I hope that what I am saying will not be looked upon as criticism only, but rather in the light of remarks from a dispassionate observer. I have no axe to grind personally, but I do hate to think that all the initiative and drive which you put into the two Departments a few years ago should be allowed to run to seed. Things want wakening up.

I do not know whether the Chairman has mentioned the ideas he told you to A.D. or the other Vice Presidents, but you ought to stop anything of the sort getting into A.D.'s head. Now have I made myself plain or only made myself a nuisance. You should return to Watford and take full charge. One day a week at the Air Supply will not make any difference. A.D. will be living at the Euston Hotel in another month's time, as he is giving up his house here, and can operate his jobs quite easily from Euston offices.

If you work from a Euston office you will become lazy, because you will not be in the heart of the business, and your capacities are worthy of full effort on behalf of the LMS

Now, having got all that off my chest, I will just let it sink in, but for Heaven's sake hold on to your full authority as V.P.

Yours sincerely
H G Smith

[N.B. The LMS head office had moved to Watford after the outbreak of war, because of the risk of damage and disruption from air-raids.]

The matter was satisfactorily resolved – in Lemon's favour, and the Board Minutes of 27 June 1940 record:

In accordance with undertakings given to Mr. Lemon when he left, he will, after a proper interval of time to make himself acquainted

with the developments under the Railway Executive Committee during the past ten months, be asked by the Board to reassume his position as Vice-President in charge of Operating and Commercial Departments.

Mr. Ashton Davies, Vice-President, who has stayed on beyond the normal retirement age to take Mr. Lemon's duties has, I am glad to say, agreed to remain on in continued charge of some of the special war time functions (Air Raid Precautions, Local Defence Volunteers, Salvage, etc.) and standing by generally to act for others. This arrangement will keep the Executive beyond its normal strength, but at a time when national emergencies may throw enormous urgent burdens upon us, we regard it as important not to give up any such ripe experience and knowledge of current railway conditions as Mr. Davies possesses in a high degree.

Lemon officially resumed his duties on 1 August 1940. However, there was little scope for him to advance new initiatives and improvements. The consequences of war meant that the

railways were struggling to maintain some form of normality in their services. Construction of all new rolling stock had come to a virtual standstill: workshops, raw materials and labour were all allocated to military, and non-railway, requirements.

The railway workshops, following requisition whilst Lemon was DGP at the Air Ministry, were allocated to work on aircraft construction and maintenance. The National Archives contain a 'brochure' entitled 'Aircraft Activities at the LMS Carriage & Wagon works and Locomotive Works', dated 24 October 1941.[386] It is a long booklet, detailing the activities in the two departments in the minutest of detail, and the name on the cover shows that it was Lemon's personal copy. The opening preamble proudly states: 'The organisation charts show the allocation of responsibilities and in this connection it should be noted that the whole of the administrative and supervisory staff are Railwaymen, with no previous experience of aircraft, while the workshop personnel was built up around about 100 skilled men, the balance consisting of workmen such as Bodymakers, Coach Finishers, Coach Trimmers,

The Grove, on the outskirts of Watford, used as LMS headquarters during the War. Hertfordshire Archives & Local Studies

Painters, French Polishers, Wood and Metal Machinists, Builders, Plumbers, and numerous other trades, together with labourers and men and women without any previous workshop experience'. The works carried out repairs to Hampden bombers; construction and repairs of Hurricane, Typhoon & Roc (Fleet Air Arm) wings; production of spares for these aircraft, and what was called 'reduce to produce'. Badly damaged aircraft were broken up so that parts could be cannibalised for future use, while the residue was recycled. The work carried out on Hampden bombers was extensive, and repairs to component parts were also sub-contracted out to other firms in the area around Derby. Overall control of this organisation was in the hands of C.E. Fairburn, Hornbuckle's supposed nemesis. The LMS workshops (and many other such shops throughout the country) had readily adapted themselves to aircraft work and shown that all the *brouhaha* about their suitability and ability was unfounded.

The railway companies were also required by the War Department to supply engines for military use. They were fortunate that the first

levy of steam locomotives, scheduled to help with the defence of France, were never shipped abroad because of the speed with which that country fell to the Germans. They were thus not lost, and could continue to be used in this country. But as the war progressed, so the military requirements increased. For example, a couple of years later, after Russia had entered the war on the Allies side, a further number of heavy engines were needed for work in Iraq, taking supplies through that country into Russia. It was not just steam locomotives that were requisitioned: many of the diesel shunting locomotives were also taken. They were used in petroleum depots (where their internal combustion engine was inherently safer) and for hauling heavy long-range guns used for coastal defence. Here, their advantage was that no smoke was emitted which would betray the location or movement of the guns to enemy observation. Some were later taken to the Middle East to work in the docks in Cairo. Whilst all of

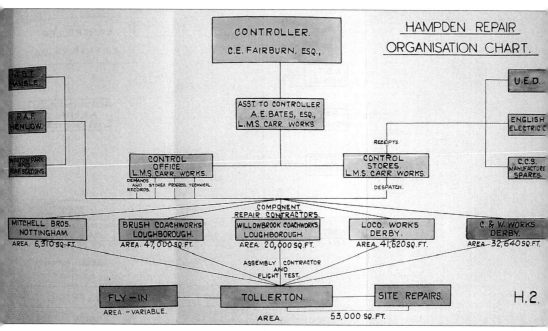

HAMPDEN REPAIR
ORGANISATION CHART.

CONTROLLER.
C.E. FAIRBURN. ESQ.,

ASST. TO CONTROLLER
A.E. BATES, ESQ.,
L.M.S. CARR. WORKS.

A.S.T.
KEBLE.

R.A.F.
HENLOW.

WOOTON PARK
AND
RAF STATIONS.

U.E.D.

ENGLISH
ELECTRIC C

C.C.S.
MANUFACTURE
SPARES.

RECEIPTS.

CONTROL
OFFICE.
L.M.S. CARR. WORKS.

DEMANDS
AND STORES. PROGRESS. TECHNICAL.
RECORDS.

CONTROL
STORES.
L.M.S. CARR. WORKS.

DESPATCH.

COMPONENT
REPAIR CONTRACTORS.

| MITCHELL BROS.
NOTTINGHAM.
AREA. 6,310 SQ-FT. | BRUSH COACHWORKS
LOUGHBOROUGH.
AREA. 47,000 SQ.FT. | WILLOWBROOK COACHWORKS
LOUGHBOROUGH.
AREA. 20,000 SQ.FT. | LOCO. WORKS
DERBY.
AREA. 41,620 SQ.FT. | C. & W. WORKS
DERBY.
AREA. 32,640 SQ.FT. |

ASSEMBLY CONTRACTOR
AND
FLIGHT TEST.

| FLY-IN
AREA. - VARIABLE. | TOLLERTON.
AREA.   53,000 SQ.FT. | SITE REPAIRS. |

H.2.

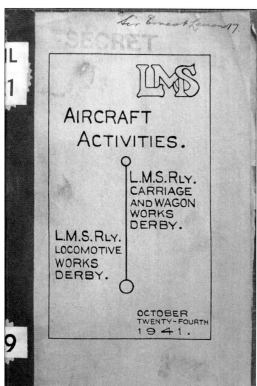

Booklet describing aircraft repair work at Derby, which includes a diagram showing the organisation of local firms involved in repairing Hampden bombers. The name on the cover shows it was Lemon's personal copy. National Archives

this was necessary for the war effort, it severely depleted the stocks of engines for home use. This was, obviously, a source of great concern to all of the big four railway companies, and representations were made to the Government through the Railway Executive Council for authority and resources to build more new locomotives. The file on the subject disappeared into the Civil Service machine, reappearing miraculously on Lemon's desk at the Ministry of Production two years later (as will be described in the next chapter).

The erosion of resources caused great difficulties, and obsolete engines that had been withdrawn from service had to be refurbished for continued use. For example, in February 1941 the Traffic Committee minutes record that 54 engines authorised to be broken up were repaired for further service.[387] Passenger requirements had also changed. Gone were the days of high-speed express trains offering the latest in luxury and comfort: now there were large numbers of servicemen demanding a cheap and basic level of service. The reality now was simply to try and maintain as good a service as possible. It was a matter of make-do and mend. And there was a lot of mending – German air-raids caused much damage to building and installations, all requiring temporary repairs.

Now that Lemon was back in charge of the Operating and Commercial Departments, he also had to accept that any decisions or initiatives he did wish to implement were subject to the strictures of the Railway Executive Committee (REC). Day-to-day management of the railways was now controlled nationally by the Ministry of Transport through the REC which H.G. Smith, a loyal railwayman, describes thus: 'The tentacles of the R.E.C. octopus were now beginning to twine round every activity of the railway transport service and, slowly but surely, the Civil Service machine was strangling initiative and resource of staff whose lifelong task it had been. The amateur was superseding the professional – unlike other games – but the political and ministerial game is so constituted under a Constitution professedly composed of amateur leaders. As 'Agents of the Minister' the R.E.C. found itself thwarted at every turn with pettifogging instructions and directions.'

Lemon was not a member of the REC which, at the highest level, was made up of the General Managers of the four main-line railway companies and London Transport. The *Directors* of these companies were expressly barred from membership and therefore Lord Stamp, who was both Chairman and President (the LMS used the title President rather than General Manager), was ineligible. Accordingly, the LMS had appointed Lemon's fellow Vice-President, Sir William Wood as its representative. As Lemon had previously been in charge of the Operating Department, he would surely have been the obvious choice to serve on the REC, but, when war broke out, he was at the Air Ministry and not available. Smith then states that Wood, whilst having necessarily to contact Chief Officers direct on matters placed on REC agendas, began to bypass Lemon. 'Pin pricks for the CHIEF' Smith called it – 'a cloud the size of a man's hand'.

Planning of Supply

UPON his return to the LMS in 1940, Lemon immediately wrote a couple of memos to Stamp.[388] The first concerned his experiences at the Air Ministry, and contained an analysis of how the Ministry of Supply went about the business of allocating raw materials for the war effort – 'the man who made the most outcry usually secured the most'. The content seems to have very little direct relevance for the railways, but was a chance for Lemon, once again, to stress the need for co-ordinated planning at the highest level. His advice on these matters was later sought by the House of Commons Select Committee on National Expenditure. In April 1941 Lemon attended a meeting of this Committee at which he repeated the conclusions he had reached from his experiences at the Air Ministry and suggested how improvements could be made. Six months later, he was called to the American Embassy to discuss the problems of war-production with representatives of their armed services and industry. Lemon summed up their meeting as follows: 'In the light of the discussion which followed it was evident the USA representatives knew all the answers to all the problems and my visit was really a waste of time'.

The second memo concerned the problems of post-war reconstruction. Once again, this was not directly relevant to his immediate work as Vice-President but, as we have seen, Lemon was in the habit of firing off memos on a variety of topics! As with the previous document, it was written at the height of the Battle of Britain and one wonders why he was already thinking so far ahead, and with such confidence. The Memo was ostensibly submitted to Stamp, but the impression it gives is that Lemon expected him to pass it on to other parties outside the LMS for general discussion, and as a way of influencing national policy. It starts:

On again taking up my duties as Vice-President I have been considering in what way my experience at the Air Ministry would be of use to the Company and to the Country, and I have come to the conclusion that, in view of our past experience when schemes have been called for by the Government for the relief of unemployment or reconstruction in its broadest sense, the best thing we could do, and in fact the only thing, would be to form a Committee of which I would be the Chairman, to consider all the post-war problems of transport as affecting the LMS and the transport systems of the Country as a whole.

He included with this document a further Memo, which set out his thinking in greater detail:

POST-WAR RECONSTRUCTION

(1) When the war is won reconstruction in its widest sense will be essential. The Cabinet on behalf of all Government Departments will have many acute problems to face with the discontinuance of war industries and the rehabilitation of trade generally on to a peacetime basis. Social services and particularly the employment question may require drastic action.

(2) Transport as an essential feature of the country's commercial effort will not be able to escape the problem, and obviously road transport, at present restricted in its scope by the necessity to conserve fuel, will probably launch out to a greater extent than after the last war in order to establish and improve its position in the transport world. It is not likely that canals will be much different in their ability to take a greater share of transport than prior to the war.

(3) Railways, having been during the war the main prop for the transport requirements of the various fighting and other Government services, will find themselves in a more difficult position than they were pre-war. The cost of the war, paid for by the various loans and taxes, etc., must obviously have eaten into the financial resources of the country as a whole, and trader and taxpayer alike will have to look around for the cheapest way of performing necessary services or obtaining necessary commodities.

(4) At present the Railways are controlled by the Government and, whilst the war is on, they are immune from any serious attack on their finances. With the termination of the war it is perhaps unlikely that they will be allowed to resume their pre-war free position as commercial concerns. It may be that there will be State ownership of Railways, or that a further grouping will be insisted upon, say, two groups instead of four.

(5) Whatever the outcome is, the problem of existence in the transport world will still be acute if shareholders or other owners are to be remunerated. It is, therefore, essential that from the Railway point of view we should be prepared with a plan, at any rate so far as the LMS is concerned, for meeting conditions which are likely to exist in another year or two years' time. Reconstruction, not entirely in the physical sense, will have to be faced, and, apart from any other consideration, the necessity for the LMS to be ready with a plan of action even for its own preservation in any nationalised or grouping system, is paramount.

(6) It is therefore suggested that a small Main Committee be appointed whose members will examine the problems impartially and without any departmental predilection, studying the future welfare of the Company as a whole and also as the most important link

Members of the Railway Executive Committee in 1940, meeting in the deep-level shelter located in the disused Down Street Station on the Piccadilly line (note the curved tunnel walls). *Left to right:* **Sir Eustace Missenden (SR), Sir James Milne (GWR), Sir William Wood (LMS), W.H. Mills (Minute Clerk), E.G. Marsden (Assistant to Secretary), Sir Charles Newton (LNER), Frank Pick (LT), Sir Ralph Wedgwood (Chairman), G. Cole Deacon (Secretary), V.M. Barrington-Ward (Chairman, REC Operating Committee).** London Transport Museum

in transport generally. Schemes of new works, improvements, modernisation of equipment, re-adjustment of facilities and working arrangements, should be tabled for submission if Government proposals for alleviating unemployment are desired, whilst proposals for meeting nationalisation or another grouping system should be ready for production at any convenient opportunity as the basis for whatever may be sponsored by a future Government on behalf of the transport requirements of the country as a whole.

Lemon then listed the various categories which he considered should be examined by this Committee. These ranged from improvements to station facilities, goods terminals, motive power depots and workshops down to simplification of paperwork. There were 14 categories in total, which covered every sphere of activity in which the Company was involved – the final one being the catch-all: 'Any other phases tending to greater

efficiency'! One category that he singled out, as an example for Stamp, was the need to obtain greater capacity from existing running lines by closing the gap between fast passenger trains and slower moving freight trains. A greater uniformity of speed for all services could be achieved by the adoption of improved braking for freight trains; drivers of these trains could then travel at higher speeds and maintain control of their trains almost up to the signals, instead of having to reduce speed a mile or so away, as was currently necessary with loose coupled vehicles. He also suggested the Committee should look at further development of Diesels for shunting. He concluded the Memo with a list of possible candidates who might serve on it.

H.G. Smith put his own perspective on Lemon's proposals, and wrote:

From the angle of relieving unemployment when the war was over with the closing down of armament factories, the railways would no doubt be called upon by the Government to suggest schemes of improvement, etc. for utilising labour, and it would be essential to have properly thought out schemes ready for such purpose rather than putting forward a list of hurriedly conceived proposals as had happened in the past. Owing to war conditions, and the restrictions placed on their activities under Ministry control, the railways would be faced at the termination of the war, in the eyes of the public at any rate, with a much reduced prestige. There would have to be, therefore, a great improvement in the quality of services rendered by the railways to retain public confidence, to survive as a paying concern in the midst of the extraordinary competition which would come from road and air transport of the future. It would not, therefore, be wise to leave such matters for consideration until the termination of hostilities. Much thought would be required in the preparation of schemes of improvement, modernisation and better methods of working.

The other challenge, of course, that Lemon's proposals faced up to was the ever-present threat of nationalisation. Under war conditions, the railways had already been effectively 'nationalised', and Lemon was probably mindful that it was the experiences gained under a similar regime during the First World War which had led to re-grouping in 1922/3. The railways had only avoided nationalisation then by the skin of their teeth, and it had remained Labour party policy ever since. Many years earlier, the *Daily Mail* reported a speech at Blackpool by Ramsay MacDonald on transport plans on 4 June 1931 in which he said 'I don't like to use the word nationalisation, but wait and see'. This caused sufficient concern to Lemon at the time that he and Harold Hartley drafted a letter from the LMS in response.

The current Minister of Transport in 1940 was Sir John (later Lord) Reith – better known as the first Director-General of the BBC. In that capacity he had seen the BBC become a public corporation, and it was his policy at the MOT to recommend a similar organisation for the railways. He encapsulated his thinking in a debate in the House of Lords a couple of years later. By this time he had ceased to be a Government Minister, but *The Times* of 18 June 1942 reported him arguing his case thus:

The question raised by LORD REITH is severely practical: how can the essential public services be worked most efficiently and made to give the best possible service at the lowest possible cost? Private ownership is apt to result in a conflict of duties, the duty of management to the public and its duty to shareholders entitled to look for dividends. Administration by Government departments subordinates every action, however small, to the Parliamentary question and therefore to civil service procedure, with its regulations and precedents, and to the rigorous detail of Treasury control, which would make efficiency in terms of production and distribution impossible. Management by corporations representing and, in the last resort, controlled by the public avoids both horns of this dilemma and offers a characteristically British method of reconciling individual freedom and initiative with the public interest.

Throughout his life Reith kept a diary and they record his day-to-day work as Minister of Transport at this time.[389] They tell of his dealings with the Chairmen of all the railway companies, but what is immediately apparent is the different relationship he had with Lord Stamp. Both men had deep religious convictions, and Reith must have felt he had found a kindred spirit. Thus we find that on 10 July 1940 Reith wrote: 'Nice letter from Horne [of the GWR] obviously very appreciative of my attitude to him. I gave it to Stamp to consider'. This was all to do with Reith's claim – disputed by Horne – that he had 'full power over the railways in every respect'. A few days later, on 12 July, he wrote; 'saw Stamp with a draft of a letter I proposed sending to Railway Chairmen . . . I saw him again in the evening after he had considered it and found him very pleased with my idea'. In contrast he dismissed Lord Hambro (who had taken over as GWR Chairman) and Sir James Milne with the words: 'rum lot they are'.

On the specific issue of nationalisation we can find that Reith prepared a paper urging public

Birmingham Central Goods Depot after the air-raid on 26 October 1940.
National Archives

ownership of the railways which was presented at Cabinet on 3 September 1940. He discussed this with Stamp on several occasions – the last being on 29 August, when he wrote: 'saw Stamp and told him what was happening, for which he was very appreciative'. However, the proposals did not get any further at the time, as they were opposed by Churchill, Beaverbrook and other Conservatives in the Cabinet. Charles Stuart, who edited the published, and abridged, version of Reith's diaries comments: 'To expect plans for a national transport system to be seriously considered at the height of the Battle of Britain was naïvely innocent'.

Exactly the same accusation could be made about the timing of Lemon's 'Post-war Reconstruction' Memo. In August 1940, the Country was standing alone against the Nazi threat – the Blitz and Battle of Britain were raging in full ferocity – and there were no indications that the Country would even survive the onslaught. A cynic might conclude that Lemon was also being remarkably naïve to state, confidently, at the outset: 'when the war is won'. And yet, it was, perhaps, this unshakeable conviction – held by people such as Lemon – which stiffened the Nation's resolve and led to the eventual victory.

Stamp replied to Lemon on 18 September 1940 that he was 'in complete accord with your main idea in your memorandum of the 1st August

on Post-war Reconstruction', but he obviously considered the proposals premature. Diplomatically he advised Lemon that, with everyone caught up with immediate urgent work, it might come as an anti-climax to have important people devoting most of their time to matters lying in the future. It was also essential that the Chief Officers should not feel that this was an extraneous nosey body settling their future for them, yet he could not expect them, at that time, to take the initial interest that was desirable. He proposed, therefore, that he and Lemon would continue to work on the plan together and then decide the psychological moment for its publication. And that appears to be as far as the proposals went at the time. Lord Stamp died in an air-raid on 17 April 1941, and it was his successor as Chairman, Lord Royden, who later revived the idea. This will be described in the next chapter.

Work for the LMS, 1940–41

APART from Lemon's monthly report on air-raid damage, there is very little in the LMS Minutes to show what occupied him for the next two years. The Board Minutes do show that, on his recommendation, authority was given for the

construction of a further one hundred 350hp diesel locomotives on 19 December 1940, at a cost of around £910,000.[390] However, work on these had not started by 24 April 1941, when the Traffic Committee could only estimate that possibly 59 would be built by 31 December 1942.[391] Because of wartime priorities, this order was suspended in 1942, and it is unclear how many engines were actually built before work stopped.

The succinct formality of these Minutes means it is therefore necessary to rely on H.G. Smith's 'Diary of No Consequence' to discover the various projects instigated by Lemon at this time. Smith therefore credited him with the decision to stop long-distance trains on the outskirts of London and wrote: 'The intensity of air raids in the London area in the autumn of 1940 disorganised train working considerably (though not to any serious extent) and to relieve local travel into and out of Euston, arrangements were made on the CHIEF'S suggestion, to stop main-line trains (except Scottish) at Watford in both directions, passengers arriving at or departing therefrom by electric trains. A most efficacious and convenient arrangement – and greatly appreciated by passengers – commenced in October 1940.' (Watford Junction was served by suburban electric stock into Euston with connections to the Bakerloo line of the London Underground system.)

The *Railway Gazette*, however, puts a slightly different perspective on the subject, as it made this very suggestion a month earlier in its issue of

Somers Town yard, alongside St. Pancras Station, full of coal wagons waiting to be unloaded. *Railway Gazette*

27 September 1940. The magazine also recommended suitable suburban stations that could be used by the other main-line companies.

The LNER also stopped trains for a while at Finsbury Park but this station was too close to King's Cross to be of any great benefit. The GWR seem to have totally dismissed the suggestion to stop their trains at Ealing Broadway, but the SR did schedule to stop express trains from the West Country at Woking. Lemon would thus appear to have been reacting to the magazine's suggestion, rather than coming up with the idea himself – a fact that Smith does not acknowledge!

Coal Supplies

COAL, of course, was the primary source of energy for the whole country, and was essential both for industry and household use. The railways were also heavily dependent on supplies and Smith tells us that:

Looking ahead THE CHIEF foresaw trouble arising with supplies of Loco. coal, and to prevent transport becoming a bottleneck with detriment to the war effort, he arranged for supplies to be obtained by sea from South Wales. Although a more expensive arrangement, the wisdom of the step was proved later; stocks were built up to about six weeks' supply (eight weeks was aimed at but not achieved). Subsequent loss of output from the mines caused enormous difficulties with the supply of domestic and industrial coal and led to voluntary rationing, but the railway position was infinitely better than it would have been, thanks to THE CHIEF'S move.

Smith does not give a date for this initiative. However, if one assumes that his 'Diary of No Consequence' is compiled in a chronological order, then it must date from soon after Lemon's return to the LMS in the late summer of 1940.

T.W. Royle in his *History of the LMS during the War* confirms that the Company did place contracts for South Wales coal, and comments:

As was to be expected, the seaborne Welsh coal when put on locomotive tenders, was very often small and dusty, and as some coalmen refused to handle it, it was confined to depots with coaling plants, which limited the range of distribution. This coal, even when mixed with other coals, could only be used for the lowest class of work, and owing to its poor condition and to the inexperience of the Firemen in its use, time was lost by engines in running. There was no shortage of the best quality coals in England, but it was not possible to obtain sufficient of the best No.1 group coal in Scotland, so the time-keeping of the Anglo-Scottish expresses suffered in consequence.[392]

Royle does not give a date for the purchase either, and it is difficult to say, therefore, whether his comments on the quality refer to Lemon's initiative, or to a later stage in the War when coal shortages were greater. Welsh coal can, of course, be of the highest quality; so it would appear that the LMS purchased a lower grade which was, possibly, all that was available. Smith does not mention the quality which, in the light of Royle's comments, puts a slightly different perspective on the benefits of Lemon's initiative.

Elsewhere in the country – as Smith implies – the situation was beginning to look grim, and as the winter of 1940 drew closer, there was grave concern, particularly in the Manchester area, of a lack of adequate supplies of coal. As usual, the blame for this, in the popular imagination, lay with the railways! The matter eventually reached Parliament, where the Minister of Transport (Reith) exonerated the railways and admitted the problems lay elsewhere – the Mines Department had not utilised the summer months with any sense of urgency to build up reserves, because of excessive absenteeism in the pits. The Government assured people that coal was now being produced in quantity, and carried by the railways. It was the unloading of wagons for onward use and delivery that caused the apparent shortages.

Before the war, the railways had been awash with thousands of privately-owned, often poorly maintained, small-capacity coal wagons. The logistics of shunting these around the system, and returning them to their owners, must have been a nightmare and taken up an inordinate amount of the railways' time and capacity. It was a situation that was ripe for change – indeed, the only benefits of the system seem to be the opportunities it now gives to model railway enthusiasts to include a variety of different wagons on their lay-outs! Wartime measures, though, had at least eliminated one part of the problem: all the wagons had been pooled, and so ownership was no longer a relevant factor. However, trainloads of coal still had to wait in sidings until laboriously unloaded by hand. Sir Ralph Wedgwood, Chairman of the Railway Executive Committee wrote an open letter to the *Manchester Guardian* in November 1940 trenchantly defending the railways' performance, giving precise facts and figures. He stated that, in the Manchester area during the previous month, there were never fewer than 3,000 wagons of coal waiting to be unloaded and, on occasions as many as 4,000. Further, for every ton of coal delivered, there had been at least four tons available and awaiting delivery. This was not enough to satisfy the critics and, on 20 November 1940, Lemon and Mr J.E. Kitching of the LNER travelled to Manchester to meet the Press. Once again, they quoted the statistics: for example, of the total of 2,838 wagons of coal delivered to one of the city's gasworks in the previous month, only 1,611 had so far been discharged. If more coal had been transported to the site, Lemon said, it would only have added to the large number of wagons already standing idle waiting to be unloaded. It was vital that wagons were used for their intended purpose – carrying fuel or merchandise – and not merely used as a convenient store in sidings. Now the only sanction that the railways possessed to encourage consignees to unload wagons promptly was to charge them a demurrage fee on overdue wagons. The Minister of Transport stated in Parliament that these penalty fees would either have to be more rigorously enforced or he would be compelled to take more drastic action. Lemon was more conciliatory, and told the Press in Manchester that 'the railways did not want to collect demurrage charges, they wanted the wagons freed for service'.

The delivery of domestic coal was a subject that Lemon had been pursuing for at least ten years – it was one of the subjects that his so-called 'Lightning' Committee had considered after their visit to America in 1930. On 28 November 1930 he had formulated his proposals in a Memorandum to the President. He envisaged a system whereby the coal merchants at a depot formed themselves into an organisation, and ordered in bulk. Coal was then delivered in uniform wagons and stored in silos for use. The wagons would be emptied into these silos mechanically, and a whole train-load could thus be disposed of within an hour. Nothing had come of these proposals in the succeeding years, despite Lemon's best efforts, because of opposition from the coal merchants. The idea, nevertheless, was a classic example of Lemon's constant quest to eliminate inefficiency and out-dated working practices.

Coal shortages in the winter of 1940 prompted Lemon to revive his proposals. Admittedly, they were not a 'quick fix' to the current problems, and it would have taken many years before such a system could have been brought into use nationwide. However, the Coal Silo Scheme, as it was known, was obviously a subject that was dear to his heart and an idea which he periodically resurrected in the hope that action would eventually be taken. Smith described it as a project 'which had grown grey or almost bald after about ten years' ineffective discussions between THE CHIEF and the coal trade'.

The National Archives contain a large file on the ensuing negotiations, from which one can trace the tortuous progress of the scheme.[393]

The earliest documents here are dated October 1940 and already refer to the project as 'an old friend'! It was actually a month earlier that Sir William Wood, his fellow Vice-President who represented the LMS on the Railway Executive Committee, re-introduced the idea into a discussion at the REC. This was two months before the shortages in Manchester became an active issue, and was either a complete coincidence or else showed remarkable foresight by Lemon. The Chairman of the REC, Sir Ralph Wedgwood, then wrote to Lord Hyndley, Commercial Adviser at the Mines Department: 'We had a discussion at the Railway Executive Committee recently in regard to the building up of stocks of coal at depots, works etc. Wood of the LMS then mentioned that his Company had for some time been working out a scheme for coal silos, the object of which was to enable coal to be discharged more rapidly and to be distributed more cheaply than at present. I asked him to let me have details of the scheme, and I send herewith for your information a copy'.

The details were set out in a Memoranda dating from 1937, the last time Lemon had tried to promote the idea, which explained the main principles:

During the last four or five years the LMS Railway have made several unsuccessful attempts to secure the co-operation of the coal trade in introducing coal silos at railway depots for improving the method of handling household coal.

The present method of transferring coal by hand from railway wagon to road vehicle, with its consequent disadvantages of increased shunting, wagon standage, congestion etc., is slow and costly and it was proposed to substitute for it a mechanically-operated system which could tip the coal into storage bunkers for subsequent withdrawal as required. The coal could in many cases be worked in train loads of 20 ton wagons, thus further reducing the cost of movement.

The railway company were prepared to bear the initial outlay of the construction of the plant, which would be operated by a company formed by the coal trade which would cover buying, selling, handling and distribution. Suitable terms were to be agreed to reimburse the capital provided by the railway company.

Plans were prepared showing alternative methods by which the contents of the coal wagons could be discharged into the bunkers from which the coal could be drawn off as desired and bagged, or fed into road vehicles if for bulk delivery.

In order to obtain the necessary experimental data to demonstrate the possibilities of such an arrangement, plans and estimates were prepared for a silo scheme on spare ground in the LMS depot at West Kensington.

The Memorandum continues with more precise technical details about the scheme, its effects and benefits. Lemon went to talk about the scheme with Lord Hyndley who asked him for a copy of the plans and what it would cost. Accordingly, Lemon sent him a break-down of the estimated 1937 costs and, seeking to capitalise on his interest, wrote that he hoped they would help in his 'consideration of this pressing problem'. However, the ensuing correspondence shows that the Government officials did not regard it as quite so pressing, and were much more cautious in their response. One such letter from the Director-General of the House Coal Distribution (Emergency) Scheme – who was appropriately a Mr Cole – reads: 'quite apart from all sorts of other difficulties and – I'm afraid – a good deal of trade opposition, (which I will try to overcome!), the lack of materials at the present time is a serious obstacle to the scheme'.

As the correspondence shows, it was the lack of available steel that was the first major problem. All such raw materials were allocated to the war effort, and none was available for a scheme which it would be hard to argue was absolutely essential to the defence of the country. However, what at first sight may seem an unimportant side-issue can sometimes have a 'knock on' effect and bring unforeseen benefits. An improvement to the supply of coal could certainly have freed railways to devote more of their energies and resources to the actual job of winning the war. But after the initial interest, Government enthusiasm seems to have waned. No further action was taken and the proposals languished until May 1941. The country muddled through the winter of 1940.

Other initiatives

T.W. ROYLE in his *History of the LMS during the War* includes a description of another initiative undertaken by the Company:

In 1940 the Government decided to import an enormous reserve of steel and iron which took the form of long billets. This traffic steadily increased until, in the winter of 1940/41, the Railway Companies' stocks of bolster and other suitable long wagons were incapable of handling the volume arriving at the ports, and a serious position arose, threatening the blockage of ports and delay to shipping.

As an emergency measure, it was then decided to improvise twin-bolster wagons by linking mineral end-door wagons together with their end-doors adjacent, removing these doors and fitting each wagon with a bolster. The wagons were not ideal, but they answered their purpose and gave immediate relief to the position.

Smith tells us that it was Lemon who came up with this simple and practical solution to the problem. According to Smith: 'The CHIEF put pencil to paper and showed Mr. Stanier how to convert end-door wagons into bolsters. Proposal to alter 1,000 agreed LMS Executive on 5th November [1940]. By 19th November C.M.E. had turned out 235 pairs; 500 pairs completed by middle of December – a good piece of work'. Board Minutes of 28 November 1940 confirm that authority was given for the conversion of 1,000 wagons into 500 twin-bolster wagons for the conveyance of steel bars and billets. A year later an order for a further 1,000 was made.[394] It is surprising that the *Railway Gazette* did not comment on this 'bodge', or illustrate it with a diagram and photograph, as large numbers were converted (not only by the LMS) and presumably they were, of great benefit both to the railways and the manufacturers for whom the steel was destined. Bob Essery in his series of books on

Canteen for workers repairing bomb damage, constructed from an LMS container on a flat wagon. Road vehicles were also similarly converted. Hardly a revolutionary idea but, nonetheless, new!
Nelson Twells

LMS wagons includes a drawing of the arrangement, but states that no drawing number was issued, no pictures are known and no running numbers have been recorded.[395]

H.G. Smith's meticulous account of Lemon's work include several suggestions that Lemon made for improvements that have not all been corroborated from other sources. These ideas covered a whole range of topics – some of which were not strictly his province – and while many of these only involved small, incidental, changes, they were nevertheless undoubtedly worthwhile. One such idea, for example, was the question of utilising the hay grown at the track side. This could be used as animal fodder and, at the Executive Meeting on 2 May 1941, Lemon suggested the use of small mowing machines similar to those used in Switzerland. It is not known whether the LMS built or acquired any such machines – but what is certain is that they didn't import them, in 1941, from the Continent! What this example illustrates, however, is that Smith's catalogue of Lemon's work is exhaustive, and shows that there is little likelihood that any work of major importance has been omitted.

Smith also mentions an innovation brought about by wartime conditions which was the use of portable loudspeaker equipment to announce the rearrangement of passenger services following air raids etc. It was found necessary to have some type of apparatus available at short notice to give out information to a particular area in order to regulate passengers or issue advice on alternative transport. Smith, rather quaintly, describes it as a 'portable pack type amplifier serving one loudspeaker and capable of being carried by one man' – but then it was a new idea! In February 1941, authority was given for the purchase of 30 sets of such equipment. At the same time Lemon authorised fitting loudspeakers at both Willesden Junction and Watford Junction stations.[396]

Another suggestion, if we accept Smith's records, was to arrange for lorries to take repair workers to the scene of damage from air-raids: much valuable time was wasted getting to and from jobs. This does not seem a revolutionary idea, but presumably had not been done before. As the men also experienced great difficulty in obtaining food whilst carrying out track repairs, he suggested the company should build mobile motor canteens for feeding them. A design was approved and a suitable number of canteens were built and stationed at central points ready for service.

Mobile Canteens for Troop Trains

THERE were also large numbers of troops travelling around the country by train – going to and from leave – and the provision of refreshment facilities for them was also an issue. There had been frequent complaints in the Press, and questions in Parliament, about the lack of facilities provided by the railways. What was needed was somewhere the troops could buy reasonably priced snacks. They did not want, or could not afford, to eat in the dining-cars. The LNER had sufficient stock to be able to introduce such a buffet service on its routes, but the LMS only had a limited supply of 'tea-cars'. As a temporary measure, Lemon suggested converting the end compartments of two carriages on each train into mobile canteens to be staffed by the YMCA and the Salvation Army. These would serve hot drinks and light refreshments at popular prices. The *Railway Gazette* reported the new facility on 24 January 1941, and gave full praise to Lemon for the idea:

Initiative in Refreshment

The LMSR. has inaugurated an important experiment in the provision of canteen facilities on trains. In view of criticisms which have been voiced both in the House of Commons and elsewhere as to the difficulties which members of the Forces experience in obtaining cheap and simple foodstuffs during long journeys, and the suggestions which have been made that more could be done to alleviate the position in this respect, it is well to be able to record that yet another step in meeting a wartime need has been made by one of the four main-line railway companies. The idea of the portable canteen which the LMSR. has put into service experimentally was conceived by Mr. E.JH. Lemon, whose tenure of office at the Air Ministry, for which he received a knighthood in the New Year Honours List, was marked by an energy and initiative which, as all who know him would expect, has quickly shown itself on his return to the LMSR. as the Commercial & Operating Vice-President. An obvious disability, the massing of troops in a railway

corridor seeking to obtain refreshments from one compartment and to return to their seats, will be overcome by one of the attendants canvassing for orders and carrying the refreshments to the men in their compartments.

The magazine then described the arrangements in detail on later pages of the same issue:

LMSR Portable Canteens

On Monday last, January 20, the Minister of Transport, who was received by Lord Stamp, Chairman of the London Midland & Scottish Railway Company, inspected at Euston station a new type of portable canteen for the service of refreshments to members of the Forces travelling by long-distance trains. The train, on which the canteen is the first of its type and which will be in experimental use for a fortnight, was the 1 o'clock from London to Glasgow (Central) which leaves Euston on Mondays, Wednesdays, and Fridays, and returns at 1 p.m. from Glasgow (Central) on Tuesdays, Thursdays, and Saturdays. The principle of the experiment is the fitting up of portable equipment in a third class compartment as a canteen, with an adjoining compartment for storage purposes. The lavatory is fitted with a portable draining board for washing up. From the compartment members of the Forces can be served with tea, coffee, sausage rolls, meat pies, sausages, and other light refreshments either through the doorway or by tray to and from ordinary compartments throughout the train. The whole of the canteen equipment has been designed so as to be readily dismantled, and it is stated that a compartment can be equipped or reconverted to its original use in the space of 12 min. The stand for the tea and coffee urns and for the hot water boiler is fitted over the seat on one side of the compartment and the store cupboard for provisions is placed over the other seat. Across the doorway is placed a folding service table; portable trays for crockery, cigarettes, and so forth are fitted above the luggage rack on each side of the compartment. Two canteens on the above model are attached to the train, one at each end, and to operate the service the Y.M.C.A.

and the Salvation Army are each providing two attendants. It is intended that one attendant will work the canteen compartment and the other will canvass adjoining coaches for orders. Although the midday service between London and Glasgow has been chosen for the initial experiment, a special feature of the canteen is that it can be fitted up very quickly in any corridor train when the need arises. The operation of the canteen and the provision of the food is being managed by the Y.M.C.A. and the Salvation Army, but the LMSR. is co-operating in the loan of its technical staff, certain of whom will be on the train during its experimental runs, and the provision of facilities for experiment. The equipment used was manufactured in LMSR. workshops.

This article was accompanied by a sketch of the layout of the canteen *(see below)*. A week later the magazine reported under the headline: 'The LMS goes all W.D.' that staid technical journalists who attended the official inspection of the new portable canteens were intrigued and a little startled to find the CME official drawing which

The layout for the temporary canteen fittings which could be fitted to a 3rd-class compartment. *Railway Gazette*

accompanied the technical brochure carried the light-hearted legend: 'Buffet, Extemporised, in 3rd Class Carr. Compt, For Troops, Sketch of.'

The magazine wondered whether other railway departments would soon be adopting this well-known War Office style for their official correspondence, so that before long a District Controller might be reporting a delay of 'minutes, twenty, to the such-and-such train, detaching wagon, mineral, with box, hot, to the discomfiture, guard of'.

Smith then recorded that the experiment showed that the portable canteens did cause corridor congestion, and the washing-up facilities were inadequate, whilst the journey was very tiring for the attendants. Buffet cars were preferable, but as the LMS had no such cars available, and no more extensive or better facilities were available, this arrangement was better than none. In April 1941, the *Railway Magazine* reported that the experiment was to become a permanent feature on certain express trains, but also reported the introduction of special third-class dining cars for troops to use on the London–Glasgow route.

Speed Restrictions

IN JUNE 1938 it had been agreed, after discussions at the Ministry of Transport, that massive speed restrictions would come into operation on the railways in the event of war. These were

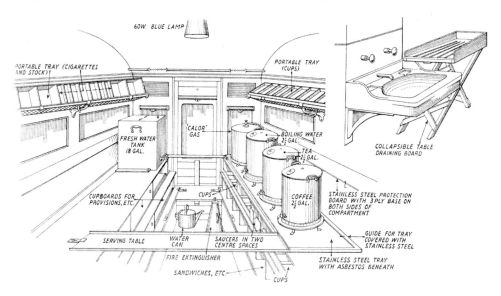

60W. BLUE LAMP

PORTABLE TRAY (CIGARETTES AND STOCK)

PORTABLE TRAY (CUPS)

FRESH WATER TANK 18 GAL.

'CALOR' GAS

BOILING WATER 2½ GAL.

TEA- 2½ GAL.

COLLAPSIBLE TABLE DRAINING BOARD

CUPBOARDS FOR PROVISIONS, ETC.

CUPS

COFFEE 2½ GAL.

STAINLESS STEEL PROTECTION BOARD WITH 3 PLY BASE ON BOTH SIDES OF COMPARTMENT

SERVING TABLE

WATER CAN

SAUCERS IN TWO CENTRE SPACES

GUIDE FOR TRAY COVERED WITH STAINLESS STEEL

FIRE EXTINGUISHER

STAINLESS STEEL TRAY WITH ASBESTOS BENEATH

SANDWICHES, ETC.

CUPS

considered necessary because of the damage and disorganisation that was anticipated from widespread air-raids. The maximum permitted speed was fixed by the Engineers' Sub-Committee of the REC from considerations of safety and track maintenance, and limits were thus set for day and night operation of passenger and freight trains, with further restrictions during an air-raid.

At the outbreak of war, the speed of passenger trains was originally fixed at a maximum between stops of 45mph, but a month later this was raised to an average of 50mph with a maximum at any point not to exceed 60mph. The limit for all trains during an air-raid was originally set at 15mph during daylight hours, and 10mph at night. Contrary to expectations, the disruption from air-raids did not immediately materialise and these restrictions were also found to be too severe. On 11 November 1940, the limits during an air-raid were relaxed somewhat so that all trains could now travel at a maximum 15mph in the blackout, whilst passenger trains, and fully-braked freight trains, were allowed to travel up to a maximum of 25mph during daylight air-raids.

The increase in war traffic on the railways, coupled with the blackout conditions and air-raid damage, meant that both passenger and freight services deteriorated alarmingly under these restrictions; and questions were constantly asked in Parliament and the Press about the poor service. Long-distance trains often arrived at their destinations three or four hours late. The LMS was rightly concerned as the blame for these delays was – in the general public's eyes – always the fault of the railway companies, and not the conditions under which they were required to operate.

H.G. Smith tells us that at the LMS Executive Meetings in December 1940, Lemon strongly urged that higher speeds than 60mph should be run in the interests of better traffic working. He could not argue his case at the REC itself as he was not a member, and so Lemon prepared a Memo entitled 'Transport and the War Effort'. This covered a wide variety of topics, but one section was sub-titled 'Speed Limits' and encapsulates Lemon's reasons for seeking change:

It is understood that the 60 mile per hour speed limit was fixed to reduce maintenance.

During the War certain risks must be taken, and it is suggested that 75 miles per hour is not an unreasonable risk. It will, of course, be necessary to differentiate between day and night operations, and it is obvious that to run at 75 miles per hour in an area where bombing is actually taking place would be taking undue risk, whilst in daylight, with clear conditions, there would be no risk.

He concludes the Memo by saying that it was the Government's responsibility to authorise an increase in the permissible speed and not individual Operating Superintendents. Presumably, Lemon envisaged this Memo being circulated widely outside the confines of the LMS and discussed at the REC and the Ministry of Transport. The REC, however, was opposed to the idea, with the main objection to any further changes coming from the LNER. However, the Operating Committee did recommend that the night-time restriction of 25mph during air-raids could be raised to 30mph; and that 'normal' speeds should apply during air-raids in daylight. However, nobody would define what they meant by 'normal'. At the LMS Executive meeting on 28 January 1941, Lemon again urged the lifting of restrictions and, on 11 February, as no clarification on what was meant by 'normal' had been received from either the REC or the Minister of Transport, he took matters into his own hands and issued orders that drivers should be instructed to make up lost time by running up to 75mph, subject to any local engineering restrictions that might be in force. On 22 February Sir Ralph Wedgwood, Chairman of the REC, questioned Lemon's unilateral instruction, and said it placed the other companies in an invidious position as it struck at the root of all co-operative action. Lord Stamp replied diplomatically.

The LMS action was noted in the *Railway Gazette* on 28 February 1941; and, a week later, the magazine reported that 'It has been decided that all classes of British main-line trains should run at normal speeds during daylight hours irrespective of air-raid alerts, and at speeds not exceeding 30mph during alerts in blackout hours'. Faced with a *fait accompli*, the REC agreed to the changes at its meeting on 4 March without comment. Wedgwood reiterated his feeling of being hurt in a further letter to Lord Stamp, calling it 'an episode which cannot be a matter of satisfaction to anyone'.

On 30 May 1941, the *Railway Gazette* reported that there had been a remarkable improvement in the punctuality of trains – particularly on the LMS. The magazine attributed this to the raising of the speed limits and commented that, as far as they knew, this was the first time in the history of the country that definite instructions had been given to enginemen to make up lost time. This last statement drew a swift riposte from the Southern Railway whose General Manager wrote to the magazine to say that the SR had issued such instructions to drivers as long ago as 1934. The *Railway Gazette* returned to the subject again on 5 September 1941, commenting:

There are few main lines in Great Britain over which a more remarkable recovery in punctuality has taken place, from the deplorable conditions of last winter, than the Western Division main line of the LMSR. It must be confessed that, with all allowance for difficulties in operation caused by lengthy night raids and alerts, the leeway to be made up on this route was exceptional; but no less exceptional has been the transformation. Drivers have taken to heart the encouragement that has been given to them to make up lost time, and some of the examples of this that have come under our immediate notice recently have been remarkable.

The Memo referred to above, entitled 'Transport and the War Effort' was actually Lemon's manifesto for the complete re-organisation of the existing system of Government control. It comes in a file labelled 'Proposals for Co-ordination of All Transport', and the subject of speed restrictions on the railways was only one small item. In this Memo, which is dated 6 January 1941, Lemon argued for greater central control of all forms of transport, proposing that the Minister of Transport should also set up National Executive Committees for canals, coastal shipping, roads, docks and air. All these Committees would then report to a Main Executive Committee, which would co-ordinate the whole mechanism of transportation nationwide. It was a planner's ultimate utopian dream. However, to this writer, the proposals seem more likely to have produced a nightmare scenario in practice, with increased layers of bureaucracy and inefficiency slowing down the making of any decisions at all.

It is also seems relevant – because of its timing – that the *Railway Gazette* of 21 March 1941 then carried a long article entitled 'Re-organisation of Road and Rail Transport in Great Britain'. No author was credited, but the article carried the sub-title: 'A railway officer submits a scheme of organisation'. The proposals it contained were a comprehensive plan for post-war re-organisation, bearing a striking resemblance to those in Lemon's memo. This scheme envisaged a management structure wherein district offices reported to regional offices who, in turn, were responsible to a central – and national – headquarters. Presumably, the author imagined that the main-line companies would become no more than regional offices, and it is hard to square this idea with their remaining as independent companies, answerable to their shareholders. At national headquarters the author proposed there would be a President supported by Vice-Presidents in charge of specific departments. Now the LMS were the only one of the four main-line companies to use these titles – so it is not too difficult to guess who must have written the article! We then find that, a couple of months later on 9 May 1941, Lord Reith, the Minister of Transport, wrote in his diary that he had 'started up a scheme for the co-ordination of all transport'. This was so soon after Lemon's memo and the *Railway Gazette* article, that it must be more than a coincidence, and certainly appears as though Lemon's ideas had found their way to Reith, and set him thinking along similar lines. It also indicates – to this writer – that Lemon did not want to return to the pre-war situation, but was quite prepared to see the LMS and the other railway companies lose their individuality in the quest for greater national efficiency.

However, these memos and articles immediately show a contradiction between Lemon's idealistic proposals and his actions. The railways *were*, after all, now being co-ordinated nationwide by a central authority – the REC. Yet, on the question of speed limits, he was chafing at having to accept a decision he disagreed with – and so he flouted it. One could argue that he did originally write that the easing of speed limits was a decision for the Ministry of Transport, and that he only acted as he did when no quick decision was forthcoming from the civil service machine. However, the Minister and the REC might very well have decided against any relaxation of the speed limits. As it was, they were presented with a *fait accompli*. One is drawn to the inescapable conclusion that Lemon would only have been happy working under a central authority if he had been running it!

The other suggestions that Lemon incorporated into his 'Co-ordination' Memo cover a wide variety of topics, and many were his old familiar war-horses. He returned to the subject of diesel locomotives for shunting – this time pointing out that, as well as being available round the clock, they did not spill light from fireboxes during black-out hours. He even ventured into the realms of science fiction – suggesting that night-time shunting could be carried out with infra-red lighting! Rather more sensibly, he urged the Government Supply Departments to give railways some form of long-range forecast of future requirements, rather than treating such matters as 'top secret'. The building of coal silos was again recommended, and in this context, he suggested that the number of men from the larger coal merchants in London who had been called up should be ascertained. Also the number of coal merchants who worked on Sundays, and whether they were being supplied with spare parts so they could maintain their lorries in good condition in order to clear the depots. He wrote that 'whilst this may seem an unimportant matter to a Priority Committee, it is vital to transport as a whole'. It was also vital for Lemon to have these sort of statistics if he was going to pursue his case for coal silos!

He also recommended that the telephone system on the LMS should be renewed, as the part inherited from the old Midland Railway dated back to 1910 and was now out of date. Any new system, he wrote, should be fully compatible with the other main-line companies 'with the object of working the railways as one unit'. There were also other indications that Lemon wanted to erode the individuality of the separate companies. In this Memo he also suggested that a full-time Central Committee should be set up to plan all railway operations. To achieve this, the Committee would need to sweep away the 'ownership' boundaries of individual companies. He continued: 'In discussing this matter with the other Railway Companies, particularly the GWR and LNER, it could be pointed out that . . . the proposals are, in fact, nothing more than a development of the 'closer working' arrangements which have already been effected'. This is somewhat devious of Lemon, and certainly shows that he was prepared to be economical with the truth to achieve his ends! Moreover, 'closer working' was something that in his view was *not* working properly.

Smith tells us that, as the war progressed, traffic working to and from the GWR became more and more difficult, and the exchange junctions in the Birmingham area were frequently becoming congested. Traffic was consequently being held up and the LMS were blamed for the delays. Of course, Smith recounts that these were all the fault of the GWR, who were urged to take remedial action. On 11 December 1940, Lemon reported to the Executive that he had given orders to block all GWR traffic and Stamp suggested that the GWR people should be invited to see some LMS Control Offices – and see how to do things properly. On 31 December 1940, Lemon again emphasised to the LMS Executive that the cross-company procedures were not working satisfactorily, and that officers should be employed full-time to address the problems, which could not merely be solved at weekly meetings. Lord Stamp had a meeting with Sir James Milne when it was agreed that officers from both companies should meet and discuss ways to collaborate more closely, but on 11 February 1941 Lemon reported to the Executive that there had been no continuous contact with the GWR and the arrangements were not working. Lemon himself went to see Milne and reported back on 18 February that their talk ought to be beneficial. However, Lemon appointed three men to work full-time as a Traffic Routing Committee. They were charged not only with analysing the traffic flow through these exchange junctions, but to re-route traffic when necessary to the most efficient and economical route.

Smith grows quite lyrical about these improvements and calls the problem 'a field which ought to have been ploughed long ago before tares grew up and choked the fruitful seed', but continues that it made 'the Operating people glad to claim the crop and forget the sower of the seed'.

Death of Lord Stamp

ASHTON DAVIES, who had retained his title of Vice-President after Lemon's return, celebrated 50 years service with the LMS and its constituent companies in March 1941. Lord Stamp presided over a luncheon of senior staff on 20 March to commemorate the event, at which both he and Lemon paid tribute to the valuable service which Davies had rendered. It must have been one of the last times that Stamp can have seen so many of his senior staff together at the same time. During an air-raid on London on 16 April 1941, a German plane jettisoned a bomb over the south-eastern suburbs. The bomb fell on Lord Stamp's house in Chislehurst killing him, his wife and eldest son instantly.

Lemon and the other three Vice-Presidents, Sir William Wood, Sir Harold Hartley and Ashton Davies all paid their individual and personal tributes to Lord Stamp in the *Railway Gazette* of 25 April 1941. Lemon wrote:

My association with the late Lord Stamp extended over a period of about fifteen years.

To get a proper perspective of his work one must go back to the amalgamation of the British railways in 1923, when such important companies as the L. & N.W., Midland, L. & Y., and Caledonian and others became what is now the LMSR Company. Mere amalgamation of a number of undertakings is comparatively simple, but to fuse them into a living organisation is quite another matter, more particularly as those railways were staffed by men of strong loyalties to their own companies, with distinct traditions and outlook, and Lord Stamp's greatest work, in my opinion, was when he succeeded in creating out of that mixture a loyalty to the new LMSR.

I would emphasise, too, how in sanctioning the enormous new equipment in order to obtain more efficient working, he realised more fully than many of us that the spirit of the undertaking was of far greater importance than the material means for working it. He will go down in history as a great railwayman, and as a very kindly chief, who, by tact, understanding and a great knowledge of human nature, got the best out of everyone with whom he came in contact.

His mind was always open to the impact of new ideas and a frequent remark was 'we cannot afford not to try that.' His gift of turning out phrases which stuck in people's minds was amazing, and one which remained with me was when on one occasion I went to him with a scheme, which comprised an entirely new outlook in technique, and which I wanted to have adopted, he turned to me and said 'as long as 95 per cent, of your white elephants turn out to be black ones, I don't mind'.

His utilisation of modern publicity technique was with the same end in view, to achieve cooperative support from all members of the staff, and through the medium of staff newspapers, talking films, etc., he got his messages over in understandable form throughout the LMS organisation.

His personality did not show itself in unnecessary forcefulness of character; he had the happy gift of cheerfulness and imperturbability under the most difficult conditions.

A great chief and a great loss.

Stamp's death was not just a great loss to the LMS, but also to Lemon. Sir Harold Hartley, who observed the working relationship between the two men at first hand, wrote in his obituary of Lemon: 'Lord Stamp's tragic death in 1941 was a great blow to him. Lemon had depended so much on Stamp's backing and encouragement and wise discrimination about his many schemes. Theirs was a most happy combination of two minds, poles apart in outlook and experience, but with trust and confidence in one another'.

Stamp's death meant that the LMS had to fill two posts – those of Chairman and President, which had been combined under Stamp. Sir

William Wood was appointed as President, which meant a slight re-allocation of duties for the other Vice-Presidents. Lemon took over responsibility for the Irish railways which had previously fallen to Wood (an Irishman). This was noted in Minute No.8500 of the Executive Committee. The relevant page of these Minutes exists in Lemon's papers, which also shows that Minute No.8501 was concerned with further canteen arrangements for troops on trains to Scotland. This second Minute has written beside it in pencil – and perhaps this is an ominous sign considering that all the official records of the Executive Committee seem to be lost – 'file in cupboard in Room 101'!!

The letters that Wood wrote to the various Department Heads informing them of the change of responsibilities illustrate another facet of war-time working conditions. The LMS, in line with Government policy, had started a massive salvage drive for all waste materials – including paper, and the backs of discarded documents from the early 1930s were used for carbon copies of these official letters. Thus we find that the copy of the letter to Frank Pope in Ireland, telling him of the management changes, appears on the back of a docket referring to a dispute in 1932 over charges for an office at Llanberis Station; another letter appears on the reverse of a docket from 1935 that had formerly only recorded that a Mr Sutton was no longer going to rent a wharf, etc. etc.

The other new appointment was that of Chairman, and Lord Royden, who had been Stamp's deputy, was elevated to the post. H.G. Smith records that Royden placed himself in Lemon's hands to arrange inspections of the line and introduce him to local officers and encourage their efforts. In his idiosyncratic style, Smith wrote: 'During the next four or five months, commencing middle of July [1941], the whole line was practically covered with The

Lord Royden, appointed Chairman following the death of Lord Stamp.
National Archives

CHIEF as mentor and the SHADOW as recorder on board the saloon, with typewriter clicking as dawn broke "o'er moor and fen, o'er crag and torrent" till the job was done'. The Scottish tour to the Kyle of Lochalsh entailed 1,300 miles in three days.

The Coal Silo Scheme (again!)

'AT THE Executive Meeting on 11th March 1941 the Coal silos question raised its head'. With these words, Smith re-introduced the subject in his 'Diary of No Consequence'. He might have added 'again', as the Scheme had been officially dormant since late Autumn 1940, when the Mines Department had considered the problem of obtaining necessary steel to be insuperable. It would seem that Lemon was giving the dying embers of the project a poke, in the hope of re-kindling the fire. Nothing came of his efforts though until May 1941, when the Deputy Under-Secretary for Mines, W.G. Nott-Bower, wrote to him:

I hope you do not think that I have gone to sleep over the coal silo proposal. This is far from the case. The Mines Department is, in principle, entirely in favour of your scheme, but at the moment the governing factor appears to be steel. There is not a single ounce available from the mining allocation, even if it were proper to divert it for such a purpose. We are also told that nothing can be spared from the railway allocation; and generally the whole steel position appears to be so tight as to afford no chance of getting the necessary supplies at the moment. If the position improves, we shall be perfectly ready to go into the matter again.

I am only sorry that such an invaluable forward step cannot be taken now.

However, the fact that the Government had officially taken an interest meant that Lemon was still willing to pursue it as far as possible. Maybe a project that had never succeeded in peace time would come to fruition in war. H.G. Smith recounts what happened next: 'Sir Andrew Duncan, President of the Board of Trade, whilst staying at the Mill House [LMS Management accommodation in Watford] chipped THE CHIEF about coal wagons standing loaded about the line, and was told about the coal silo scheme and inability to get the Mines Department to push it with the trade, when Sir Andrew agreed forthwith to provide priority for the steel required.'

This was a positive step forward. The Department of Mines came under the control of the Board of Trade, and Duncan, who had been Chairman of the British Iron & Steel Federation before his appointment to the Board of Trade, apparently felt he could 'pull strings'. The project was given a new lease of life!

Nott-Bower confirmed Duncan's interest in the Scheme in a Memo to Lord Hyndley on 29 October 1941 – a year after the initial interest in the Scheme:

At his weekly meeting yesterday, the President announced that he had recently met Sir Ernest Lemon who had discussed with him his project for erecting an experimental coal silo. The President said that he approved the scheme in principle and had told Sir Ernest Lemon to go ahead with it. Sir Ernest Lemon rang me up this morning and said that in accordance with the President's authority, he was proceeding at once to obtain a tender from the firm which does most of the LMS constructional work. The scheme is to be the West Kensington Scheme, and the silo is to be erected on LMS land and is to be so designed that it will be possible, if desired, to move it elsewhere later on. I asked Sir Ernest whether the necessary steel priority would be applied for on the LMS allocation, but he said that this could not be done as all their extra steel was needed for repairs of bomb damage. He is therefore relying on us to obtain an addition to the Mines Department allocation (assuming that we can't squeeze it out of our present quantities). As soon as he has heard from the contractor, he will be communicating with us about this. He anticipates that it should take about six months to erect the plant.

Another writer has then added:

There is no hope of finding a spare 1,000 tons of steel from the present allocation to the Mines Department and I do not look forward to appealing successfully to the Materials Committee for an additional amount for such a project.

The country's supply of steel is insufficient to meet all the present Service and civilian demands and the amount allocated to the Mines Department is barely enough to meet our production requirements, particularly in view of a potential shortage of timber for propping purposes, for which the only practical substitute is steel.

Nott-Bower wrote to Lemon at the beginning of November telling him the procedure he would have to follow to acquire the necessary steel, now that Sir Andrew Duncan had given the Scheme his blessing. This would involve making a formal application to the relevant Licensing Officer at the Ministry of Works and Buildings (MWB), which the Mines Department would support. It would then be considered by several MWB Sub-Committees for approval. However, he warned Lemon that: 'The Prime Minister has recently insisted on a drastic reduction of the country's building programme and no project will get through unless it can be shown to be "vital and urgent". A good case will have to be put up showing the advantages and savings to be made in transport, labour and other ways'. He urged Lemon to try and get Lord Reith to take a personal interest in the project, as well as Duncan. By this time, Reith had left the Ministry of Transport and was now Minister of Works and Building. Reith's diaries show that Lemon followed this advice and that, on 19 November, he 'lunched with Lemon at Euston about silos'.[397]

The application was presumably made, and Lemon started to deal with other aspects of the scheme. One immediate problem was the site at

Silos for bagging domestic coal in the USA. Picture from S.H. Fisher's official report of the 1933 visit to America with the *Royal Scot*.
National Archives

West Kensington which was, at the time, covered by a storage dump of 8,000 tons of coal belonging to the Ministry of Works. This would have to be moved to an adjoining site which, Nott-Bower warned him, would not be easy to arrange as the London County Council (LCC) had earmarked that particular area for static water tanks.

Surprisingly, up to this point, no official meetings had been held with the coal merchants whose working practices would be radically changed. Lemon and Nott-Bower had the first meeting with Mr John Charrington, the largest coal merchant using the site, on 12 November 1941, to explain the scheme.

Lemon told him that, as soon as the plant was ready, it would be taken over and operated by a private holding company representing the three or four large coal merchants at present using the depot. Lemon thought that he would possibly chair this company. In the meantime, the LMS would give notice to all the merchants that the silo was going to be built on the land at present occupied by the sidings, turntables, etc. that they used; and that, as soon as the silo was ready for operation, no merchant would be able to obtain any coal from that depot except through the silo operating company. Lemon also stated that it was necessary, for the economic operation of the silo plant, that one or two other LMS depots in the immediate vicinity would be closed down so as

to concentrate the demand at West Kensington. These were the depots at Kensington High Street and Warwick Road – a mile or so to the south.

Charrington, of course, already knew about the proposals, unofficially, from contacts at the House Coal Distribution Scheme and, while he did not dismiss them out of hand, said he had no doubt that they would evoke strong opposition from many quarters. Nott-Bower asked him, as the next step, to prepare a formal response setting out the principal difficulties that he expected; and in his notes of this meeting wrote 'Sir Ernest Lemon is tending to take the bit between his teeth over this Scheme, and I think we shall have to be careful that we are not dragged along too fast. I do not propose to do anything more until I have received Mr. Charrington's memorandum'.

The necessity of committing his thoughts to paper made Charrington a good deal more conscious of the difficulties involved. Yet, as the Scheme was a private initiative by the LMS, he did not think it necessary at this stage to consult any of the other Merchants. The Government over-ruled his opinion as they felt that such a radical departure from present procedures meant important principles were at stake. For example, it was accepted that 'soft' coal would not be suitable for use in the silos, and there would also have to be a reduction in the number of different grades of coal. They were also worried about the disturbance to existing trade relationships, both at the merchants' end and the collieries.

And so consultations started with the Society of Coal Merchants, which meant the involvement of yet another Committee – the Merchants' Consultative Committee. Meanwhile Lemon was pressing ahead: on 4 December he reported to Nott-Bower that the site had been cleared and on 20 December that contracts had been let with the construction company who were to build the silos. There were to be 8 hoppers, each of 250 tons. The LMS would stand the total capital cost of construction which, it was estimated, would need about 750 tons of steel. Lemon now emphasised that the West Kensington Scheme was essentially an experiment, designed to prove that the present system of coal distribution was entirely out of date, and that the silo system resulted in a substantial gain both in terms of transport and of retail distribution. This is the first time that the word 'experiment' was used.

The affected coal merchants eventually drew up a list of objections, some of which appear to have substance, but others now seem trivial. For example, they foresaw that all the different merchants would have to pool their sacks, which was 'impractical'. They thought that more petrol would be required for deliveries if two of the secondary depots were closed, and there would be delays in loading; also that collieries might take the opportunity to send bad coal to the silos. However, their main objection was that the silos would damage household coal, which accounted for over 85% of the trade from the depot. They had no objection to silos for industrial use.

They were also worried about the constitution of the new company to run the Scheme, and their position within it. Charrington backed the plan that it should be managed by two or three of the largest merchants at the site, as a larger body would never be able to agree on anything, although he denied he was seeking to gain any personal preferment by this. Smaller merchants were not happy, and demanded an equal say in the management. Rather ingenuously, Lemon suggested that Sir Alfred Hurst – Nott-Bower's superior – had volunteered that the Mines Department would draw up the constitution and smooth over all the difficulties. This was news

to Nott-Bower, and he was having none of it. He replied to Lemon on 29 January 1942:

So far as I am aware, it has always been clearly understood that the Silo Scheme, both on the constructional and operational sides, was a private enterprise. It is true that it has the active support of the Government, and that the President of the Board of Trade and the Secretary for Mines are prepared to render every possible assistance to the promoters of the Scheme. At the same time, it is a little difficult to see how we can give direct help until there is some preliminary agreement as to the method in which the Scheme is to be operated and the persons who are going to do it. I do not think that there is, at present at any rate, any suggestion that the Scheme should be operated as a Government undertaking by the Mines Department, and we are awaiting notification that there is a group of coal merchants ready to take it on as an experiment.

He circulated a departmental note containing the ominous observation: 'Mr. Charrington's enthusiasm for this Scheme is rapidly decreasing, mainly because he thinks Sir Ernest Lemon is not fully conscious of all the difficulties involved, and is rushing ahead much too fast'.

The records show that this was Lemon's last involvement with the project. At the beginning of February 1942 he was laid up in bed with a sprained ankle. The negotiations were taken over by Sir William Wood, as the new President of the LMS. He chaired a meeting with the affected merchants at the beginning of March 1942, when all their objections to the Scheme were discussed. These were now set out in twelve separate categories. H.G. Smith describes them as 'every snag the representatives could think of'. As the merchants' apprehensions increased , the Government's commitment appeared to grow stronger. By now the Ministry of War Transport was involved, and at a joint meeting with the Mines Department on 16 March resolved:

1. Mines are convinced that methods of receiving and delivering coal at depots are archaic, extravagant and urgently in need of reform.

2. They approve the proposal of the LMS to construct silos and demonstrate the advantages of modern methods.

3. They consider that the plant should be designed to serve ultimately the whole trade done at South Kensington and High Street depots.

4. As this change will revolutionise the methods of the coal trade and restrict the choice of customers, it involves many experiments in practice which can only be solved by trying them out. Mines therefore favour starting with a plant to deal with approximately half the trade done at these two depots, but designed so that it can be readily extended to deal with the whole trade.

5. They urge that LMS should start construction of these silos at once, and will give the Ministry of War Transport their full backing to procure the necessary labour and material and by recommending the new methods to the coal trade and the public.

Although one assumes that Lemon's sprained ankle was only a minor inconvenience, there were signs that his health was, again, a cause of concern. He was also now heavily involved with a new project that was posing problems of its own: post-war railway reconstruction, (which will be discussed in the next chapter). On 27 March 1942, Lord Royden, the new Chairman of the LMS, wrote to him: 'I have been much worried for some time about your health', and urged him to go off and have a week's holiday. Lemon took the advice and went to Mullion Cove in Cornwall. On 8 April, he wrote to Royden saying that he intended to stay for longer than he had originally intended, to which Royden replied that he should stay until he was thoroughly fit. Lemon therefore missed the final death throes of the Coal Silo Scheme.

By the beginning of April 1942, the Government was imperative that discussions must stop and a decision taken on whether to proceed or not. Accordingly, on 5 April a meeting was held attended by representatives of the Mines Department, the LMS, the Ministry of War Transport and the Merchants' Consultative Committee.

All the arguments for and against the Scheme were rehearsed yet again, until Sir William Wood finally announced: 'The LMS were definitely not prepared to proceed with the present scheme in the absence of full and willing co-operation by the merchants. It was clear from what had been said that this was not forthcoming: so that the scheme must be abandoned.' And that was that. There were vague mutterings about reconsidering the project after the war was over. But the scheme was dead; after Lemon had worked on it for 18 months.

Now it is conceivable that Wood's ultimatum was intended to call the merchants' bluff. The records show that up until this point, he had officially been as enthusiastic about the scheme as Lemon. However, if this was the case, it did not have the intended effect. It was left to Sir Harold Hartley to tidy up the loose ends, and cancel the contracts with the constructors. There is nothing in the records to show Lemon's reaction to this turn of events, but he must have been furious. It was not that the scheme foundered on the difficulty in obtaining the necessary steel, which was the original problem. This must have been satisfactorily overcome. It was the merchants' intransigence to changes in their established working practices that caused the whole scheme to collapse like a house of cards. Nott-Bower in an earlier Memo had referred to the Scheme as 'this apparently heaven-sent opportunity of driving in the thin end of the wedge'. But neither he, nor anybody else, was prepared to push it any further. A more resolute attitude by either the Government or the LMS might well have negotiated a way round the merchants' objections, and found compromises that they were willing to accept. Nevertheless, it must be accepted that, at an early stage, Lemon did not spend sufficient time and effort in engaging the good-will of the traders. Rather he concentrated on the technical and engineering aspects. Indeed, it could well be that he was relying on the Government to push the project through as an emergency war-measure, and thus circumvent the necessity for bothering about the concerns of the merchants. This was a surprising oversight for a man who constantly stressed the need for proper planning.

ELEVEN

The End of a Railway Career, 1942

I N THE late Autumn of 1941, Sir Thomas Royden, who had succeeded Lord Stamp as Chairman, turned his mind to the problem of reconstruction that the LMS would face at the end of the war. and asked Lemon if he had given any thought to the subject. Lemon told him that he had prepared a memo on the subject for Lord Stamp in August 1940, and gave him a copy. Royden realised that its analysis of the problem was exactly what he wanted and, on 4 December 1941, discussed the matter with Lemon asking him to take on the task of preparing proposals for the post-war reconstruction of the LMS in all its phases, including the possibility that the railways might be nationalised and brought under some form of Government control, or amalgamated into a smaller number of groups. Royden expressed his fears that this extra work, on top of his other Vice-Presidential commitments, would be too heavy a task; but Lemon – who, of course, was still grappling with the Coal Silo Scheme – assured him that this would not be so. Royden thought the matter should not be handled by any set committee, but that particular individuals in the various departments should be brought in as required. It was also understood that it would not be possible, at the outset, to incorporate in the proposals anything more than what the LMS should do to bring its own house into the most efficient state; but when this was done, it would be a basis for adjustment with anything the other companies prepared.[398]

The Railway Companies Association Commission

LATER that month, Royden raised the subject with colleagues from the other main-line railways at a meeting of the Railway Companies' Association (RCA). He circulated Lemon's Memo, and found that the other Chairmen had also started to consider the matter. They discussed the desirability of setting up a special Commission, with members drawn from all the different companies, to examine and report upon the problems which they faced. This seemed an eminently sensible suggestion, and Lemon appeared to be the obvious person to appoint as Chairman. Royden put the idea to him, strongly urging him to accept. He told Lemon that, in his opinion, the work of the Commission would be of the utmost importance and that he was the only man capable of undertaking such a task. He assured him that the work would be supported in every way by the Chairmen of all the Companies involved. As the position was intended to be a full-time appointment, it would mean that Lemon would have to relinquish his Vice-Presidential responsibilities again, but these could be re-allocated. The following morning Lemon informed Royden that he was willing to become the independent Chairman of the Commission. However, so that he would not totally lose touch with what was going on at the LMS, he arranged that copies of all the weekly statistical returns should continue to be sent to him, and he continued to attend Board Meetings.

On 18 December, H.G. Smith tells us that Royden probably unofficially told the other LMS Directors of these developments at the Board luncheon. On the 23rd, he then called a meeting of all the Chief Officers of the LMS to tell them what was happening, and asked them to give Lemon all possible assistance. Smith quotes Royden as saying: 'He has undertaken an

Lemon intended to keep an eye on LMS operations while he was working for the Railway Chairmen's Commission. This memo shows the daily statistics that he was accustomed to receive as Vice-President.

Lemon's personal papers

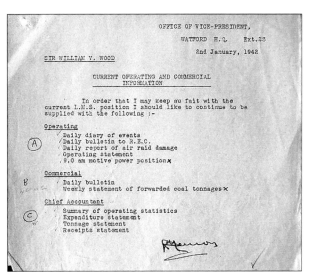

unenviable job and I sympathise with him. I look upon this task as the most important problem facing the railways today, and I do want you to help him all you can.' It was not only Royden who foresaw difficulties ahead. The Minutes of the LMS Board Meeting in February 1942, which officially recorded Lemon's secondment to this new post, predicted that the work 'would make considerable call on Sir Ernest's tact'.

In view of the later problems that Lemon had to face – notably from Sir James Milne of the GWR – it is worth commenting here that the only file in the National Archives dealing with this whole subject is Milne's GWR file. There is no equivalent in the LMS records.

On 1 January 1942, Lemon attended a meeting at Liverpool Street of the Chairmen and Deputy Chairmen of the four main-line companies, who all indicated they welcomed the idea of the Commission and would give it their full support. Sir Ronald Matthews of the LNER, who chaired the RCA, stated that this new Commission would be known as the 'Railway Companies' Association Commission' and its remit was ' to enquire how the efficiency of the railways can be improved in the broadest sense by schemes of post-war reconstruction and re-organisation'. However, Lemon found that the RCA had added an important caveat to the proposals in his original Memo. In this he had acknowledged that the railways should plan for the possibility of nationalisation or, at least, amalgamation into a smaller number of companies. This, naturally, caused a problem for the Chairmen, and Matthews stressed that the Commission must

work on the assumption that the four companies would go back after the war to their individual entities, with their separate financial responsibilities. It might be thought that, by this, the Chairmen were being ostriches – and refusing to face up to the inevitable. However, as Chairmen, they were primarily responsible to their shareholders for the continuing existence and well-being of their companies and, presumably, hoped that the Commission would devise schemes for such radical improvements that they could claim the railways were perfectly competent to put their own house in order and meet the intensive competition which would undoubtedly arise from road and air. They could not be seen to be actively planning for their own demise. The Coalition Government, with its enthusiasm for nationalisation, would cease to exist at the end of the war – and the *status quo* would be re-established. And so there was a hidden political agenda behind the Commission's work.

Lemon gave each of the Chairmen a folio containing a list of the problems which he thought might be suitable for consideration. The following day, Sir Ronald Matthews wrote a personal letter to Lemon confirming the decision at the meeting, concluding 'My colleagues and I are very appreciative of the whole-hearted manner in which you have placed your knowledge and experience at the disposal of the Association for the carrying out of a task, the successful performance of which is vital, not only to the railways and their proprietors, but to the country as a whole'. Lemon replied, saying: 'This is a job after my own heart and I hope I shall be able to do it to your satisfaction. It will be very useful if you can attend the first meeting, and I will let you know the date as soon as possible. I await the names of the representatives of the Commission and will arrange for the minutes and memoranda to be sent to you for distribution as you suggest.' The letter continues: 'With regard to the provision of the necessary Secretariat; I should like my Assistant, Mr. H.G. Smith to be with me as he has worked with me for the past ten years and knows my outlook and methods'. We can therefore rely on the accuracy and authenticity of the scrupulous records which Smith kept, and which still exist in Lemon's personal papers. They record a sorry tale of intrigues and squabbles that followed this optimistic start.

The Commission's formation was announced in the newspapers on 8 January, to general and favourable comment. Lemon gave further interviews where he emphasised the desirability of avoiding any political colouring by the newspapers of the Commission's work, and that he wished to avoid the possibility of any jealousy arising between the individual railway companies, as he had been seconded to undertake the work in an impartial manner for the general benefit of the railway industry as a whole. Some of the topics the Commission was expected to address were obvious enough – for instance, further electrification and the rebuilding of stations. Others were remarkably ambitious: the *Financial Times* stated on 12 January:

As is well-known, Lord Reith's Ministry of Works is considering re-planning of towns damaged in air raids, and part of the schemes produced will provide for better roads in built-up areas. Some of the properties damaged have been beside railway lines, and Sir Ernest Lemon's Commission will take the opportunity of devising plans for improvement in the lay-out of tracks which will be possible in view of the clearance of property. Much-needed improvements have been held up in the past

due to the presence of property or the prohibitive cost of its acquisition.

Lemon's papers show that he did, indeed, discuss the matter with Lord Reith, who he called 'an old friend'. Reith's diary for 8 January 1942 records his appointments during the day: 'Then Sir E. Lemon who has been appointed to look into post war planning for railways. Quite clever of them to have done this on their own and I expect the Transport Ministry to be rather annoyed.'[399] As described in the last chapter, Lemon had lunched with Reith in May 1941, when he was Minister of Transport, to discuss the coal silos scheme – a fact that was baldly described in Reith's diaries without further comment. So how well did Lemon know Reith? It is when one looks into Reith's early life that a surprising connection can be found. Reith, like Lemon, had also been an apprentice at the North British Locomotive Works. He was five years younger than Lemon, and it is unlikely that they would have met at the time. Nevertheless, within the distinguished portals of the Athenaeum Club – of which they were both members – they would have discovered a common link from the past, and it seems perfectly possible that each could have influenced the other's thinking. As already mentioned, Reith was a firm believer in nationalisation and so, since many of Lemon's ideas reflect Reith's beliefs, we have to consider Lemon's personal attitude to the subject. On the one hand he was a loyal servant of the LMS and committed to safe-guarding their future interests. On the other, his proposals for greater integration between the main-line companies could only lead, by a logical extension, to some authority having over-all national control. Maybe he did not intend this authority to be in the hands of civil servants. This is what Reith had achieved for the BBC.

Lemon wrote to Sir Ronald Matthews, outlining the discussion he had with Reith, and astutely flattered Matthews by giving him all the credit for setting up the Commission:

Lord Reith told me how delighted he was to read the announcement in this morning's paper and congratulated you upon the step which you had taken and said 'I think this is a very clever move on the part of Sir Ronald Matthews'.

**First meeting of the Railway Chairmen's Commission
in the Euston board-room on 15 January 1942.
Sir Ronald Matthews *(centre)* welcomes the members – *(from left to right)*
F.J.Wymer (SR); K.W.C. Grand (GWR); E.J.H. Lemon; Sir Ronald Matthews;
C.K. Bird (LNER); T.E.Thomas (LPTB); H.G. Smith (Secretary).**
Lemon's personal papers

He outlined to me the machinery of planning which had been set up, both officially and unofficially, and I said that in my view it was essential that before any of these Planning Bodies developed their ideas to anything approaching the final stage, they should consult the Railway Companies so that transport could be focussed into its proper place.

Lord Reith undertook to cover this and at once dictated a note of instruction to his people.

He told me in confidence that certain proposals for post-war reorganisation of the railways, both financial and practical had already been pigeon-holed at the Ministry of War Transport, and I told him that following your instructions I was proceeding with my enquiries on the assumption that the railways would resume their individual status after the war period. Lord Reith was very helpful in his remarks, and promised to assist in any possible way that he could. I thought you would like to know this.

Reith obviously appreciated the political motives of Sir Ronald Matthews in setting up the Commission although, at the same time, he hinted that decisions had already been made for post-war reorganisation. Nevertheless, the railway companies pressed on with their plans, and everything seemed prepared for the Commission to take a radical new step in planning for the future. But it was not to be – although there was no hint of this in the first official meeting of the Commission on 15 January 1942. This was held at Euston, and Sir Ronald Matthews was present to make an opening statement. In this, he reiterated the reasons for the formation of the Commission, and suggested that before long the work would become a full-time job for everyone engaged, as the remit had been drafted in the widest possible terms. He emphasised again that the Commission should work on the assumption that the railways would return to their independent status after the war, and then touched on a detail, which he may have considered of little importance, but became the nub of the whole problem with the subsequent operation of the Commission.

Matthews explained that the inspiration for the Commission had come from the *Chairmen* of the railway companies, not from the General Managers who were representing their companies on the Railway Executive Committee, responsible to the Ministry of War Transport for the day-to-day management of the railways. If they had been nominated to serve on this Commission, their position 'might have become somewhat delicate with the Ministry'. Accordingly the members were subordinate officers: F.A. Pope (LMS), K.W.C. Grand (GWR), C.K. Bird (LNER), F.J. Wymer (SR) and T.E. Thomas (London Transport). The General Managers would be given time to assess and criticise the recommendations of the Commission, but all final decisions would be taken by the Chairmen.

Matthews left the meeting, and a general discussion then took place on the ways and means to enable the Commission to function satisfactorily, and particularly the relations which would exist between it and the domestic planning organisations already set up by the Companies under the authority of their General Managers. Lemon stressed that, whilst the Commission itself would not concern itself with the detailed working up of schemes, each company in preparing its own proposals on any particular problem should be observing practices which were the best amongst all the companies. To achieve this, there would have to be some liaison between the Companies at all management levels, otherwise the contribution of the Commission would not be of maximum benefit. He asked the members to think the matter over and examine the tentative list of subjects he had circulated, and submit the items they consider should be investigated at the next meeting; after which the

question of priorities could be decided.

With hindsight, one can now appreciate that the constitution of the Commission was deeply flawed from the outset, and the problem, basically, was that its members were being asked to serve two masters – the Commission and their General Managers. They did not have the authority to make the decisions that Lemon expected of them. As junior officers, they could only refer recommendations to their own General Managers, and feared their career prospects might be blighted if these incurred their displeasure. Lemon obviously expected that a spirit of goodwill would over-ride these problems, but this did not happen. The members of the Commission immediately split into two groups. On one side were the LMS and the LNER; on the other were the GWR and SR. The latter two obviously feared that the LMS and LNER, in the persons of Lemon and Sir Ronald Matthews, were seeking to dominate and monopolise the situation, and were deeply suspicious of their motives. H.G. Smith summed up the situation:

The Commission was, for all practical and effective purposes, hamstrung after the first Meeting, in spite of Sir Ronald Matthews' statement of aims and hopes and his blessing at that Meeting, for as soon as the Minutes were issued to the General Managers, Sir James Milne [of the GWR] asked THE CHIEF to see him and thereupon raised a quibble on the wording of the Organisation Chart, which was only a tentative draft (and really prepared for LMS domestic purposes). Moreover, he said he would not allow any G.W. officer to give evidence before the Commission, and further, all problems to be tackled by the Commission should be first approved by the General Managers.

A pretty kettle of fish, and so soon after the Chairmen had given an open remit to the Commission with their unqualified approval.

January 1942 onwards was but a succession of frustrations and binding arrangements by the General Managers to restrict any initiative or unfettered action on the part of the Commission. The promising infant had developed into an anaemic brat and would do no credit to the Commission.

As Smith indicated, the first 'quibble' arose from the Minutes of this first meeting. Sir James Milne objected to the use of the word 'Executive' in the draft Organisation Chart. He insisted that the Commission would have no executive status, but was purely advisory. Lemon immediately conceded that this was an unintentional error, and no more than a legacy from an unrevised LMS document. However, it was clumsy not to have noticed the mistake, and added to the general air of mistrust. Milne's other complaints were more substantial, and Lemon himself wrote an account of their discussion, a copy of which he forwarded to his own Chairman at the LMS, Lord Royden:

He then went on to the point that Sir Ronald Matthews had made, which was to the effect that the Commission should be in a position to consult anyone connected with the railways whom they thought might help in the investigations. Sir James very strongly objected to this and said that he absolutely refused to allow any of his officers to give evidence before the Commission, and that the only contact that I, as Chairman, should have with any of the other railway companies should be through the Members of the Commission representing the individual railway companies. I strongly protested against this point of view, as I thought it was contrary to the whole spirit in which the Commission had been set up, namely, that there was going to be a common pool of ideas and further, that if the procedure outlined by Sir James were adopted, I, as Chairman, would be having views expressed by Members of the Commission on matters in which they themselves had had no personal experience; I should not, therefore, be in a position to question anyone for the purpose of elucidating points that were not clear, or suggesting other lines of thought to them. As I am the independent Chairman seconded to the Railway Companies' Association and am not acting in my capacity as Vice-President of the LMS, I thought this was not the right method

of dealing with the various problems with which the Commission will have to deal, and I told Sir James so. Whilst the conversation was at times heated it was, on the whole, friendly.

His third point was that before the Commission tackled any problems they should submit a list of such problems in order of priority for the General Managers' approval.

He has, I understand, also instructed Mr. Grand not to attend any further meetings of the Commission which I may convene until the meeting of the Chairmen on Wednesday, 28th January, as he wishes to get the whole procedure clear. I gathered that Sir James was speaking on behalf of the other General Managers and our own President [i.e. Sir William Wood of the LMS].

After further correspondence, and with Lemon's acceptance, the points raised by Milne were placed on the agenda for discussion at the Chairmen's next meeting. They agreed that it should be made clear that the Commission was purely an advisory body; and that the Commission should tabulate, in priority order, the problems they proposed to tackle. The Chairmen would then give their approval after consulting their General Managers. They also agreed to change the name of the Commission to 'The Railway Chairmen's Commission'. Milne crucially agreed to soften his stance over the question of other officers being allowed to give evidence, and that appeared to be a satisfactory compromise.

The Commission held its second meeting on 13 February. The Minutes of this meeting are concise, occupying one page of foolscap paper, and cover two topics. The first records that the members considered that, before they could formulate any proposals for investigation, they needed some estimation of the traffic the railways would carry after the war. As this was a totally unknown quantity, Lemon suggested that they collate data from past experience as a starting point. The second item in the Minutes merely records that they decided to correlate the long list of suggested subjects for investigation under simplified headings.

What is much more revealing, however, is the digest that Smith wrote of the discussions that took place. In contrast with the Minutes, this takes up over twelve pages of foolscap. Lemon started discussions by suggesting that the first topic they should consider was the continued use of private owners' wagons. Mr Bird (LNER) immediately observed that until they had an idea of post-war requirements, they might be formulating schemes for traffic that would not exist. It would therefore be difficult to consider any item unless they knew what Government policy was likely to be. Mr Wymer (SR) followed this by saying that the indications were that it was unlikely that the railways would return to their own individual control. And so the discussion had immediately turned to the subject of nationalisation, although this was the one topic they were expressly forbidden from considering. Lemon stated that the railways should aim to provide the very best service, whatever the form of ownership. To which, Wymer replied that anything they might do would, in fact, make nationalisation easier – and then added that, in many instances, it was now quicker to travel by car anyway. Time and again, Lemon urged the members to think positively, and suggested other topics for priority, such as improved telephone communications, the proper lighting of marshalling yards or making better use of locomotives, but every time the 'what if?' question was raised, and the conversation inexorably returned to the subject of nationalisation. History, of course, has shown us that they were right to be so concerned, but at the time it must have seemed to Lemon that he was surrounded by defeatists.

The representatives also complained that their companies just did not have the staff, or staff of the necessary quality and ability, to work on schemes for the Commission. This contrasts with Lemon's blithe assertion that the LMS could find up to 200 experts to work for him; and that the costs of these people would be negligible, compared with the great financial issues involved. The other members, however, seemed totally over-awed by the scale and complexity of what they had been asked to do. They constantly pointed out how so many of the problems were inter-related, and that it was therefore impossible to decide on a list of priorities. The brief Minutes show how little the meeting actually achieved. However, there *was* one un-minuted success – they unanimously agreed on a design for their headed notepaper!

They also agreed to meet fortnightly in future, and scheduled the next meeting for 27 February. The Minutes were duly circulated – using the Commission's new title of Railway Chairmen's Commission; and another rumpus broke out. Sir Charles Hambro, Chairman of the GWR, stated that he was not prepared to accept the change of title; and until the matter was sorted out Mr Grand would not attend any further meetings. Mr Wymer (of the SR) also wrote to Lemon, saying that until this matter had been cleared up, he would be unable to attend any meetings. 27 February was cancelled.

Exasperated and despondent, Lemon wrote to Sir Ronald Matthews at the beginning of March. His letter starts:

I have been giving a great deal of thought to the question of the future activities of the Commission in view of the unfortunate situation which has arisen, and am taking the liberty of putting the following before you.

I have come to the conclusion that the best plan would be for the Commission as now constituted to be disbanded because the proper atmosphere or spirit which should animate everyone has, for some reason or other, been vitiated, and in my opinion, if success is to attend the efforts of any Commission, the spirit of its members should be co-operative in every way; there should be no hesitation in supplying information or ideas and no question of personal jealousies or thoughts as to future prospects in the railway service, etc.

The name of the Commission has been recently altered to 'Railway Chairmen's Commission' and it seems to me therefore its constitution should be Directors and not Officers (who are naturally answerable to their own General Managers). In view of this I would suggest to you that at your meeting tomorrow you elect two Directors from each company to serve as the Commission.

They will of course require advice on the problems which will have to be dealt with and, if it were acceptable to you and to the other Chairmen, I should be quite willing to act in this advisory capacity, as I have of course already been seconded by the LMS Board for the purposes of the Commission when it was first set up.

It is perhaps an impertinence on my part but, if I might make suggestions as to the Directors who could serve, I would suggest those who have close associations with industry and preferably the engineering industries; they should also be young, as in the future they may have to defend the question of private ownership of railways, and if they have served on this Commission, and had the advantage of handling facts and other information through the medium of the Commission, they would be in an excellent position to discuss the wider issues either in the House of Commons or outside it; at any rate they would have the ammunition to meet party propaganda such as that now being put out by the Labour Party, e.g., Mr. George Ridley's pamphlet on the railway situation.

Matthews and Lemon discussed the situation the following day, when Matthews said that he did not think it possible to put Directors on the Commission. And there the situation rested. Meanwhile, as was mentioned in the last chapter, Lemon's health was suffering and, in April 1942, he went to Cornwall to recover. It was not a good start to the year. Not only was the Coal Silo scheme coming to an ignominious end, but he was now seemingly blocked by yet another impasse.

While Lemon was recuperating in Cornwall, the General Managers held an informal meeting after Lord Ashfield, head of the LPTB, received an 'off the record' briefing that it would be in their interests to start taking future policy seriously. He advised the companies to examine the matter under several possible alternatives:

(a) Amalgamation into one company.
(b) Continuance as four separate companies –

with, or without, reshuffling of penetrating lines.
(c) Either of these two plus road transport.
(d) Formation into public utilities on the lines of the LPT.
(e) Sub-division into semi-autonomous areas.

This galvanised the RCA into action. They formed another Committee to address this particular problem, chaired by Eric Gore-Browne, Deputy Chairman of the SR. At the same time, they took the opportunity to re-affirm the terms of reference for Lemon's Commission – which also returned to its original title – and confirmed its members would remain unchanged. Lemon's brief remained 'to examine how the efficiency of the railways could be improved by schemes of reconstruction and re-organisation'; whereas Gore-Browne was now charged with preparing proposals 'for post-war reconstruction which would appeal to the public imagination, overcome difficulties which had arisen from road transport competition and meet present criticisms'. Gore-Browne was also asked to 'give special regard to private ownership in relation to the public interest'. It was decided that the work of this second committee should receive no publicity.

Sir Ronald Matthews wrote to Lemon in Cornwall on 17 April, requesting a meeting when he was fully recovered, and a date for the beginning of May was fixed. Lemon also wrote to his Chairman, Lord Royden, telling him of developments with Matthews and of his intended return. The drafts of these two letters exist in Lemon's personal papers. They are handwritten in pencil and contain alterations and additions – but it is not Lemon's handwriting. It is unlikely that he would have asked some unknown person to help him write confidential documents, and suggests that Hermione was with him in Cornwall. No sooner had all this been settled than Lemon received a letter, forwarded from London, asking whether he would be available for part-time work on a new Industrial Panel that the Minister of Production was setting up. This is the subject of the next section of this chapter, and so will be described fully there. Lemon was probably glad to be offered an opportunity to get away from all these other problems, but before he could accept had to clear the matter with Sir Ronald Matthews and the RCA. They did not stand in the way of his acceptance, and Matthews advised him that, with regard to the work of the Commission, the 'best thing to do was to maintain masterly inactivity'.

The work did not come to a complete halt, however, and in June 1942 the General Managers approved a list of suggested topics for examination, as follows:

(1) *Organisation*
   (a) Elimination of working restrictions between Companies
   (b) Improved telephone, etc. systems of communication
(2) *Commercial*
   (a) Central Rates Offices (Goods, Minerals and Passenger)
   (b) Simplified charging arrangements
   (c) Modernised station amenities
   (d) Possible unification of Marine interests
(3) *Operating*
   (a) Best lay-out for motive power depots, marshalling yards and goods terminals
   (b) London Cartage and Receiving offices
(4) *Technical*
   (a) Measures of standardisation to be adopted in each branch of railway industry
   (b) Combination and centralisation of Technical Research Departments
   (c) Engineers' reclamation depots
   (d) Improved lighting standards for all purposes
(5) *Special Subjects*
   (a) Post-war continuance of Inter-Company Wagon Control Committee
   (b) Extension of continuous brakes to wagon stock
   (c) Substitution of oil boxes for grease boxes

Before Lemon took any action he sought to clarify the situation. He pointed out that unless the atmosphere round the table changed, there was no point in even starting to look at these topics. Furthermore, the Commission might now find themselves at odds with whatever recommendations Gore-Browne's Committee was going to make. Nevertheless, so that some progress, at least, could be made while he was away at the Ministry of Production, Lemon called the third meeting of the Commission for 10 July. It was now seven months since he had started work on the project, and so far it had achieved nothing! The notes that H.G. Smith made of this meeting show that they discussed all the topics on the list of priorities at considerable length, and various members promised to look at certain aspects in greater detail. However, Mr Grand (GWR) said he failed to see how anybody could give a considered opinion at the present time on any of the subjects before them; and that his General Manager, Sir James Milne, was in agreement with this view. He confirmed that the GWR had prepared no information for the Commission as they did not have the staff to do the work. And so, as the records show, the atmosphere round the table had certainly not changed! The meeting therefore limply concluded that until Gore-Browne's Committee came up with some guidelines as to the directions the railways would follow after the war, there was little point in doing anything further. The question of any further meetings was left indeterminate, and shortly afterwards Mr Grand tendered his resignation.

Lemon put these problems aside and turned his attention to the work that he had been asked to do for the Ministry of Production.

The Industrial Panel of the Ministry of Production
The 'Changeover' Report [400]

IT WAS on 23 April 1942 that Oliver Lyttelton, Minister of Production, wrote to Lemon asking him to become a member of the Industrial Panel that he was setting up under the chairmanship of Mr Robert Barlow. According to H.G. Smith, this was in direct response to an approach from Colonel Llewellin, Minister of Aircraft Production, asking for an investigation into the delays which occur when a firm changes over from production of one type of aircraft to another. Llewellin considered the matter to be urgent and specifically suggested that Lemon might be the man to carry out the investigation.

Before proceeding any further, it is relevant to describe (very briefly) what had happened at the

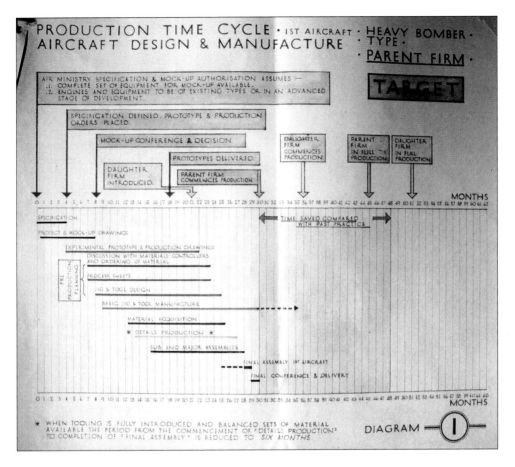

Gantt chart showing the various phases in the design and construction of a bomber aircraft, attached to Lemon's 'Changeover' Report. Henry Gantt was one of the originators of 'Scientific Management' whose principles Lemon followed throughout his career.
National Archives

Air Ministry in the two years following Lemon's departure in 1940. When Churchill became Prime Minister in May 1940, following the fall of France, one of his first actions was to form the Ministry of Aircraft Production (MAP) with Lord Beaverbrook at its head. Most writers and commentators now accept that Beaverbrook was a disastrous appointment. He disregarded the painstaking collection of statistics, and the sober assessment of production figures that could be realistically achieved from them – which Lemon and Freeman had set up. Lemon's erstwhile deputy, Buchanan, summed this up in December 1942 when he wrote: 'There was a good central planning and progressing unit before Beaverbrook's day, but he had it largely dismantled'.[401] Instead Beaverbrook surrounded himself with 'fair-weather' cronies and ran the Ministry on his

own personal charisma, constantly exhorting the workers to greater efforts and making exaggerated forecasts of the number of planes that would be produced. Freeman had eventually been promoted sideways in November 1940, exasperated by Beaverbrook's style of management, to another job in the RAF. Beaverbrook eventually moved on, after a year in office, on 1 May 1941. He was succeeded as Minister of

Aircraft Production by John Moore-Brabazon who, in turn, was replaced by Col. John Llewellin on 22 February 1942. It is indicative of the state that the MAP had reached that it was now unable to carry out its own investigations into production problems. The Ministry of Production (MOP) was a newcomer to the scene, only formed in February 1942, and still without a clearly-defined role. The first Minister of War Production, as he was originally titled, had actually been Lord Beaverbrook, but he resigned after only two weeks in office. A month later, upon the appointment of Lyttelton, the name was changed to Minister of Production.

Lemon received Lyttelton's letter while he was still convalescing in Cornwall. It might seem with hindsight that it was reckless to even consider accepting yet more work, but he must have felt the extended break had achieved the desired results. He replied to Lyttelton by telegram from Cornwall on 25 April accepting the offer. Formal application was then made to the Railway Companies' Association for his release. The Minister informed them that Lemon's duties on the Panel should not require him to devote more than 14 to 21 days per year to this work, and approval was given. The LMS and the Ministry of War Transport also had no objections, and Lemon started work at the MOP on 7 May. His precise terms of reference on this first project were to investigate:

(a) The minimum period in which a parent firm can design and bring into production an aeroplane of new design.

(b) The minimum period in which this new design, or any existing design, can be brought into production by the daughter firm.

(c) Achieving (a) and (b) with a minimum loss of effective man hours.

[The phrase 'daughter' firm is self-explanatory: they were firms who were later contracted to build a particular aircraft from plans and drawings supplied by the parent firm. It was the supply of these duplicate drawings that often led to delays.]

Lemon secured the services of two accountants from the LMS to help him collate statistical evidence – one from Derby, the other from Wolverton – and they spent the next month visiting a representative selection of aircraft factories and collecting information. At the outset Lemon stated to all the aircraft firms that he was not holding an inquest, but was merely endeavouring to find out the weaknesses of the present arrangements and recommend changes where necessary. His previous experience at the Air Ministry, and the contacts he had made then, undoubtedly helped him in this task. It is indicative of his reputation for fair dealing that the firms were willing to supply all possible information, and agreed that it would be to the benefit of everyone if some standards could be laid down. Moreover, they accepted that, in the past, there had been too little planning when such changeovers had taken place and the outcome had been a serious loss in production of aircraft. Lemon's team discovered there had been a striking example of this at the Rootes' factory at Speke in Liverpool, during the changeover from Blenheim to Halifax production.

Before completing and submitting his report, however, the MAP referred another investigation to the Industrial Panel at the beginning of July 1942. This involved delays to the 'Barracuda' aircraft required by the Fleet Air Arm. Having obtained an extension to his release from the Railway Companies' Commission, Lemon was appointed to this second project (which will be considered separately later in this chapter), and immediately started work. It was thus not until August 1942 that he submitted his 'Changeover' report to the Minister of Aircraft Production.

Apart from its recommendations, the report is interesting for the style of its language, which is remarkably forthright. The very first recommendation bluntly reads: 'Introduce a time-table such as is set out on Diagram No. 1 and insist on this time-table being kept by all concerned'. A rigorous time-scale is defined for each phase of design, development and production. By this means, Lemon states that: 'new bomber aircraft can be brought into production in 30 MONTHS instead of FOUR YEARS, which latter time has been taken with most of the existing types'. However, he did acknowledge that 'The times set out on the diagrams represent ideals which

- 16 -

Comparative Data for Airframes

	Handley Page Halifax	Shorts Stirling	A.V. Roe Lancaster	A.V. Roe Manchester	A/Whitworth Albemarle	Bristol Beaufighter	Westland Whirlwind	Hawker Typhoon	DeHavilland Mosquito
1. Air Ministry Specification and Date of Issue	P.13/36 8 Sep.1936	B.12/36 15 Jly.1936	No Prototype	P.13/36 8 Sep.1936	18/38 1 Sep.1938	F.17/39 4 May 1939	F.37/35 15 Feb.1936	F.18/37 9 Mar.1938	B.1/40 15 Mar.1940
2. Date Requisition for Prototype passed to D.of C.	9 Apr.1937	6 Feb.1937	Direct Production order by D. of E. 15 Nov.1940	9 Apr.1937	Direct Production order by D. of E. 13 Nov.1939	Direct Production order by D. of E. 24 Feb.'39	5 Dec.1936	2 Nov.1938	Direct Production order by D. of E. 29 Jan.1940
3. Production Specification and Date of Issue	1/P1 12 Aug.1938	1/P1 17 Jly.1939	1/P1 23 Aug.1941	25 Jly.1938	-	-	F37/35/P1 17 Jun.1939	Typhoon 1/P1 3 Oct.1940	-
4. Date of First Flight	25 Oct.1939	May 1939	Feb.1941	21 Jly.1939	20 May 1940	17 Jly.'39	11 Oct.1938	Mar.1940	24 Nov.1940
5. Date of Completion of Prototype trials at A.& A.E.E.	27 Mar.1941	5 Aug.1940	10 Oct.1941	31 Jly.1940	14 Jun.1941	31 May '41	29 Jun.1939	18 Dec.1940	22 Jun.1941
6. Date of first Production Order	7 Jan.1938	11 Apr.1938	6 Jun.1941	1 Jly.1937	13 Nov.1939	Jun.'39	5 Apr.1939	14 Oct.1939	1 Mar.1940
7. Size of first Production Order	100	100	450	200 (Red. to 157)	198 (with Gloster)	300	200 (Red.to 114)	500 (with Gloster)	50
8. Date of delivery of First Production Aircraft	Oct.1940	May 1940	Oct.1941	Sep.1940	Sep.1941	Apr.'40	Jun.1940	Jun.1941	Jly.1941
9. Aircraft Deliveries for first six months after delivery of first production aircraft 1 2 3 4 5 6	2 3 3 4 6 8	1 4 4 6 9 8	3 13 25 24 25 ¼	3 11 6 10 9 15	1 1 3 6 9 ✕	2 5 23 15 21 25	3 1 3 1 8 5	2 6 12 - 7 11	4 4 4 9 17
10. Date of First Operational sortie	10/11 Mar. 1941	10/11 Feb. 1941	3/4 Mar. 1942	24/25 Feb. 1941	-	14 Oct.'40	14 Jan.1941	-	18 Sep.1941
11. Date first Squadron formed	5 Nov.1940	2 Aug.1940	Dec.1941	Nov.1940	-	9 Sep.'40	13 Sep.1940	11 Sep.1941	-
12. Date first Squadron became Operational	Mar.1941	6 Feb.1941	23 Feb.1942	Feb.1941	-	14 Oct.1940	14 Jan.1941	-	-

✕ 6th month not yet completed.

have not yet been achieved by any firm in this country'. When the report was circulated by MAP to the various manufacturers for their comments, many of them demurred at this scenario, claiming that the timings were, indeed, impossible ideals, and did not take into account the many problems that always delayed a project in reality. However, these ideals *were* achieved with the production of the de Havilland Mosquito aircraft.

Lemon accepted that, for various reasons, there would always be a loss of productive man-hours when a factory changed from one type of aircraft to another. One reason was that the workers would deliberately go slow, in order to establish the piece-rates that they considered reasonable. Together with other losses due to rectification of mistakes and unfamiliarity with the new type, he estimated the minimum loss to be in the order of 1¼ million man-hours – or, for the sake of simplicity, about 30 Lancaster bombers. It is interesting how we always find this type of comparison useful, and the size of Wales or the length of London buses are other examples which immediately spring to mind! However, Lemon had many immediately practical recom-

Comparative data showing the time-scale that was actually achieved in the design and construction of different aircraft. Note the speed with which the Lancaster and Mosquito were delivered.
National Archives

mendations to make. One such was that only one type of aircraft should be in production at any one factory, and that more prototypes of new aircraft should be built in order to speed up tests – at least three for land-based aircraft; and up to six for those destined for the Fleet Air Arm. This would enable the different proving tests to be carried out simultaneously, and any modifications embodied at an early stage in production.

He also showed that the quickest ways to get improved machines was to adopt variants of existing types, thus automatically using a large number of the existing jigs and tools. In this context, Lemon quoted the speed with which the two-engined Manchester bomber was converted into the four-engined Lancaster. No prototype was built – the order was placed in November 1940, and the first production aircraft was completed in June 1941. This policy is now generally reckoned as one of the major factors which helped to build the RAF's eventual supremacy in the war. The three main stumbling blocks to greater speed in production, however, were still floor-space, delays in the drawing offices and tools. For the first of these, Lemon could only urge that more floor-space was still needed, and that improved assembly techniques should be adopted. He acknowledged that individual firms were devising initiatives to speed up the production of drawings, but still urged that there should be more pooling of resources, and greater use of sub-contracting of drawings to suitable outside firms. Lastly, he devoted a considerable amount of space to the problems of acquiring, and using, jigs and tools. These were essential when so much unskilled labour was being used. However, as 70% of the jig and tool making capacity in the country was already taken up by MAP, and new dies were taking up to nine months to produce, saturation point had probably been reached. He recommended it was necessary to identify those areas where jigs and tools were absolutely essential, and those where other methods could be used. To illustrate the point, he did an analysis of several Spitfire components and showed that it was only cheaper with a purpose-built press tool, if more than 1,000 units were required. For quantities less than 1,000 it was cheaper to use bench tools. Accordingly, he recommended that a closer study should be made to see how the resources of the skilled men who made these tools could be better used, and urged that more training schools should be set up by the Ministry of Labour to produce such men.

Lemon's final recommendation was that there should be a Central Development, Planning and Progressing Section at the Ministry of Aircraft Production to ensure that the scheduled change-over was moving strictly to time-table; it would also be possible to anticipate difficulties and take prompt steps to neutralise any adverse effect on the time-table. One wonders what Lemon privately thought about the task he had been set. The report reads as a manifesto of how the Ministry of Aircraft Production should be run. The facts and recommendations presented therein embody the attention to detail that Lemon had endeavoured to instil while he was at the Air Ministry, and which had subsequently lapsed. Indeed, one could believe that, if he had remained there as Director-General of Production, such a report would not only have been immediately available to the Minister, but would have been constantly under review.

After the report was concluded, Lemon fired off a series of memos about specific items of interest he had discovered while visiting the factories. One of these concerned the continuous assembly line that had been built at Phillips & Powis in Reading. Although all aircraft were built on a progressive system, this was, apparently, the first instance where *all* the techniques of assembly line production had been thoroughly incorporated.

Lemon listed the many advantages:

By reason of the machines moving forward after a definite time interval, the men working on a particular station take a pride in seeing that their job is completed in the allotted time.

The method acts as an automatic foreman, keeping both Management and men keyed up because any shortages at one station may throw out of gear the whole line, and both Management and staff try to prevent this taking place.

It is possible to install all labour-saving appliances at much less cost than if the assembly was spread out over the floor.

He strongly recommended that similar techniques should be used elsewhere. He also drew up a table showing the man-hours needed to construct the different types of heavy bomber, demonstrating that the airframe of a Lancaster took half the time required for a Halifax, and a third of the time required for a Stirling. This caused the MAP to question their priorities, and to consider what other considerations might govern the continued production of the Stirling.

Barracuda Report [402]

BEFORE Lemon had completed his 'Changeover' investigation the Minister of Aircraft Production, Col. J.J. Llewellin, asked him, at the beginning of July, to look into another matter: the delays in

the production of Barracuda aircraft for the Fleet Air Arm. These were being constructed by Fairey's in Stockport in conjunction with associated 'daughter' firms. Lemon had visited Fairey's on 21 May in the course of the 'Changeover' investigation and was the obvious choice to undertake this work. However, he was aware that, before he could accept, there were certain formalities to be dealt with: his official position was actually quite complex. He was still employed (and paid) by the LMS, who had seconded him to the Railway Companies Association. They, in turn, had released him to work for the Ministry of Production's Industrial Panel, where he was carrying out an investigation for the Ministry of Aircraft Production! Aware of this, and in order that the proper procedures should be seen to have been observed, Lemon circulated a memo around the Ministry of Production later in July, which reads:

On Wednesday afternoon the 1st [July], the Minister of Aircraft Production called to see Sir Ernest Lemon and amongst other things, introduced the subject of the Barracuda programme of production which was giving him some concern. He asked Sir Ernest whether he would undertake the investigation into this and Sir Ernest replied that he was now working under Sir Ronald Matthews on the post-war reconstruction problems for the main line railways and that it would be necessary therefore for the Minister to get

The prototype Barracuda under construction. National Archives

into touch with Sir Ronald for his agreement to the proposal. The Minister said that he would do this, probably through the Minister of Production. Correspondence accordingly took place and Sir Ronald Matthews agreed to Mr. Lyttelton's suggestion that Sir Ernest should continue work on behalf of the Minister for another two or three months.

It is interesting that Lemon here rather glosses over his involvement with the Ministry of Production, when he was only appointed to carry out the work for MAP as a member of their Industrial Panel. And it was the MOP who sought and obtained the necessary permission. Lyttelton wrote to Llewellin: 'I have now received Sir Ronald Matthews' confirmation that he agrees to the release of Sir Ernest Lemon for a further spell of almost whole time work with Barlow's Industrial Panel. I have told them that what we want are Barracudas rather than a number of reports, and I know they propose to tackle the job in that spirit'.

Lemon was now officially cleared to start the investigation which would involve four firms in the so-called Barracuda Group: Fairey's in Stockport; Bolton and Paul; Blackburn's of Brough, and Westlands.

Llewellin wrote to Lemon on 3 July, setting out what he wanted the investigation to achieve:

The whole of this production needs to have a grip taken on it from the centre of the Group ...You have my complete authority to take any necessary step to co-ordinate and improve this production, except that, of course, financial expenditure will have to be approved at Headquarters here. There should, however, be no difficulty or delay about that and I will certainly see that anything that you consider necessary is done.

The one outstanding fact is that you go to this work with the complete consent of the four Companies concerned. I thank you very much for agreeing to undertake it. I wish you every success.

To help him in his task, Lemon asked that J.S. Buchanan should temporarily move from MAP to join him. Buchanan had been Deputy Director-General to Lemon during his two years at the Air Ministry 1938–40, and had remained in touch. As has been noted previously, they met for lunch in September 1941.

This investigation was a totally different matter from the unfinished 'Changeover' investigation. There Lemon had been asked to look at a general problem affecting the overall policy of aircraft production. As was mentioned earlier, he was not seeking to apportion blame to individual firms, but to suggest improvements. Here, however, he was specifically called in to look at the failings of a particular Group of companies. He would thus be performing the role that he found so objectionable when Treasury officials investigated his Production Department at the Air Ministry in December 1939. In that case, however, he was aggrieved to find that his Department was being superficially assessed by people he considered unqualified. Here, he would surely have argued that he was eminently suited to do the job. One wonders, nevertheless, whether he was aware of the irony of the situation, especially in the light of the major reforms he instigated?

The first fact to emerge from the investigation was that all four Managing Directors unanimously denied that they had ever received official notification from the Defence Committee of the priority for the Barracuda. They complained that in the absence of such notification they were unable to bring home to the sub-contractors the urgency of the situation. They also complained that some of their sub-contractors, who were also working on other types of planes, were being urged to give these preference with the concurrence of MAP officials.

As requested by the Minister, Lemon's report was produced quickly, and was presented on 21 July 1942. This starts off by listing the failings that he had uncovered, and virtually every aspect of the production process was found to be at fault. There were delays to drawings, materials, machining, tools and labour; and the first conclusion was that the programme as issued to the firms was incapable of execution. He would therefore pursue further what could realistically be achieved; but, for the guidance of the Admiralty, he predicted that the output of Barracudas by the end of the year would be approximately fifty.

Lemon then observed that it was evident, for one reason or another, that the Group had found it impossible to co-ordinate their efforts. To overcome this he recommended that a Group Co-ordinating Office be established at Manchester. Lemon stipulated that the men chosen as co-ordinating staff must be of first-class ability and, importantly, that they had the power to make decisions on behalf of their firms. Was this a lesson he had learned from the Railway Commission? All the firms welcomed this idea which Lemon claimed would be productive to the interests both of the firms themselves, the Ministry of Aircraft Production and the Admiralty. To start this organisation on the right lines he arranged with the LMS for C.E. Fairburn to be seconded to the Ministry to establish the office. Fairburn, who Lemon obviously rated highly, was now the Deputy CME and, as has been previously mentioned, in charge of the organisation repairing Hampden bombers at the Derby works.

Lemon also recommended that a firm of consultants be brought in to re-organise all sections of Fairey's clerical work. Finally he pointed out that the firm were also building another two aircraft for the Fleet Air Arm at their headquarters in Hayes, Middlesex. These were the Firefly and Firebrand, and Lemon suggested that the problems should be considered jointly. The productive capacity of the firm could mean that priority for one would affect production of the other two. He offered to investigate the position of these other two aircraft, if required.

Lemon's overall conclusion was that, in his opinion, the whole trouble with the Barracuda had arisen through inadequate planning before the programme was issued to the firms, and this was a question of policy which should receive serious consideration by the Minister.

Having delivered this report, Lemon then returned to completing his 'Changeover' report, and one can now appreciate that many of the recommendations this contains had been brought into sharper focus in the light of his experiences at Fairey's.

Developments with the RCA Commission during August 1942

LEMON was not able to abandon all of his commitment to the Railway Companies' Association Commission (RCA) while he undertook this work for the MOP, and desultory correspondence was exchanged and meetings held. Matthews and the other members of the RCA considered that none of the problems remitted

to the 'Lemon' Commission (as it was now generally called) was involved to any great degree with the future structure of the railways. This was a totally separate issue to be considered by Gore-Browne's 'Special Committee'. It was felt that, notwithstanding the anticipated difficulties, Lemon's Commission should proceed with all the subjects remitted for their consideration to the fullest extent possible.

The General Managers agreed to review the proposed subjects. On 12 August, they produced a simplified list and arranged for preliminary memoranda on each of the subjects to be prepared. At the end of the month, Sir Ronald Matthews told Sir James Milne of the GWR, that, once again, he had received certain information 'from the political angle' stressing the extreme importance of getting on immediately with post-war plans, and Sir James had replied that there would be no unnecessary delay in the matter. On 1 September, the memoranda were allotted to different Companies, and the list of subjects, as now constituted, for the 'Lemon' Commission to investigate is shown in the table below.

Topics to be considered by the RCA Commission. The only result of eight months' deliberations.

Subject	Memorandum to be prepared by –
Elimination of working restrictions between Companies	Engineering Committee
Central Rates Offices (Goods and Minerals)	LNER
Central Rates Offices (Passenger)	Southern Railway
Best lay-out for motive power depots, marshalling yards and goods terminals	LMS
Combination and centralisation of Technical Research Departments	LMS
Engineers' reclamation depots	LNER
Post-war continuance of Inter-Company Wagon Control Committee	LMS
Extension of continuous brakes to wagon stock	GWR
Standardisation of Stationary and Forms	Ad hoc Committee drawn from all 4 Companies
First Class Travel: Question of the desirability of abolishing the present system of First and Third Class accommodation and the introduction of a basic charge for all travel with a special supplemental charge for the use of superior accommodation.	Passenger Superintendents

One item had thus been deleted from the list – the substitution of oil boxes for grease boxes. But two others had been added – the standardisation of stationery and, most surprisingly, the possible abolition of first-class travel.

Lemon, however, was still concerned with the atmosphere of ill-will that dominated the Commission's meetings thus far. As he considered that no progress would ever be made on an all-company basis, he suggested to Matthews the possibility of the LMS and LNER 'going it alone'. Matthews could not agree to this, and Lemon went to talk the matter over with his own Chairman, Lord Royden, and President, Sir William Wood. He suggested that perhaps the stage had been reached when he could be recalled from the Commission to take over purely LMS work again. Both Royden and Wood were anxious to avoid any suggestion that the Commission had been sabotaged by the LMS. They felt it was essential that these post-war problems should be tackled, and they could not see who might do the job if Lemon were to cease to be the Chairman.

And so Lemon remained in charge, awaiting the promised memoranda which were being prepared before taking any further action. However, he was not personally spending that much time on this work, as he was preoccupied with a succession of other investigations for the Ministry of Production, which occupied him through the Autumn of 1942.

Torpedo Inquiry[403]

THE first investigation was into the management of the Royal Navy torpedo factory in Greenock.

Lemon and the Hon. J.K. Weir were allotted the task on 11 September. Weir was a Scot and the son of Viscount Weir who had been adviser to the Air Minister, Viscount Swinton, in the regime before Lemon joined the Air Ministry. After a visit to Weymouth to familiarise themselves with methods at the factory there, Lemon and Weir travelled to Scotland to investigate the two factories on the Clyde estuary. They found that the root cause of the trouble was due to the management being in the hands of Naval Officers who did not have the necessary training

and experience for executive industrial positions. They considered it would be a mistake merely to replace them with other officers. What was needed was a complete overhaul of the management, and they recommended a structure of new appointments which would have to come from outside industry. In order to carry out this reorganisation, they recommended the Admiralty should appoint a firm of Production Consultants. No names were mentioned in the report, but the MOP file shows that this caused an immediate difficulty. The only acceptable organisation that fitted the criteria was G.& J. Weir Ltd – the family engineering firm of which J.K. Weir was a Director. As it turned out, this was of no consequence: the Admiralty did not follow up their recommendations. They ignored the advice in the report, and replaced the Superintendent with another Naval Officer, although they did appoint a Production Manager as recommended.

Fairey & Co., Hayes, Middlesex

ON 2 September, the Minister of Aircraft Production asked the MOP's Industrial Panel to look into yet another production problem: this time with the Hamilcar glider and Firefly aircraft being built by General Aircraft. As the Firefly was designed by Fairey's, and General Aircraft was only a 'daughter' company in the project, one might have expected Lemon to have undertaken the investigation but this did not occur. The Managing Director of General Aircraft was E.C. Gordon England, and the Industrial Panel's Chairman has written on the back of the letter from MAP 'not Lemon or Buchanan – Lemon is Gordon England's brother-in-law'.[404] This is patently not true, as the genealogical research carried out for this book shows, but the investigation was nevertheless carried out by other members of the Panel. Rather confusingly, the National Archives have indexed this file as the 'Firefly' investigation. Because of other commitments, the investigators only looked into the delays with the Hamilcar glider, and did not look into the problems with Firefly production at all. However, Lemon did become involved with the delays to this aircraft when he was asked to extend his investigation into Fairey's operations at its headquarters in Hayes. The original request was made directly to Lemon by a Mr Dunbar at the MAP on 14 September, and led to a minor 'spat' between the Ministries involved. The Firefly was another aircraft for the Fleet Air Arm, and Sir Henry Self, on behalf of the Ministry of Production, wrote to the Admiralty telling them that the approach was out of order.[405] The proper procedure was to get the Ministry of Aircraft Production to channel such a request to him. His Minister could then approve the request and pass it on to the Industrial Panel for consideration. Such niceties are important! After this brief hiccup, and an exchange of letters between the two Ministers, Llewellin and Lyttelton, to resolve the matter, Lemon was officially appointed to the task. It was, after all, a logical continuation of his work in Stockport, and he had made the self-same suggestion at the conclusion of his report into the Barracuda problems.

Presumably the decision for such an investigation was prompted by a letter from the resident RAF Overseer at Hayes, dated 8 September, to the MAP which detailed the lamentable state of affairs at the factory there. This letter, which Dunbar forwarded to Lemon, starts off:

My general impression of the organisation is that it lacks completely any sense of urgency; there appears to be no desire to get on with any job at a speed greater than the peace-time tempo; there is no drive either from the Directors or Heads of Departments, none of whom attempt to plan or think ahead, and whose first and chief consideration is to shift the blame on to someone else – usually MAP – in fact the greatest output is 'alibis' and much time is spent in making them watertight.

The Overseer continued to list the many failings of the Company, which led to workers being left idle at their benches and machines. He apportioned the blame for this on the Works Manager who, he claimed, was incapable of filling the position effectively. This gentleman, he stated, did not tour the shops during working hours to see the actual conditions which prevailed, but invariably made his tour during the lunch hour. Thus he did not see the employees at work

and had to rely on information provided by the heads of departments – who misled him on many occasions, as was obvious to all at the weekly production meetings.

Dunbar's letter was written on 14 September, the very day that Lemon and Weir started the Torpedo investigation. It must, therefore, have been a while before he was able to turn his attention to the matter. But his first action was to appoint the same firm of industrial consultants who had been advising in Lancashire to carry out a similar investigation at Hayes. Meanwhile, changes were being effected at Fairey's in Stockport, and there were periodic problems which involved Lemon. In October, for example, he found that supplies of raw materials were not coming forward in the quantities which he had requested. Letters passed to and fro, and Lemon was told, basically, that as the Barracuda was not a fighter aircraft, its production had to take place within the Government's overall strategy, and there were now other more immediate needs.

Joint Supply Staff (MOP)

THE work that Lemon was carrying out for the Ministry of Production was obviously highly appreciated and valued – to such a degree that the Minister, Oliver Lyttelton, approached the LMS with a further request for Lemon's services. Lyttelton 'had it in mind' to form a Joint Supply Staff (JSS) which would control production of all supplies for the armed forces, and wished to appoint Lemon as its head. Although the plan was in its infancy, he wrote to Lord Royden on 23 September, explaining his reasons for the approach at such an early stage:

The success of such a Joint Supply staff would largely depend upon its being guided and supervised by a person having the right standing, experience and qualifications.

I feel sure that Sir Ernest Lemon possesses these qualities in a unique degree and that he would be outstanding in such a capacity. The purpose of this note is therefore once again to seek your kind indulgence in the hope that you will feel able to allow Sir Ernest to assume this new responsibility if the scheme should finally be approved.

At the moment it is in a purely provisional and preparatory stage but it would be extremely helpful if Sir Ernest could guide its formulation and translation into concrete shape. Indeed, if it is finally approved and you agree to his undertaking the position indicated above, it would seem most important that he himself should actively share in the shaping of the outline of the organisation before matters progress too far.

I should perhaps add that the scheme, once established, would entail a substantial demand upon Sir Ernest's time but this should not preclude his continuing with such special activities as you may deem advisable to ensure that his knowledge and experience are still available to your Board.

The LMS Board considered this request at their Meeting the following day, and it was agreed that Lemon could be released for this work. The Minutes also record that he would retain his status as Vice-President in full while with the Ministry.

There were, of course, many committees already in existence that were charged with planning war production programmes, but these were generally linked to specific sections of the armed forces. There was also a Joint War Department on which representatives of the Supply Ministers, the Minister of Production and all the Services collated the requirements for the conduct of the war. However, there was no over-all body charged with looking at production *problems*, and this was the gap the new JSS was intended to fill. One can sense the influence of Lemon behind this whole project. The idea was encapsulated in a letter to Lyttelton, signed by Lemon and Henry Self, dated 28 September 1942.[406] This contained a dossier setting out the plan in detail, and referred to earlier discussions and Lyttelton's provisional approval. This dossier is no longer in the file at the National Archives, but Lemon's personal papers contain Self's draft terms of reference, which sets out the whole *raison d'être* for such a Department. Included in this document was an 'Annexe',

written by Lemon, entitled 'Phasing of Production' which contains the following:

We have now reached a stage in the war when it may be said that the bulk of capital expenditure on workshops and machine tools has been completed, and that we are now, and (unless the ceiling of the war effort is put up) shall for the rest of the war be making, what may be regarded as consumable articles. I mean warships and aircraft down to shells and uniform.

All these things have a different fabrication period; and it is essential to avoid locking-up too much of the available raw material resources in articles manufactured long in advance of the time at which they are actually required.

Assuming that the shell and filling factories are fully equipped and have sufficient capacity to provide the assumed rate of supply which meets Army and Navy and Air Force requirements, then shells, for example, can be fabricated in, say, four weeks from the time the materials are put in hand in the shell factories. On the other hand aircraft, aircraft carriers and other items, take a much longer period and the decisions must be taken and, raw materials provided much longer ahead.

A consideration of these problems, under the current system, involved many different Departments – such as the Central Priority Committee, the Materials Committee, the Ministry of Supply, the MAP, the Admiralty, etc. The proposal was that this co-ordination should be planned by a central staff – such as the JSS. A final draft of the proposed Terms of Reference, and a tentative organisation chart, was completed on 27 October. This was considered at a meeting on 13 November attended by Lemon, officials of the MOP and representatives of every Supply Department that could possibly be affected by the proposals. The outcome of the meeting was that the representatives of the Supply Departments were happy with the *status quo*. They considered that there was no gap in the inter-departmental machinery already set up, and no case existed for a proposed Joint Supply Staff. Accordingly, on

17 December, Lyttelton's Council agreed to adopt as an alternative a Progress Report Centre. In view of this development, Lyttelton wrote to the LMS Chairman, Lord Royden, on 23 December:

The plan for a Joint Staff has not been found feasible in present circumstances and, by arrangement with the Supply Departments, I am establishing a new progressing department within my own Ministry. The new organisation will function departmentally and will gather together its material from departmental and inter-departmental sources. This will entail control of the organisation by a departmental head who will himself have to exercise detailed supervision and work very heavy hours on a full-time basis. Moreover, it will not be an appointment which will have the same scope for special advisory functions as were previously in mind for Sir Ernest Lemon.

As these arrangements came into shape, Sir Ernest himself agreed with our view that it would not be reasonable to ask him to undertake these detailed responsibilities which would not be compatible with his status and special experience. He very generously asked us to proceed with the arrangements for a departmental appointment without regard to the previous suggestion that he should function as head of a Joint Staff.

I am now writing to let you know that the departmental arrangements are being made on this basis and to explain the circumstances which prevent me from using Sir Ernest's services in the manner previously hoped

I hope that you will be willing to allow Sir Ernest to continue, as heretofore, as a member of the Industrial Panel of my Ministry and that we shall, in this way, have the benefit of his special knowledge for problems as they arise *ad hoc*. As you are aware, we have endeavoured to avoid making too heavy demands on members of the Panel and they should not involve more than the equivalent of roughly one day per week.

Please forgive me for having put you to so much trouble in this matter. I should greatly have

wished to take advantage of your readiness to release Sir Ernest if the Joint Staff project had proved practicable.

H.G. Smith commented: 'Thus died the germ of a real Joint Supply Staff being brought into practical operation. One might give a new twist to that famous phrase of the Prime Minister: "Never before has so much been said about so little by so few". The mice had been at work!'

At first glance, this is a neat and wryly cynical summation of the proceedings, but on closer examination makes no sense. Surely, it would have been more appropriate to write 'Never before has so much been said about so little by so *many*'?

Meanwhile, Lemon was concerned with other investigations.

Small Arms Ammunition[407]

ON 2 October, Lemon attended a meeting at the MOP to consider matters arising from the recommendations of the Lever Committee investigation into production of Small Arms Ammunition. It was felt that the report had been compromised by the Chairman's difficulty in getting any agreement on recommendations that implied adverse criticism of current departmental practice. Lemon agreed to study the papers to see if any further action was needed. This was a precise example of the work proposed for the Joint Supply Staff, and Lemon is minuted as again emphasising the importance of proper phasing between different programmes, which he did not believe was given sufficient attention. For example, he reported, there was no point in building yet more aircraft, if there was not enough ammunition for their guns.

On 6 October, he concluded that he was satisfied that, on the production side, no action was required. However, that still left the issue of closer collaboration between 'user, formulation of requirements, design and development, and production'. On this he suggested that he should call together representatives of the Service and Supply Departments to discuss the matter further. However, by the end of November, no such meeting had been held – largely because of the somewhat elusive nature of the Agenda. That was presumably the end of the matter.

Babcock & Wilcox[408]

ALSO dealt with by Lemon during October 1942, was an investigation into the delays with orders placed with Babcock & Wilcox in Scotland. The output of this heavy-engineering firm encompassed a wide range of products. Not only did they make boilers for Admiralty ships, but other products included gun-carriages, torpedo cases, tank turrets and depth-charge throwers.

There had been considerable correspondence between the Ministry of Supply, the Admiralty, the Ministry of Production and the firm over delays in delivery; but the real point was that the firm were overloaded with orders and had not been able to obtain any ruling on the priority these orders should receive. The crunch came with an order placed for steam boilers that were required for export to Russia. As this was a prestigious order for our (now loyal) ally, the Ministry of Supply demanded that it receive absolute priority, which threw the firm into a quandary. Every other government department was making the same demands. An impasse seemed to have been reached.

The situation was referred to the Industrial Panel, and Lemon was asked to look into the matter. Once again, this was a problem that a Joint Supply Staff could have sorted out at an earlier stage. Lemon decided that the obvious way to resolve the problem was to hold a meeting attended by representatives of the firm and all the government departments involved. All concerned would sit down around a table and thrash out the problem. Presumably, it had never occurred to anyone to do this before.

The meeting was eventually held on 22 October, and chaired by Lemon. This revealed how each Ministry had been pushing its own orders, regardless of other considerations. The meeting therefore agreed an order of priorities – the Admiralty's requirements for boilers was given equal first priority with the Russian order. Other orders would have to be accommodated as and when possible. The meeting was also an opportunity for the firm to air some other grievances – in particular the loss of skilled workers who were being called up for Military Service. They pointed out, as an example, that the Admiralty was calling up skilled workers for service as naval ratings who would have been far better employed in building the boilers for the ships they required. The recommendations made at the meeting were adopted and H.G. Smith records that 'the firm were greatly relieved'. Lemon had been assisted in the collection of detail by the two LMS accountants who had helped with the 'Changeover' Report, and the firm asked that they should continue to give further assistance, which was arranged.

Possibly the last piece of business to come Lemon's way at the Ministry of Production occurred some time in November 1942. By chance, a file which had been washing around government ministries for two years finished up on Lemon's desk. It concerned the railways and H.G. Smith, in idiosyncratic style, recounts the sequence of events in his 'Diary of No Consequence':

THE CHIEF at LMS Executive 12th November, 1940, urged that 100 additional locomotives be built in anticipation of next year's requirements. Recommendation for 262 (including 20 Diesels) already authorised to be implemented, similarly with 2,399 wagons agreed. Also desired to build 100 Diesels, and agreed to obtain authority for these at next Board.

Chief Operating Manager seriously concerned about locomotive position seeing programmes so much behind, and workshops taking on more war work. THE CHIEF got busy again as matter had been under discussion since September, and on 3rd December he submitted comprehensive memo to Executive Committee.

Matter dragged on with R.E.C. until July 1941 when Sir William Wood submitted a memo setting out four-companies position (noted at Executive Committee July 4th) and further discussed at Railway Executive Committee July 8th. A further and more detailed document prepared August 29th.

Meeting of President and THE CHIEF and Officers same day and latter were requested to take all steps to make engines more quickly available at sheds, including alteration of examination period. R.E.C. on 3rd September submitted memo to Sir Cyril Hurcomb on position and need for more engines. And so the matter went on, backwards and forwards between the R.E.C. and the Ministry of War Transport, more figures being added to more.

Whilst at the Ministry of Production in November 1942 a file of papers came along to THE CHIEF on the loco. building programmes of the railways, a thick file too, reports and memos, and arguments carried on between M.W.T. and Ministry of Supply, and then to MOP for decision. A day or two later a man from the Lord President's Office came to see THE CHIEF and produced sheets of statistics on traffics and engines under repair and reasons for and against the particular number the railways ought to have. September 1940 to November 1942, words, words, words, instead of engines.

Inevitably fireworks began to pop and THE CHIEF assisted in the constellation to the dumbfoundment of the poor emissary from the Lord President, who no doubt now realised the inefficacy of a statistical mind against the irresistible force of an engineering personality. He returned much chastened, satisfied that further arguments pro and con were unnecessary.

How the matter stands now (January 1943) Heaven only knows!!

President of Institution of Production Engineers[409]

IN THE autumn of 1942 Lemon became President of the Institution of Production Engineers, which was celebrating 21 years of existence. His appointment had been announced some months earlier, and he was officially installed at the AGM on 23 October – a day after the Babcock & Wilcox meeting, described above.

Sir Oliver Lyttelton, Minister of Production was the Guest of Honour at the AGM, and affably started his address by noting how many familiar faces he saw among his audience – of whom many were actively working for his Ministry.

He mentioned several in particular, including Lemon who he described as having 'carried out some highly important studies for my Ministry and for the Supply Ministries in the field of war production'. But as he then explained – to laughter from the delegates: 'my idea of organisation is that other people should do my work, and that, where they are successful, I should take the credit, but where things go wrong I should have the opportunity of saying that it was their fault. You will have realised already, however, from the names which I have just mentioned, that I have very successfully developed this policy and that, because all these names are such household words, by getting them to do my work I have shown that intelligence and foresight for which His Majesty's Government is so justly famous.'

Lemon's speech, as reported in the Institution's *Journal*, was a slightly rambling affair. One of his proposals was that the Government should set up a Staff College for senior management, as had been done for the Armed Services. He observed to the Members that:

a number of the difficulties which you meet today are the result of a lack of pre-production planning on the part of this country before and during the war. It seems to me that, if it is necessary to have a Staff College for the Army, a Staff College for the Air Force and a Staff College for the Navy, it is equally important, if not more so, that we in this country should have some sort of Staff College as part of the governmental machinery.

I say that for this reason. All the industries which go to make up this enormous war potential are very complicated, and it requires a long training to understand the sequence in which the various processes should be carried on. It is no use, for example, putting up factories unless you know that the raw material and all the ancillary industries necessary to make, shall we say aircraft, are there. If there was a constant interchange through some sort of Staff College, as I have called it, so that certain people were taken from industry in peace-time and trained, they could be ear-marked to go back immediately on the outbreak of war into Government service to carry out the various plans which had been worked out. I think that that would be a tremendous gain.

Lemon then turned his attention to the problems of post-war planning, and dismantling the enormous machine of war-production. Although this was 1942, and the war was by no means won, it is interesting that, as far as Lemon was concerned the outcome was not in doubt, and he was already looking ahead for future problems, and ways to solve them.

Railway Companies' Association Commission

ON 28 October 1942, Lemon held the fourth meeting of the Railway Companies' Association Commission. This had not met since 10 July despite the urgency which was constantly been reiterated. However, in fairness, since 1 September they had been waiting to receive the specific memoranda that had been allotted to the various General Managers. Lemon was obviously reluctant to return to these railway problems, especially as the idea that he should head the proposed Joint Supply Staff at the MOP was still very much alive. He suggested to his President, Sir William Wood, that possibly Ashton Davies could be made an alternate Chairman, so as to leave him more free for his other duties. This idea was acceptable to the RCA and it was left that Lemon would notify them when his position with the JSS was confirmed. Lemon therefore chaired the meeting on the 28th, which had new representatives from the GWR and London Transport. They also had a new topic to discuss: the standardisation of freight train brakevans. This had been suggested only a few days before, and there was immediately a conflict of interest as only the GWR and SR used brakevans with sanding apparatus as standard practice. The discussion on this matter, although lengthy, appears to have been amicable, and they decided the LMS should build four prototype brakevans – with sanding apparatus (!) – and then subject them to trials on each Company's lines. The only other subject they were able to discuss in any detail was the standardisation of stationery. Here some progress had been made by an *ad hoc* staff

of redundant clerks at the Railway Clearing House. However, it was agreed that no progress could be made in accountancy forms until the financial status of the post-war railways was known. The members also acknowledged that some changes had already been made by their Companies as a war measure, and because of the limited supplies of paper, but these were intended only to be temporary. It was not possible to consider any of the other subjects as the Memoranda had not been completed. Further meetings would therefore be arranged when these were received.

Freeman returns to the Ministry of Aircraft Production.

ON 19 October 1942, Sir Wilfrid Freeman returned to the MAP.[410] Accepting the fact that it would have taken him a week or so to establish the true situation at the Ministry, the following hand-written letter, which was discovered in Lemon's personal papers, was probably written some time in November. Parts of this letter were quoted in the chapter describing Lemon's resignation from the Air Ministry in 1940. Unfortunately, the document no longer contains either the date or the writer's name, address and signature as the relevant sections have been cut off. It reads in full:

I spent some time with W.F. this morning and we discussed matters with complete candour. He tells me that he had no idea, until he went into M.A.P., of the ghastly state of affairs there, – but fully realizes it now. The breakdown of Buchanan has been a serious blow to him for, as he said, he is himself not an expert on production. 'I have, however, grasped the main principles', he said, 'and Lemon taught me all I know.'

He is naturally nervous about the powers of MOP and thoroughly appreciates that Self – and you, not Lyttleton [*sic*], are the people who matter in that Ministry, – and, though nervous, he seemed to think that the public interest is safer in your hands than in Lyttleton's!

He agreed with me that very serious damage to the national interest can be avoided if he

I spent some time with W.F. this morning and we discussed matters with complete candour. He tells me that he had no idea, until he went into M.A.P., of the ghastly state of affairs there, – but fully realizes it now. The breakdown of Buchanan has been a serious blow to him for, as he said, he is himself not an expert on production. "I have, however, grasped the main principles", he said, "and Lemon taught me all I know."

He is naturally nervous about the powers of M.O.P. and thoroughly appreciates that Self and you, not Lyttelton, are the people who matter in that Ministry, – and, though nervous, he seemed to think that the public interest is safer in your hands than in Lyttelton's!

He agreed with me that very serious damage to the national interest can be avoided if he and you can work together in complete confidence, and promised me that he would do everything possible to re-establish the partnership between you. So it's up to you to make it as easy as possible for him to do so, – and it isn't easy for him since he is a proud man.

I think that I made him understand that, if you two were working together, any increase in the powers of M.O.P. will be found of real and positive advantage to him in his present position under a dud Minister in a rotten Ministry.

Letter describing the chaotic state at the Ministry of Aircraft Production (identified as written by Austin Hopkinson MP, in Autumn 1942).
Lemon's personal papers

and you can work together in complete confidence, and promised me that he would do everything possible to re-establish the partnership between you. So it's up to you to make it as easy as possible for him to do so, – and it won't be easy for him since he is a proud man.

I think that I made him understand that, if you two were working together, any increase in the power of MOP will be found of real and positive advantage to him in his present position under a dud Minister and a rotten Ministry.

Perhaps the reason that Lemon removed all means of identification from the letter was because of the wild indiscretions that it contained. It is not easy to judge who could have written it – it is easier to tell who didn't! Obviously it was not written by any of the people directly referred to,

which eliminates both Ministers: Llewellin (who must have been the 'dud' Minister) and Lyttelton. It is also difficult to date precisely. Llewellin was replaced as Minister by Sir Stafford Cripps on 22 November – shortly after Freeman's return – and, although Freeman did not immediately get on well with him, a rapport was soon established. This seems to confirm that the letter can be dated to early in November 1942.

The identity of the writer came with the realisation that Sir Harold Hartley had used a similar phrase concerning Freeman's indebtedness to Lemon in a letter to Sir William Haley, editor of *The Times* in 1955. This was written after Lemon's death and informed Haley that Sir Henry Self had agreed to write an appreciation of Lemon's work at the Air Ministry for the newspaper. Hartley wrote 'Austin Hopkinson told me last week that Wilfrid Freeman once said that he owed everything to Lemon'.[411] Hopkinson was a back-bench MP representing Mossley in Lancashire from the 1920s right through to the end of the Second World War. In all that time he sat as an Independent, resolutely refusing to follow any party line. He was a keen pilot and his knowledge of flying led to his strong support for rearmament, especially of the RAF. He held no official Government posts but used his influence as a free-thinking back-bencher wherever possible. He was also a member of the Athenaeum Club, like all the protagonists in the matter, which is undoubtedly where the remark was made. An examination of his handwriting immediately confirmed that it was indeed Hopkinson who wrote this letter.[412]

It is interesting to see that Hopkinson considered Self and Lemon to be the dominant force in the Ministry of Production, and not the Minister, Oliver Lyttelton. It was exactly at this time (13 November) that Lyttelton's plans for a Joint Supply Staff, with Lemon at its head, were squashed. It looks as though there was a lot of wheeler-dealing and political machination going on behind the scenes, and there were those who wished to curtail Lemon's importance and influence. The letter also confirms the allegation made by Bulman (see earlier) that Freeman and Lemon had fallen out towards the end of his period as DGP. The phrase 'it won't be easy for him since he is a proud man' implies that Freeman was, in some way, at fault. The partnership was never resumed however, and the reason for this can be explained by what happened next to Lemon.

Hopkinson's letter also tells us that, since Lemon started work on the Barracuda investigation in July, his colleague, J.S. Buchanan, had suffered a nervous breakdown, although this is not mentioned in any of the correspondence in the relevant files. It is perhaps not fully appreciated today what strains the war put on those in administrative positions. We are aware of the horrors faced by the fighting man and sometimes forget the pressures under which those away from the front-line also operated.

Lemon had also been working under enormous pressures. For the previous six months he had been driving himself remorselessly. He had only just recovered from a breakdown in health when he agreed to take on a continuous load of work for the Industrial Panel at the MOP. This had involved a great deal of travel, and there had been times when he was juggling with two or three projects simultaneously. He had also been struggling to make any sort of progress with the Railway Companies' Commission. This must all have had an effect on his health. However, there is no reference to his being unable to carry out any work because of sickness. As has been mentioned earlier in this chapter, Lemon attended the meeting at MOP on 13 November when the Joint Supply Staff proposal fell through, but it is perhaps an ominous sign that there is no record of his active involvement with any new project throughout November.

However, at the beginning of December, he did turn his direct attention to the Firefly problem, and the reorganisation of Fairey's in Hayes. Lemon called the companies involved in the project – Fairey's, General Aircraft and Aero Engines – to a meeting at Hayes on 9 December. Fairey's were able to report that, as a result of the on-going re-organisation of the Barracuda group of manufacturers in the North, they had already appointed new Production Managers at both their Hayes and Stockport branches. Lemon proposed that they should now follow the same pattern as he had instigated there, and set up a Group Co-ordinating Office in Hayes. This was accepted, and the minutes of the meeting show that the remainder of the time was spent in discussing and organising the practicalities. Two days later – on 11 December – H.G. Smith records that Lemon was unwell. His exact words were: 'forced to lay up'. No mention is made of the precise nature of this illness, and so, as an immediate reaction, one might well suppose that it was nothing particularly serious. Lemon appeared able enough on the 15th to write to Sir Stafford Cripps, the new Minister at MAP, telling him of the action he had taken at Fairey's, explaining that this followed the request by his predecessor, Colonel Llewellin, to examine the Firefly problems. However, although Lemon must have dictated the letter, he didn't sign it: it was signed by H.G. Smith. Moreover, a meeting of the RCA Commission which Lemon had called for 16 December, after receiving memoranda from the General Managers on four of the other subjects to be investigated, was cancelled.

Lemon also did not attend the LMS Board Meeting on 17 December. Despite all his other commitments he had attended every other meeting throughout the year, and it was on this occasion that the LMS Board of Directors decided that now was the time to consider seriously whether to terminate his employment as Vice-President. This is not recorded in the Board Minutes, but the date can be deduced from the Special Minutes of 25 February 1943, when the financial details of his pension payments were decided. It would have been remarkably quick off the mark of the LMS to have discussed his future with the Company if he had only become unwell six days earlier. So one has to believe that the signs of an impending break-down had been apparent for some time.

Smith laid all the blame for Lemon's collapse on the problems with the RCA Commission. This does not quite seem to fit the order of events as they have been described in this chapter. The last meeting of the Commission had been six weeks earlier, and was not particularly fraught. Since that time, other things had been at the fore-front of Lemon's attention – notably the reorgan-isation of Fairey's at Hayes and the cancellation of the projected Joint Supply Staff. Nevertheless, Smith concluded his 'Diary of No Consequence':

The effect of all this caused THE CHIEF much disappointment and irritation of mind, so much so that in December, 1942, he had to lay up. The doctor's diagnosis was that his trouble arose from the frustration and manner in which, as Chairman of the Commission, he had been compelled to function, and the Doctor strongly urged THE CHIEF to be quit of it, and that the LMS should utilise his services and abilities in some more suitable and satisfying direction. Lord Horder, who was brought into consultation, confirmed this in more restrained but no less emphatic terms. The CHIEF discussed the matter with the President, who the following day saw the Doctor, and then placed it with the Chairman,

who stated that it would be for the Board to make the decision.

The breakdown in Lemon's health was far more serious than his secretary H.G. Smith was prepared to indicate – and it soon becomes clear that he had suffered a complete nervous breakdown. On 22 December the Harley Street consultant, Lord Horder, wrote to Lemon with his diagnosis:

Dear Sir Ernest,

It is good to be able to assure you that there is no evidence you are suffering from any organic disease. Your present disability is entirely due to prolonged strain and frustration.

The anxiety of the last four years, with the attendant wear and tear of your mental equipment, have resulted in a disorganisation of your blood pressure; this disorganisation is capable of adjustment only by an adjustment of the causative factor. It thus becomes imperative that the necessary steps be immediately taken to allow you to be engaged upon such mental activities, of a creative nature, as will give you peace of mind and an achievement of your objective. Should you not attain this desideratum, I must warn you that the alteration in your blood pressure is liable to develop into an organic and permanent condition.

I think you will see from the above that I consider relief from your permanent disability lies in the hands of yourself and your colleagues. In the meantime it is essential that you should spend a period of approximately six weeks away from work.

Lemon discussed his future with the President, Sir William Wood, who came to visit him. Although he wrote to Wood: 'Thank you so much for coming to see me and for your help', Wood was really the bearer of an ultimatum. And by the end of the year, Lemon had accepted that he must offer his resignation to the Board, and await their decision. Not only was his career with the LMS at an end, but all the other work that had involved him during 1942 was to finish as well.

TWELVE

Retirement and Recovery, 1943–1945

So far as Lemon's position at the LMS was concerned, H.G. Smith obviously felt there had been ominous signs that the writing had been on the wall for some considerable time. He recorded in October 1942 that the Chairman had asked Lemon to give up his room at the Mill House in Watford. This House was a senior management 'facility' that Lemon was conveniently using as his private address for all official business. In formally accepting the offer of his knighthood in 1941, he had quoted it as his private address; and in several of the replies to congratulatory letters which he received following this honour he described the house as his 'mess' for the duration of the war. It was undoubtedly a convenient location as LMS headquarters had also temporarily transferred to Watford, but it is also further confirmation that he was no longer living at Northchurch Hall, only a few miles away.

The Chairman, Lord Royden wrote:

My colleagues on the Board of the LMS Railway often ask to be put up at the Grove Mill House or the Old Mill House on the occasion of their visits to London to attend the Board or for other purposes. The room you used to occupy is generally vacant but I have hesitated to put anyone in it without first letting you know. It would facilitate matters if you could let them know at the Old Mill House some time in advance if you were contemplating spending a night there. It would be awkward if there were two would-be occupants for the same room!

A reasonable request, to which Lemon replied:

I will arrange to remove my belongings from the room I have occupied at the Mill House as soon as I have time to come out and collect them. I am sorry if you have been put to any inconvenience.

Nevertheless, one wonders if there were any other reasons – apart from medical ones – that influenced the attitude of the LMS Board to Lemon's situation. The first point to make is that he had not actually done any work for the Company since the beginning of the year, when he was seconded to the Railway Companies Association. From May, he had been working virtually continuously for the Ministry of Production. Moreover, on 17 December 1942, when the Board first discussed the subject, they had not been informed that the MOP plans for Lemon's involvement with the Joint Supply Staff had fallen through. Lord Royden was only officially informed about this on 23 December, and so the expectation could have been that Lemon was unlikely to return for some considerable time.

It is also true that Lemon's position as Vice-President had been uncomfortable since his return in 1940. Wartime restrictions meant that the railway was simply trying to maintain its best level of service under the circumstances. There was little scope for Lemon's enthusiasm for new projects and initiatives. In fact, he had achieved little success with any new projects, as is demonstrated by the Coal Silo fiasco and the impasse with the Railway Companies' Commission. He had also not taken kindly to the restrictions in operating practices placed on him by the Railway Executive Committee. During his absences, Ashton Davies had stepped into the Vice-President's shoes and fulfilled his duties adequately. The LMS might well have felt that they just didn't need him any more. At 58 years old, he was two years away from the official retirement age, and his health was fragile.

However, there is one other point that may have prejudiced the general feeling against him, and tainted his reputation within the LMS. This was his affair with Hermione Mervyn. A senior executive at British Rail (now retired), who worked for the LMS at this time, recalled that rumours circulated through the Company regarding the scandal of an affair between a married Vice-President and another member of Staff that precipitated his resignation. There is, of course, no hint of this in any of the official records and it seems unlikely to be the prime cause. Nevertheless, society in those days was remarkably puritanical about such matters. Sir Wilfrid Freeman had feared that his promotion prospects at the RAF would be compromised when he divorced in the 1930s, and if such an atmosphere was prevalent in the Air Force, it probably also existed in other large organisations such as the LMS.

However, it is impossible to tell from this distance in time how many people were aware of his relationship with Hermione. She had left the railway in 1937, six years earlier – unless she returned in some capacity as part of the war-effort. It must have been apparent, though, to senior executives that he had left his wife, as it would have been difficult to disguise the fact that he was no longer living at Northchurch Hall. Whether Lord Stamp was aware of the situation is impossible to discover. He would surely have disapproved, but there is no evidence of any cooling in their relationship before his death in 1941. It may be that Lemon and Hermione did manage to keep their affair a secret – and all that was generally known were rumours.

Financial considerations do not seem to have been a problem, as secret minutes of the Board Meeting on 25 February 1943 show. These record the pension and financial settlement that the LMS agreed to pay:

The Chairman reported that as agreed at the meeting of the Board on 17th December last he had seen Sir Ernest Lemon and informed him of the wish of the Board that, having regard to the condition of his health following his special work for the Ministry of Air and Ministry of Production in the last 4½ years, and the likelihood that he would not be fit for further railway work for some time to come, he should retire from the Company's service at 31st January rather than remain on leave.

He had arranged that the Company would pay Sir Ernest a pension for his life of £3,200 per annum from 1st February 1943, payable on the last day of each month, and a lump sum of £8,533 being the benefits he would have received from the Superannuation Fund had he retired at age 60 on his present salary, together with a further lump sum payment of £3,567 as compensation for loss of office, his salary ceasing on 31st January.

(Under the rules of the Superannuation Fund Sir Ernest receives on retirement for refund of his contributions a sum of £3,900 and the total payments received by him are thus £16,000, equal to two years salary, and a pension of £3,200.)

At the same time as Lemon was discussing his future at the LMS, he received word from the Ministry of Aircraft Production that his services in the re-organisation of Fairey's were no longer required. The timing of this decision may have been a complete coincidence, not influenced in any way by his illness, but merely indicative that the new regime of Sir Stafford Cripps and Sir Wilfrid Freeman at the MAP were seeking to put their house in order, and take such matters back into their own hands. Cripps visited Hayes on 19 December, and then wrote to Lemon:

Many thanks for your letter of the 18th December enclosing the notes of a meeting which you held at Hayes on the 9th December, with representatives of all the firms concerned, about the establishment of a Firefly Group Co-ordinating Office. I am glad to see that you have been attacking the Firefly problem on the lines which you adopted in handling the Barracuda problem.

I have been giving a good deal of thought during the last few days to problems connected with Fairey, Hayes. There is no doubt that the absence of Sir Richard Fairey in America has left the management in a rather weak state. To meet this situation, I have proposed, and the Board of Faireys have approved, the appointment of Mr. G.E. Marden as Deputy Chairman and Managing Director. Mr. Marden will have my full support in any necessary measures of reorganisation.

While dealing with these matters, I have had to consider whether it is right, now that the management of the parent firm has been strengthened, to continue the arrangement by which you, a member of the Ministry of Production, are placed in charge of the measures for bringing Firefly production into a state of efficiency, and have come to the conclusion that the arrangement made by Colonel Llewellin ought to be terminated. The chain of responsibility ought henceforward to be direct from Mr. Marden to this Department.

I can assure you that this change implies no disagreement with the preliminary measures which you have taken as regards the Firefly Group.

I take this opportunity to thank you for the time you have given to and the efforts you have made to solve the production problems of the Barracuda and Firefly.

On 4 January 1943, Lemon was 'up again', and replied to Cripps:

Thank you for your letter of the 28th December, and I am glad to hear that you are in agreement with the preliminary measures I have taken as regards the Firefly Group Office.

I note that now, in view of the changed circumstances at Hayes through the appointment of Mr. Marden, you consider the arrangements made by Colonel Llewellin with me should be terminated. It is further understood from telephone conversation with your office that your letter is to be read as applying to the Barracuda also.

In view of the altered circumstances I feel sure you will agree that the men who have been assisting me with the Barracuda problem may go back to their own jobs. These comprise Mr. C.E. Fairburn, the LMS Chief Mechanical Engineer at Derby, Messrs. Smith, Wollaston and Haynes, loaned from the LMS Company, and Mr. Roberson loaned to me by Sir George Beharrell personally.

It would be pleasing to record that the work that Lemon and his team had done at Fairey's – and, of course, the ensuing work of Cripps and Freeman – sorted out the problems. However, correspondence in the Admiralty files from November 1943, eleven months later, showed that this was not the case. A despondent official at MAP then wrote to the First Lord of the Admiralty explaining why no Fireflies had been produced in the previous week:

With reference to your note of the 17th November about Firefly production. Fairey's failure to make their programme last week is reported to be due to a shortage of ailerons, but it might equally well have been due to a shortage of almost anything else; by that I mean that the planning at Hayes is still so chaotic that if it is ailerons this week it will probably be rudders next week and elevators the week afterwards, and so on to the end of the year.[413]

It was also on 4 January, that Lemon replied to his Chairman, Lord Royden:

I thank you for your letter of the 31st December. So far as the Industrial Panel is concerned I am afraid there has been some misunderstanding, as I am quite willing to remain on the Panel for any ad hoc duty which the Minister may require and for which my special knowledge may be of use.

As regards the Commission, in view of the way that things have developed I feel there is little chance of my endeavouring to influence its policy or course. I would, therefore, rather be freed from the Chairmanship of it, and you will no doubt be willing to obtain Sir Ronald Matthews' concurrence.

My thirty two years' experience with the LMS has convinced me that I can with confidence leave the question of my future in the hands of your good self and the Directors.

I am up again to-day and my Doctor wishes me to get away to the country as soon as possible, and I hope to achieve this by the end of the week.

Although his work at Fairey's had come to an end, Lemon still intended to be available for any future work that the MOP Industrial Panel might require of him. However, the records show that he was never asked to undertake any further investigations – and the work of the whole Panel virtually came to an end a few months later. It existed theoretically in name until the end of the war, but was offered no more investigations.

Lemon's resignation from the Railway Companies' Commission was accepted, with regrets, by Sir Ronald Matthews; and it was agreed that Ashton Davies would take over the Chairmanship.

H.G. Smith, ever the loyal servant, records that, on 28 January 1943, the Board ratified both Lemon's retirement and Ashton Davies' appointment – and commented: 'An Autolycus of 68 supplants a Knight Bachelor of 58: St John Ch.5 v. 41' *

There is no mention of Lemon's resignation in the LMS Board Minutes. They do not carry any acknowledgement of his departure, or tribute to his years of service – as one might reasonably expect. Company policy seems to have been that tributes were only recorded for departing Directors and, although Lemon attended Board meetings, he did so as a Vice-President, not a Director. The only indication that he had left the LMS has to be inferred from the re-allocation of his duties, which *is* recorded. Sir William Wood's file of correspondence as President also shows that he informed the other senior officers of

[* I receive not honour from men]

G.L. Darbyshire's appointment as Vice-President without even mentioning Lemon's departure. It is a curiously discourteous omission.

Lemon's resignation was announced in the Press at the beginning of February 1943, and H.G. Smith penned this tribute in a letter to the *Railway Gazette* of 10 February:

SIR, – In taking leave of Sir Ernest Lemon, who was my Chief for the past ten years, I do so with feelings of regret and pride; pride, in that I enjoyed and retained his confidence in every way; and regret, that no longer will his invigorating personality be with us on the LMSR. As his personal assistant since 1932, I worked with him in the closest intimacy on all the problems he had to tackle, and they were many.

He was the mainspring behind the developments in all phases of traffic working on the LMSR., inaugurated from 1932 to 1938, with benefits which placed the company in a most favourable position for handling the enormous war traffic which commenced to flow in 1939.

A man of forthright temperament, frank and without guile in all his dealings, he was the essence of loyalty to colleagues and officers alike, and looked only for the same loyalty in return. Essentially friendly at all times, cool in weighing up a problem and giving his decision, requiring no fuss to be made on his account when travelling about the line, he preferred seeing and talking to men at their jobs rather than reading long reports from them. One of his dicta was that the profits of a business are made on the workshop floor, and efficiency on the station platform or goods shed deck had a similar application. He was a great Chief in every way; he got a lot

H.G. Smith,
Lemon's Secretary and
Personal Assistant while
he was Vice-President.
Railway Gazette

227

of good work done and did not mind who got the credit for it. Coupled with these qualities was a large charity of understanding, and an appreciatory word of encouragement for everyone who worked for him. His heart was in the LMSR and will always so remain.

Sir Harold Hartley's papers show that a decision was made at the luncheon following the Board Meeting on 25 February that a presentation should be made. At Lemon's request this was a silver salver with the facsimile signatures of the Chief Officers – and a spirit kettle. These were presented to him at the luncheon held a month later on 29 April.

It was H.G. Smith who wrote to Lemon's sons to tell them of their father's retirement – and not Lemon himself, which may be significant. Smith's letter of the 20 February 1943 to Dick, who was serving in the Army in India starts:

You will no doubt be surprised to receive the enclosed extracts from 'The Railway Gazette' this week, which indicate that your Father has retired from the LMS. I am very sorry indeed that this has happened, and it is a long story. Briefly the reason given him for being compensated is that he did not fit in the Watford organisation. The real reason behind it is, however, the fact that the Railway Companies' Commission, of which he was appointed Chairman twelve months or more ago, has never been given a real chance of working in a practical way. We have been subjected to all kinds of restrictions on the part of the General Managers – don't pass this on to any of your G.W. colleagues, or it might have repercussions – and your Father has been in a continual state of frustration and mental irritation as he realised how impossible it was to get a proper job done as was intended in the first place.

In December he was far from well, and has since then been under the Doctor. There is no physical illness, but just a question of strain and worry and he is at the present time in a Nursing Home undergoing toning-up treatment. He should be all right again in a week or two's time.

Smith concludes:

I have not said anything to your Mother, and it is quite likely she does not yet know, although there was a brief statement in 'The Times' and 'Daily Telegraph' last Saturday.

I saw your last Airgraph, and am glad to hear that you are going on well and hope you are keeping in good health.

Smith's professional relationship with Lemon was at an end, and with it ended the careful compilation of records of his work. Although Lemon's papers do contain some evidence of his later life, the information is patchy and possibly incomplete – much has had to be ferreted out from other sources. As Lemon was estranged from his wife, very little information remains in the family.

We can, however, deduce that Lemon took his doctor's advice to leave London. His son, David, referred to a 'cottage in Saffron Walden' in a letter to his brother, written after Lemon's death. Lemon's personal papers also contain a letter from Frank Pope in July 1943 telling him of a package awaiting collection at Audley End Station, which serves the town. The exact address, however, remained a mystery (as no Electoral Rolls were collated during the war) until it was discovered that the first post-war Register still lists him and Hermione at Bulls Green Cottage, Arkesden.[414]

The village of Arkesden lies a few miles from Saffron Walden, in the north-west corner of Essex, close to the border with Hertfordshire and Cambridgeshire. Bulls Green Cottage is situated outside the village at the end of a narrow lane and remains remarkably isolated and remote. It can hardly have changed in 50 years, and must have been an oasis of peace and quiet, where Lemon could recover from the pressures of the previous years. The present owner knew of Lemon's connection, and told the author he was reputed to have planted the row of cedar trees in the garden and to have had the telephone put in. This was the only modern amenity in Lemon's time – an electricity supply was not put in until many

The silver salver presented to Sir Ernest Lemon on his retirement from the LMS.
Family

years later. The spirit kettle would undoubtedly have come in handy!

One wonders whether Hermione chose the location? Although she and her family had been Irish for generations, 'Audley' was a family name, carried by both her brothers and other relatives. Certain correspondence, however, continued to be addressed to 34 Acacia Road, St John's Wood, showing that Lemon still used the house as a London base.

Lord Horder's advice to Lemon at the beginning of 1943 was to refrain from any work for six weeks, and one might expect to find evidence that he gradually resumed work in some field or other as the year progressed. But one searches in vain. It seems extraordinary to have to accept that, after the frenetic activity of 1942, he did nothing at all for virtually a year – but that seems to be the case. The breakdown in his health was obviously far more serious than anyone expected. It also shows that the LMS had been remarkably prescient in deciding that he should retire, although one hopes that their decision did not aggravate his condition.

President of the Institution of Production Engineers

THE one position that Lemon did still hold was President of the Institution of Production Engineers. Council Meetings, which were not necessarily in London, were held every three months, and the Minutes of the meeting held on 19 March 1943 record that 'owing to the indisposition of the President, it had not been possible to approach him on the subject of post-war reconstruction, and it was therefore decided to leave this matter in abeyance'.[415]

The Minutes show that he did attend a meeting on 24 September 1943, at which he 'regretted his absence at previous meetings due to ill-health, but hoped he would be able to attend more regularly in the future'. In fact, this was the only Council Meeting that he *did* attend in the two years that he was President. The Institution's *Journal* then shows that he chaired the AGM on 29 October 1943 when the meeting concluded with Lord Sempill declaring: 'I do not know whether I shall be ruled out of order by the President, but as he has just come back from a long period of illness, due to heavy war work, I will ask you to give him a hearty cheer. We are very glad to see him here, and we hope that he will keep fit and well and be with us at all our future meetings, as I am sure he will.'

A week later, on 5 November 1943, Lemon was well enough to travel to Lincoln for the inaugural meeting of the Lincoln Sub-section of the Institution. Once again, it was announced that he had been very ill – and his opening remarks, which were printed in the Institution's *Journal*, even imply that his attendance at the meeting had been in some doubt. He announced that he had no written speech and was just going to talk off the record. It thus gives us a unique opportunity to hear his personal philosophy, in his own words – what had motivated his thinking and what now concerned him. These are very much the thoughts of an older man who was now able to acknowledge his shortcomings, and was seeking to pass on his wisdom to a younger generation. After the customary opening niceties he said:

My main object tonight is to examine the position of Production Engineers and what they really mean in this country. Are the engineers doing what the farmer does? Are they producing two blades of grass where one grew before for, as the Americans put it, the best engineer is the man who can produce for one dollar what the other takes two dollars to produce. You have produced tools, you have increased production, and you have made it possible for the Army, the Navy and the Air Force to fight, and that is to your everlasting credit.

I am particularly concerned with what we are going to do in the future. The problem of the people coming back from the war, and the swinging over of industry to its normal channels are going to be more serious problems than building up the war potential in this country.

We have a number of Governmental interests that are planning for post-war, but as one of my former Directors once said to me, 'The profits of a business are made on the floor of the workshop'.

Bulls Green Cottage, Arkesden. Photograph taken in the early 1950s. David Ahn

You will have in this country an enormous engineering potential, far and away more than you had before the war. It has not been built in the ordinary channels of trade because we either had to do it or we went down. You, as Production Engineers, are the people who can speak to those in authority on what can be done. We cannot afford to break this potential up. We have to regulate it by turning over to new forms of production. We cannot tolerate the attitude of mind that says let us see about winning the war first. Are we going to sit back and say let us wait until peace comes before we can think of our future?

I know that the engineer in war-time has a heavier load than he can carry, yet he must now begin to consider the post-war position. If we start at the beginning and we say, 'well, what is the first thing to do?' We shall have to get on the world's markets. A lot of us want to know what these markets are, what products we can sell, and how we can sell them and how we can manufacture them at such a price that we can sell at a reasonable profit. I would like to leave that thought with you. Those are the lines on which I am thinking, and about which I am worrying.

People, apart from engineers, do not really know how long it takes to build up a sales organisation, to make the tools, and whilst we may say that is the Government's job, I do think we could go back to the old characteristic of

helping ourselves. We must help ourselves, and there is no use leaving it to somebody in Whitehall who doesn't know the problems. Each of us has to think what we are going to do with this war potential that has been developed.

Taking our young Production Engineers, I would like to appeal to you as your President, to bring the young men in here to have discussions, to try and train their minds on thinking on the right lines, and by the interchange of ideas with them you will find that they will learn while they talk.

We are a comparatively young Institution, but I look forward to the day when the Institution obtains a Royal Charter. Whilst we want research and academic discussions, it all boils down eventually to: 'Can I produce these things cheaper than the other fellow?' That is done by the people who guide you, and I should like you if you can to bring in younger men. The next time we come down to see you I hope we shall find that the membership has gone up to at least 200 as a result of your efforts. If you are big and you have a big membership, and if you represent a large interest, you can make yourself felt, but if somebody says what is the membership of the Production Engineers, and you say 3,700, against the Mechanicals 15,000, well, you have got to get up somewhere near so that you can speak with an equal voice in the gateway, and the gateway after the war will lessen too.

Try, then, to bring in the younger people, and stir up their minds. I think the motto of the Production Engineers ought to be: 'Why? Why do you do it this way, why can't we have another way?' If we have done it like that for twenty years why can't we change it? Never be afraid of making mistakes. I have as you know had a long experience, and I have changed from one job to another, and I expect I shall keep on doing so.

There is one other thing I would like to say to you, and I should like the Lincoln people to do it. It ought to be possible for the youngsters to read all the current literature on Engineering, and I would like to suggest to you that you form a really decent library. One of the books I have in mind more than anything in my work is an American book called 'The twelve principles of efficiency'.[416] You can take that book and apply the principles outlined there to any job you are doing. Try and get the general principles embedded in your minds so that your natural approach to any problem is such that first of all it is scientific. In these you have many minds at work, and it is not merely your own experience. It is the experience that is recorded from all over the world. Give these youngsters a chance to have some sort of rivalry which they can enjoy and from which they can benefit. Secondly, encourage them at your meetings to talk, and don't do what I sometimes do, gibe, when somebody does something, but treat them kindly, encourage them to talk, because after all is said and done, thoughts are only caught by words. Words are really only a sort of cage in which you catch your thoughts. I well remember the time when I could never get up at a public meeting without my voice going. I was thoroughly scared as a young man. It was only a question of practice and encouragement and the older really ought to encourage the youngsters, because ideas are curious things, and on them depends what the engineering industry of this country is going to be.

Having said that, I think that is really about all I have to say. I am very glad indeed to have had the opportunity of addressing you tonight.

Gentlemen, you have a marvellous job to perform in the engineering industry of this country. All life depends today on what the engineer does, so be proud of your profession, make it better, and see that you make yourselves felt. Make it a virile organisation which reacts on the counsels of the country.

Engineering Industries Association

THERE were further indications that Lemon felt it was time his opinions were heard again in a forthright speech to the Engineering Industries Association at their luncheon on 23 February 1944. His speech again addressed the problems of post-war reconstruction with particular reference to management and research. He related the thinking that led to the establishment of the LMS School of Transport, and the benefits it had brought in the short time of its existence before the outbreak of war. He recommended other large industries to follow the example of the LMS and set up their own Staff Colleges. He acknowledged this would be impossible for smaller firms, but thought some form of 'grouping' might be possible. He considered that training for management should start at the same time as apprentices were learning their craft. Not only should they be taught technical skills, but seen as potential managers. Although there were existing classes in administration at institutes and colleges, something more was required and he proposed the creation of a University of Commerce.

Lemon then moved on to his second topic – research. Once again, he started by relating what had been done, and why, by Sir Harold Hartley and the Scientific Research Committee at the LMS. He urged everyone to look at current methods and practices and ask the question 'Why?' Why was it done this way? Was there not a better solution?

To finish, Lemon considered two aspects of post-war conditions that the engineering industries could not necessarily solve for themselves, and these remarks were very much directed at Government policy. He asked what was to be done with the vast capacity of factories that had been newly built for the war effort and said:

The date and occasion when this photograph was taken is unknown. *Left to right:* Lemon, C.K. Bird (LNER), unknown, Sir William Wood. Lemon's personal papers

'I hope some very hard thinking is being done as to the uses to which these well-equipped establishments can be put for producing goods other than aircraft and munitions'. He proposed that here was an opportunity to demolish many of the the country's obsolete, slum factories and for the Government to rent out these surplus modern factories to businesses at a modest rent. In his opinion, it would be wasteful merely to 'mothball' them.

In his concluding remarks, he made a further recommendation to the Government. He recalled that Churchill had been in the forefront of those who, before the war, had pressed for a Ministry of Supply. Lemon suggested that this Ministry, or the Ministry of Production, should now be equipped with a permanent Industrial General Staff, who would – like the Military – plan for peace and war. If this had existed before 1939, he thought that industry would have been better prepared, and able to react faster to wartime requirements.

This speech was widely reported in the Press, and many papers state that a lively discussion followed.[417] The *Liverpool Daily Post* however, under the headline 'Aircraft Expert "in the dark"', started its report – 'The admission that he had "no knowledge" of what was going on in Government departments regarding the change-over from war to peace-time production' was made

by Sir Ernest Lemon . . . in London yesterday. Mr E.C. Gordon-England, the pioneering racing motorist and aviator, who presided, said: 'If that is true it is a very severe criticism of the attitude of the Government. If eminent men such as he have not been drawn into consultation, who is going to do this reconstruction?'

These remarks must have been made during the discussion, as they do not appear in the text of Lemon's speech, which still exists among his personal papers. This original draft is interesting for another reason. Lemon crossed out one whole section dealing with coal silos and the inefficient labour-intensive methods that the coal suppliers were still using, indicating that he did not deliver this section in his luncheon address.

However, a week after it had reported Lemon's speech, on 10 March the *Railway Gazette* carried a further article entitled 'Transport in the Future – Some considerations of post-war needs, from a speech by Sir Ernest Lemon'. There is no mention of when this speech might have been made, or where it was given, and it must be questioned whether it was ever delivered.

It incorporates the text that Lemon wrote about the use of factories after the war verbatim. Crucially, it then contains the text about coal silos – even to the extent of including the same grammatical error and spelling. Both read: 'Every transit unit, whether wagons, locomotives, airplanes or ships, are only earning money when they are in movement' and spell the word 'shute' thus, rather than 'chute'. It appears to be an exact transcript, copied out from Lemon's draft. The rest of the speech – if indeed it ever was a speech – is concerned with the electrification of railways and use of diesel power. This is not mentioned in any of the press reports after the luncheon on 3 March.

Whatever the truth of the matter, this second speech does contain some interesting information about Lemon's thinking on the future of the railways. He started by admitting past failings. Rail transport had had more than a hundred years of historical and traditional background, he said, and due to its former monopolistic character, acquired a good deal of stolidity and perhaps inertia, a reluctance to modernise with the passing of the years. However, during the decade prior to the war, he asserted, much leeway was made up. He still maintained that diesel power was only suitable for shunting purposes, but he was more positive about electrification. It is cleaner, an undoubted advantage for passengers; the locomotives can run for longer before servicing; and the time taken in climbing gradients is reduced. He posed the question: 'What is going to be the future of electrification for railways in this country?' and answered: 'My reply is that frankly I do not know. It is purely an economic decision'.

He then moved on to the vexed question of coal silos. At a typical LMS depot, he says, there were possibly 27 different coal merchants dealing in 20 different classes of coal, drawn from 150 different collieries. He continues: 'When I pass through Baker Street on a bus, I am appalled by the labour effort at the coal dump there; coal manhandled at the railway depot, and then when required again laboriously shovelled into a lorry'. He expressed the hope that, one day, distribution centres could be designed and equipped like a modern factory, where power was employed in every way as a substitute for manual labour.

He also ventured that he 'would like to see the customers get rid of their critical attitude towards the railways and substitute for it a co-operative spirit'. A vain hope – we still like to blame them for all our problems to this day!

The newspaper reports of Lemon's speech caused a personnel administration firm in London to write to him suggesting a meeting. The writer reminded Lemon that they had met in 1942, and expressed appreciation of what he had said in his address. This letter exists in his personal papers, but it is not known if anything came from this approach. However, there is further evidence that Lemon was seeking to pick up the reins and find some other activities to occupy him. In May 1944, he discussed the matter with Harold Whitehead, who ran a firm of Industrial Consultants, over lunch at the Athenaeum Club. Lemon appears to have been looking for some role in post-war Anglo-American relations, and supplied Whitehead with a list of names of his former contacts. Whitehead responded enthusiastically to the suggestion, and wrote to Lemon at his London address in Acacia Road, St John's Wood on 26 May 1944, confirming that they would meet again. He also asked whether, in the meantime, he could hold onto the papers on mass production, modernisation and mechanisation that Lemon had given him, commenting that they were too meaty to read through briefly and that he also wished to get some of his staff to read them.

As Coal Silos were very much on his mind, Lemon tried to revive his plans for the old scheme, and privately raised the matter in conversation with an old acquaintance, Sir Frank Tribe. Tribe was a civil servant, and must have known Lemon since the days when he was at the Air Ministry. At that time, Tribe was working for the Ministry of Labour, and would have been involved in the labour requirements that were needed for the expansion of aircraft production. In 1944 he had moved on and was now the Permanent Secretary at the Ministry of Fuel and Power. He was, one assumes, totally unaware of the earlier history of the silo scheme and wrote to the Mines Department that Lemon: 'had ideas which should lead to a vast improvement in the system of coal distribution and enable the price of coal to be reduced. His proposal broadly was that there should be big dumps under Government control fitted with mechanical cranes etc., and railway facilities. Trucks could be turned round in a very short time.' The Mines

Department looked out the old files and refreshed everyone's minds on the subject, but reiterated that there were formidable objections which had so far proved insuperable.[418]

And then, on 13 July 1944, *The Times* carried an article 'from a correspondent' entitled 'From Colliery to Cellar'. This discussed the need for improved methods in the distribution of household coal after the war was over. It stated that 'since the war a proposal has been examined for delivering the coal straight into silos or bunkers at depots'. Amongst the other suggestions, which largely mirrored Lemon's original proposals, was that coal wagons could thereby be increased in capacity to 20 tons (the precise figure that Lemon had used in his original memorandum of 1940). Having been fobbed off a month or so earlier, Lemon was outraged. He telephoned the Mines Department the following day, and this is how Nott-Bower recorded their conversation in a Memo – which is quoted in its entirety. It is interesting to see how, after two years, some of the background information has been subtly altered by Nott-Bower to give a different perspective on the case. Memories can sometimes be very short:

Sir Ernest Lemon rang me up this afternoon about the article entitled 'From Colliery to Cellar' in yesterday's 'Times', with particular reference to the paragraph marked 'X' in the attached copy. I have not previously seen this article.

Sir Ernest was in a state of indignation which to begin with approximated to hysteria and for which, even now, I have great difficulty in accounting. The burden of his complaint is that this paragraph obviously refers to the West Kensington Coal Silo Scheme, which Sir Ernest himself originated and developed in great detail, and which he put to the Mines Department two or three years ago. As result, we had a series of discussions with Sir Ernest and a private group of coal merchants, headed by Mr. John Charrington. Discussions were conducted privately, as the coal merchants concerned felt that the general body of coal traders in London would be opposed to the scheme and that it would be undesirable to

have it generally talked about unless and until some working arrangement could be devised to get the scheme into operation as a private venture. After several meetings, the matter was brought before the President of the LMS who, after hearing a full account of the proposals, came to the conclusion that the Company would not be justified in putting up the capital required.

Sir Ernest Lemon was not present at the meeting at which the President arrived at his decision. Personally, I think that the decision was justified, if only because the coal merchants who had taken part in the private negotiations were themselves lukewarm and nervous about the whole thing.

Sir Ernest now complains that the mention of this scheme (although not by name) means that someone – either we or the coal merchants or even the railway company have blown the gaff. For some reason or other, he regards this as a personal insult and he is threatening to go (a) to Mr. Barrington Ward [Editor of *The Times*], (b) to Mr. Aneurin Bevan and tell them all about the scheme and how much work he put into it. He also proposes to tell them that he laid the whole scheme before the Mines Department, who are in possession of all the plans and details. This, of course, is quite true. Sir Ernest admits that we were very helpful in our approach and did everything we could to facilitate agreement between the LMS and Mr. Charrington's group. None the less, he appears to regard us as criminally responsible for the failure of the scheme to come into operation, because in the last resort we did not use our compulsory powers.

I pointed out to Sir Ernest (a) that his own President, after hearing the full account of the negotiations, had turned the scheme down, and (b) that whatever the merits of this scheme, it could not possibly work without full co-operation from the merchants concerned, and (c) that we should not have been justified in using compulsory powers for what was in its essence a post-war development project (and a very admirable one), unless we were satisfied that the use of such powers was fully justified in the interests of war effort. We had in fact no reason to think that, even if the scheme could have been forced through, it would have had any appreciably advantageous effect on coal distribution in the area concerned. It might indeed have caused a great deal of confusion for the time being.

With regard to (a), Sir Ernest said that this cut no ice with him because the President was an accountant, and could not be expected to understand a practical proposal of this kind! We (the Mines Department) ought to have taken the advice of the practical man over the head of the accountant. As to (b) Sir Ernest admitted that the merchants were unreliable, but said that the scheme ought to have been carried out whether they liked it or not.

This is how I left things with Sir Ernest (although at the end of our conversation he had cooled down a bit). I should have thought that the worst he is likely to do is to write to the "Times", and I am bound to say that so far as my memory goes, I am satisfied that the Mines Department did all that it could reasonably be expected to do. I have no doubt at all that Coal Silos will have ultimately to form an important part of reorganised post-war coal distribution machinery, and Sir Ernest Lemon is entitled to every credit for the prolonged efforts he made to get this innovation accepted long ago, but I really can't see anything in this "Times" article which justifies his extreme indignation and in particular his animosity against this Department.

Apparently Lemon calmed down after his outburst, and took no further action. The files carry the sardonic comment: 'I have no doubt he would like to make certain that everyone knew that he put up the proposal originally'. And there the matter finally rested, although the files show that they were periodically taken out for consultation until as late as 1949.

Another example of Lemon's anger at events beyond his control comes from a family anecdote. It must date from the later stages of the war, and was told to Lemon's granddaughter, Amanda, by

her father David. David had progressed through Oundle School and followed his brother to Balliol College, Oxford, where he read law. After a year at university, he volunteered for the RAF and became a bomber pilot. Amanda was told that Lemon apparently had a blazing row with Churchill over the lack of adequate protection for aircrews. He wanted the RAF to follow American practice and put a sheet of armour-plate under the pilots' seats to protect them from anti-aircraft fire. Churchill point blank refused, and Lemon said that he was needlessly wasting the lives of expensively trained pilots. This story has not been verified from any other source but, as a bomber pilot, David is hardly likely to have invented it. It cannot date from the earlier period when Lemon was at the Air Ministry, as Churchill was not Prime Minister, nor were the practical consequences of the RAF's bombing campaign then apparent.

Lemon resigned as President of the Institution of Production Engineers at the AGM in the Autumn of 1944, and was made an Honorary Member in June 1945. The war draw to its close, and on 27 September 1945 Stafford Cripps wrote to Lemon officially thanking him for the work he had done on the Industrial Panel at the Ministry of Production – in 1942.[419]

It is apposite to quote Lewis Ord at this point. In 1944, his book 'Secrets of Industry' was published. It was an assessment of British and American industrial methods and practice as they had developed over the previous 100 years, and he found little to commend in the British way of doing things. In the foreword he quotes one of his American sources as follows:

The British got into a jam because they did not know how far they were behind and tried to prepare for war on the cheap. They are doing the same thing again. They do not know how far they are behind industrially, and the industrial leaders are taking care that the British Government and the British people shall not find out. Their plans are to avoid spending money and continue things as they were. They are trying to win a peace on the cheap.' He paused for a minute or two. 'Those fighting British, men, women, and children, they compel admiration. They deserve a better fate.'[420]

Ord writes that this made a profound impression on him, and was a major factor in his decision to write the book. Of the British post-war plans for industry, he wrote:

Many well-to-do men have had to live on capital during the war. Some industrialists are planning to secure the maximum possible profits after the war so as to recoup their losses in some measure. The most effective means of increasing profits is to raise prices. The most effective means of raising prices is first to prevent competition and price cutting. This can best be accomplished by trade associations with compulsory membership and with strong legal powers over their members. Then prices can be raised and maintained at will and work allocated among members. Some plans put forward conform to these requirements.

Second only in importance to increasing profits, in the view of some persons, was the need for a plan to avoid heavy capital expenditure after the war and to maintain things in industry as they were. To accomplish this result it would be necessary to convince the British public that British industry was fully efficient and therefore did not require radical change. Some British industrialists appeared to be confident of their ability to do this successfully. It would require active propaganda on the excellence of British industry and the suppression or refuting of evidence to the contrary. My American friends told me that this has been successfully accomplished in the past, and that under war-time conditions, when criticism was more difficult, it should be even more effective.

Perhaps the British people were not so gullible after all – and this was yet another reason for the Labour victory in the 1945 election. It is interesting to speculate if this pecuniary trait was, or indeed is still, a major factor in Britain's economic and industrial malaise.

THIRTEEN

Post-war and final years, 1945–1954

AT THE END of the Second World War, Lemon moved back to the county of his birth. He and Hermione left Saffron Walden and bought Cliff House in Charmouth, on the Dorset coast, and are recorded there in the 1947 electoral roll.

Lemon's granddaughter Christine – daughter of his eldest son Richard – has fond memories of a visit to Cliff House as a young girl. Richard had resumed his career with the GWR which had been interrupted by the War and, in the summer of 1949, he and his family were based in Exeter. Christine and her mother went to visit Lemon in Charmouth. He was, she says, very good with children and remembers how he told her about the rabbits she might see if she stood very still, as dusk fell, in the garden room which had two huge windows overlooking the lawn. She – and he – stood fascinated as, lo and behold, one by one the rabbits popped out. It was years later that Christine realised how Hermione had kept very much in the background, busying herself with preparing food, so that her presence went unnoticed by the young girl.

It is also from this time that we have further evidence that Lemon still kept in touch with his brothers and sisters. A letter that his former secretary at the LMS, H.G. Smith, wrote to him in 1946, contains the line: 'I hope Mrs. Hunt has not had any increased trouble with her eyes'. Mrs Hunt was his eldest sister, Elizabeth Sarah– eight years his senior – who had married the policeman John Hunt in 1901. She had been a widow for many years: her husband retired from the police force in 1923 due to ill-health and died a couple of years later. Although the couple had at least one son, Lemon would appear to have

been closely concerned with her welfare. In 1945, she was the sole occupant of 34 Acacia Road, St John's Wood – the house that Lemon used during the latter stages of the war as a *pied-à-terre*.[421] It may be that she acted as Lemon's housekeeper for his London property while he and Hermione lived in Saffron Walden.

We also know that he kept in contact with his younger brother, Albert James. Albert remained in Okeford Fitzpaine all his life, working there as the village carpenter, and his son Frederick, told the author that 'Uncle Ernest must have visited Okeford quite frequently, as the Staff at Shillingstone Station were at pains to tell me of the 'red carpet' treatment that was called for when he arrived by train. Presents always materialised at Christmas, but I think both these and the visits stopped at the beginning of the war'. Fred's wife had an uncle who was station-master at Evercreech Junction. Fred recalled that this uncle told him 'Lemon often used the station, and "what a smasher" his wife was. His description in no way fitted Aunt Amy, but we didn't enlighten him!'

Lemon was now in his early 60s, and faced the classic quandary of a retired man. He was bored if he had nothing to do, but not in robust enough health to undertake anything too taxing. He probably hoped that, with the country at peace, he could occupy himself by sitting on the Board of various firms and maybe serving on the occasional Government Commission. And, for a while, that is what happened.

On 22 March 1947 the *Glasgow Herald* announced that he was to become a Director of Scottish Aviation, and this was officially confirmed at their AGM on 25 April. The company was based at Prestwick airport in Ayrshire and, during the war, had been heavily involved in aircraft fitting and maintenance work. Lemon would certainly have had dealings with them while he was at the Air Ministry. Their interests now included the conversion of Douglas aircraft for peace-time use as passenger planes, a franchise for Bell helicopters and operating charter flights. With the formation of the British Overseas Airways Corporation (BOAC) and British European Airways (BEA), they were no longer able to offer scheduled passenger services in this country. However, they operated scheduled services through companies in which they held a majority interest in Greece and Luxembourg.[422]

In July 1948, Lemon visited Canada again. He travelled on a Canadian Pacific liner, the s.s. *Beaverburn*, on 10 July from Liverpool bound for Montreal.[423] The passenger list shows that another passenger was a Miss Doris Challis, of whom more anon. She was described as a secretary, and one can infer that she was accompanying Lemon because their reservations carried successive ticket numbers.

When they arrived in Montreal, Lemon was interviewed by the Press. As a Director of Scottish Aviation and an 'expert on rail and air transport', he was immediately quizzed about the Berlin airlift, which had started a few weeks earlier. Although he disclaimed any status as an expert on such matters, he is quoted in the Montreal *Daily Star* as saying that the airlift was obviously too expensive to maintain in the long run, and that talk of shipping in coal by air seemed impractical as it would be frightfully expensive.[424] The interview appeared under the headline: 'Declared Test of Allied Power – Sir Ernest Lemon Feels It Is Too Expensive to Last'.

The article then moved on to the reasons for Lemon's visit:

'I thought I could retire', said Sir Ernest today with a smile. 'But I found it hard to settle down after so long in harness, I've come out this time for a rest – I've not been well – and to visit old friends in the railways and new friends in aviation. There have been many changes in the ranks of railway administrators since I was last here'.

Studio portrait of Lemon from 1949.
Lemon's personal papers

So, in 1948, he was still talking about having not been well and, it has to be said, he certainly does not look a fit man in the photograph that accompanied the interview. But then, newspaper photographs are notoriously unflattering!

Standardisation[425]

ON 20 October 1948, an old colleague from the Ministry of Aircraft Production during the war, Sir Archibald Rowlands, wrote to enquire whether Lemon was interested in a project that the Government was proposing to set up. Rowlands was now the Permanent Under-Secretary at the Ministry of Supply and his letter starts:

As you know we are responsible in the Ministry of Supply for sponsoring the activities of the engineering industry so that it can make the maximum contribution to the economic welfare of the country.

We have been considering what steps should be taken in the interests of productivity to secure a greater measure of standardisation and simplification by eliminating unnecessary variety in the products of the industry and its component parts.

Rowlands concluded:

The purpose of this letter is to ask whether you would be prepared to take on the job of Chairmanship of the Committee. I do hope so. It is not going to be an easy job and in the initial stages, at any rate, it will require a great deal of energetic action on the part of the Chairman. We have not yet asked anybody to be members of the Committee, since, obviously, that would be a question which we would like to discuss with the Chairman, when appointed.

Perhaps Lewis Ord's analysis of the industrial problems facing this country in his book *Secrets of Industry* had not fallen on stony ground. Ord's book must have had a considerable impact as it was reprinted three times, and the last edition came out in 1949.

Lemon visited Rowlands on 22 October, and then confirmed that he was willing to accept the offer. His letter of acceptance states that, in view of the fact that this would be a full-time job, he would resign his Directorship of Scottish Aviation. However, it is by no means certain that he carried this out as his name continued to appear on the Company's letter-heading as a Director and he is still listed in Handbooks such as *Kelly's* as late as 1952.[426]

In November 1948, the Minister of Supply officially announced Lemon's appointment as Chairman of the Committee, with the following terms of reference:

To investigate, in consultation with the British Standards Institution and appropriate organizations, the methods by which manufacturers and users of engineering products determine whether any reduction in the variety of

MINISTRY OF SUPPLY

REPORT OF THE COMMITTEE
FOR
STANDARDIZATION
OF ENGINEERING
PRODUCTS

LONDON : HIS MAJESTY'S STATIONERY OFFICE
1949
NINEPENCE NET

The last project of Lemon's career
British Library

products manufactured is desirable in the light of technical, commercial and other considerations; to report whether these methods are adequate and what, if any, further measures should be taken by industry or by the Government to ensure that such simplifications as are determined are put into effect.

Anyone who has ever struggled to assemble a piece of flat-pack furniture, with its unique assortment of grommets, widgets, nuts, bolts, screws and washers will find Lemon's report makes interesting reading. Although it was written nearly 60 years ago, they may also reflect on what little notice has been taken of his Committee's recommendations!

It is not necessary to analyse the Report that Lemon and his team submitted in great detail in a book such as this, and a brief description of its findings will suffice. The Committee's Report was signed by all its members, but one can immediately see the influence of Lemon throughout. The whole Report is a credo of Lemon's beliefs, and a description of everything he had been working towards throughout his career. Many of the examples quoted come directly from his railway experiences.

Lemon's Committee was known as the 'Committee for Standardisation of Engineering Products', and its title is perhaps slightly misleading. The word 'standardisation' implies uniformity, which is not what the Committee were asked to consider. In fact, they defined three principles that governed their thinking – the 'three Ss' – Specialisation, Simplification and Standardisation. Specialisation was the process whereby particular firms concentrated on a limited number of products. Simplification reduced the number of types of such products, and Standardisation meant that these products met the required criteria or 'standards'.

The Government commissioned the Report, at this time, for several reasons: firstly, the country was still rebuilding its manufacturing base after the war, and they wished to seize the opportunity to modernise British industry, and not revert to old, inefficient, practices just because 'that was the way it was always done'. Secondly they also wanted the committee to look at the effects of nationalisation, which had created some new, and very large, institutions in the public services; and finally they were asked to report on the workings of the British Standards Institution, and study ways to strengthen the process whereby standards were set.

Lemon and his team started their Report by looking at the situation from a historical perspective, and the reasons for the great variety of similar products. They traced the origins back to the Industrial Revolution. Ever since then, this country had been in the forefront of technical innovation – which had provided the foundation for its industrial greatness. It was this tradition of undertaking continual development, and applying the results to the production of high-quality goods, which led to the great variety of products available. The implication of the Committee's terms of reference, however, was that a reduction was desirable, and a considerable amount of space is devoted to the topic in the Report. This states that *unnecessary* variety is inefficient and uneconomic, and leads to higher prices for the consumer. Lemon's team say that it was not generally realised how much money could be saved by concentrating on long, uninterrupted production runs and eliminating the manufacture of small batches of similar items. They illustrate this – rather surprisingly! – with the production of paint tins. The manufacturers had taken the decision in 1948 to pack paint by volume, rather than by weight, and had reduced the 'inordinate number of containers' to five

An advertisement from before WWII showing how paint was sold by weight
Paint & Wallpaper magazine

standard sizes. A year later, one manufacturer had already made a saving of £100,000.

Conversely, the Report also states that many manufacturers did not cost their products accurately, so that benefits of mass-production were not reflected in the price. In this context, Lemon's team stated that consumers would gain if, for example, the dimensions of electric motors were to be standardized. Those made by different manufacturers would then become interchangeable. Manufacturers, however, preferred to compete with each other, and offer to meet the exact specifications of customers, in the knowledge that such customers would be forced to return to them for maintenance, overhaul and replacements. Many firms also believed that a move to bulk production would reduce their reputation for quality. Consequently, they were reluctant to incur the costs of re-equipping and re-tooling – in many cases preferring to stay with long-established production methods that were in use before automatic machinery was developed.

It is interesting, 60 years on, to see what products were chosen by Lemon's team to illustrate these particular points – and, apart from electric motors, ball-bearings crop up more than once! Once again, Lemon's team recommended that a range of standard sizes should be defined. In this instance, they recommended that Standards for ball-bearings should be set in both imperial and metric measurements. This is the only mention of metric sizes in the entire document, despite a whole section listing the advantages of their proposals to the export trade. However, in those days the majority of exports were to the Empire or Commonwealth, where imperial sizes were still the norm. Nevertheless, Lemon's team recommended that, 'when simplified ranges or standards were determined, the acceptability of the products to the export market should be born in mind, so that such ranges would be equally suitable for use both at home and abroad'. They illustrated this with another example from the railways, and said they were informed, for instance, 'that there was frequently a divergence between the railway signalling equipment used at home and that purchased by overseas users – with the latter taking the more modern equipment'. They suggested that the 'industries concerned should give the fullest consideration to this and to other similar cases'.

Lemon and his team stressed that they were not seeking to standardize the end-products. What they were seeking to identify were those areas where constituent parts, or even raw materials, could be produced to a defined standard. They quoted the example of electrical plugs, sockets and wiring – where specifications had already been set. Individual manufacturers were still free to design their products as they wished, as long as they were compatible with the defined standards. On the other hand, as an example of an area where several different, and overlapping, specifications existed, they cited the boiler-making industry. Here, there were different standards for the steel plate used in marine, land and locomotive boilers. These differences were unnecessary and led to inefficient and wasted production.

The Committee therefore considered closely the rôle of the British Standards Institution (BSI) – the body charged with setting these standards. The Committee soon found that, if the BSI was to remain the authoritative body, it would not only need to expand in size, but its funding would have to be greatly increased. In 1948/9 the BSI received just under one third of its income from the Government, with the rest coming from industry. Lemon's team calculated that the total income was not even sufficient to cover the costs of the experts who attended their meetings. Accordingly, a few months after inception, on 8 February 1949, they produced an interim report: that an expansion programme should be approved and the Government should hold urgent talks as to how this was to be financed.

Lemon and his team then considered the process by which Standards were set, and whether it could be improved. The decision that a Standard was necessary had traditionally been a voluntary one, agreed between the manufacturers and users – and they saw no reason to change that. The problem was how best to represent the views of the users. If a user belonged to a small, clearly-defined, group, it was a relatively simple matter to reach agreement, and define a Standard. Such a case was the coal-mining industry, where the specialised equipment that was needed would not be used elsewhere. However, when a product was used by many different users, the problem became more difficult. Not only did the process take longer but, in practice, the proposed criteria were constantly being watered down to a 'common average' in order to suit the varying requirements of the different parties. These compromises were unsatisfactory for all concerned, and meant that the Standard became largely meaningless. In this case, Lemon's team recommended that several grades of Standards should be adopted.

This may seem to be a direct contradiction to Lemon's earlier strictures on the unnecessary duplication of Standards, as was the case with industrial boilers, but there are obviously exceptions to every rule!

They had other suggestions for co-ordinating the views of users. This was especially relevant where the users were individuals who had no collective voice, such as in the farming industry. There was no organisation to represent their interests in pressing for standards in the machinery they used. Even something as basic as the dimensions of road wheels for agricultural implements had not been standardised. The Report recommended that such professional bodies as did exist should be persuaded to interest themselves in these matters. If no such body could be found, then one should be formed specifically for the purpose.

However, there were certain other areas where manufacturers alone, and not the users of the final product, were primarily responsible for standardisation. Such an area was the manufacture of cars. Anyone buying a car was not greatly interested in the technical aspects or dimensions of wheels and tyres etc. Their concern was only that such components should be readily available, interchangeable, and as cheap and efficient as possible. Lemon's team acknowledged that this problem must be left to the manufacturers and their suppliers.

Lemon's team then turned their attention to the new nationalised industries. If exports were ignored, these industries were now absorbing one third of the country's total engineering output. The fear was that they would use their size to dominate procedures in setting standards; or that they would unilaterally settle standards for the equipment they used without regard to other people's interests. Such actions would only lead to opposition from other manufacturers, and a further multiplicity of standards. Lemon's team were also concerned that the nationalised industries should learn to co-operate amongst themselves, and illustrated this with another example that involved the railways: the delivery of coal to power stations. As we have seen in an

earlier chapter, this was a subject that Lemon felt passionately about!

This case is described in great detail in the Report as an important, but typical, example of the benefits of properly co-ordinated standardisation. Three separate nationalised industries would be involved; and the Report recommends the 'possibility of utilising high-capacity bogie rail wagons (say, of not less than 40-ton capacity) fitted with vacuum brakes, for coal and mineral traffic. The use of such large wagons – which can lead to considerable economies in the cost of transport – has hitherto been hindered by the fact that the loading and unloading facilities at collieries, power stations, industrial establishments etc. have been designed for existing wagons and, in general, these are too small for large wagons to be used. The opportunity now exists to work out broad dimensional standards for the loading, transport and unloading equipment for heavy mineral traffic to enable high

SHELL MEX HOUSE,
LONDON, W.C.2.

23rd June, 1949.

My dear Jack,

Many thanks for your letter.

We are very grateful to you for having undertaken this task for us and for having carried it through with the energy, skill and thoroughness which is characteristic of you.

If industry plays its part I am satisfied that the reports of your Committee will be prominent landmarks on the road to greater productivity, on which so much depends.

I am also very grateful for your offer to give us further help in this field should the occasion arise.

I should like to think that I can look to you again for any help we may require of you in other fields. It was a great joy having you as a colleague once more, even if for so short a time.

I am very glad to have your tributes to Cass and Whitehouse, who are among the most promising of my younger people.

Yours ever,

Archi

Sir Ernest Lemon.

Letter from Sir Archibald Rowlands following completion of the Standardisation Report. Was (Ernest) Lemon always known as 'Jack' to colleagues?
Lemon's personal papers

capacity wagons to be used in the future. It is particularly important to make such decisions now when so much development and rebuilding is in hand or projected.'

The Government did not pigeon-hole the Report, but actively promoted its recommendations, as later documents at the National Archives show.[427] The railways also took full note of Lemon's conclusions. E.S. Cox, describing railway policy following nationalisation in 1948, wrote: 'The second decision was to go all out for common practices and technical standardisation, which only a unified technical direction would make possible. In this the wishes of the Executive were strongly reinforced, if not inspired, by a Government-sponsored committee under Sir Ernest Lemon whose report emphasised the need for standardisation of manufacture'.[428]

And so, 60 years on, we can look back and see what it all achieved. Many of the conclusions and recommendations now seem to be simply common-sense. However, they were obviously new ideas at the time, and needed to be spelt out in detail. However, there is one aspect of Lemon's report that has been a signal failure. And that is the hope that simplification would lead to an interchangeability of components. How many people have had to throw away an article because some small minor component has broken? Car manufacturers, in particular, seem to delight in making each model uniquely different – and not only the components, but the tools to service them! What Lemon and his team never foresaw were the changes that would come from the global market we now live in. Our consumer society has had to accept – albeit reluctantly – that when a product breaks down it is cheaper to throw it away and replace it than to repair it.

The Committee published its report in the autumn of 1949, and the Minister, G.R. Strauss, wrote to Lemon on 4 October to thank him for his valuable work. As a result of the recommendations in the earlier interim Report from February of that year, the Board of Trade had already appointed Lemon in July 1949 as a member of a further Committee specifically to investigate the Organisation and Constitution of the BSI. However, he resigned from this Committee on 16 May 1950 'owing to business commitments', and on 30 May, was appointed Managing Director of the South Western Industrial & Water Corporation.[429] This latter company had been going through a turbulent period as it diversified its interests. *The Times* reported that there had been a 'cleavage on the Board of Directors' and it had been necessary to adjourn the AGM. The word 'Water' was soon dropped from the Company title, and its main interests then seem to have been pressure cookers and central-heating boilers. However, it is doubtful if Lemon ever took up this appointment as his name never appears in the Corporation's later records and, as we shall see, health problems were to dominate the rest of his life.

It is in the autumn of 1950 that we enter the final phase of Lemon's life and, with very few personal records to substantiate the details of these last years, the sequence of events has had to be deduced from whatever sources can be found. We can certainly tell that Lemon left Dorset and was admitted to Westminster Hospital in London. The immediate cause cannot be confirmed, and it is perfectly possible that this was due to a recurrence of the blood pressure problems that had caused his breakdown in 1942 – brought on this time by intensive work on the Standardisation Report. However his death certificate in 1954 tells us that at some earlier time he had a prostate cancer removed, and this seems a much more plausible reason for his admission to hospital. Lemon certainly must have felt his condition was life-threatening and, on 7 December 1950, made his Will, witnessed by a Ward Sister at the hospital. On a happier note, on 4 November, when he was already in hospital, his younger son David was married at Marylebone. David had resumed his law studies at Oxford after the war, and by this time had qualified as a barrister. Amanda remembers her mother, Wendy, telling her how the newly-married couple went to visit Lemon immediately after the ceremony. Wendy wore her wedding dress to show him and the Ward Sister exclaimed 'We haven't had a bride in here since the Peruvian Ambassador's daughter'.

On discharge from hospital, Lemon moved into a flat in De Walden Court, New Cavendish Street with David and his new bride. Significantly, perhaps, there was no sign of Hermione, although she could have been living discreetly close by. One would have hoped that he would make a successful recovery from such an operation. However it is apparent that for the rest of his life Lemon was a semi-invalid. In those days the treatment of cancer was in its infancy and, although the primary source could be surgically removed, there were no effective drugs for long-term treatment and prevention. In Lemon's case, the cancer eventually spread into his bones, and it was only a matter of time before this proved fatal.

David and his wife left London in 1951 – he had taken up commercial law and his career took him to Oldham in Lancashire, where their daughter, Amanda, was born. Lemon is still listed in New Cavendish Street, but the only other occupant of the flat was called Ellen Birchall. Nothing more is known of her, and she may well have been a nurse-companion. Lemon left the flat in 1952, and it was only as this book was being completed that his next whereabouts were discovered. The 1953 Electoral Roll lists him at the Athenaeum Club in Pall Mall (which he had given as a contacting address for some years in *Who's Who*). This cannot have been just a temporary base, to be listed thus, but his permanent home. It is sad to consider that his life had come to this.

What happened next is even more difficult to ascertain, as Lemon directed his Executors to destroy, at their discretion, all his personal papers after his death. Not only was he estranged from his wife, but contact with his sons was also now sporadic: David, as already mentioned, had moved away from London – first to Oldham and then to Birmingham. Meanwhile, his elder son Richard had left the GWR to take up an appointment in 1950 with East African Railways. He and his family were living in Kenya and only visited this country occasionally. Lemon's granddaughters were still only children, and their fathers, like many others of their generation, were curiously reticent about passing information on to them as they grew up. There is thus a complete lack of direct information that has been handed down within the family about the following couple of years, apart from some isolated corres-

pondence following his death on 15 December 1954. In truth, these indicate that there is little to say: apart from one final twist in his private life, his final years seem to have been spent in a gradual decline until the inevitable outcome.

After Lemon's death, Sir Harold Hartley wrote a letter of condolence to his son Richard, in which he said: 'It was terribly sad to watch him going downhill in recent years. Everything went wrong for him'. Richard had to be informed by post about what was happening in England and, fortunately, some of this correspondence has survived.[430] Richard replied to Hartley: 'His sudden death was, of course a great shock to me because even though when I was at home eighteen months ago he seemed to be failing – and still more so in the early part of my leave last year – he seemed to be making very good progress when we saw him last July'. This shows that, as early as the summer of 1953, his health was of grave concern. He did not attend the Memorial Service for Sir Wilfrid Freeman at St Margaret's Westminster on 30 June 1953 for example.

Hartley's remark that 'everything went wrong with him', however, implies that it was not only Lemon's health that was suffering, and we can deduce from the two letters that David wrote to his brother in Kenya, to tell him of their father's death, that Hermione had certainly left him. The first letter contains an account of the events on the day Lemon died and the funeral. The second describes his financial situation, as David understood it, and the terms of his Will. It is not possible from this correspondence to tell exactly when the relationship broke up, but the picture that emerges from the oblique comments is that the house in Charmouth was sold in 1952, when Hermione 'took her pick of the furniture'. She moved to a flat a few miles away in Bridport, and was living there by November of that year. It is still not known where she might have been living in the years 1950–2 but, as we have seen, the records show she was certainly not living with Lemon in New Cavendish Street.

What caused the split will never be known, but it is inconceivable that his admission to hospital was the sole cause. Hermione had stood by him throughout the recovery from his breakdown in

1942. However, his latest health problems might well have led to tensions that she was unable to cope with. He was probably not an easy patient. His former colleague at the LMS, Frank Pope, also wrote a letter of condolence to Richard, in which he said: 'I'm so sorry his last years were clouded by unhappiness through illness and consequent inactivity'. The inactivity must have been especially galling to a man who had been bursting with nervous energy and ideas all his life.

David said in his letter to Richard that their father had made an independent settlement for Hermione, which did not appear in his Will. He did not know the details, and could not reasonably ask the solicitor to tell him. Apart from the Charmouth furniture, he thought that Hermione must also have received 'the proceeds from the sale of the cottage in Saffron Walden'.

It was this letter that provided enough clues to unravel all the details about Lemon's private life after the breakdown of his marriage. It was the discovery of their names in the Charmouth Electoral Rolls that first identified Hermione's surname. Up until this point, Lemon's grand-daughters only knew her Christian name. It was then a chance discovery to find out that she had been an LMS employee. The reference to Saffron Walden was the first indication that the couple had lived there during the war, later confirmed by the 1945 Electoral Roll. Without this one letter, Lemon's later life would have remained a mystery.

Lemon did not die at the Athenaeum Club – or a hospital close by – but in Woodcote Grove, Epsom. This is another surprise: why, and when, did he make the move? Woodcote Grove is a large mansion on the slopes of the North Downs leading up to Epsom race-course. It is now the headquarters of W.S. Atkins, the engineering conglomerate but, at the time, was owned by the Marchioness of Crewe – widow of the Marquess who had died without heir in 1945. The property was not being used by the family, and was only occupied by a skeleton staff. Consequently it was rapidly falling into disrepair.

Despite the expectation that the Marquess of Crewe may have been connected with the railway that so dominated the town, he had never been a Director of the LMS. There is therefore no obvious connection between him, or his heirs, and Lemon. Nor is there any evidence that the house was being used as a private nursing home although, as it is only a few hundred yards from Epsom Hospital, that seemed a possibility. Lemon's death certificate shows that his death was certified by a Dr R. Mellon of Ashtead, Surrey who had a general medical practice in the area, but the Medical Registers show that he had earlier been a surgeon in the Department of Genito-Urinary Medicine at Guy's Hospital in London. This must surely be more than an unrelated coincidence, and suggests that Mellon may have arranged for Lemon to have further post-operative treatment for the prostate cancer close to where he lived. Lemon's name, however, does not appear in the Electoral Rolls at Woodcote Grove, which does suggest his stay there was a short one.

Lemon's grand-daughters were told that, in his final days, the only relief he could get from the unrelenting pain was to take larger and larger doses of morphine, which he was apparently able to get through a personal contact. Christine's mother also told her that, towards the end of his life, he was drinking two bottles of whisky a day, in the belief that the alcohol would enhance the effects of the copious amounts of morphine he was taking.

Lemon's actual death was surrounded by confusion and a most unpleasant scene. His son David received a telephone call about 7.30 in the evening at his home in Birmingham, telling him the end was near. He and his wife arrived in Epsom at 1.30 in the morning. Lemon was already unconscious and died an hour and a half later, on 15 December 1954, unaware of their presence. The death certificate shows that he died of heart failure and anaemia caused by the secondary bone cancer. David described what happened next in the letter to his brother:

We found Doris Challis in full charge, half drunk and hysterical, having sacked the two previous nurses and engaged a new night nurse . . . After he died we had a most unpleasant time dealing with Doris Challis, who had been through all his things removing we know not what. Anyway Wendy [David's wife]

A somewhat unkempt Woodcote Grove in 1957. Bourne Hall Museum, Epsom

managed to get back the various small items of furniture which she had removed, though there was no watch amongst his belongings and not a penny piece in cash. We subsequently found out that he had drawn £60 in cash on the day before he died – I wrote to Doris and stated that if she did not account for the money, I would take steps to trace it . . . This produced the desired result and the estate is now £40 better off than it would have been.

As mentioned earlier in this chapter, Doris Challis accompanied Lemon on his visit to Canada in 1948; and so, whatever relationship they may have had went back at least six years. In 1948, the passenger list gave her occupation as 'secretary', but the events described above imply that she was now more closely involved. What is certain is that, as far as the family were concerned, both she and Hermione were very much *personae non gratae*. Both were persuaded – with difficulty, David reported – not to attend the funeral.

The funeral took place at Golders Green Crematorium and the niceties were observed, as was seemly for such a figure on such an occasion. The service was attended by the legitimate family members: Lady Amy, son David and daughter-in-law Wendy, brother-in-law Thomas Hornbuckle, together with friends and colleagues from the

LMS, Air Ministry and other Government departments for which Lemon had worked.

Both Frank Pope and Harold Hartley wrote appreciations of Lemon's work on the railways which were printed in *The Times*. Hartley sent a letter to David telling him that he had felt compelled to write a personal tribute 'as I owed so much to his help and encouragement in my early days at Euston'. He describes Lemon in this letter thus: 'He had a most remarkable brain, logical, creative and imaginative. I always regretted that he had not had the advantage of a training in pure science. He had so many of the attributes that make up a first scientist [*sic*]'.

Hartley's personal papers at Churchill College, Cambridge show that he was also concerned that the paper should publish an appreciation of Lemon's work at the Air Ministry.[431] The obvious people – Kingsley Wood and Wilfrid Freeman – were both dead, and Hartley approached several people on behalf of 'poor old Lemon' before he found someone who felt qualified to write a tribute. The description of Lemon seems slighting, but cannot have been intended: merely an expression of genuine regret at his sad decline. It was Sir Henry Self, who had worked alongside

Lemon at the Air Ministry and Ministry of Production, who eventually wrote the tribute (see chapter 8). In thanking Self for his contribution, Hartley wrote that all that remained now was to get Lemon into the *Dictionary of National Biography* – and it was he himself who wrote the original entry.

There is one final puzzle – David wrote to his brother that 'the financial position is not as bad as I thought it would be'. Lemon earned exceedingly well at the LMS and had a generous pension and yet David says his only assets, apart from Northchurch Hall where Lady Amy was still living, were about £400 in cash. The family must have been aware that his money was ebbing away at an alarming rate and, as it turned out, the cash bequests in his Will to both of his sons could not be met. Northchurch Hall was bequeathed to Lady Amy for life, but the family had already decided it would have to be sold. David asked his brother whether he should immediately accept an offer of £11,600, or push for a better offer nearer £15,000. When Probate was granted on the Will, Lemon's estate was valued at £14,266 10s 3d gross – clearly showing that the bulk of this came from the value of Northchurch Hall.

So where had all the money gone? Inflation may have reduced the value of his pension, and an unknown amount must have gone in the settlement to Hermione and, possibly, in a similar one to Doris Challis. One also assumes that Lemon had continued to support his wife and sons in all the years after the marriage broke down. Lady Amy did not come from a wealthy family, and her only personal income was from certain small holiday properties she owned at Studland in Dorset. We also know that Lemon had supported his sons at university, although both Richard and David referred to being hard up while students. Richard apparently once mentioned this in conversation with his father after he had graduated. Lemon was quite upset, saying 'Why ever didn't you ask for money if you needed it? I only kept the allowance down because I didn't want it to appear that you had money to burn'.

But in the last years of his life, it looks as though Lemon felt he *did* have money to burn. He bought Doris Challis a car – and his granddaughter Christine remembers being told that all his meals were sent round to the flat in New Cavendish Street from Mirabelle's restaurant in Mayfair. While this may be a slight exaggeration, it implies a reckless disregard for economy. These are not the actions of a man who was worried about money. It also shows that neither Lemon, nor anyone else who might have been living with him, was interested in cooking! He must also have had considerable medical expenses. Although the NHS had come into existence after the War, he had probably always had private treatment in hospital, and David's letter shows that he was, subsequently, also paying for constant nursing care. Perhaps this just goes to show how quickly these expenses can eat up one's income.

It was a sad and squalid end to a man who had risen to the very heights of his profession, and served his country well in a time of great crisis.

FOURTEEN

Personality

I N researching a biography, one starts off by trying to establish as many precise facts and dates as possible, in order to build up the sequence of events in the subject's life, career and achievements. Although time-consuming work, the records eventually yield up nuggets of factual information. What these cannot tell you is anything about the more personal side of the subject's character and personality, without which any biography is incomplete.

Lemon died over 50 years ago, and any colleagues with stories to tell and memories to recount have also now died. Lemon's grand-daughters hardly knew him – they were still children when he died – and the memories of Lemon's nephew Frederick are mainly of Lady Amy after the break-up of the marriage. Nevertheless, a certain amount of anecdotal evidence has been found, which permeates through the previous chapters and helps to give a more rounded picture of Lemon as a man – notably in the tribute written by his loyal Secretary, H.G. Smith, published in the *Railway Gazette* when he retired from the LMS. Smith was as close to him as anyone within the Company, and saw him in all his many and varied moods.

There is more information to be found in the obituaries written after his death. Sir Henry Self's tribute to his work at the Air Ministry has already been quoted in chapter 8, but both Sir Harold Hartley and Frank Pope wrote appreciations of his work at the LMS which illustrate sides of his personality. Hartley described this as 'forceful' and Pope referred to his 'restless and creative mind and immense energy . . . Nothing could be done quickly enough for him, and he exerted

relentless pressure on the officers responsible for work that was receiving his attention. The word 'why?' was constantly on his lips. He accepted nothing on face value, and he was not a comfortable person to be with at any time. But he got results.'

Lemon was, undoubtedly a hard taskmaster, and expected the highest standards and commit-ment from those around him. Amanda, his granddaughter, recalled a train journey as a child over a particularly rough section of track. Her mother said to David: 'Your father would never have tolerated this'. Apparently, on Lemon's inspection travels around the line, he would place a glass of water on the table in the carriage and, if it slopped, would have something pertinent to say on the subject to the permanent way department. Undoubtedly Lemon ruffled a few feathers – it is not possible to be a hard taskmaster without so doing! In any large organisation there will be cliques and factions, and ambitious men jockeying for power. It was not his job to be universally liked, and it is only to be expected that he made enemies. When Amanda's mother, Wendy, told her father that she wished to marry Lemon's son David, he apparently said 'Why do you want to marry this man. His father is hated the length and breadth of the railway'. This must have been said in 1950, eight years after Lemon had left the LMS. Yet still the resentment remained. There were obviously many within LMS who felt embittered towards him.

There is, however, one further source, which shows us the voice of Lemon himself – the correspondence with well-wishers following his knighthood. Many of these incoming letters and telegrams give the well-wisher's personal

A modern photograph of The Old Mill House, Grove Mill Lane, Watford on the edge of The Grove estate, which Lemon referred to as his 'mess' in 1941. In 1942, he was asked to relinquish the room that was permanently reserved for him (see p.224). Author

perspective on his achievements, which adds to our knowledge of how he was viewed by his colleagues and associates. Lemon replied to them all – some had handwritten replies, and no record of these exists, but the remainder of the replies were typed by Lemon's staff. A number of them contain a deprecating apology for this along the lines of: 'I never believe in doing something by hand which can be done by machine' or 'I am having this letter typed because I still believe in labour-saving devices', which succinctly sums up Lemon's approach to every aspect of his work. His letter to Lord Rootes expands on this theme, showing that he still felt a twinge of guilt in so doing: 'I am having this letter typed and frankly I do not know why it should be considered wrong to use labour-saving devices in replying to one's friends but evidently it is. I think I am going to start a society for the abolition of shibboleths. Firstly, why all personal letters should be replied to in one's own fair hand – mine is not fair in any case and secondly, why one must tie a dress tie rather than use a made-up one which could be put on in half the time and save temper, time and trouble – a nice alliterative sentence'.

With so many replies to write (or rather dictate) many are formulaic in content, but wherever possible Lemon adds a personal touch – picking up on a comment in the well-wisher's letter, or adding a few handwritten words at the end. He appears to be genuinely touched that so many employees of the LMS who occupied quite humble positions should write to him, and went out of his way to tell them that their letters meant as much to him as any of the others. On one such reply to an employee of his old Carriage & Wagon works in Derby, Lemon has added the handwritten words 'Good old C & W'. He received so many letters that they cannot all have been written by sycophants.

He has a nice touch in self-deprecation as well – he writes to the head of English Electric: 'To have praise from one's peers is indeed as Kipling says, "a very heady wine" and I must be careful, having read all the letters of congratulations, to put them all away and not read them again until I am a doddering old man'.

There is also much good-natured 'joshing' and banter. His reply to Lord McGowan, for example, contains a reminder of a previous sweepstake on the horses: 'It is hoped that if not in 1941, we shall be able in 1942 to run a Grand National Special again when I shall have pleasure in making you draw the winners. You let me down rather badly over Golden Miller after having drawn it for me and then not seeing that it won. What is the good of being Lord McGowan if you cannot arrange for the favourite to win?' Air Marshall Sir William Mitchell humorously asked him why he couldn't run his 'bloody trains on time', to which Lemon retorted 'why don't you stop the b***** Germans from bombing them'. This was followed by an invitation to stay at the Mill House in Watford – 'our mess for the time being' – and meet Lord Stamp, Harold Hartley

and other colleagues. Many of the letters to the more senior Establishment figures end this way – or at least with the words 'we must meet for lunch again soon'.

Senior figures at the RAF, aircraft manufacturers, politicians and civil servants alike all paid tribute to his work at the Air Ministry – Bruce-Gardner 'whooped with joy' – and all wrote that the honour of a knighthood was well overdue. Esmund Milward, who was working at the MAP, even considered it an apology for the treatment Lemon had received from the Government. Any past differences were forgotten: there is a telegram from Sir Wilfrid Freeman, and a particularly warm letter from Freeman's wife, Elizabeth. Many of these letters include the phrase 'when the story can be told'.

Unfortunately, it has taken over 50 years for this to be fully realised, but the author hopes that this biography goes some way to redress the balance.

One of hundreds of letters which Lemon received congratulating him on his knighthood in the 1941 New Year's Honours. Stanier wrote on the day of the official announcement, 1 January, but forgot the year had changed! Family

FIFTEEN

Postscript

THROUGHOUT the years that Ernest Lemon and his wife were separated, Amy remained at Northchurch Hall, involving herself in local activities. The Women's Institute met at the house, and, as has been previously mentioned, she was an active member of Berkhamsted Golf Club, being Lady Captain there in 1935. During the War, she had evacuees billeted with her, and both the Home Guard and St John's Ambulance Brigade used parts of the house and out-buildings.

She and Lemon never divorced, and she was apparently happy to use the title of Lady Amy after her husband's knighthood, but it is not known how much contact existed between Lemon and his wife and sons. Amy's letter to Sir Harold Hartley, thanking him for attending her husband's funeral (see earlier), started: 'Your words to me years ago were "keep a stout [*sic*]" & they were no less comforting than your saying on that day "you have your boys well established". Few if any will know how much of that devolved on me. Well, anyway I tried to do my best'.[432]

It is, perhaps, surprising that Lady Amy remained in touch with several of her estranged husband's relatives. Lemon's nephew, Frederick, recounted how Lady Amy still kept in contact with him and his family. Fred was an apprentice in 1942 at RAF Halton. This was only just up the road from Berkhamsted, and he spent several Sunday afternoons with her. He described her as 'a very kind and pleasant lady who always managed to fill my empty stomach'.

At the end of the War Northchurch Hall was in a state of neglect and disrepair and, in 1946, Lady Amy started to convert the buildings of the Home Farm into dwellings. She continued to live in the main house, however, until after her husband's death. Both of her unmarried sisters, at one time or other, also lived with her there –

Florence in 1952 until her death a year later; and Mabel continuously until she died in 1955. After Mabel's death, Lady Amy finally moved out of the Hall into a property on the Home Farm, which she had converted, called Lea Hurst. Fred and his wife Eileen visited her there about 1960. Northchurch Hall was sold for demolition, and the land was redeveloped into the Park Estate. Lady Amy's granddaughter, Amanda, still has some of the furniture from Northchurch.

However, Lady Amy also owned several properties in and around Studland Bay in Dorset, and a house in Bournemouth where her unmarried sisters, Florence and Mabel, had lived before they moved to Northchurch. One assumes that these were purchased with money from her husband.

Lady Amy died in 1966, at which time both of her sons were working abroad – Richard was still in Kenya, and David was in Australia with his family. In a brief Will, she distributed her property among her sons, their families, and her sister Margaret Hornbuckle. She also decreed that Alice Andrews, a niece of her late husband, should continue to have a week's holiday at a cottage she owned at Studland Bay, Dorset. Alice Andrews was a (married) daughter of Albert James Lemon, and one imagines that this arrangement had existed for some years, possibly even from before Lemon's death. It was a generous act of Lady Amy to continue with the arrangement – especially as it was for the benefit of a distant relation of her estranged husband.

Hermione continued to live in the flat at St Swithin's Court in Bridport until her death in 1971. She died of a heart attack following hypothermia. It seems slightly unusual to suffer from hypothermia in August – but there was no inquest. She did not leave a Will, and her death was registered by the undertaker.

Curtain Calls

IT WAS by a set of curious chances that I came to write this book. At the outset, I had little knowledge of railway history, and had certainly never heard of Sir Ernest Lemon. What I knew of railways in the steam era was basically limited to the engines whose numbers I collected as a boy in the 1950s – coincidentally, in north-west London, on the mainline out of Euston. Although I graduated with a Degree in Engineering, my adult life was spent as an opera singer, and for over 25 years I was a principal tenor at the English National Opera. I came to this project, therefore, purely by chance, and with an open mind.

I was introduced to the subject by my brother-in-law Keith Harcourt, who *does* have a lifelong interest in railway history. But that is not the beginning of the story. Keith's involvement also came about by chance. The sequence of events started when Amanda Robinson, one of Lemon's granddaughters, approached Colin Divall, Professor of Railway Studies at York. She had inherited Lemon's personal papers from her father, and wished them to be put to use. Divall passed them to one of his postgraduate students, Rachel Moore – and she, in turn, asked Keith (a friend of hers) to help with some preliminary research.

Keith was immediately interested as it was clear that, although Lemon had been a major figure in the management of the LMS, little information about him was readily available. He decided to investigate further and, as I had some experience of historical research, soon asked me to help with specific queries. It was apparent to me that Lemon's importance stretched way beyond his work for the railways. His entry in the *Dictionary of National Biography* showed that he was a figure of national importance through his work at the Air Ministry before the Second World War; and it was this area where I originally concentrated my research.

Keith made contact with Amanda and Lemon's other granddaughter, Christine Broomhead, and it turned out that both ultimately hoped that Lemon's papers and memorabilia could be used for a biography. Commitment to a full biography took the project to a different level, and it was clear that, in order to do justice to the subject, considerably more original research needed to be done. Although Keith's knowledge of people within the railway fraternity whom one could approach for particular advice was of great value, he too had many other commitments, and so he graciously yielded overall responsibility for the research to me.

Lemon decreed in his Will that his executors should destroy, at their discretion, certain of his private papers, and his archive is therefore not large. Nevertheless sufficient remains to shed new light on his workings at the LMS and the Air Ministry. I was then particularly fortunate in discovering, in Sir Harold Hartley's papers at Churchill College Cambridge, additional information about the Management of the LMS, which contradicts many long-held beliefs and assumptions.

Finally came the task of collating all the information and writing the book, which I was happy to undertake. It is very much the culmination of research which Keith originally started and inspired, and my thanks are due to him, Amanda and Christine for all their encouragement and support.

It is hoped that Lemon's personal archive will eventually be deposited in the Institution of Mechanical Engineers.

Terry Jenkins
January 2011

Lord Stamp's Criteria for the LMS Executive Committee

The following document can be found in Sir Harold Hartley's papers at Churchill College, Cambridge. It carries a note dated 30 January 1946 – 'The attached was written by Lord Stamp many years ago for the benefit of his Vice-Presidents and Senior Executives, and is circulated at Sir Harold Hartley's request as a guide to the executives of B.E.A.'

(Hartley was the first Chairman of B.E.A., which was formed at the end of WW2)

It is possible that this is not the complete text of Stamp's memorandum – as it is not dated or signed – but merely a copy containing the first eight clauses. It ends, conveniently, at the bottom of a page. This may suggest, therefore, that Stamp would have subsequently continued, and defined the particular areas of responsibility for each Vice-President etc. – this would be of no concern to the BEA Executives.

Memorandum to Vice-Presidents

In the following notes I sketch out my present views as to the functions of the Executive and of the Vice-Presidents respectively, and as to their relations to their Departments and to each other. It is impossible to be precise upon every point in advance, and the answer to many conundrums must be found in practical working, but this will form a basis for our initial discussions on procedure, etc.

1. The Vice-President and his Chief Officers.

Time and experience devoted

(1) One of the advantages we hope to secure from putting the general managership into commission, is that each Chief Officer shall have a General Manager who has, first, the type of mind and experience which will be of real help to each Chief Officer concerned and, secondly, time to give to him and his problems. At present, if the General Manager is full of affairs of a 'general' character, or dealing with problems put up by other departments, months may go by without a particular department having any eye over it at all. It might be slack or inefficient, but the General Manager has not the time and, perhaps, not the special knowledge, to take the initiative and to keep a watch over its activities, laying down a programme of returns or reports and studying them for signs of strength or weakness.

On the other hand, the Chief Officer is very likely full of suggestions on which he would like consultation and approval, but cannot get them for lack of time or direct interest.

Threefold Capacity

(2) Under the new arrangements the Vice-President is to be, <u>first</u> and foremost, the <u>consultant</u> of his Chief Officers, looking at the matters of their Departments not in such detail, but with broad relation to what he knows of the whole problem of the railway, and the policy of the Executive and of the Board, in such a way as the Chief Officer, thinking mainly and naturally of the success of his department, can never be expected to do.

In the <u>second</u> place, he is an 'authoriser' with powers to delegate, to settle questions himself, or to make recommendations, respectively, according to certain defined limits, on lines which we will lay down by experience.

In the third place, he is a critic, and should keep such a watchful eye over the work of the departments and the way they are dealing with their problems, as will keep any departments that might otherwise be slack, self-conscious and keen. Interference with the technical methods of a Chief Officer in carrying out his duties, particularly where these technical methods take on a professional character, is to be deprecated and only resorted to in very special cases. Once having decided the thing that has to be done and the Chief Officer having promised a given performance, precisely whether it is done under one specification or another, must always remain the responsibility of the Chief Officer of the department, though doubtless, if the proper spirit prevails, that Chief would be glad to avail himself, on his own initiative, of any advice or criticism that a Vice-President with technical or special knowledge, could afford.

Sharing Responsibility

(3) The Chief Officer has many disagreeable duties to perform, e.g., to turn down personally proposals and requests from men with whom he is in daily contact, and to make preference of one over another. On the human side it is a great help to him if he can do a little 'passing the buck' and put some of the onus or odium upon his superior officer: I think that the Vice-President should not be unwilling to lend himself to this to some extent, and might be prepared, if a Chief Officer puts to him a proposal with the 'pros' and 'cons' leaning hard on the 'cons', to help him very much by driving it home and taking the decision himself where it is a disagreeable one, to help his Chief Officer.

Co-ordination

(4) One of the most important functions of the Vice-President is to promote co-ordination at an earlier or lower stage than has hitherto been found in practice. In the past there have been two opposite vices. Proposals have been put up to the General Manager 'signed, sealed and delivered', and necessarily refined to the last point – a stage at which it is humanly difficult to make modifications, or retreat from positions,

without some loss of dignity, and it has been for the General Manager to call in, by way of destruction and criticism, other departments affected. Such other department may be either more tender than it would otherwise have been if the scheme had not been cut and dried, and then it may only put up points of overwhelming criticism and not minor adjustments: or it may revel in the attitude of the critic, which is not the true atmosphere of co-ordination. The second class of difficulty is where an officer is going to put up a proposal and he knows by contact with a brother officer that when it is put up it may be opposed. Not fully sure of his ground and his power to carry it, it remains in his bosom and he does not present it at all. It will be for the Vice-President to know, as far as possible, what proposals are incubating in his departments, and to make arrangements and suggestions for co-ordinate consideration before he, himself, passes judgment on them. In other words, the Vice-President's vision penetrates a little further down into the machine than the General Managers could, and he guides proceedings into co-ordination at a rather earlier stage. In the same way, but in far fewer case, Vice-Presidents will themselves clear up much in the way of co-ordination before things are considered by the Executive; much more before they are put to the Board. The Vice-President should encourage his Chief Officers to feel that through him, as their representative, their views are effectively presented to, and considered in, the final counsels.

II. The attitude of the Vice-President and Executive Committee to each other.

Individual responsibility

(5) Just as the existence of the Vice-President does not rob the Chief Officer of the responsibility for the success or failure of a department (i.e., the Chief Officer cannot shelve from his own shoulders, the executive running of his department) so the Executive Committee will not tell the Vice-Presidents, or his Chief Officers, how to do their job. When the Vice-President has brought his problem to the Executive, and expressed his own views and

heard the general reactions of his colleagues, it will, in the ordinary way, still be for him to say 'yes' or 'no' and whether he will go on in the way he has suggested. He takes the responsibility for the decision – reassured doubtless, if their comments have been favourable, but realising that his responsibility in making good is all the greater if they have expressed any doubts about the course. I should, of course, reserve my right as President, after hearing all the views, to take the responsibility of a decision myself, and say that a thing should, or should not, be done, despite the feelings of the individual Vice-President.

I should also, in carrying a proposal to the Board, feel it incumbent upon me in matters of great importance, when making a definite recommendation to the Directors, to say if my Committee were not unanimous, and to explain the doubts of any members. But the Executive Committee is not to be in the position that things are taken to the Board only on a majority vote, or are necessarily taken on a majority vote. The responsibility of the final recommendation must be mine, but I shall be fully open and above board with the Directors about it. There will, of course, be a considerable area of recommendation (to be defined) in minor matters which I shall hope the Board will take from the Vice-Presidents direct, without my intervention or detailed knowledge, otherwise my position will be still a 'bottle neck'.

Spirit of Committee

(6) I am particularly anxious that the spirit and proceedings of the Executive Committee, while businesslike to the point, shall be informed [informal?], conversational, and as easy as possible for the mutual exchange of views. We want no set speeches and no spirit of 'face saving', or 'climbing down', to be prevalent. We shall keep a minute of our proceedings, but not a detailed record of all our cross talk. For example, it will be quite common for one of us to take the position of a devil's advocate merely for the purpose of testing a thing out on its weak side, and not from any desire to score or to upset the proposal. In short, we want the

proceedings to be such as are possible with a small group of three or four, and impossible for a large committee of twelve or more where strict order and rules must prevail if the committee is not to become a bear garden.

General knowledge and interchangeability

(7) In committee the Vice-President will become aware of all the big problems of the Railway and not merely of his own, and general strength is to rest in the fact that for the first time there will be brought together on such problems three or four different types of thought and wisdom. Hitherto an officer has had no responsibility whatever for what is going on elsewhere and, at the same time, has exercised the right of trivial and irresponsible criticism on it in private conversation. Now he will have the right and duty of responsible criticism and review and agreement over a wider field than his own activities.

Initiation of considerations

(8) The Vice-President must never forget that the essence of this scheme is that he has no departmental executive responsibilities; he is primarily a thinker and a reviewer; an authoriser, an adviser and consultant, and not a man who takes the responsibility daily for a hundred executive decisions in letters and commands. The Vice-President will naturally bring to the Executive proposals which come to him that he is inclined to think should go forward, but the Executive Committee is not to be a valve opening only one way. Ideas will be engendered there, and the Vice-President will push them down for elaboration and suggestion into his departments. Moreover, the Executive Committee is not to be a ground for the mere discussion of positive recommendations by the Vice-President. It will be his duty, before he turns down any proposal that is strongly urged by a Chief Officer, to ventilate and explain his proposed negative to the Executive. The Chief Officer must feel that his idea has a full 'show' and, if necessary, the Chief Officer should be called to the Committee to expound it, when the Vice-President, with adverse views, feels he might not do justice to it.

The re-organisation of LMS Management following Lemon's appointment as Vice-President

A copy of this Memo from Lord Stamp can be found in Sir Harold Hartley's papers at Churchill College Cambridge.

<u>21st June, 1932.</u>

ORGANISATION

The organisation of an amalgamation of different Companies forming the London Midland and Scottish Railway is, of course, a matter of stages. In the first place, the organisation had to be such as to ensure that the different sections of the amalgamated Company continued to function efficiently, and that changes should be made gradually so as to avoid dislocation. Put in another way, the question of organisation of a large concern such as ours must be dealt with in three major stages:–

FIRST. All practices and methods must be reviewed and dealt with centrally to enable different conditions on different sections to be comprehended.

SECOND. Comparative examinations of practices and methods must be made, so that standards may be laid down for the whole or for parts of the undertaking.

THIRD. Having instituted standard practices, greater decentralisation of certain activities becomes possible. In other words, decisions can be made as to what sections of the organisation shall be centrally managed, and what can be decentralised.

We have passed through the first two stages, and we are now ready to take action with regard to the third stage.

It is of great importance in a large undertaking that the organisation in certain respects shall be such as to provide elasticity by means of a decentralised control (for example, in commercial matters it is desirable in view of the industrial conditions and competition today). It is equally of importance that certain other parts of the organisation shall remain centrally controlled if the economic advantages of amalgamation are to be obtained (for example, purchasing of stores and accounting operations).

I feel that the time has arrived when in the matter of traffic operation, the solicitation of business, and in the ordinary day to day maintenance of plant and equipment, greater decentralisation and fusion of resources locally is required, from the points of view of:–

(a) giving as quick and as close a contact with the public as possible, *and*

(b) fusion of interests and resources with a view to obtaining team work in a given locality, and of economy in administration.

The Company provides fine passenger and freight services. Every effort must be made towards obtaining customers to use them and the organisation designed to facilitate revenue earning. We must create the best sales organisation we can.

At present, the organisations of certain depart-ments do not dovetail into other departmental organisations – districts are not co-terminous: local headquarters are not at the same places, etc. Each department has in the past designed its organisation individually and more co-ordination of resources is required.

I have had under consideration for some time past the question of closer contacts between the departments themselves and between the Company's Commercial Officers and our customers. You will be aware that a step in this direction was taken recently by the appointment of one Vice President to control departments formerly covered by two. Investigations I caused to be made by a special committee appointed last year show that economies can be obtained by a closer fusion of interests locally, and I propose to follow up the appointment of Mr. Lemon by a reorganisation of the Operating and Commercial Departments. This will necessitate a remodelling of the administrative structure of the present organisation, which I will explain a little later in greater detail; but, in addition to this, I propose to give practical effect to the conclusions my Vice Presidents and I have come to in regard to area management.

Area management means that one Officer in an area will be in charge of :

(a) Solicitation of business.

(b) Traffic Operation.

(c) Day to day maintenance of plant and equipment.

Its advantages are briefly as follows:–

(i) All traffic getting activities in one area are in one department.

(ii) All expenditure down to the smallest detail in one area can be related to the revenue, and both are under one authority.

(iii) Co-operation between the staff, whether engaged on traffic getting or on working it, or on maintaining plant, can be achieved and the whole of the staff in a given area fused into a team, who can be enthused into pulling together for the good of the Company as whole.

Under such an organisation in its complete form the Railway is split up into a number of areas, in each of which there is an Officer in charge who is responsible for everything connected with the movement of trains, including the running repairs to locomotives and rolling stock, and the maintenance and upkeep of all way and works, signals, outdoor machinery, etc. These Officers in charge of areas are responsible to Headquarters for the same functions as regards the whole railway. The main principle is that there shall be only one authority in each area in charge of commercial business, rolling stock, operating, locomotives, signals and track, and that he can give orders concerning everything connected with the movement of traffic and the maintenance of rolling stock, plant, buildings and permanent way. He has such technical officials under him as may be necessary for the different classes of maintenance for which they are responsible to him, and not to a Departmental Head.

The area system of organisation enables men to obtain a general experience of the different branches of railway working, thus fitting them for the higher managerial and administrative posts. Moreover, all officers irrespective of their particular work are 'Transportation' Officers, and have an interest in the activities of the railway as a whole in their area.

As regards the relationship of the Headquarters Officers to the Officers in charge of areas, the Chief Mechanical Engineer and the Chief Engineer are responsible for design, works practice and research, and lay down the standards to which maintenance of plant and structures is carried out. Similarly, through freight and passenger services are arranged by the Chief General Superintendent but the Area Officer can alter, withdraw or institute services local to his area, keeping in mind the net revenue position.

An important point in the application of the principle of area management to this Company would be that in the case of accounting, the units of the Chief Accountant's organisation would supply to the Area Officer all figures that he requires for managerial purposes, but the control of the accounting staff and methods would remain the responsibility of the Chief

Accountant: costing would be carried out independently by the organisation of the Chief Accountant. In the same way, as regards staff questions, the Area Officer would refer to the Chief Officer for Labour & Establishment for decisions on matters of policy and principle as is now done by the Heads of Departments. Thus in these two respects – accounting and staff – there would be a departure from the present clear policy of the Company.

Scotland lends itself to an experiment in Area Management. It is a self-contained unit with Divisional Officers of each department in charge of different activities, with varying degrees of autonomy on purely local matters. I intend therefore to appoint a

CHIEF OFFICER FOR SCOTLAND

(or Manager for Scotland)

He will be in charge of all Departments in Scotland, and will report direct to the Vice Presidents.

The Chief Engineer, the Chief Mechanical Engineer, Chief General Superintendent, and other Officers at Headquarters will be responsible for standards, for research into particular problems, and for giving guidance to the Chief Officer for Scotland for the traffic and technical staff under him. The exact demarcation will be the subject of further enquiries, and a main object will be the elimination of formal references of local questions to headquarters.

The Chief Officer for Scotland will be responsible for net revenue. His responsibilities will be to keep the gap between revenue and expenditure as wide as possible by means of local control and fusion.

HEADQUARTERS CONTROL

The control of the Operating and Commercial activities of the Company under the Vice President (Commercial and Operating) will also be altered, and the following appointments made:–

The VICE PRESIDENT (Railway Traffic Operating and Commercial) will be assisted by the following principal officers:–

(i)   Commercial Manager.

(ii) Operating Manager.

(iii) Estate Manager.

(iv) Mineral Manager.

The functions of these Officers will be as follows:

(i) *Commercial Manager.*

The solicitation of all traffic by rail, road, and water: the maintenance of close contact with the trading and travelling public: freight and passenger rates and fares: carriage accounts, claims, rebates, etc: and the responsibilities now vested in the Overseas and Continental Traffic Manager: publicity and advertising in all its phases including trade advertising.

The Commercial Manager will be assisted by a Passenger Manager and a Freight Manager, a Publicity Manager, and such Assistants as may be required, including a Rates & Charges Assistant for all traffic.

(ii) *Operating Manager.*

The administration and control of all movement of traffic by rail and road: the handling of passengers, freight, and mineral traffic at stations, depots and docks: motive power: cartage and road transport generally.

The Operating Manager will be assisted by an Operating Superintendent and a Superintendent of Motive Power, and Cartage and Station working Assistants as required.

(iii) *Estate Manager.*

The administration and control of all the Company's land and premises, including sales, purchases and leases: in fact the present functions of the Land & Estate Agent and the like letting functions of the Chief General Superintendent and Chief Goods Manager in England and Wales, with the added responsibility now vested in the Chief Goods Manager and Mineral Manager of private sidings negotiations and agreements.

(iv) *Mineral Manager*

The Mineral Manager's functions will remain as now at any rate for the time being, except as regards certain estate responsibilities as mentioned under (iii) Estate Manager.

OTHER ORGANISATIONAL CHANGES

In due course changes in the line organisation will have to be made. The areas and functions of the District Commercial Officers (i.e. District Goods Managers, District Passenger Managers, and District Goods & Passenger Managers) will have to be reviewed and the changes made last year were consistent with this course.

Similarly, it will be necessary for the line organisations of the other departments, such as the Chief Engineer's, Signal & Telegraph Engineer's, and Land & Estate Agent's to be dealt with so that they may be organised in such a way as to provide close contact with the commercial organisation.

This is an important point so far as the future organisation of the Railway is concerned. If departmental boundaries are the same, a common interest between the District Officers in the different Departments is created; comparable statistics and costs can be produced, and the local departmental Officers can work far more together as a team than is possible at the present time.

During the year 1931, the system known as 'budgetary control' was introduced. Under this scheme, expenditure is rationed to departments and subsequently split into departmental areas. Owing to the differences in organisation as between departments, it has not been possible to provide in each area comparable figures of expenditure and revenue for different departments. Moreover, one of the main objects of budgetary control is the co-ordination of revenue and expenditure by area, but it has not been possible to do this owing to the differing types of organisation in force in the departments.

CONCLUSION

To sum up, in all amalgamations, it is necessary in the initial stages to centralise on a considerable scale in order that standard principles and practices may be adopted. The time has now arrived, however, when decentralisation can, with advantage, be effected so as to enable questions to be settled with a minimum of delay, and so that Headquarters may be relieved of as much detail as possible, thus enabling concentration to be given to major problems and research.

References and Footnotes

HART = Churchill College Archives, Cambridge:
Sir Harold Hartley's papers
RG = The *Railway Gazette* magazine
TNA = The National Archives
WEIR = Churchill College Archives, Cambridge:
Viscount Weir's papers

Chapter 1: Birth, origins and early life
1. All the relevant censuses can now be viewed online.
Parish records are at Dorchester Archives
2. Date unknown, possibly *c*.1936/7. The author is
grateful to Peter Tatlow of the LMS Society who
brought this paper to his attention and furnished
a copy
3. *Evening Standard,* Tuesday 28 June 1938, p.6
4. *The Times*, 23 December 1954, Obituaries p.9
5. Letter from Mrs Margaret Porritt, née Stirling.
7 Jan. 1941, Lemon's personal papers

Chapter 2: The Midland Railway and LMS, 1911–1929
6. This appointment and subsequent promotions,
together with the salaries paid, can be found in
Lemon's Employment Card at the Midland Railway
(TNA RAIL 410/1890). Issues of RG etc. carried
announcements of promotion
7. The *Derbyshire Courier* and *Derbyshire Times* both
carried reports on 19 October 1912
8. Supplement to *London Gazette*, 7 June 1918
(p.6705)
9. RG, 4 January 1918, pp.12–16
10. www.steamindex.com – Sir Henry Fowler
11. Presidential Address to the Railway Students
Association, London School of Economics,
8 December 1927 – see RG, 16 December 1927,
pp.745 and 763–4.
12. Midland Railway Study Centre, The Silk Mill,
Derby: Ref. no.10379 (506.04.04) 'Report to General
Manager on Messrs Reid & Anderson's Visit to
America, Aug.–Nov. 1919'
13. Lewis C. Ord, *Secrets of Industry*, (George Allen &
Unwin, 1944) – Chapter 2: 'Origin and Principles of
Mass Production', pp.15–25
14. The phrase 'Scientific Management' was actually
coined by the US lawyer, Louis D. Brandeis, seeking a
snappy title to embody Taylor's principles. He used it

in the so-called Eastern Rates Advance case in 1910
while opposing the US Railroads desire to increase
freight rates. (See 'Letters of Louis D. Brandeis',
Vol.3, pp.240–1)
15. E.J.H. Lemon, 'Railway Amalgamation and its
effect on the LMSR Workshops'. Paper read at the
Morning Session 8 July 1930 – Institute of Transport
Conference – Glasgow. Printed in the *Journal of the
Institute of Transport*, July 1930, p.421. (Digest of paper
also printed in RG, 11 July 1930)
16. 'Modern Methods in Railway Carriage Building
and Mass Production of Railway Wagons', *Engineering*
magazine 12 Oct. and 28 Dec. 1923, published as a
separate abstract 1924
17. H. Ellis, *British Railway History 1877–1947*
(George Allen & Unwin, London 1959) p.361
18. RG, 1 July 1938, p.1
19. E.J.H. Lemon, *Journal of the Institute of Transport*,
July 1930, p.421 (see footnote 15)
20. *The Locomotive*, 15 December 1924, p.393
21. see RG: 7 March 1924, p.332
22. Lemon, *Journal of the Institute of Transport*, July
1930, p.420 (see footnote 15)
23. RG: 11 July 1930. Report of the paper read by
Lemon at the Institute of Transport Congress,
Glasgow, 1930. 'Railway Amalgamation and its effect
on the workshops'.
24. The last entry for him in the Derby Electoral Roll
at this address is Autumn 1924
25. see *Derby Daily Express*, 2 March 1925, p.6; and
RG, 6 March 1925
26. The *Derbyshire Times*, Sat. 7 Feb. 1925
27. E.S. Cox: *Locomotive Panorama Vol.1* (Ian Allan
1965) p.77
28. 'A Progressive System of Railway Wagon
Building', *Railway Engineer*, April 1928, p.6
29. He is first listed at this address in the 1928
Directory, compiled in 1927
30. TNA RAIL 418/23 Minute 327, 28 March 1928
31. TNA RAIL 418/23 Minute 380, 28 Nov. 1928
32. RG, 11 July 1930, p.62 (see footnote 15) – a
description of the carriage repair facilities appeared in
RG, 8 July 1927, p.42
33. RG, 24 February 1928, p.245
34. Ref. nos DY4567–71 in KWIC Index
35. RG 22 June 1928
36. TNA RAIL 418/23. Minute 440, 26 June 1929
37. TNA RAIL 418/7, Minute 2062, 27 June 1929

38. *Modern Transport*, 24 August 1929, pp.3–4
39. TNA RAIL 418/5, Minute 1061, 26 February 1925
40. Patent No. 363,887 (application date 13/2/1931, complete accepted 31/12/1931)
41. TNA RAIL 418/24 Minute 620, 24 June 1931
42. TNA RAIL 420/236, Licence to use certain inventions
43. Colin Divall: *Industrial Research on the London, Midland & Scottish Railway, 1923–1947*, Institute of Railway Studies, 1998
44. see the Annual Army Lists at TNA
45. C.E.C. Townsend, *All Rank & No File*, Royal Engineers, *c*. 1965
46. E.J.H. Lemon, *Journal of the Institute of Transport*, July 1930, p.435
47. Ord, *Secrets of Industry*, Chapter 9: British Mass Production pp.92–3

Chapter 3: LMS, 1930–1931
48. Quoted in booklet commemorating the opening of the LMS Research Laboratory, Derby, 10 December 1935, p.1 (TNA ZLIB 6/158)
49. RG, 7 February 1930
50. TNA RAIL 418/13: Special Minutes of the Board of Directors
51. RG, 7 March 1930, pp.364–5
52. HART Box 87, Correspondence 1930–40 (S)
53. HART Box 73(1), LMS Papers
54. TNA RAIL1007/486
55. Copies at TNA Ref. ZPER 49
56. This can be consulted in the Knowledge Centre of the Chartered Institute of Logistics and Transport (CILT (UK)) in Corby
57. TNA RAIL 1007/486 'Report of the Committee on Steel Rolling Stock', p.3
58. RG, 23 April 1926 'New Steel Coaching Stock, London Midland and Scottish Railway' pp.582–4
59. TNA RAIL 1007/486 p.12
60. *Ibid*, p.9.
61. *Ibid*, Appendix B
62. TNA RAIL 418/105 'Reports to the Board 1932 No.8 – Carriage Renewal Programme'
63. Report of the Committee on Steel Rolling Stock – Part 2, Freight Stock, p.4
64. Office Central d'Etudes de Matériel de Chemins de Fer (OCEM)
65. TNA RAIL 1007/486 Appendix A by C.R.E. Sherrington
66. see RG, 11 July 1930, pp.58–61. Lemon became a member of the Institute of Transport on 8 December 1930, and served on its Council from 14 May 1934
67. HART Box 73(1), LMS Papers
68. C. Hamilton Ellis, *The Midland Railway*, Ian Allan 1953
69. Cox, *Locomotive Panorama*
70. *History of the West Coast Main Line – The LMS Era*. www.virgintrainsmediaroom.com

71. www.steamindex.com
72. J.E. Chacksfield, *Sir William Stanier, a new biography*, Oakwood Press 2001, p.47
73. HART Box 73(1), LMS Papers
74. TNA RAIL 418/169 – Minutes of the Advisory Committee on Scientific Research
75. E.J.H. Lemon, 'Rationalisation on the LMSR' – paper read at the Institute of Transport Congress, Buxton, 1 June 1932 – published by the LMS in *Modern Developments on LMS Railway*, TNA ZLIB 6/78, p.11
76. HART Box 73(1), LMS Papers
77. *Ibid*
78. see – Colin Divall (1998): *Industrial research on the London, Midland & Scottish Railway 1923–1947*.
79. HART Box 59, 'Confidential Memos to keep'
80. TNA RAIL 418/13
81. *The Times*: 3 January 1955, Obituaries p.8, Some writers have erroneously attributed the name 'Lightning Committee' to the later triumvirate of Vice-Presidents: Hartley, Wood and Lemon
82. See Lemon's personal papers
83. TNA RAIL 418/7, Board Minutes, 27 November 1930, Item 2367

Chapter 4: Chief Mechanical Engineer, 1931
84. Denis Griffiths, *Locomotive Engineers of the LMS*, Patrick Stephens 1991, p.100
85. Supplement to RG, 16 September 1938, p.45
86. E.A. Langridge, 'Under 10 CMEs – No.6, E.J.H. Lemon', *Stephenson Locomotive Society Journal*, Vol.54, No.641, December 1978
87. TNA RAIL 418/49 – Minute 1138 (25 February 1931) and Minute 1191 (20 May 1931)
88. TNA RAIL 418/23 Minute 522, 30 April 1930
89. 'Rationalisation on the LMSR', paper read at the Institute of Transport Congress, Buxton, 1 June 1932 (see *Modern Transport* 11 June 1932, also published in *Modern Developments on LMS Railway*, TNA ZLIB6/78, p.13)
90. Cox, *Locomotive Panorama*, pp.78–83
91. E.J.H. Lemon, 'Pioneer work in locomotive standardisation', *c*. 1936/7?) – copy in author's possession
92. TNA RAIL 418/104, Reports to the Board 1931, No.9 *Locomotive Position*
93. See also TNA RAIL 418/49, Locomotive & Electrical Committee Minute 1150, 25 February 1931
94. Cox, *Locomotive Panorama*, p.79
95. Roland C. Bond, *A lifetime with Locomotives*, Goose & Son, 1975, pp.91–2

96. 'Rationalisation on the LMSR', paper read at the Institute of Transport Congress, Buxton, 1 June 1932 (see *Modern Transport* 11 June 1932, also published in *Modern Developments on LMS Railway* TNA ZLIB6/78 p.12)

97. TNA RAIL 1007/277 *Use of Engines*, Memo to the President, 13 November 1930, pp.10–11

98. TNA RAIL 418/49. Locomotive & Electrical Committee, Minute 1227, 27 July 1931

99. TNA RAIL 1007/277, Memo to President, 13 November 1930, *Use of Engines*

100. quoted in Minutes of Tour No.7, 16 October 1934, 'Visits from Headquarters to different sections of the line 1933–39' (TNA RAIL 421/69 p.3)

101. TNA RAIL 418/107, Reports to the Board, No.21, 20/11/1934 – Locomotive Construction Policy

102. Lemon's personal papers

103. TNA ZLIB 6/80 p.27. This booklet is a reprint of articles from RG, April 16, 23 and 30, 1937

104. Chris Hawkins & George Reeve, *LMS Engine Sheds (Vol.1)*, Wild Swan 1981, p.5

105. TNA RAIL 418/49

106. TNA RAIL418/79: Traffic Committee Minutes 1931, Vol.5, No.2771

107. Referred to in *Memorandum to the Chairman* 16 June 1937 (Lemon's personal papers)

108. TNA RAIL 418/70, Minute 1150 of Locomotive & Electrical Committee, 25 February 1931

109. J.B. Radford, *Derby Works and Midland Locomotives,* Ian Allen 1971, p.197

110. 'LMS Heavy Oil Engined Shunting Locomotive' RG 1932, Vol.57, No.23

111. see Traffic Committee Minutes: No.4159, 19 December 1934 and No.5015, 25 November 1936

112. Dennis Monk M.I.Mech.E latterly a Senior Engineer at Derby Works in conversation with Keith Harcourt

113. TNA RAIL 418/104, Reports to the Board 1931 (No.16)

114. WEIR 10/10

115. HART Box 59, 'Confidential memos to keep 1930–1'

116. TNA RAIL 424/4, Ministry of Transport Committee – Main Line Railway Electrification, 1931

Chapter 5: Vice-President, 1932–1933

117. TNA RAIL 418/13, Special Minutes of the Board

118. H.C.B. Rogers, *The Last Steam Locomotive Engineer – R.A. Riddles*, George Allen & Unwin 1970 p.61

119. For example: Denis Griffiths, *Locomotive Engineers of the LMS, Patrick Stephens,* 1991, p.101

120. Chacksfield, *Sir William Stanier*, p.47

121. HART Box 87, Correspondence 1930–40 (S)

122. O.S. Nock, *LMS Steam*, David & Charles 1971, p.144

123. Rogers, *The Last Steam …*, p.146

124. TNA RAIL 418/13, Special Minutes of the Board of Directors: No.2734, 27 October 1932

125. TNA RAIL 424/28. *The Times* article 'Servants of the Public', 20 Sept. 1938, p.39, omitted the Chief Officer for Labour & Establishment in members of the Executive

126. HART Box 73(1), LMS Papers. The full text of this memo is given in Appendix A

127. Memorandum to the President, 16 June 1937: Mechanisation of Marshalling Yards (Lemon's personal papers)

128. TNA RAIL 1007/494. The Minute is filed with papers relating to the rebuilding of Euston Station

129. TNA RAIL 424/28

130. TNA RAIL 1007/277, Memo to President, 13 November 1930 'Use of Engines'

131. HART Box 73

132. The full text of this memo is given in Appendix B

133. Paper to the Institute of Transport, Buxton 1932 (TNA ZLIB 6/78 p.8)

134. also quoted in Lemon's Paper to the Institute of Transport, Buxton 1932 (TNA ZLIB 6/78 p.9)

135. Bond, *A Lifetime with Locomotives*, p.96

136. TNA RAIL 418/8 Minutes of Board Meetings, Item 2607, 28 January 1932

137. *Evening Standard*, 28 June 1938, p.6

138. e.g. 9 March 1934 (RG: 16 March 1934, p.479)

139. see RG, 4 November 1932

140. see Army List, May 1932 (Appointment also announced in *London Gazette* and RG)

141. TNA ZLIB 6/78

142. This paper was printed in *Modern Transport* on the 11 June 1932. Digests appeared in the national press, e.g. *The Times*, 2 June 1932, p.11

143. TNA RAIL 418/169, Item 183

144. see RG, 12 February 1932, pp.209–11

145. TNA RAIL418/169: *Minutes of Advisory Committee on Scientific Research*

146. see Lemon's personal papers; and RG, 1 July 1932 pp.9–12

147. Memo to C.R. Byrom, 16/11/1932, LMS Ref. C.O.142/10/14 (Lemon's personal papers)

148. These were: Aston, Buxton, Bescot, Devons Road, Edge Hill, Farnley Junction, Lancaster, Longsight, Monument Lane, Patricroft, Rugby, Springs Branch, Stoke and Walsall

149. Both memos given LMS Ref. C.O.137/5/2 (Lemon's personal papers)

150. TNA RAIL 421/69: 'Visits from Headquarters to different sections of the line 1933–39. Tour No.1'

151. Hawkins & Reeve, in their series of books *LMS Engine Sheds*, describe in great detail the rebuilding and modernisation work that was carried out

152. TNA RAIL 418/81: Traffic Committee Minutes 27 June 1934, Item 3953

Chapter 6: Vice-President 1933–1938, part 1

153. TNA RAIL 418/8 Minutes of Board Meetings, Item 2721, 29 September 1932
154. The Report on this visit was written by S.H. Fisher (TNA RAIL 418/208)
155. HART Box 84, Letters 1951–61
156. Original in Lemon's personal papers
157. TNA BT26/1027/1–12: Incoming arrivals, Southampton
158. e.g. Byrom arrived back at Liverpool on 17 June
159. 'LMS Film Propaganda', Memo to the President 21 November 1933 (Lemon's personal papers)
160. Report – Lewis C. Ord, 'Mechanisation of Goods Sheds', 3 March 1934, p.16 (Lemon's personal papers)
161. Lemon's personal papers
162. RG, 30 March 1928, p.468
163. TNA ZPER37/22 – Modern Transport 26/5/1934, p.10
164. see Traffic Committee Minutes: Nos 4310, 4446, 5154 & 5373
165. RG, 5 February 1937, p.252
166. Patrick Whitehouse & David St John Thomas, LMS 150, David & Charles 1987, p.82
167. Lemon's personal papers
168. Memo to the Chairman, 19 January 1935, Ref: C.O.291/1/13 (Lemon's personal papers)
169. Traffic Committee Minute 4223, 27 February 1935 – approved by the Board 28 February
170. Traffic Committee Minute 5035, 16 December 1936 – approved by the Board 17 December
171. Traffic Committee Minute 5676, 27 July 1938
172. see Traffic Committee Minute 6697, 26 February 1942
173. TNA RAIL 421/69: 'Visits from Headquarters to different sections of the line 1933–39'
174. TNA RAIL 421/69, Tour No.8, Item 218
175. Traffic Committee Minute 5579, 27 April 1938
176. Information accessed at AncestorsOnBoard.com and Ancestry.co.uk (also see TNA BT26, BT27 & website)
177. The Times, 3 January 1955, Obituaries p.8
178. HART Box 73
179. see RG, 16 March 1934, p.479
180. see RG, 22 November 1935, p.887
181. TNA RAIL421/16: 'Freight Transportation in Container Trucks', LMS Goods Department internal publication
182. Memo: 'Mechanisation of Goods Yards', 23 March 1933 (Lemon's personal papers)
183. W.J. Cunningham, 'British Freight Services', included in J.A. Droege (ed), Freight Terminals & Trains, McGraw Hill, New York, 1912
184. Cunningham pp.200–1
185. Roy Horniman, How to make the Railways pay for the War; or The Transport Problem Solved, George Routledge, London, 1919, p.24

186. 'The World', 30 March 1909, quoted in Horniman, p.58
187. 'Rationalisation on the LMSR', Paper read to the Institute of Transport Congress, Buxton, 1 June 1932 (see Modern Transport, 11 June 1932; and TNA ZLIB6/78 p.7)
188. Memo to the Chairman dated 23 October 1933 (Lemon's personal papers). No copy of Ord's interim report of similar date has been found
189. T. Hornbuckle, 'Application of Diesel Engines to Rail Traction', Proceedings of the Diesel Engine Users Assoc., 1936, quoted in Cox, Locomotive Panorama, p.155
190. Traffic Committee Minutes 1933, Vol.6, No.3389; quoted verbatim by H.G. Smith, 'The Lemon Papers'
191. e.g. RG, 28 December 1934, p.1079. Established sources such as Cox and Radford are confused on these, and subsequent details
192. Reported in RG, 8 March 1935, p.458
193. TNA RAIL 418/82 24 July 1935, Item 4433. NB: the original order was for 250hp engines
194. Other sources give this engine No.7059 (which is chronologically more appropriate). However, Fairburn in his 1941 paper to the Institution of Locomotive Engineers gives it No.7079; and allocates No.7059 to the first of the ten A-W engines
195. Traffic Committee Minute No.4570 (27 November 1935)
196. Cox, Locomotive Panorama, p.155
197. T. Hornbuckle, 'Application of Diesel Engines to Rail Traction', paper read before the Diesel Engine Users Association, 11 November 1936 (copy at the Institution of Mechanical Engineers, London) pp.9–10
198. C.E. Fairburn, Diesel Shunting Locomotives. Paper presented before the Institution 30 April 1941 in Journal of the Institution of Locomotive Engineers, 1941, pp.180 & 182
199. RG: 22 November 1935, p.886, 'Golf: Eastern Command v. LMSR'
200. L.H. Short, 'Service operation of an LMSR Diesel Shunter', RG 12 July 1935, p.86. This article had previously been published in the English Electric Journal
201. Anon, 'The New British Diesel Shunters', Diesel Traction Supplement, 1936 – RG Vol.64 No.12 p.585
202. Hornbuckle, 'Application of Diesel Engines …'
203. see RG, 12 February 1932, pp.209–11
204. see RG, 22 February 1935, pp.340–41 & 351
205. 'New Down Marshalling Yard at March, LNER', RG, 24 February 1933, p.245
206. Lemon's personal papers
207. TNA RAIL418/208, S. H. Fisher, 'American Visit of LMS Officers, May 1933 – Notes made on certain operating practices and problems' p.21
208. ibid
209. H.G. Smith: Lighting of Marshalling Yards (Lemon's personal papers)

210. TNA RAIL 418/97 Works Committee Minute No.3289, 22 November 1933
211. H.G. Smith, Mechanisation of Marshalling Yards (Lemon's personal papers)
212. Memo to the Chairman: 'Mechanisation of Marshalling Yards – Toton', 16 June 1937 (Lemon's personal papers)
213. Supplement to RG, 21 May 1937, p.27

Chapter 7: Vice-President 1933–38, part 2

214. Information accessed at *AncestorsOnBoard.com* and *Ancestry.co.uk* (also see TNA BT26, BT27 & website)
215. HART Box 84, Letters 1951–61
216. Whitehouse and Thomas, *LMS 150*, p.40
217. TNA RAIL 426/9 p.68
218. TNA RAIL 1007/494
219. TNA RAIL 418/170 & 171, *Advisory Committee on Scientific Research*
220. LMS Ref. C.O.401.27.2, 'Road Competition: Pipes from Swadlincote', 2/6/1932 (Lemon's personal papers)
221. Traffic Committee Minute No. 5006; Mechanical & Electrical Engineering Committee Minute No.1101
222. TNA RAIL 422/24
223. LMS Ref: C.O.401, 'Shock Absorbing Wagons, Appendix C', 7/11/1938 (Lemon's personal papers)
224. see *The Times*, 26 May 1937, p.18
225. Lemon's personal papers
226. A description of these trials can be found in Rogers: *The Last Steam Locomotive Engineer*, p.65–9
227. *Glasgow Herald*: 17 November 1936, p.13
228. TNA RAIL 421/204 – Anonymous newspaper cutting kept by G. Royde-Smith
229. see *Steam Railway*, 1980 – also quoted in Andrew Roden, *The Duchesses*, Aurum, 2008, p.31
230. O.S. Nock, *Great Locomotives of the LMS*, p.247
231. Rogers, p.78
232. see RG, 12 November 1937, p.816
233. Lemon's personal papers – LMS ref. C.O.393.7.51
234. Traffic Committee Minute 4776, April 1936
235. Traffic Committee Minute 5361, 27 October 1937
236. TNA RAIL 421/69; Report of Tour No.23, Item 731
237. Letter to Byrom 15 January 1937, LMS Ref. C.O.313.3.1 (Lemon's personal papers)
238. TNA RAIL 418/83: Traffic Committee Minutes, 24 November 1937, Items 5427 & 5428
239. Lemon's personal papers
240. Diesel Engine Users Association, *A General Review of the Development of the Diesel Engine during 1936*, p.36 (copy at the Institution of Mechanical Engineers, London)
241. RG: 12 August 1938, p.310; also see RG 4 August 1939, p.124 & Fairburn's paper 1941 p.180

242. see www.derbysulzers/awglobal
243. Cox, Locomotive Panorama, p.155
244. RG supplement: *Diesel Railway Traction*, 15 April 1938, p.769
245. RG diesel supplement: 17 February 1939, p.26
246. RG supplement: *Diesel Railway Traction*, p.775
247. Copy in Lemon's personal papers
248. TNA RAIL 418/109, Reports to the Board 1936, No.6 – this includes photographs of the building in Crewe that was first proposed as the site for the School
249. See *Daily Express*, 6 November 1936, p.11
250. 'LMSR Derby Staff College Scheme', RG: 6 Nov. 1936, p.739
251. 'Scheme for the First Railway Staff College' RG: 6 Nov. 1936, p.775
252. *Derbyshire Advertiser*, 24 September 1937. 'Investing the Human Element'. Cutting in Barbara Cramp's Scrapbook available at Derby Silk Mill Museum
253. '*LMSR Derby Staff College Scheme*' RG, 6 November 1936, p.739
254. *Derby Evening Telegraph*, 19 April 1937 – 'By our Railway Correspondent'
255. W. O'Keefe, 'A course of Instruction at the School of Transport, Derby', *Journal of the Permanent Way Institute*, 1951, Vol.69, Part 3
256. *The Times*, 15 January 1937
257. RG: 'The LMSR School of Transport', 29 July 1938, pp.206–9
258. *Ibid*, p.227
259. B. Cramp, *School of Transport Derby*, Derby Silk Mill Museum
260. RG: 25 February 1938, p.388
261. TNA has copies of Passenger Station Working, Goods Station Working, Cartage & Salesmanship; Refs. ZLIB 6/73–6
262. Lemon's personal papers
263. TNA BT 26/1145/69–78 (although marked 40)
264. HART Box 87(O) letter dated 13 Feb. 1938 from TRM
265. RG: 11 November 1938, p.837
266. *Modern Wonder*, Vol.3 No.54, w/e 28 May 1938, p.2

Chapter 8: The Air Ministry – the run-up to War, 1938–1940

267. TNA AIR 19/35
268. WEIR 19/1, p.112+
269. WEIR 19/13 p.72
270. WEIR 19/13 p.37–9
271. TNA AVIA 46/93
272. TNA CAB 104/78
273. TNA AVIA 10/144 EPM 58(38), Agreement to appoint Overseers taken at 120th Meeting, 30 March 1938
274. TNA PREM1/251

275. M.M. Postan, *British War Production*, p.18. History of the Second World War series, HMSO, 1952

276. WEIR 19/18, pp.140–6

277. *The Times,* 13 May 1938, p.8

278. TNA AVIA 20/429

279. TNA AVIA10/91, Secretary of State's Panel of Industrial Advisers

280. TNA AVIA 46/93/21A

281. TNA AIR 6/34, Minutes of 127th Meeting, 21 June 1938

282. TNA BT26/1162, No.15 *Incoming Arrivals*

283. TNA AIR 2/3771

284. *Evening Standard,* 28 June 1938, p.6

285. Letter from Eric Robinson, Bush House, Aldwych – is this the BBC conductor? This, and subsequently quoted letters, from Lemon's personal papers

286. The indexes to the TNA baldly state that the Air Council held no formal meetings. However the Council *did* meet weekly, and the Minutes can be found listed as 'RAF Expansion Measures' Ref AIR 6/34★

287. TNA AIR 6/54, Notes of decisions taken at meetings

288. TNA AIR 20/430, Types of Aircraft towards Scheme 'L'

289. TNA AIR 6/35 p.23 – Minutes of 131st Meeting, 12 July 1938; also AIR6/54, E.P.M. 135(38) with annotations in Lemon's handwriting

290. see N.H. Gibbs, *Grand Strategy*, HMSO, 1976, p.586

291. TNA AIR6/34, p.201 – Minutes of 129th Meeting, 5 July 1938

292. TNA AIR 6/35, p.16 – Minutes of 131st Meeting, 12 July 1938

293. TNA AIR 6/34, p.203 – Minutes of 129th Meeting, 5 July 1938

294. TNA AIR 6/35, p.18 – Minutes of 131st Meeting, 12 July 1938

295. *Ibid*, p.50 – Minutes of 132nd Meeting, 19 July 1938

296. TNA CAB 21/517 – Expansion of RAF, C.P. 106(35), 20 May 1935

297. TNA AIR 6/39 p.253, Minutes of 179th meeting, 4 August 1939

298. Letter to Kingsley Wood, 2 December 1939 (Lemon's personal papers)

299. TNA AVIA 46/91, Letters to Prof. M.M. Postan, 9 & 15 July 1943. See also: J.D. Scott & R. Hughes *The Administration of War Production*, HMSO, 1955, pp.386–8; and Lewis C. Ord, *Politics and Poverty*, Mayflower Press, 1948, p.121

300. TNA AVIA 46/97, E.P.M. 127 (38) – reference in AIR 6/54, 134th Meeting

301. TNA AIR 2/2944 – organisation chart; list of personnel also published in AVIA 46/30/14A & /15A

302. Sir Henry Self, 'Obituary of Sir Ernest Lemon', in *The Times*, 17 January 1955, p.10

303. Letter to Lemon, 23 April 1940 (Lemon's personal papers)

304. Postan, *British War Production*, p.464305. Letter to Sir Samuel Hoare, Secretary of State for Air, 8 April 1940 (Lemon's personal papers). A similar description of proposed duties can be found in Bruce-Gardner's correspondence (TNA AVIA 46/93)

306. Minutes of this Committee are in TNA AIR 2/3291

307. TNA AIR 6/34, Minutes of 127th meeting, 21 June 1938, p.160,

308. *The Times*, 17 January 1955 – the full text is printed at the end of Chapter 9

309. TNA AVIA 46/91, letter to Prof. M. Postan, 15 July 1943

310. TNA AIR 19/35. Letter dated 29 June 1938 from Vickers

311. see Postan, *British War Production*, p.22 and Scott & Hughes, *The Administration of War Production*, p.386

312. see *The Times* report, 26 May 1938, p.9

313. TNA AVIA 46/91/1A, Interview with Sir Henry Self, 13 October 1942, p.3

314. TNA AIR 6/35, Minutes of 134th meeting, p.106, 7 September 1938

315. TNA AIR 6/35, Minutes of 139th meeting, 18 October 1938, p.267

316. TNA REF, EPM 127 (38) clause 41

317. TNA AIR 6/35, Minutes of 134th meeting, 7 September 1938, p.105★

318. TNA AIR 6/34, Minutes of 129th meeting, 5 July 1938, p.185

319. TNA AIR 6/35, Minutes of 136th meeting

320. see M.M. Postan, *Design & Development of Weapons*, p.169

321. TNA EPM 127 (38) clause 44

322. TNA AIR 6/35, Minutes of 133rd Meeting, 26 July 1938

323. for example, see: Stephen Bungay, *The Most Dangerous Enemy*, Aurum, 2000, p.80

324. TNA AIR 6/35, Minutes of 136th meeting, 22 September 1938, p.176,

325. TNA AIR 6/35, Minutes of 137th meeting, 27 September 1938, p.215

326. TNA T 161/923

327. TNA AIR 6/352, Minutes of 140th meeting, 25 October 1938, p.215

328. TNA AIR 6/54

329. TNA AIR 6/36, Minutes of 141st meeting, 1 November 1938

330. TNA AIR 6/38, Minutes of 162nd meeting, 28 March 1939

331. Correspondence in Lemon's personal papers

332. TNA, AVIA 46/93/46A, letter to Freeman from Bruce-Gardner dated 10 January 1939

333. TNA AIR6/36, 146th Meeting, p.137. Also AIR20/429, P.I.A.15

334. Postan, *Design and Development of Weapons*, p.38 footnote 3

335. TNA AIR 6/54: EPM 138(38) p.2 – presented at 136th Meeting
336. TNA AIR 2/3291, Minutes of the Air Council Committee on Supply, includes the Minutes of this Meeting
337. TNA AIR 20/429, Minutes of 6th Meeting of Industrial Panel, 21 November 1938
338. HART Box 21
339. TNA AIR 6/37, Minutes of 151st Meeting, 24 January 1939, p.7
340. As reported in *The Times*, 16 February 1939, p.17
341. TNA Cabinet Committees, ref. CAB 59/5 Book 27
342. All correspondence from Lemon's personal papers
343. TNA AVIA 10/310, DGP Directors' meeting, 27 March 1939
344. TNA CAB 60/50

Chapter 9: The Air Ministry – War, 1939–1940

345. TNA AIR 6/58: EPM 120 (39); comments in AIR 20/366. AVIA 46/30/17A contains a long analysis of the progress of the expansion plans under Lord Swinton (Letter from Mr Abrahams to M.M. Postan 19 July 1942)
346. TNA AIR 6/58 – EPM 136(39)
347. TNA AIR 6/58 – EPM 130(39), Report presented 24 July 1939
348. TNA AVIA 10/310, DGP's Meetings
349. TNA AIR 10/91, verbatim report of PM's Advisory Panel of Industrialists, 17 July 1939
350. TNA AVIA 10/310, 21st Meeting of DGP's Directors, 14 August 1939
351. TNA AIR 6/58 – EPM 128(39), 179th progress meeting, 4 August 1939
352. Letter from Kingsley Wood to Stamp, 14 September 1939 (Lemon's personal papers)
353. Letter from Stamp to Lemon, 26 September 1939 (Lemon's personal papers)
354. TNA AVIA 15/40, Reorganisation on the outbreak of war
355. TNA AVIA 10/29. Reorganisation of AMDP's department, Memo from E.F. Cliff to Freeman 4 May 1939
356. TNA AIR 6/40 – Minutes of 186th Meeting, 10 October 1939
357. TNA AVIA 46/500
358. TNA AVIA 10/31
359. As recounted by his granddaughter Amanda in conversation with the author
360. TNA AIR 6/40, Minutes of 186th Meeting, 10 October 1939; also AVIA 15/40, DGP's meeting, 2 October 1939
361. TNA AVIA 10/31, correspondence dated 1 December 1939
362. *The Times*, 13 December 1939, p.8
363. Letter to Sir Wilfrid Freeman, 2 December 1939 (Lemon's personal papers)
364. *Ibid*365. Letter from Kingsley Wood, 9 December 1939 (Lemon's personal papers)
366. TNA AVIA 10/310, Minutes of DGP's meetings 18 January 1940
367. TNA AIR 6/41, Minutes of 194th Meeting, 13 February 1940, p.97
368. *Ibid*, Minutes of 197th Meeting, 26 March 1940, p.189
369. Anthony Furse, *Wilfrid Freeman*, Spellmount, 1999, p.110
370. Later in the year, Lord Beaverbrook, after he became Minister at the newly-formed Ministry of Aircraft Production, removed the Castle Bromwich factory from Nuffield's control and it was taken over by Vickers
371. Letter to Sir Samuel Hoare, Secretary of State, 8 April 1940 (Lemon's personal papers)
372. TNA AIR 6/41, Minutes of 198th Meeting, 9 April 1940
373. Letter from Sir Samuel Hoare, Secretary of State, 22 April 1940 accepting Lemon's resignation. (Lemon's personal papers)
374. Furse, *Wilfrid Freeman*, p.114–15
375. McNeale (ed), *The Memoirs of George Purvis Bulman*, No.31 Historical Series, Rolls-Royce Heritage Trust) p.260
376. Letter dated 23 April 1940 (Lemon's personal papers)
377. McNeale, *The Memoirs ...*, pp.247–8
378. *Ibid*, p.252
379. HART Box 21, Personal Correspondence 1951–3 [sic], Letter from Sir Harold Hartley to Professor J.A. Jewkes, 29 December 1955
380. Court Circular – as reported in *The Times*, 27 April 1940, p.9
381. Letter from Sir R. Glyn, 5 January 1941 (Lemon's personal papers)
382. *The Times*, 17 January 1955; p.10

Chapter 10: Return to the LMS, 1940–1941

383. RG: 17 November 1939, p.647
384. Cox, *Locomotive Panorama*, p.155
385. Chacksfield, *Sir William Stanier*, p.123
386. TNA RAIL 421/149
387. Traffic Committee minutes, Item 6442, 27 February 1941
388. copies of both memos in Lemon's personal papers
389. Lord Reith's diaries are held at the BBC Written Archives Centre, Reading. The entries quoted do not appear in the published version, which has been heavily abridged
390. TNA RAIL 418/11: Board Minutes 19 December 1940, Item 4212; also Traffic Committee Item 6441, 27 February 1941

391. Traffic Committee minutes, Item 6485, 24 April 1941
392. TNA RAIL 418/201
393. TNA POWE 16/263
394. see also Traffic Committee minutes Item 6373, 29 November 1940 & Item 6630, 27 November 1941
395. R.J. Essery, *Illustrated History of LMS Wagons, Vol. 1*, Oxford Pub. Co., 1981, p.119. Peter Tatlow illustrates such a conversion in his book on LNER wagons, but dates it pre-war (?)
396. Traffic Committee minutes, Item 6692, 26 February 1942
397. This entry does not appear in the published version, which has been heavily abridged

Chapter 11: The End of a Railway Career, 1942

398. TNA RAIL 258/549, and Lemon's personal papers
399. This entry does not appear in the published version, which has been heavily abridged
400. The report can be found in AVIA 46/88 (TNA). Matters arising and reactions in BT 28/423
401. TNA BT 28/542 – Progress Reporting, Talk with Major Buchanan 12 December 1942 – also further comments by Professor Jewkes on the state of affairs at MAP
402. TNA BT 28/422,
403. TNA BT28/425, and Lemon's personal papers
404. TNA BT 28/424
405. The Firefly investigation is included in the Barracuda file, BT 28/422 (TNA)
406. TNA BT28/541. Also see Scott & Hughes, pp.460–1
407. TNA BT28/545
408. TNA BT 28/477
409. Records of the Institution are now held at the Institution of Engineering Technology. Copies of their *Journal* are at the British Library
410. A description of the procedural wrangling and negotiations that preceded this can be found in the biography: Furse, pp.243
411. HART Box 21, Personal Correspondence 1951–3, Letter to Sir William Haley 5 January 1955
412. An example can be found in the Tameside Archives Centre, Ashton-under-Lyne, Lancs

Chapter 12: Retirement and Recovery, 1943–1945

413. TNA ADM 1/15003
414. 1945 Electoral Roll: Copy at Essex Record Office, Chelmsford, Ref: C/E 2/8/23 p.1
415. Copy at the Institution of Engineering & Technology

416. Harrington Emerson, *The Twelve Principles of Efficiency*, first published in 1913. Emerson was a disciple of Taylor and introduced Scientific Management to the US railroad industry, notably on the Atchison Topeka and Santa Fe. The book is still in print
417. Various articles on 24 February 1944; RG 3 March, p.227; *The Engineer* and *Engineering* magazines 3 March etc.
418. TNA POWE 16/263
419. Lemon's personal papers
420. Ord, *Secrets of Industry*, pp.12–13

Chapter 13: Post-war and final years, 1945–1954

421. 1945 Electoral Roll – qualifying date, 30 June 1945; Elizabeth Sarah Hunt died in 1947 aged 79
422. *The Luxembourg Bulletin* for Mar/Apr 1948 gives a comprehensive account of the firm's history and activities at this time
423. Outgoing passenger lists are now available on-line
424. Copy in Lemon's personal papers
425. Report published by HMSO, draft copy in TNA SUPP 14/141
426. Scottish Aviation was incorporated into British Aerospace in 1977, and nobody seems to know where – or if – any records from this period still exist
427. See TNA BT 195/1 and 195/2
428. E.S. Cox: *Locomotive Panorama, Vol. 2* Chap. 1, p.1
429. TNA SUPP 14/333
430. Letters to Richard in Africa at this time remain in the family's possession. Richard's reply to Hartley is in HART Box 84 (Letters 1951–61)
431. HART Box 21: Personal Correspondence 1951–3

Chapter 15: Postscript

432. HART Box 84, Letters 1951–61

Index